MRS. FISKE

And the American Theatre

MRS. FISKE

And the American Theatre

by

ARCHIE BINNS

IN COLLABORATION WITH

OLIVE KOOKEN

CROWN PUBLISHERS, INC.

New York

Letter from Bernard Shaw to Mrs. Fiske
on page 99 reproduced by permission of
The Public Trustee and The Society of
Authors, London, England.

MANUFACTURED IN THE UNITED STATES OF AMERICA

List of Illustrations

Foreword

Some months ago the publishers sent me Archie Binns's manuscript to read. It filled me with a special delight because it seemed to me that he had caught the spirit and the fire of America's unquestionably greatest actress. How Alexander Woollcott, an old critical admirer, would have cherished *Mrs. Fiske and the American Theatre*! From my childhood to the end of her life I saw every play she was in if I were within a hundred miles.

Having examined the source material, I feel that Archie Binns has told the Fiske story very completely and very well. The account of her childhood and early acting in New Orleans and in the Deep South is authentic as well as deeply touching. You learn to know all the Madderns and enjoy them in their precarious triumphs and all too many financial disasters. It is the story of the theatre in the Deep South and in the Eastern Mississippi Valley in the Sixties and Seventies of the last century. Mr. Binns has captured the atmosphere of the towns and cities in which they played as well as the climate of the actors and their productions.

It has been more than twenty years since the great exponent of Ibsen and the modern theatre died. All this time I have been waiting as one of her admirers for a biography to emerge. For a long time, even almost up to his death, I expected Harrison Grey Fiske to supply that need. Many times at my desk in the Theatre Collection of the New York Public Library overlooking the greenness of Bryant Park, I conferred with Mr. Fiske as he talked to me of the book he planned to write about his beloved and famous wife. Remembering the literary style of the old New York Dramatic Mirror which he for so long edited and published, I expected a distinguished if naturally biased account of Mrs. Fiske's career in the theatre. It never came. Then I later learned that he had not seriously considered a biography of his wife alone but contemplated his own autobiography. This was left unfinished and unready at his death. The manuscript fell into the hands of friends but it was far from ready for publication. Years later Archie Binns undertook this labor of disinterested love for a great actress whose distinguished career was still unchronicled in Biographia Dramatica Americana. He has unquestionably written the definitive Fiske biography.

GEORGE FREEDLEY

Preface

It seems unaccountable that it should be necessary to explain who Minnie Maddern Fiske was. It is also frustrating; she was so much and so many different things that a summary can only nibble around the edges and dislodge a few crumbs.

It is rudimentary to say that Mrs. Fiske was an American actress. She was the most purposefully American of them all; she discovered her own native playwrights; she took her productions, the best of their time, to the farthest reaches of the continent and to Americans who never saw Broadway; and she battled for ideals far beyond the confines of the theatre.

But a eulogy is the last thing Mrs. Fiske would have welcomed. She once observed that an actor who was applauded had only himself to blame. And often in her productions she almost obliterated herself so that others could shine. The most she would have approved about herself would have been crumbs of unbuttered truth.

In Mrs. Fiske's complex life there were facts that can be simply stated: she was born in the theatre and died in the theatre; she was born in relative poverty and died in the same. In the years between, from 1864 to 1932, she enriched the lives of two generations of playgoers, and she touched the ways of thinking of millions who never saw her.

These are simplifying facts about a great American woman. There are also complicating ones. In her long stage career she was two very different people. There was the unlettered Minnie Maddern whose cradle and playhouse were behind the scenes in the theatre: the child actress; the star of hoydenish melodramas who was praised as "frolicsome and vivacious without being vulgar"; the girl crooner who made "In the Gloaming" the hit song of a decade.

Then there was Mrs. Fiske, who was one of the best minds of her time: the acknowledged leader of the American stage for a generation, a skilled and successful playwright, an actress who was rated with Duse and Bernhardt, a producer who was probably the best outside Europe, the triumphal champion of Ibsen in America, the discoverer of some of the best American playwrights of the early twentieth century. The list could be continued almost indefinitely, but for the sense of humor that was Mrs. Fiske's it is already too long.

"Dear! dear! How seriously we take ourselves!" she used to say on such occasions.

It was not a pose. Mrs. Fiske would have listened with more pleasure to her accomplishments in other fields, like the important role she played—not on the stage—in introducing modern and humane cattle cars, and her campaign in behalf of the egret. Ornithologists had written them off as doomed to extinction at the hands of plume hunters —and when Mrs. Fiske had done her work, no woman in America would have been found dead wearing an egret, and the birds were multiplying by the thousand.

Mrs. Fiske had a good sense of values. What stage accomplishment could compare in satisfaction with the knowledge that she had saved a lovely species from extinction from this earth?

The interests closest to her heart led to places where there was no applause, but the shy follower of St. Francis of Assisi observed that "Theatres, too, can be holy places."

Mrs. Fiske lived that belief. For a generation, she was the conscience of the American theatre. When the Syndicate made the theatre a commercial monopoly, she stood against it, most of the time alone, for twelve long years. At the height of her career Mrs. Fiske played in burlesque houses, skating rinks, disused churches and abandoned halls; her tours were hardly more comfortable than the campaigns of Joan of Arc. Like Joan, she won the victory—and paid its price. The "best years of her life," when she could have amassed a fortune, were given to the best cause of which she knew: the freedom of the American theatre. She won that freedom, and ended with nothing. Nothing? Did Joan of Arc end with nothing? Did Mrs. Fiske? She had ample wit to understand that every life is expendable, and must be spent. Why not for what its owner values most—however invisible such values may be to others?

Mrs. Fiske's last audiences saw her dying on the stage. (Though she could no longer eat, she still had to pay rent.) When her voice and steps faltered, some of her audience cried out that the play must be stopped. But a play—and an integrated life—must go on to its appointed end. Quite suitably, the play was a comedy. Mrs. Fiske had the gift of being able to laugh at many things, including herself. Laughter, which gives perspective, did not desert her.

CHAPTER 1

The big house set back on Baronne Street had known brighter days. Its broad galleries shaded by great oaks and magnolias, its wide lawns and slave quarters, bespoke a gay life. But in 1863 New Orleans was an occupied city, and war and the stern voice of the widow Maddern left no room for frivolity.

Sundays in the big house began with early rising, grace before and after breakfast, followed with a two-by-two pilgrimage to Christ Church on Dauphine Street; after the service there was a two-by-two return, grace before dinner, discussion of the sermon during the meal, and grace afterward.

There followed the one Sabbath relaxation which Mrs. Maddern permitted—reading of the Scriptures. Her three daughters had never known any other kind of Sunday. But to her hot-blooded son-in-law, Tom Davey, the day was torture.

Davey's bachelorhood had never been ruled by the days of the week; when he and his cronies had used up the hours of one day, they borrowed from the next. That freedom ended with his marriage to Lizzie Maddern. Now he fidgeted with an unlit cigar while Mrs. Maddern read aloud from the Gospel according to St. John.

Sometimes the reading ended in time for Tom Davey to manage a smoke—but this evening it went on until the clock whirred and began striking seven. Then the lady closed her Bible.

"We must not be late."

The women put on bonnets and shawls and fingerless gloves while the man squeezed into his coat and gathered up his gloves and tall hat. The dim hall mirror reflected their images as they passed: Mrs. Maddern tall and straight, her widow's black setting off her pale aristocratic profile; Emma Maddern, still in her teens, with her youth glowing quietly in staid surroundings; Lizzie Maddern Davey, like a frail young nun, more soul than body; and Tom Davey, small and quick and wiry, hawk-nosed, with flaming red hair—a firebird walking with mourning doves.

Tom Davey had been a ploughboy in England, too frail for that kind of work, and with too much imagination. He educated himself, saved the price of a steerage ticket to New York and there got a job as callboy in a theatre.

Davey's friends labeled him the maddest wag since Yorrick, but in the theatre he was better known for his fiery temper. His energy soon brought him a promotion from callboy to prompter. On his first evening Davey stood proudly in the entrance, prompting conscientiously for the leading man, who did not know his lines and was sticking at every speech; Davey's anger rose with each appeal for "the word, my boy, the word." The manager of the company had come into the entrance unobserved, and stood directly behind the new prompter, glaring at the book.

"The word, the word!" the actor implored for the last time.

"The word!" Davey shouted. "There's the prompt book!" and he threw the book at the actor. The manager seized Davey by the neck and flung him after the script.

"And there's the prompter!"

Tom Davey was still a firebird; but the widow Maddern who had temporarily caged him was no ordinary woman. A Northern fleet had captured New Orleans two years before, but Mrs. Maddern had arrived before the gunboats; the doom of the city might have been foretold by her brisk housekeeping and her vigorous disregard of the subtropical climate, the exotic foliage, and the air of pagan indolence that lingered over the city.

Tom had married Lizzie the year of Mrs. Maddern's arrival in New Orleans; and neither he nor the city had been the same since.

Evening church bells were ringing as the widow Maddern halted the little procession at the stage door of the St. Charles Theatre. Inside, the women went to their dressing rooms and Tom Davey to his office, snapping off the end of his cigar on the way as if it were his mother-in-law's head.

Mrs. Maddern, the barrier between Tom and Lizzie, had not always been a kill-joy. In her romantic youth in England she had scandalized her aristocratic parents by marrying Richard Maddern, a poor young musician from Sadler's Wells, and they had cut her off with one shill-

2

ing. Half a dozen years later, with their six children, the young couple had sailed for America, where their last child, Emma, was born. Maddern taught music to his brood as soon as they were old enough to hold instruments and with them he organized the Maddern Family Concert Company. In out-of-the-way theatres in the Midwest and South Tom Davey had met the Madderns, lost track of them, and seen them again, the musical couple and their seven musical children, living a romantic story!

Mr. Maddern led the orchestra; his wife played the piano; Emma, just big enough to hold the sticks, beat the drums. But it was Lizzie, the cornetist, whose soulful eyes captured the callboy's heart.

Richard Maddern was dead now and his sons were leading orchestras of their own; Mary, the staid trombonist, was on her way up the Mississippi with a traveling company; the others were in New Orleans.

The dreams of the ardent ploughboy had led to marriage and stage management, without all the expected fulfillment. They were presenting *Seven Sisters*, and Tom Davey had to piece out his war-thinned cast. As he waited in the wings for his cue, his stately mother-in-law swept past, and the ruler of the stage cringed under the shell of the lowly Snail.

Later that Sabbath evening Tom Davey watched his wife on the stage. Powdered and rouged, with shining eyes, in spangled tights, she led the ballet as the Spirit of Life. Lizzie's dresser was her mother, whose faith in God was equaled only by her conviction that the play must go on.

The spectacle went on, and Davey watched the Lizzie with whom he had fallen in love, a dancer beckoning to his ardent heart. But Mrs. Maddern, who had helped her daughter into her costume, also helped her out of it and into her nun-like street clothes. Off stage Tom Davey never quite found the Spirit of Life.

The company was kept busy presenting a new play each evening, including Sunday, with extra morning rehearsals in Shakespeare for a famous matinee idol billed to appear in March; in the brief hours at home Mrs. Maddern coached Lizzie, who was to be the visitor's leading lady.

The famous actor was presented to a house packed with homesick Union soldiers, free men of color, emancipated slaves, and the new poor and the new rich: Creoles stripped of their wealth and Northern profiteers. The stage offering was the comedy *Money*, and the star was John Wilkes Booth.

3

John Wilkes Booth was matinee idol to more than his audience. The players found him uncommonly gentle and considerate; the nearest he came to finding fault with any of their work was to suggest that it might be more effective done some other way.

The season ended in June with a revival of *Seven Sisters*, Lizzie Maddern again playing the Spirit of Life. She was then two months pregnant. In the fall there was a new stage manager and Lizzie was missing from the company, although Emma was still there, and Davey appeared as an actor on the stage which he had once ruled.

On the night of December 19th, while Charles Couldock was appearing in *The Willow Copse* at the St. Charles, there was flurry and grim tension in the house on Baronne Street where Mrs. Maddern boiled water and prepared sterile cloths for her daughter's confinement while she kept a critical eye on the midwife. The frail Lizzie, tired from overwork and financial worry and troubled by the conflict between her mother and her husband, was in poor shape for the ordeal. Patiently and without complaint she exerted herself, while the blue veins stood out on her forehead and perspiration rolled onto the pillow. She was sure the reluctant baby must be a giant. Actually it was only a mite, with a glint of red in its hair. When Lizzie was able to open her eyes she feasted them on the perfectly shaped little head and dainty features. But when the baby clenched its fists and drew its whole body up for one fierce cry, there could be no doubt that the imperiousness of the grandmother and the impulsiveness of the father were to govern the child's life.

The baby was christened Marie Augusta Davey; but the theatre-minded women of the family soon changed that to Minnie Maddern, in imitation of their idol, Maggie Mitchell, the "cute" star of the day. For half a lifetime the name and the limited ambition which it represented misdirected the talents of a genius.

By the fall of 1865 the War Between the States was over—and so was Tom Davey's eclipse. Once again he was stage manager at the St. Charles, and Lizzie was back too. While she was on the stage she kept little Marie Augusta in a champagne basket in her dressing room, where Grandmother Maddern watched over her. Between the acts Lizzie nursed the baby. And visiting stars came in to see little Marie Augusta: Laura Keene, on her slow decline from fame; the Charles Keans on the last engagement of their farewell tour of America; Lawrence Barrett, an old friend of Tom Davey and the Madderns and the new actor-manager of the Gaieties Theatre; and young Lotta

Crabtree, the darling of California mining camps, accompanied by the grim-visaged, poker-backed Mrs. Crabtree—all of them in pursuit of fame or fortune, or clutching at those things as they slipped away from them in the shifting sands of the theatre.

The widow Maddern was wont to remind her daughters that the wage of sin is death, though in softer moods she commuted it to suffering, for lesser sins. So it was, and the wage was paid.

The sins for which the Maddern daughters suffered had been committed before they were born. They were the sins of the theatre in the days of Garrick, Cibber and Kemble. The drama then had been a bawdy affair, egged on by coarse and turbulent audiences. It was through no eccentricity that Garrick, about to die on the stage, was waited on by an attendant who spread a piece of carpet for the hero's fall. The carpet saved on cleaning expenses by providing a relatively safe place amid the garbage of sucked oranges tossed on the stage by eighteenth-century gallants. Verbal garbage, too, was tossed across the footlights by the male animals in the pit; and actresses often made coarse retorts to coarse remarks. Off stage, actresses found refuge from the pit, but not from the gallants who crowded into their tiring rooms and made ribald anatomical remarks. In those days it was taken for granted that every famous actress was the mistress of some famous man, and lesser actresses were pawed by lesser men.

The bawdier days of the theatre passed with the century, but their flavor was kept fresh by those who disapproved. Inveighing against sin was so much in fashion that information did not have to be up to date; nineteenth-century ministers who professed never to have seen a play thundered against the theatre of an earlier day, giving—and presumably having—the impression that it was still flourishing around the corner. In America, where such things had never been, timid mothers of daughters and equally timid heads of colleges forbade their charges to witness theatrical performances, and men about town, hoping there was something in all the talk about sin, hung around theatres to see if any could be found, or produced.

Since the 1840's Mrs. Maddern, with her children, had toured America, or camped within walking distance of the stage door. Few people were better informed about actual conditions, but her daughters were in a suspect profession and they had to keep themselves above a mountain of suspicion. Even for blameless young women it was an exhausting climb.

The theatre in which the Maddern sisters lived down the sins of other people in other times was strenuous enough in itself. At the St. Charles, the company presented a different play every night. The day began with two hours of morning rehearsal in the dirty-gray daylight of the unlighted stage, in an atmosphere of dust and burned gas that aggravated Lizzie's asthma. In hot weather the rehearsing company sweltered in street clothes; in cold and wet weather they retained shabby greatcoats and shawls, and sometimes fenced or gestured with wet umbrellas. Six days a week the stage of the St. Charles accumulated dust; early on the morning of the seventh it was drenched with buckets of water and scrubbed down. Sunday morning rehearsal was held in an atmosphere or miasma of icy chill. The elder Booth, rehearsing there, had caught a deathly cold, and on the way home to Maryland he had died alone in his stateroom on a river steamer. A few days before the birth of Lizzie's daughter, a young man of the stock company had caught a less famous chill and died of pneumonia.

Morning rehearsal was followed by three or four hours of studying new parts or brushing up on old ones. The evening performance, which began at eight and lasted three or four hours, was enlivened by gaslights and an audience. A great visiting star might fill the orchestra and the three balconies, rising tier on tier to the high ornate ceiling and turning the theatre, as the star saw it, into a glamorous stage-set. For the company the stage had less glamor; and behind the scenes there was still less. With every possible foot of theatre devoted to auditorium and stage, an actress's dressing room was a mean cubbyhole, furnished with the occupant's trunk, a wash basin, a gas jet, a piece of mirror, a rough board shelf and a chair. There were also pegs for her wardrobe: a black velvet dress, a white satin and a simplicity muslin. That was the wardrobe of a leading actress; with it she was equipped to play every role from Lady Macbeth to Julia in *The Hunchback*. Minor actresses were less lavishly supplied.

In the greenroom there were the comforts of chairs, companionship and relative quiet; gentlemen were forbidden to wear their hats or talk vociferously, under penalty of a fifty-cent fine. In theory, the actress who had been on her feet through morning rehearsal, and who might have spent the afternoon pacing the floor as she studied her role, could relax in the greenroom while waiting for her cue. But callboys were a careless lot; and there was a three dollar fine for making the play wait. Conscientious actresses—less often actors—waited in the wings, where no chairs were allowed. Often they waited in tears

6

of exhaustion—ready to go on with a display of mock fatigue, sprightliness, or with laughter, as the scene required.

Stars were a law unto themselves, but middle-class stage people as the Madderns knew them were mostly a sober and dedicated lot, the children and grandchildren of actors, with the stamina developed by several generations in the theatre. Fewer but more conspicuous were the stage-struck who had envisioned a life of ease and glamor—and bruised themselves on hard reality. Sometimes they gave up and went to hell through pettishness, giving their more enduring fellows a bad name.

The public's misconceptions were helped along by the fact that actors largely kept to themselves, partly from lack of time and energy to mingle with the public, sometimes from lack of funds. Often, on a precarious tour, the members of the traveling company had little to sustain them but their pride. The manager of the troupe might solve his problems by saying, "Why speak of salaries when blackberries are ripe?" But actors living on blackberries or the equivalent were not in a position to be good fellows with the public. Most of all, actors kept to themselves because acting was less a livelihood than a way of life.

In a country as wide and varied as America, audiences were less of one stamp than were the actors. At one extreme was an audience recalled by Joseph Jefferson. In the hinterland of Mississippi, traveling by wagon, the family company gave a request performance in an open barn, twenty-five miles from any town. The seats—chairs and benches and logs—were under the night sky, and they were filled with farm families none of whom had ever seen a play before. The bill was *The Lady of Lyons* and a farce, *The Spectre Bridegroom*. The performance began by candlelight that was presently extinguished by a rising wind, and the play went on in the light of a harvest moon, with the audience talking among themselves in voices of awe and wonder; and sometimes they interceded in behalf of the threatened heroine. It was such an audience as must have once gathered in an English courtyard to witness the first miracle play, and its reactions were as pure.

At the other extreme was a performance given at the St. Charles in the palmy days before the War. It was a benefit performance for Eliza Logan, popular in New Orleans. The seats had been sold at auction, and the boxes were filled with Creole aristocrats, and beauties blazing with diamonds.

The play was *Lucretia Borgia*, with Eliza Logan in the title role, and a splendid supporting cast. Near the end of the final act, with the audience tensely silent, Gennarro raised his glittering dagger to stab the murderous Lucretia. As he was about to say "die!" a beautiful Creole belle almost threw herself out of a stage box, shrieking:

"Oh, oh, don't kill Miss Logan! She's going to be my bridesmaid tomorrow!"

Amidst the laughter of the audience and the ruins of the scene, the girl shrank back, and the unnerved Gennarro made a stab at Lucretia, who obligingly died. Thereupon, the Creole belle stood up in her box and lowered to the stage a pair of carrier doves bridled with white ribbons and bound together with a diamond bracelet; in their bills was a white envelope for Miss Logan, with cards for the belle's wedding. The curtain fell on the tragedy with the white doves perched on Lucretia's body, and the audience in tears of excess laughter.

Other cities had other ways. When the staid Mary Maddern was up North she often appeared at the Bowery Theatre, where she had carved a small niche for herself. In the sixties the Bowery was the last American theatre with a pit. There, newsboys and ragpickers could see the performance for a few cents; and dirty urchins hawked apples, oranges, peanuts and candy.

The Bowery boys were noisy in their applause, but they had a true reverence for drama and melodrama. None of the debris of vended food was tossed on the stage though performances were given in the earthy reek of peanuts, which Mary could never abide with good grace.

The regular New York theatres were an actor's and producer's dream. New Yorkers were ardent playgoers, and every good production was welcomed by plentiful and well-behaved audiences. There was no welcome for bad productions or bad acting, but even they were allowed their day of grace. On the fringe of the theatre there were would-be actors who could not ordinarily appear in safety on the boards. By trial and painful error they learned that New Yorkers full of turkey dinner were unwontedly tolerant. Accordingly, around Thanksgiving, the hopeful ones hired disused halls and put on plays which the citizenry attended because it had become a tradition. For obvious reasons, the day-of-grace Thespians were dubbed "turkey" actors. Later the term was applied to unsuccessful plays.

Out West, in Ohio and Illinois, audiences had the uncouth habit of stamping their approval, raising clouds of dust; but everywhere

Americans were kind to good productions. They were also resentful of being "sold," and audiences expressed their resentment in varied ways. Swindlers and incompetents floated down the Mississippi, stopping at small towns and matching their wits and heels with audiences that returned to a second performance with rotten eggs and cabbages and dead cats. City audiences were content to hiss bad actors from the stage—but not always. In New York in the sixties, theatre speculators began the tradition of sending out third-rate companies advertised as the original cast of some metropolitan hit.

One of the early fraudulent exports was a "famous French company." Unhappily, none of the riffraff was competent in the language; more unfortunately, the company was sent to Montreal, where it was greeted by a theatre packed with French Canadians.

The curtain rose, and the opening exhibition of bad acting and worse French was met with icy silence. As the play limped on, the "sold" audience began to boil, first with a hissing sound, and then with an ominous rumble. The trembling actors were showered with wadded-up programs, then overshoes; women contributed spare articles of clothing, and men went out in search of munitions. They returned with items which suggested that if words would not break the actors' bones, sticks and stones would. The actors fled the bombardment, and the drop fell. An apologetic manager appeared before the curtain—and ran for his life under a shower of missiles. The pit then engaged in a free-for-all fight for the honor of France, and seats in the family circle were torn up and sent crashing to the stage. The ladies began to leave in terror; the pit united in singing the "Marseillaise," then began another free-for-all.

The "original cast" never reappeared on the stage, and when the theatre was finally cleared, it was in poor condition.

During the War, Southern soldiers had little opportunity for playgoing; but in Yankee-held territory theatres were often filled with Union soldiers with wartime manners. They wore their caps or campaign hats, smoked in the theatre, spat tobacco juice, hung their legs over the backs of spare benches, and sloped their rifles with fixed bayonets toward the stage with an uncomfortably thorny effect.

In truth, the soldiers were good-natured audiences, but they did not choose to be taken for granted. War had disconcerted them, and they saw to it that some of the disconcertion was passed along to stage civilians. The soldiers were generous in their laughter, applause and bouquets, but they bestowed them perversely. They watched comedies, intent but unsmilingly, applauding at all the wrong places; they laughed their way through tragedies, applauding the villain; and they threw the heroine bouquets that were awkwardly timed and placed in relation to what she was doing—renouncing the vanity of the world, murdering someone or dying.

Soldier audiences were articulate in their way, testifying that the world was turned upside down.

With some additions and deductions, the plays of those years had their origins in England. There was no international copyright law, and it was cheaper to pirate a successful work than to pay for an unproved one.

Popular among the plays inherited or borrowed from England were the works of Sheridan; dramatizations of Scott's and Dickens' novels and Tennyson's *Enoch Arden*, the innumerable plays of Dion Boucicault; Bulwer-Lytton's perennial *Lady of Lyons*; Colman's *The Iron Chest*, which was the elder Booth's greatest play; and Sheridan Knowles's famous comedy, *The Hunchback*.

Among the exceptions—plays paid for in England or written in America—were some of the most successful in theatre history. For a lump sum, Dion Boucicault had written the version of *Rip Van Winkle* which kept Joseph Jefferson for the rest of his life. Clifton Tayleure's dramatization of *Uncle Tom's Cabin* founded an industry in which thousands of actors and bloodhounds labored; his *East Lynne*, borrowed from an English novel which borrowed from a German play, was a favorite of emotional actresses and road companies, drenching decades of playgoers in mawkish tears. Tayleure had many other successes.

Of briefer success in those times were plays in which the staging overshadowed the acting, like *Ogarita, or the Sea of Ice*, which began with a sailing ship frozen in the Arctic sea, and the aurora borealis flashing overhead. Popular for a little while were "protean" dramas, in which an actress appeared in rapid succession in six different roles and two sexes, speaking in six different dialects. Sometimes there were two actresses playing the game, further confusing the audience and making a double mincemeat of histrionic ability.

Above solid modern plays, old favorites and passing novelties, there was Shakespeare. His plays were the chief vehicles of the great, like the Booths and Charlotte Cushman; indifferent actors felt ordained to mouth his roles, and mountebanks, swindling their way down the Mississippi, paid garbled tribute to the Bard.

In the respite of the Civil War, soldiers occasionally yawned through Shakespeare, and voiced their preference for a naked woman Mazeppa strapped to the back of a galloping horse. But Shakespeare was generally as unquestioned as the Bible, with which his works were linked —and realistic stars offered relief from the classics. At the St. Charles, Matilda Heron played *Medea* one night and *East Lynne* the next; and Booth followed *Othello* with *The Lady of Lyons*.

CHAPTER 2

One of Minnie's earliest recollections was of a Southern city where her mother had a season's engagement as a dancer. The two shared a hotel room, and when Lizzie Maddern went to the theatre in the evening, she left Minnie with a colored nurse called Loo. After Loo put the child to bed, she would tell her stories until she fell asleep; and when Minnie woke in the morning, her mother was beside her.

Minnie believed that Loo stayed with her every minute until her mother came home. She accepted it as an immutable fact until she woke one night in the big silent room. There was no Mama and no Loo— only a dim light on the table. She was alone in a shadowy world, where she had been deserted.

She scrambled out of bed and began to tug on stockings and shoes, crying bitterly. As she struggled into the rest of her clothes, her terror changed to indignation at Loo, who had not kept her promise. Indignation gave her skill, and at last she was dressed, except for her hat. It, alas, was hanging in the great black wardrobe. But not for worlds would Minnie open the doors of the terrible wardrobe filled with nameless fears. Hatless she ran from the room and down the stairs, and slipped out of a side door of the hotel.

Minnie had not gone far before she found herself in a world of bright lights and gay crowds and confusion. The street was lined with noisy cafés and long rows of shooting galleries. Through doors open to the warm night she saw gaily colored, fantastic targets. Upstairs, in brilliantly lighted places, men were playing games. At intervals, through the noise of the crowds, the crack of rifles and the clang of bullets on targets, there was the triumphant shout of "Keeno!"

Minnie stopped in the doorway of an especially gorgeous establishment where men talked and laughed in rich cigar smoke, and other men with rifles fired into the heart of a beautiful Columbine.

One of the men came over to ask what she was doing out so late. She told him, with returning indignation, how Loo hadn't kept her promise, and she was going to the theatre where Mama was playing. Minnie had no idea where the theatre was, and when the gentleman offered to help her find it, she trotted along beside him.

At the theatre her new friend held her up to the box-office window, where she was confronted by the surprised face of the manager. There followed a conversation over Minnie's head; then the manager came out of the office; Minnie's escort shook hands with her and went away. The manager summoned a young man who took her around to the back door of the theatre and set her in a chair in the wings. The curtain was up and she had a good view of the stage. What followed is best told in Minnie's words:

A sort of transformation scene was in progress. Presently I espied my mama, dressed as a fairy and in the act of slowly rising from a gigantic water lily. I was very much pleased. Jumping from my chair, I ran to her and began to explain about Loo. The audience seemed delighted with my appearance; Mama stuck half way in the water lily; and the curtain fell with undue haste upon my most successful debut.

Mama discovered that it was Loo's habit to spend an hour or two with congenial friends while she was supposed to be watching at my bedside. We found her in a state of great excitement when we got home. There were tears galore, and lamentations, in the midst of which I went haughtily to bed. Next day I told my mother about my experiences in the shooting gallery and she decided that thereafter she would take me with her to the theatre each night.

Those evening walks to the theatre were very pleasant. It was great fun to pretend that I was blind as we went along. I would close my eyes tight and Mama would lead me along, saying, "Now a step up, now a big one down." Sometimes she would play a trick on me and tell me to "take a high step up" while we were on the level pavement, and then we would both laugh heartily.

We entered the theatre through the stage door and had to traverse a long dark passage before reaching the stairway which, branching off to the right and to the left at the top, led to the stage on one side and to the dressing rooms on the other. It was while walking along this long, damp passage that I learnèd to know and to love the smell of the theatre—that odoriferous medley of gas, paint, and mold dear to the hearts of all true children of the stage—as familiar to them as the salt breeze to the sailor.

In the dressing room I was put to bed in a trunk. Mama turned

13

the trunk around so that the raised lid shielded me from the light. I am sure the audience never guessed at that little domestic scene in the quiet dressing room of the pretty young actress.

I thought my mother the prettiest lady in the world. Often I found myself watching her furtively while I pretended to be sleeping, and when she went out I would lie quietly looking about the room. The theatre dressing rooms of that day were poorly furnished; boxes served as dressing tables and an actress's wardrobe usually consisted of half a dozen gowns of cheap material. It seemed to me that Mama's room was very dirty. One night when she came in with her usual caution, she found me gravely scrubbing the shelf with a whisk that I had soaked in soapy water. Mama was terribly distressed to find me awake at such an unholy hour, and I stood in danger of being consigned again to the tender mercies of Loo. But now the dust was on my wings; I had inhaled the beloved ether; it was deep and safe in my lungs. It would have been as unnatural to keep me from the theatre as to forbid the duckling his bath.

Minnie was three at the time. Next season the family was together again, on the road. Tom Davey was manager of a traveling company which included Lizzie.

It required a special art to tour the hinterland of the impoverished South, and Davey was an artist at itinerant management; the company did not starve to death, and the manager was credited with discovering Mississippi and Arkansas towns whose existence had not previously been suspected.

Minnie enjoyed that precarious tour. She skipped around behind scenes, helped set the stage and work the properties; she knew every line of the repertory. Minnie was already a trouper, though she had not yet appeared on the stage. But she became so insistent about having a public appearance that presently her mother made her a little Scotch costume and, in the interval between the tragedy and the farce, Minnie came on stage and sang "Jamie Coming over the Meadow," after which she danced a Highland Fling—a performance in the best tradition of the Maddern Family Concert Company.

A few weeks later, still only three years old, she made her first appearance in Shakespeare. The company was playing unsuccessfully at Little Rock when a visiting tragedian borrowed her to play the Duke of York to his Richard III.

The tour completed, the Daveys returned to the Baronne Street house—poorer than when they started. But Minnie had learned the ways of the road, and she had won a pint-size reputation as a Shakespearean actor. Soon after they came back to New Orleans, the famous

Irish tragedian Barry Sullivan engaged Minnie to play the Crowned Child in *Macbeth*.

As usual with a visiting star supported by a local company, the play was hastily put on, with only one rehearsal before the first performance. Minnie had been offhand about learning her lines; at rehearsal she stuck hopelessly, but she tried to make come true the old stager's declaration that by evening she would be all right. However, she did not know what old stagers did between shaky rehearsal and performance, and that evening she was no better prepared:

> The play had gone very well up to the time of my entry; but as I came up through the witches' caldron—a funny little ghost with bristling red crop and a white nightgown, holding a branch in my hand—the audience burst into a roar of laughter. This unexpected greeting somewhat shook my self-assurance, and I stood before the great actor and spluttered, "Be lion-mettled, proud, and take no heed where perspirers are."
>
> Poor Mr. Sullivan ground his teeth. "Take her down!" he growled. "T-a-k-e her down!"
>
> The trembling stage manager ordered my descent into the caldron right in the middle of my exhortation.
>
> "O-o-oh!" he cried, holding his head in anguish.
>
> "Why did you pull me down?" I demanded. "I wasn't through."
>
> That night in his dressing room Mr. Sullivan sat me on his knee, and promised that if I would study my lines for the next performance he would buy me some lollipops. I didn't know what lollipops were, but they sounded good; so I acquitted myself with pride on the following night and, I got my lollipops.

A little later Minnie appeared with Lucile Western, the emotional actress who lived her roles.

> I can close my eyes now and in the conjured darkness see a woman with a brilliant, flashing face, a noble head, and sturdy shoulders pacing up and down in the deserted green room. I am sitting quietly in the corner watching her as she paces to and fro, her hands clasped nervously, her brows knitted, and great tears coursing down her cheeks. . . . We are wise in our generation. The old-fashioned way was too wearing; it killed this woman who is pacing restlessly before me.

It also resulted in wear and tear on others. Once when Minnie was acting the part of a little boy who died, Miss Western, the mother, nearly dislocated one of Minnie's arms in her frenzy of grief.

The steamboats that carried members of Minnie's family to distant theatres also brought them back—all but Tom Davey. His misfortunes on tours increased the tension at the Baronne Street house, where he felt himself an unsuccessful son-in-law rather than the proud husband of the Spirit of Life. In his fiery outbursts of temper he clashed more and more frequently with Lizzie—and finally he went away up the Mississippi and never came back.

One of the steamboats brought Uncle Richard Maddern, who came to lead the orchestra at the New Orleans Academy of Music. While he was there, Minnie acted at the Academy in a glow of stage fire and first love.

I had my first beau—five years old and very handsome. He was the youngest member of a talented acrobatic family that had been brought to the theatre as a feature in a grand spectacular revival, *The Ice Witch;* in it I played the Sun God, making my entrance from the clouds in a golden chariot. My lover thought it great fun to climb into my gorgeous car with me, hide down behind the painted horses, and tickle my ankles as I slowly descended in all the majesty of gold dust and red fire and waved my sceptre over the ballet kneeling on the stage below.

We had sworn eternal fidelity every night and Wednesday and Saturday matinees for several consecutive weeks when my acrobatic Romeo met with an accident which betrayed our rendezvous.

One night, in climbing into the chariot, he had the misfortune to catch his tights on a nail, and the result was a dreadful rent from thigh to ankle. To avoid an explanation was impossible. I heard his mama (she was French and very quick tempered) exclaim angrily, "Never again dare to go in zat m-i-s-e-r-able car! If you tear ze tight once more, I make you eat zem! Sar!"

I went mournfully about my business in the next scene, a "Drill of the Amazons" where I was the Captain. I had to march directly to center front under the watchful eye of my Uncle Richard, who was leading the orchestra and directing the drill. I can still see the horrified expression in my uncle's eyes and his frantic gestures to me as, with Willie's howls ringing in my ears, I crept dejectedly forward, head hanging, eyes brimming, shield drooping, and spear trailing behind like a long silver tail.

My vogue developed so fast that presently Mr. Bidwell, the veteran manager of the Academy at New Orleans, put on *Uncle Tom's Cabin*, and my name as Eva was placarded about the town in letters taller than myself. I used to measure myself against the posters and swell with the magnitude of my name; and to this day I remember Little Eva's thrill while going up to heaven in a soap box.

When I was six Mama and I came to New York; Laura Keene had asked me to play Willie Lee in her production of *Hunted Down*. I had reached a new height in my career: instead of seeking parts, managers came seeking me. My salary ranged from fifty to seventy-five dollars a week—a goodly sum for those days. I used to deposit most of it each week at the old Bowery Savings Bank, where I was known as the Little Depositor.

Miss Keene was very fond of me. Every day my nurse took me to her apartment at the Grand Central Hotel, where I would play for an hour, and where frequently there was a new toy for me. When Miss Keene went upon a short tour she insisted that I accompany her, and, as it was impossible for my mother to leave the city, the great artist took me under her personal charge. She would not leave me out of her sight for a moment, insisting that I sleep beside her, not only at the hotels, but also in the sleepers of the railway trains when we traveled by night.

During the run of *Hunted Down*, Carlotta LeClercq gave a perform-ance of *A Sheep in Wolf's Clothing* at the French Theatre on Four-teenth Street, borrowing Minnie for the role of Sybil. Miss Keene had agreed to the arrangement, but she snubbed the child actress when she returned—perhaps because Miss LeClercq had billed her:

LITTLE MINNIE MADDERN
Her First Appearance on Any Stage

The misstatement of obvious fact was only less surprising than the apparent faith in the drawing power of inexperience—though on poster paper it established Miss LeClercq's claim to the discovery of Minnie Maddern.

Minnie recalls her part in a bona fide discovery on the New York stage:

After a while there came to town a graceful young fellow with terribly wicked eyes and a great shock of curly black hair. He produced a piece called *Carl and Hilda*, in which he played Carl and I Hilda, his little sister. I have a distinct recollection of the first night of the play and of a scene we played together. . . . Carl puts me into my little bed, gets his guitar, and sits beside me to sing me to sleep. The lights are turned low as he sings softly and for the first time a simple lullably—a gentle, tender melody which some-how quiets the turbulent audience, steals up under its vest and into its heart.

Joe Emmett, the singing comedian, woke up next morning to find himself famous!

Minnie Maddern had taken New York in her stride and was becoming a well-known little actress, but her mother's engagement ended and the two returned to New Orleans; it was several years before they saw New York again.

When Minnie was eight her mother went to Pittsburgh, leaving the child with her grandmother. The staid Sabbath atmosphere of the Baronne Street house was oppressive, and Minnie wept for her mother. Her aunts tried to cheer her with a new puppy, but she was inconsolable; finally they put her on a train for Pittsburgh, with the fat puppy, Dixie, in her arms. As Lizzie was not in good health at the time, they did not inform her for fear she might worry about the child's traveling alone. Of that experience Minnie wrote:

> I arrived in Pittsburgh very early one morning. I didn't know where my mother was staying, but I knew she was with the Furbish Fifth Avenue Company and I knew Mr. Furbish; he would be staying at the best hotel in town. I climbed into a cab with Dixie in my arms and directed the cabby to drive me to the best hotel, which turned out to be the Monongahela.
>
> I had picked the right place. The desk clerk directed me to the Furbish apartment, and in answer to the sleepy query that followed my knock, I said,
>
> "It's Minnie!"
>
> Mr. Furbish threw open the door. "My God! Minnie!"
>
> He and Mrs. Furbish welcomed me and gave me breakfast; then they took me to a house on Diamond Street, where my mother was staying. The moment when she opened the door and I rushed to her arms remains one of the high spots of my young life.

After a second unsuccessful attempt to leave Minnie, Lizzie took the child with her on engagements.

Next year mother and daughter were again in New York. There Minnie played Prince Arthur in a magnificent production of *King John,* with John McCullough, Agnes Booth and Junius Brutus Booth, Jr.

On one engagement, when Edwin Booth was the visiting star, Minnie begged her mother to take her behind the scenes so she might see him. Lizzie found a place for her to hide in the first entrance from which Booth had to take his cue.

Breathless, Minnie waited:

> Then he came—in clanking armor he came and stood just beside me. Of course he didn't see me. But my lot was quite perfect with-

out that. Here, near enough for me to touch, stood the great Edwin Booth. Then my heart stood still—my idol was about to speak.

Giving an impatient hitch to an ill-fitting part of his armor, he spoke and I caught his soft exclamation:

"God damn it!"

Not long after this Minnie was visiting in Cincinnati, and when the time came to go home, John Havlin, a family friend, arranged for her to go back to St. Louis in the private car of Madame Modjeska. It was a happy experience, and long afterward it had pleasant repercussions.

CHAPTER 3

When Minnie was ten, she toured as Prince Arthur in John Mc-Cullough's production of *King John*, and in the fall of 1875 they played at the Detroit Opera House. Upon their arrival the manager, a sharp-faced little man with flaming red hair, caught Minnie up in his arms and kissed her. The surprised child tried to draw away, but he reassured her.

"Minnie, don't you remember me? I'm your father!"

Minnie had forgotten she had a father, it was so long since she had seen him. After his divorce from Lizzie, Tom Davey had drifted to Detroit, where he became manager of the Opera House, a position he held for many years. He married and raised a second family quite peacefully. But in one sense the turbulent Welsh farm boy remained in transition the rest of his life—he made his home in Windsor, Ontario, and commuted daily across the international boundary to Detroit.

Tom Davey treated Minnie like a little princess during that engagement. He gave a party for her in Windsor, where she met newspapermen and critics, as well as his own intimate friends—a party that indirectly smoothed her way in Canada to the end of her acting days.

For Lizzie the way had never been smooth. Early in her discordant marriage she had begun to suffer from asthma. When she kept her baby in the dressing room, she used to tiptoe in after the dance, in spangled skirts and blonde curls and painted cheeks, trying to quiet her heavy breathing lest she disturb her child. By the time Minnie was fourteen, Lizzie's asthma had become acute. She was unable to lie down during one entire winter, but she never complained and she was never once absent from the cast. She was playing in St. Louis at the time, while Minnie attended the Ursuline Convent School. On March 25, 1879, Lizzie wrote to Robert Stevens, stage-manager husband of her sister Emma:

Dear Bob,

I learned of your whereabouts from Alice who was here last week. At that time I was very busy getting ready to go out of town to support a young novice rejoicing in the euphonious appellation of Schmitt. During my absence Minnie went to Cin^{ti} to visit some school friends, also to see our own folks. . . Mr. Havlin brought Minnie back in Modjeska's car and as there were several old acquaintances in the party she had a very pleasant time. . .

Bob, I am going to take advantage of your kind offer and ask you to lend me about $50, if you can easily spare it. I can return it when I get to New York. All well and hope you are the same. With kindest regards I remain very truly yours

Lizzie Maddern

Near the end of the summer of 1879 Lizzie took Minnie to New York, where they shared a house with Bob and Emma Stevens. As Lizzie's health was failing, her sister undertook to prepare Minnie for a full-fledged stage career. One of Emma's first acts was to take her niece to the Booth Theatre to see the great Adelaide Neilson in *Twelfth Night*.

A few weeks later, with her devoted Aunt Emma and Uncle Bob, Minnie stood in the autumn rain as her mother's coffin was lowered into a grave in an uptown cemetery. Elizabeth Maddern had ended her valiant stage career fifty dollars short of breaking even.

Minnie was on her own now. That fall she appeared in Hooley's *Juvenile Pinafore* at the Park Avenue Theatre in New York. She was an engaging and daring Ralph Rackstraw, and the operetta ran for a hundred performances. But Minnie dismissed it lightly and let Ralph Rackstraw drop from the record of her youthful roles. An all-juvenile cast offended her sense of the theatre.

At the close of *Pinafore* Minnie joined her aunts Emma and Mary in Cincinnati, where she had many theatre friends. One of them was the rough-and-ready John Havlin. He believed in Minnie's future, and he talked her into the company of Barney MacAuley, who was about to star in *A Messenger from Jarvis Section*.

Barney MacAuley was a nervous actor who believed that a star should be "wrapped in the solitude of his own originality." Minnie played a muted Clip and tried not to divert attention from the star, but her daydreaming and carelessness about clothes were her undoing, and MacAuley's. Sometimes he would find that the attention of the audience had deserted him for Minnie Maddern, who was absent-mindedly stepping out of a petticoat or some other garment which had come off at the wrong moment.

After such a mishap MacAuley would have an agonizing scene with Minnie.

"Miss Maddern, is it impossible for you to keep your clothes on?" and failing to get any convincing reassurance, he would end with the despairing admonition: "*Lock* your clothes on! *Bolt* them on!"

Once the daydreamer missed her cue: instead of coming to the rescue of the hero, who had been bound and gagged by thugs, she let him writhe in silent agony when he should have been declaiming his great speech—the ultimate of an actor's frustration.

After the curtain Minnie was ordered to stand before the entire company while MacAuley recited his wrongs:

"There is no scoundrel who would have merited the treatment I had this evening from this young person . . ."

Minnie remembered the speech all her life, but even while it was being delivered she lost sight of the fact that it had anything to do with her.

While Minnie was neglecting the business at hand she was formulating her own theories of acting. She thought actors on the stage should behave like people. She was humiliated by the antics of "emotional" actresses who smashed vases, tore down draperies and rolled on the floor, with the idea that they were showing their emotional depths. Audiences are not blind or hard of hearing. Sometimes a small voice can be heard most truly, and the smallest gesture can be the most telling —or the gesture that is never made, only started.

Actors who were too noisy in their grief drove audiences into their shells. The more an actor held back his grief, the farther the audience came out of its shell, with all its senses alert for the small sound of a breaking heart. With perfect acoustics and the right acting, Minnie thought, the actress could hold back all her grief except one tear, and the sound of that lonely little splash would be answered by a flood from the audience. The audience, not the actress, should supply the tears.

Minnie also believed that actors should talk like people, but whenever she groped for the right word, the prompter shoved the word at her as if she didn't know her lines, and she ended by speaking so rapidly that no prompter could get ahead of her.

When Minnie and MacAuley parted company, John Havlin took the young actress under his own management and starred her in a

22

play written by Charles Callahan, a local newspaperman; it was an imitation of Lotta Crabtree's flimsy plays and it was a failure.

Havlin was a determined man. He followed with another play of the same type, by the same amateur playwright.

Fogg's Ferry, Callahan's new effort, was even more like one of Lotta's plays, with some grand effects. Havlin decided to take it directly to New York.

Fogg's Ferry opened at Abbey's Park Theatre, New York, on May 15, 1882. Minnie was launched as a star to the full accompaniment of newspaper publicity, posters and folders and souvenir programs, cheering friends, and extravagant bouquets. When the golden dust had blown away, the critics judged Minnie and the play on their individual merit. The opinions were unanimous: Minnie Maddern would go far; *Fogg's Ferry* had gone too far already.

Of all the reviews, the one that thrilled the young star most appeared in the weekly *Dramatic Mirror*. The reviewer found Minnie's acting perfectly natural, and he predicted a brilliant future for her. The comment on her naturalness meant that her belief about actors on the stage acting like people had found its way into her work. The recognition meant all the more because it came from the *Mirror's* editor. The owner-editor had a stately name—Harrison Grey Fiske. People spoke of him as young—but people called anyone under thirty "young." Minnie didn't believe he was young until the opening night when the stage manager pointed out celebrities in the audience. Harrison Grey Fiske was big and impressive, with an air of being born to evening clothes—but he *was* young. To be exact, he was twenty, having been editor of the *Dramatic Mirror* since he was seventeen!

Though the critics damned *Fogg's Ferry*, the public liked it and the play was off to a long run and a national tour, which began in Boston.

An incident of the Boston engagement was prophetic. Two young men met in the lobby; both were short of stature and of funds, but long on dreams. They had seen Minnie Maddern in *Fogg's Ferry;* one ventured a spark of praise for the new star; the other responded with a brighter spark, which in turn encouraged the first to use even more glowing terms. It grew until the first young man borrowed two dollars from his friend, rushed to a florist and bought an armful of flowers, then hurried back to the theatre, bent on placing Miss Maddern under his management. In the theatre alley he almost collided with what seemed like a duplicate of himself, flowers and all. The two

23

marched in grim silence on their identical missions; at the stage door there was a dispute as to whose flowers and offer should go in first. The dispute led to a scuffle, then to a pitched battle which brought Minnie Maddern out to join the cheering spectators.

It was a lively little drama, but no one recognized it for what it was —future theatrical giants battling over the future leader of the American stage. There is some doubt as to whose damaged flowers were first through the stage door, but tradition has it that they were Charles Frohman's, with David Belasco's a close second.

Actually they were second and third. During the New York engagement another young man had been captivated by Minnie's acting; also he was personally smitten. Critics had found her cute, captivating, magnetic, and one of them had described her as "a little delicate wisp of girlhood, all luminous intensity, verve, and spirit, fine and sheer as a mist of lace." The girl, with her glorious red hair, deep blue eyes shining out of a delicate, wistful face, was all those things and more to the young man. He swore that he would keep her in sight until she became his wife, and a star under his management.

The young man, Legrand White, was not badly situated for making good his vow. He was a handsome and dashing scion of the Whites of piano company fame. He was also a competent musician and a well-known xylophone player in vaudeville. At the time of White's infatuation he was living with his family in Brooklyn. He told no one about his vow. But his mother and four sisters were only mildly surprised when he joined the *Fogg's Ferry* orchestra as drummer and went on tour with more enthusiasm than the job seemed to warrant; Legrand was an ardent youth, given to sudden and strong impulses, and called the "black sheep" of the family although there is no evidence of any wrongdoing.

In Boston, when Frohman's and Belasco's battered flowers were sent in to Minnie's dressing room, others, in good condition, were already there from Legrand White. On the long tour there were many more as the dashing young drummer laid siege to Minnie's heart and filled her head with dreams of stardom in a finer play than the present crude melodrama.

There were other hints that Minnie deserved a better vehicle. In Cleveland she received a note and a book from Lawrence Barrett, the Eminent Tragedian. Barrett was an old family friend, but such an austere man that Minnie was apprehensive over what he might say about *Fogg's Ferry*. All he said, however, was that he understood she was appearing in a financial success. He trusted she was in good health —and he was sending her a play which he believed would reward her thoughtful reading.

The play was *A Doll's House* by Henrik Ibsen. It seemed a strange thing for a great Shakespearean actor to recommend. It had only three acts, and no soliloquies or asides; the only way one knew what the actors were thinking was from what they said to one another, and their lines were like ordinary conversation. There was no action, although things happened in a quiet and disconcerting way.

Minnie put the little volume in her carpetbag with a baffled feeling. She believed actors on the stage should behave like people. That ought to make the play right for her, but it didn't. After all, actors had to have something dramatic to work with, and *A Doll's House* didn't even feel like a play!

With undiminished box-office receipts, *Fogg's Ferry* toured through the remainder of 1882 and all of 1883. By late March of its second year it had traveled as far west as the Rocky Mountains.

At Tabor's Grand Opera House in Denver, Minnie was welcomed by an enthusiastic audience, with a special demonstration from Eugene Field, who applauded vociferously from a stage box. Minnie thought he was making fun of her, until he leaned over the edge of the box and threw a large bouquet of violets at her feet. The flattered girl smiled gratefully and stooped to retrieve the flowers—only to have them snatched away on a thread which Field had attached to them.

Eugene Field couldn't let Minnie go without further proof of his waggish affection. For the close of the Denver engagement he engineered a testimonial luncheon at which the "gentlemen of the press" presented her with a pair of "diamond" earrings the size of walnuts— and about as valuable.

Fogg's Ferry went on to San Francisco and started back across the continent, with Legrand White painting Minnie a word picture of the fame and happiness they would share together. He never wrote home anything that was a clue to his devotion to the company. But one spring night in Brooklyn one of his sisters dreamed that Legrand brought home a bride with glorious red hair. The dream was so vivid that she told it to her mother and sisters, declaring that it was too real to be a dream.

An afternoon or two later the doorbell rang, and there was Legrand, with a dainty wisp of a girl whose mass of red hair was as glorious as any ever dreamed of.

25

Legrand introduced Minnie Maddern, his fiancée and future star.

The Whites took Minnie to their hearts, arranged a home wedding, and did their share in making the young couple's dream a reality.

Reality for Minnie was living in Brooklyn with her in-laws while they wrestled with the practical details of starring her in a suitable play. The play itself was less of a problem than plays had often been. Minnie and Legrand were wisely agreed that there would be no more imitations of Lotta Crabtree. They had a play written to order by Howard Taylor, managing editor of the *Dramatic Mirror*. It was called *Caprice*, a graceful, sentimental play with songs.

Production of *Caprice* was another matter. Legrand had assumed, correctly, that his family would finance the play, but their funds were limited. Minnie's dreams, on the other hand, were unbounded. She envisioned a perfect production with the best cast that could be assembled. Differences of opinion arose and had to be smoothed out. But things were on a workable basis until Minnie announced her choice of a leading man—Henry Miller, the highest-paid male lead of the day! Immediately the Brooklyn house was thrown into turmoil. Through the long hot days of summer the family argued the wisdom of such an expense. Legrand sweated between two fires. His mother alone saw the whole picture, in which more than money was at stake. The marriage of the unawakened young star and the ardent Legrand was on shaky ground, and it was not being steadied by prolonged family argument. Mrs. White became Minnie's staunch ally; she quieted disagreements and ruled in favor of Henry Miller, and to economize on the cost of the production she made all of Minnie's costumes.

Caprice had its premiere in New York at the New Park Theatre, prettily staged and generously cast. It was a smooth production, but its financial success hung in the balance for a long time, and in the White household nerves remained at the snapping point. After repeated quarrels Minnie and Legrand finally separated, and the rift was never healed. Legrand was married twice more, the second time to another actress.

The prime cause of trouble in the White household was the large salary paid to Henry Miller; Minnie was unyielding in her insistence that he was essential to success. Yet it was not Miller's work, but her own interpretation of the part of Mercy Baxter, that made *Caprice* outlive in memory a hundred better plays.

At the end of the first act the humiliated Mercy consoled herself by singing "In the Gloaming." Other actresses would have rendered the ballad while standing at the footlights, but Minnie remained in the stage picture—crouched on the hearth, looking into a glowing fire that lit up her vivid hair.

It was a daring innovation, but the public was enchanted by the picture and by the young star's wistful, tender singing.

Caprice toured all during 1884, and would have continued longer except for the bank crash and panic of that winter. It was the nation-wide tour that made "In the Gloaming" a popular song for decades, and for many who heard it, a lifetime memory. Fifty years afterward George Brasfield of Petersburg, Virginia, wrote to Harry Fiske:

> I have listened to Grace Moore tonight sing "In the Gloaming," from Hollywood. I have heard her and many others sing this same song many times. Each time I am delightfully reminded of Minnie Maddern. When I was a small country boy I heard her sing this song in the old Masonic Theatre in Nashville, Tennessee, many years ago, and the song amid the scene is as vivid to my mind now as then.

The song amid the scene that made a lifelong impression on a country boy in the South was no less effective in Northern cities. Recently a New Yorker observed that the site of the Park Theatre is buried twenty stories deep under an office building, but when he thinks about it the right way, the skyscraper disappears and there rises in its place the old Park Theatre, with a girl crouched by the hearth, and the firelight playing on her pale face and vivid red hair while she sings for an old man as she sang for the child, "In the gloaming, O my darling—"

CHAPTER 4

For Minnie, home was where other Madderns were. In childhood it was the house on Baronne Street, then dingy housekeeping rooms in St. Louis, and later a hotel suite in Cincinnati, headquarters of Aunt Emma and Uncle Bob. The pattern was interrupted by her marriage, but after her separation she returned to her family.

The Stevens' headquarters shifted with the changing fortunes of the theatre. At the end of her long tour in *Caprice*, Minnie joined her aunt and uncle at Larchmont, New York. Coming home to a house in the country was a new experience. She had seen most of North America from train windows, but her intimate knowledge of it was limited to city parks and the gardens of convent schools.

Larchmont, on the Boston Post Road twenty miles from New York City, was an unhurried village where broad lawns made room for carriage houses and summer retreats under big trees. To the south a wooded slope descended to the clear waters of the harbor, and across the Sound lay the blue shore of Long Island. To the north and west, village streets became country lanes, and spacious grounds blended with estates and farms that undulated over the rolling Westchester hills. Brooks flowed through rocky glens, and half an hour's walk from the railroad station the sunny hills and groves darkened into Saxon Woods with their miles of primeval forest.

In many ways Minnie was poorly equipped for her new surroundings. She had never learned to swim or ride horseback or play games; she didn't even know how to dress suitably for the outdoors. Driving was one of her few accomplishments and at Larchmont she made the most of it, borrowing her uncle's pony and little yellow cart and driving madly over the country roads and lanes, her hair streaming out like flame in the wind.

"All you need is a black cigar," Aunt Emma observed, "and you'd look like Lotta Crabtree!"

Lotta used to wear down her excitement after a performance by driving and smoking furiously. In part, Minnie's own mad driving was hero worship.

But Minnie could enjoy the country in quieter mood, too; she had a gift for walking without tiring and for being alone in silence without being lonely. At such times she felt renewed confidence in her ability to do things on the stage. She had been a star almost from infancy and she had just completed a nationwide tour in *Caprice*, but instead of glowing with a sense of accomplishment, she was plagued by the consciousness of unused powers. In all her stage life, it seemed, she had been walking on the outskirts of success.

Summer evenings at Larchmont Minnie's future was discussed with Uncle Bob and Aunt Emma; sometimes they were joined by Doctor and Mrs. Shepard, who were neighbors as well as devoted friends. In those discussions the elders agreed that Minnie was ready for a debut in a substantial play.

Minnie welcomed the decision and hoped they could find a play and a director in sympathy with her methods. Eugene Field had once classified Minnie as a perfect example of the "MacKaye belief." Steele MacKaye, inventor, playwright, actor, producer, director and teacher, was the American prophet of the Delsartean school of acting. He had recently finished the Lyceum in New York; Minnie had not seen it, but she had heard that it was the most modern theatre in the world.

Here was a director on whom they could all agree; but MacKaye was bankrupt and about to lose his theatre.

Loyal Doctor Shepard came to the rescue; he put money into the treasury of the Lyceum and arranged for its opening with Minnie in a play to be provided and directed by Steele MacKaye. The young actress was to choose her own cast.

The evening after the signing of the agreement Steele MacKaye arrived at Larchmont. He was slender and dark—strikingly like Edgar Allan Poe, and as ill-fated.

One of MacKaye's disastrous experiences had been with the theatre-minded editors of *The Churchman*, the Reverend Mallory and his brother. They engaged MacKaye to build, manage, and write plays for the Madison Square Theatre. Their contract, which he signed without reading, indentured him forever at a salary of thirty-five dollars a week and gave the brothers the rights to everything MacKaye produced.

The indenture clause was illegal, but when MacKaye broke with the Mallorys they claimed his play *Hazel Kirk*, then in its third year of production, and they removed his name from the play. He got no credit for its authorship—nor did he get any of the seven million dollars which it earned in its thirty years of continuous production.

Steele MacKaye was born to troubles, but he forgot them in his rush of ideas. He knew the very play to reveal Miss Maddern's talents— Sardou's *Andrea,* which he would rewrite into an American play to be called *In Spite of All.*

In after years Minnie wondered at her audacity in casting *In Spite of All.* For her stage husband she chose the celebrated Eben Plympton, who was equally at home in Shakespearean tragedy or modern comedy. Plympton was startled by the brash proposal, but Minnie signed him as confidently as if she had been hiring a cook, and went on to engage the distinguished John Lane for another part.

For the role of the prima donna, Minnie secured the vivid Selina Dolara, English comic-opera queen, who had been one of the first Carmens of Bizet's opera.

There remained one more important role—Antonius Kraft, the impresario. Minnie's choice for Kraft was the young English actor Richard Mansfield, trained for both opera and stage. Mansfield had sung in the first touring company of *Pinafore.* In New York he had been sensational as Baron Chevalier in *A Parisian Romance.* After that he had gone into total eclipse.

In an impressive hotel room, Minnie had her interview with Richard Mansfield. He was a short young man, punctilious, in immaculate clothes somewhat too large for him, and his square-cut face was whiter and more sunken than she remembered it.

He had planned to return to London for the fall season, Mansfield told Minnie. However, he would consider the role of Antonius Kraft and let her have his decision in a day or two. On second thought, he would postpone his return to London and accept the role.

Actually, Mansfield did not have the money for his next meal; after months of slow starvation he was being saved from despair by Minnie's offer.

News of the *Andrea* production leaked to the Mallorys, but the only announcement from the churchly brothers was to the effect that the Madison Square would not open until September tenth. MacKaye, feeling the pressure of his opening date, was reassured by the announcement; he postponed his play for a week. Then the Mallorys announced the opening of their theatre on August thirty-first with Madame Janish in Sardou's *Anslema* (another name for *Andrea*), which the company had been secretly rehearsing night and day.

MacKaye then sought out Agnes Ethel, in the hope of buying the right to a play named *Agnes,* which Sardou had written for her. But Miss Ethel had sold her rights to Kate Claxton, and the chase led back to Larchmont, where Miss Claxton was living. There, for five thousand dollars, Steele MacKaye purchased, in Miss Maddern's name, the right to produce *Agnes* in America.

At the Madison Square Theatre, a few hours before curtain time, the Mallorys were stunned by an injunction against their presenting a play to which Miss Maddern had the exclusive American rights; *Agnes* and *Andrea* and *Anslema* were all the same play. The court order gave Madame Janish the right to produce *Anslema* for a week under stringent conditions which included securing Miss Maddern's permission and paying whatever royalty she demanded. Minnie had it in her power to obliterate the rival production. Instead, she granted Janish permission to appear ahead of her, and asked only the usual royalty, thereby impairing her own chances but satisfying her Maddern conscience.

At the Lyceum Theatre, Minnie stepped into a new age. She went there on a hot summer day, but the theatre was refreshingly cool, and the smell of burnt gas was missing. MacKaye moved a lever in the prompter's box, and the stage was flooded with the first electric light ever used in a theatre.

Notice, Miss Maddern, how this switch revolutionizes acting. The actor no longer has to come down to the footlights to be seen.

Here is something that will eventually save thousands of lives. MacKaye lowered the world's first asbestos curtain—his own invention.

And here is the stage curtain of the future. Instead of rolling down like a window shade, two velvet drapes swept out and down from the proscenium arch.

This lever allows the Lyceum to open at eight-thirty instead of eight. MacKaye moved a lever, and the stage rose like an elevator, and a second stage, completely set, took its place.

Notice the seats in the auditorium—they fold back, making it easier to get in and out. The rack underneath is for a man's hat.

This is a coupon ticket. The patron keeps the stub, with the row and number of his seat. . .

Minnie wondered how a building could be so cool on such a hot day—and MacKaye's monologue gained impetus.

The air is fortified with ozone and circulated by fans. In summer it passes over cakes of ice, in winter over hot radiators. . .

Most of MacKaye's innovations were soon adopted everywhere—

but not all of them. Forty years afterward, on draughty stages and on stifling ones, Minnie looked in vain for the air conditioning which Steele MacKaye had demonstrated in 1885.

In her brush with Madame Janish, the green young actress had risen above her famous European rival in generosity and dignity; in her role of Alice Clendenning, the critics noted the same mixture of greenness and maturity. The New York *Sun* wrote that Miss Maddern outraged all her art and won all the sympathies in the same role.

In the *Dramatic Mirror*, Harrison Grey Fiske wrote romantically of Minnie's sparkle, piquancy and magnetism; of her ever-changing great deep violet eyes, her rich golden-red hair, and her clear, soft, brilliant skin.

A few evenings later Minnie was pleasantly aware of Mr. Fiske sharing one of the lower boxes with an important-looking stranger. In the three years since the young editor had been pointed out to her, Minnie had made two long tours of the United States, fallen in love, and entered an unhappy marriage which ended in separation.

After the performance, as Minnie was hurrying along the narrow passage to the front of the theatre, Steele MacKaye stepped out of one of the boxes and asked her to meet some friends.

MacKaye escorted the young star into the box. She found herself in the presence of Harrison Grey Fiske and his companion, Henry Arthur Jones, the English playwright. Jones had just arrived to supervise the rehearsals of *Saints and Sinners*. He told her that the first thing he had wanted to see in New York was her performance. He had heard great things of her, but he hadn't been prepared for such genius. He was sure it hadn't been any hardship for his escort to see the play for a second time.

Mr. Fiske interrupted to say that it was the third time, and he expected to see it a fourth. He had been an admirer of Miss Maddern's work ever since he had seen her as Prince Arthur, when she was nine and he was twelve.

She asked lightly if he had been editor of the *Dramatic Mirror* at the time.

No—not until several years afterward, Mr. Fiske told her—but he was there to discuss her work, not his.

Minnie was always reticent about her work, and now she was inwardly flustered; after a few pleasantries she hurried away—elated over her meeting with the famous young editor.

In Spite of All brought the realization of dreams to several people.

32

Three years earlier, in a theatre alley, young David Belasco and young Charles Frohman had battled over which should be the first to offer Minnie Maddern a contract. When *In Spite of All* was taken to the same Boston theatre, Charles Frohman went along as Miss Maddern's manager and David Belasco as stage manager.

Another young man who felt the expansive touch of the play was Richard Mansfield. His gloom during rehearsals was partly dispelled by critics' predictions that the role of Antonius Kraft would live in theatre history, and as the run continued, Mansfield began to dream once more of fame and fortune on the American stage. After a rousing personal success in Boston, his confidence rose to such heights that in Philadelphia he deserted the company to rush back to Boston and sing the role of Koko in a tremendously successful production of *The Mikado*.

In Spite of All closed soon after Mansfield's desertion, having played and toured less than six weeks. Financially it was a failure, but some of its by-products changed American theatre history: one was the meeting of Minnie Maddern and Harrison Grey Fiske; another was the circumstance that instead of returning disillusioned to England, Richard Mansfield remained to become one of America's greatest actors.

Among those who did not benefit from the production was its creator, Steele MacKaye; he lost the Lyceum that fall and was never able to complete another theatre.

In the summer of 1886 Minnie was back at Larchmont; she drove less and spent more time walking in the fields and woods, where she dreamed of what she wanted to do in the theatre. In mid-August the rural quiet was interrupted by a church fair. Minnie presided over a booth with a stagelike counter, where she sold photographs of theatre notables, among them one of Harrison Grey Fiske.

Minnie had written Mr. Fiske requesting an autographed photo and inviting him to the fair; his reply had come unexpectedly from Mamaroneck, three miles away, where he was living at his parents' country place and commuting to the city. A previous engagement prevented his attending the church fair, but he enclosed a photograph by Sarony and a check.

The photograph showed a particularly well-groomed and confident-looking young man with large, regular features, luxuriant moustache, light eyebrows and thinning hair which accentuated his high forehead. Minnie wanted to buy the photograph herself, but the young editor

33

was an eligible bachelor and a reputed millionaire, and his picture was snatched up at once.

Minnie wondered whether Mr. Fiske had been unable to attend the fair, or didn't want to, till one afternoon shortly after, he answered her question by riding over on a bay thoroughbred to make a neighborly call.

He and Minnie talked for an hour on the wisteria-shaded porch. He asked to see the book she had been reading, and was surprised that an actress should be partial to Thoreau's *Walden*. He wanted to talk theatre, and he was surprised again to discover the young woman who got such true effects on the stage was reluctant to discuss her methods.

Minnie was puzzled by Harrison Fiske's seeing the theatre as a glamorous place. For all his knowledge of plays and players, he wasn't of the theatre; he thought of it as a pleasant place to linger—instead of a quicksand where one had to keep moving to survive.

The two observed blind spots in each other, but in many things they saw eye-to-eye; and Mr. Fiske called twice more before Minnie began her autumn tour of 1886 in *In Spite of All*.

The progress of Minnie's friendship with the young editor was leisurely, and her progress in the theatre was more leisurely still; sometimes it seemed like retrogression.

Following the revival of her two earlier plays, Minnie appeared in out-of-town productions of *The Puritan Maid*, *The Professional Beauty* and *Lady Jemina*—plays that were born, and died, in the provinces. New York, which the child Minnie had taken for granted, became a dream city, receding into the distance.

When Minnie wasn't playing, she lived at Larchmont, sometimes with the Stevenses and sometimes with the Shepards. She continued to spend much of her time close to nature, but she spent even more with books, trying to make up for her inadequate schooling, which she contrasted unfavorably with that of the fortunate and polished Harrison Fiske.

The young editor continued to call at intervals. He was generally announced by the expectant whinnying of his horse; Minnie would run to the gate, where she let the bay nuzzle her pocket for sugar while she welcomed the rider. It was a dignified friendship, and to Minnie's romance-minded relatives it progressed too slowly. They had almost given up hope when, after two years, she surprised them by applying to the Wayne County, Michigan, courts for a divorce from Legrand White. She had never used her married name, so the granting

34

of the decree, on June 25, 1888, made little external difference. But the family's hopes revived.

During Minnie's Larchmont years, the baby Emily Stevens grew to be an observant little girl. One day Minnie heard the front door burst open and the five-year-old Emily hailed her:

"Co' Minnie! Co' Minnie! Here comes the Big One!"

Minnie dashed out to see Harrison Fiske riding up the lane. The "Big One" suited him well: a big, handsome young man sitting easily on his bright horse in the June sunshine.

She met him at the gate, and as soon as he dismounted he began telling her that on the way from Mamaroneck he had been taking stock of his life. He would be twenty-six in July, and it was high time for him to think of marrying. He had been thinking of it, and he realized how right it was for a man to be married—and for a woman, too.

Minnie stroked the horse's velvety nose.

"Whom were you thinking of marrying?"

"I was thinking of you."

It was a blunt proposal, and the setting in broad daylight provided no opportunity for sentimental demonstration. But if Minnie was disappointed she gave no sign, and Harry interpreted her silence as consent. They talked of other things while she petted the horse affectionately.

Neither one referred to their engagement until a later visit. Then Harry asked Minnie what she planned to do after they were married.

She had been thinking of that searchingly, and she told him: she would leave the stage and be a full-time wife.

Minnie was twenty-three; she had been on the stage nearly all her life without finding herself. Her interests were modern and American, and the kind of play she wanted did not seem to exist. She was tired of travel and a hundred discouraging things about the stage; at best it was an imitation of life, and she looked forward to graduating into reality.

Minnie's plan to retire broke the jinx that had kept her off the New York stage for four years. In the spring of 1889 she appeared at the Madison Square Theatre in the lead of *Featherbrain*—a farce which purported to show that men love women for their stupidity.

Featherbrain was symbolic of the plays which had helped Minnie's decision to leave the stage, but some good things came of it: the young actor Wilton Lackaye made a great hit as the jealous Portuguese nobleman and was boosted on his way to fame; and Minnie's sparkling performance inspired a theatrical prophecy from Nym Crinkle—Minnie Maddern would one day play Becky Sharp.

Featherbrain did not outlast the spring; in the fall Minnie returned to *In Spite of All*. She and Harry Fiske had set their wedding date for March of 1890; late in January she ended the tour at the old Grand Opera House in Toronto.

Harry came up from New York to see Minnie's unheralded farewell to the stage, and after the play he took her to dinner at the Queen's Hotel, where she was staying. This circumstance inspired the Toronto legend that they became engaged that evening in the Red Parlor of the Queen's. In substantiation it is pointed out that when the Queen's was to be torn down to make room for the Royal York Hotel, Mrs. Fiske asked for a public movement to preserve it as a landmark. Actually, Minnie Maddern's farewell appearance occurred near the end, not at the beginning, of the betrothal of a travel-weary young star and a journalist who was an unaccountable mixture of worldly polish and high-minded ideals.

CHAPTER 5

The boy editor of the *Dramatic Mirror,* who sometimes took off his kid gloves to fight barehanded for the underdog, was born into a gentleman's world. The elder Fiske had prospered in the hotel business, and he and his wife were able to give their sons the best their judgments could discern. Except when they traveled in Europe, the Fiskes wintered in New York City and summered in the country—usually in Maine. In the process of giving their sons the best, they exposed the boys to the inevitable experiments in education.

Harry began his formal education in a kindergarten newly imported from Germany. He was still wearing dresses, but the ruling passion of his life had already sprouted. The seed had been planted earlier when his nurse took him to Barnum's Museum at Broadway and Ann Street; there he saw his first play, *Joseph and His Brethren,* in the Moral Lecture Room, where the wily Barnum presented such things for those who had moral scruples about the theatre.

Harry found the play enchanting, and his enthusiasm was rewarded with a toy theatre. This proved so much to his liking that he turned away from learning the alphabet and devoted himself wholly to the theatre—until his exasperated father smashed the toy and threw it in the fire. The result was so disastrous that Mr. Fiske relented and bought a new and larger theatre, and Harry's enthusiasm gained momentum.

Kindergarten was followed by tutoring at home; then a school on Forty-second Street, run by Mrs. George Vanderhoff, wife of the retired English tragedian. It was an experimental school with honor system and unusual freedom, but parents were uncertain about a school where boys were not whipped; presently it closed and the pupils scattered.

For Harry the path of education now led downtown to Dr. Chapin's Collegiate Institute at Sixth Avenue and Fourteenth Street. The

Institute had none of the rich flavor of the theatre that had found its way into the Vanderhoff schoolroom, but only a wall separated it from the Theatre Française, later known by the names Lyceum, Fourteenth Street, Haverly's, and, until recently, as the Civic Repertory Theatre.

It was while he was enrolled at the Institute that Harry Fiske first saw Minnie Maddern. She was playing in *King John* at Booth's Theatre with Junius Brutus Booth, Jr., and his wife Agnes. For Harry the truest note in the play was struck by Prince Arthur, played by "a pale-faced child of nine with big eyes, startling red hair, and a haunting voice."

Minnie lived the role as if she were at the moment of unfolding of ancient events, speaking lines that had never been spoken before. Harry kept the program with his cherished possessions, where it remained until his death.

The elder Fiske believed that boys should have a taste of the sterner stuff of life. He kept fine horses, and he required his sons to spend a part of each summer on horseback. At the end of one summer on the Maine coast, Mr. Fiske gave Harry and his brother Theodore permission to ride their horses home to New York. The boys had not asked for it, but they made the autumn jaunt across four states and they arrived home in good health.

The following September Harry and his brother had the adventurous idea of buying a twenty-one-foot sloop and sailing her home from Maine. Their mother protested, but Mr. Fiske added a one-eyed Maine fisherman to the crew and waved them good-by. At the end of eleven sometimes-hazardous days, the boys reached home, vindicating their father's belief that young gentlemen neither broke their necks nor drowned before their time.

The pursuit of learning occupied only a fragment of Harry's energies. He had a printing press, and one of his earliest enterprises was the writing and publishing of a monthly paper. It flourished for a time and was followed by a series of short stories, written under the influence of Poe and published, under the influence of his mother, in a Massachusetts newspaper owned by an uncle. Later, Harry was an irregular correspondent for the Raleigh *Observer*, owned by a friend of his father.

While still in his teens, Harry was appointed dramatic critic of the Jersey City *Argus*, and he plunged enthusiastically into his first job which was not the product of family money or influence. So he supposed, until the paper had one of its periodic financial seizures.

Then he learned that the *Argus* was in debt to his father, and his appointment had been a by-product of the debt. His enthusiasm died with the discovery.

About this time Mr. Fiske bought a hundred-acre country place at Hyde Park on the Hudson. At the beginning of summer the family migrated to their new estate with servants, horses and carriages. The boys sailed their sloop up, and Harry spent most of the summer exploring the river from Poughkeepsie to Kingston.

Near the end of the second summer on the river, the younger members of the family came down with malaria and they were hurried back to New York City. At the end of the year, still plagued by malaria, Harry passed his examinations and was ready to enter New York University, but the family physician prescribed a trip abroad instead.

Harry sailed for Europe in June, aboard the crack liner *Spain*. A flock of girl-friends who accompanied him on board made the most of the occasion by kissing him good-bye, and at the last moment one of them impulsively took off her heart-shaped locket on its gold chain and clasped it about his neck.

The girls departed; but as the liner was standing out past the Statue of Liberty, Harry was startled by a lovely mocking voice near him:

"Romeo, Romeo! wherefore art thou Romeo?"

He turned to face a tall, beautiful woman—Fanny Davenport, New York's favorite actress. She had burst into stardom two years before in *Pique*. Harry had worshipped her from a distance ever since, and now here she was, admiring him.

Miss Davenport had observed the schoolgirls' tender leave-taking and she was twinged with jealousy. She told Harry the scene had been charming—but clearly she didn't think so. The girl who had bestowed the locket had triumphed over all the others; now the actress triumphed over the girl by removing the locket from around Harry's neck.

"You are too old for such juvenile sentiments," she told him as she tossed the keepsake into the Atlantic.

The young man was overwhelmed by this sign of Miss Davenport's affection and he swore eternal love for her. She responded with similar vows, and they became engaged. To be sure, Fanny Davenport was nearly ten years Harry's senior, and she had a husband from whom she was separated but not divorced. But the locket at the bottom of the ocean bound Harry to the glamorous actress, and the engagement, play-acting or real, continued for years.

In London Harry indulged in sight-seeing and playgoing with

Fanny and her family, met Ellen Terry and went coaching with the elder Sothern. But a wave of homesickness overtook him, and he returned to spend the rest of the summer with his family in Maine.

That fall Harry entered New York University, and shortly thereafter he submitted an article to a new theatre paper, the New York *Dramatic Mirror*. His article was accepted, and he continued to contribute to the promising young paper during the remainder of his freshman year. The following year he was assigned to do special interviews with playwrights and actors.

The *Mirror* assignment was more daring than it sounds. On entering the university, Harry had had to sign a pledge not to frequent theatres or other unholy places. His interviews for the *Mirror* were public proof that he had broken his pledge. But the authorities said nothing.

While still a sophomore, Harry decided to make journalism his career. At about the same time he was offered the chance to buy one-third of the *Mirror's* stock.

The elder Fiske had wanted Harry to finish college, but he believed that a boy old enough to choose his profession was entitled to make his own decisions. So he purchased the third interest in the paper for his son, who thereupon left the university to become editor of the New York *Dramatic Mirror*. He was then seventeen—by some years the youngest editor in New York.

Along with the editorship, Harry inherited a crusade against another New York dramatic paper, sometimes referred to as the *Vulture*. That journal rested on the solid foundation of a research department which delved into the private lives of theatre people and catalogued moral imperfections. When a subject ripened into prominence, he would be offered a choice: his portrait in the *Vulture* for a large fee; or anything from a deftly-placed smear to a bludgeoning attack.

When Harry took over the *Mirror*, he stepped up the war on the *Vulture;* those who had been threatened, or forced to buy protection, supplied a steady trickle of potential ammunition. The circumstance made a seventeen-year-old the father-confessor to erring actors and actresses, but the young man took it in his stride. With the accumulation of information he became more specific in his charges, and the *Vulture* replied with abuse and threats of libel action.

The battle had no dramatic climax, but the campaign had its effect. With everyone aware of the *Vulture's* methods, erring actors cooled to the idea of paying for portraits which would advertise the fact that they had something to conceal. As the *Vulture* was reduced to impotence, its circulation and advertising declined, and eventually it disappeared from the scene.

Early in his editorial career, Harry made the acquaintance of Edwin Booth; that gentle and reticent public idol was generous in his encouragement of the young man's efforts, and Harry valued the friendship as one of the happiest experiences of his life.

One day in the second year of his editorship, Harry was faced with a sudden crisis. He owned one third of the *Mirror* stock; another third was owned by a theatrical man who favored using the paper to promote his own enterprises. The remaining third belonged to Colonel Lewis, a man who, like Harry, believed in an editorial policy without favoritism and without fear. Except for exerting his influence in favor of the young editor, Colonel Lewis let the *Mirror* take care of itself while he dabbled in Wall Street—where ex-President Grant rode to work each morning in a gilded carriage, and where watered stocks were booming in preparation for a crash.

On the morning in question, the Colonel burst into the office with the news that he was engaged in a big deal and it would take every dollar he could raise to cover his margins; if Harry could raise twelve thousand dollars in cash by the following morning, he could have the Colonel's share in the paper; if not, the Colonel would have to sell to the third partner, who was eager to buy.

Harry depended upon his father for financial backing, but his family were traveling in the South and Harry's urgent telegrams failed to locate them. Everything he could raise on his own account fell ten thousand dollars short of the required amount, and the friends with whom he felt free to discuss the situation did not have that kind of money.

On the morning of the deadline which he could not meet, Harry was putting his desk in order when a messenger handed him an envelope. It was from the Hotel Brunswick, and in it was a check for ten thousand dollars together with a note from Edwin Booth explaining that a friend had told him of the crisis at the *Mirror* office. There was also a postscript: *Use this and let's not mention it when we meet.*

A week later Harry got in touch with his father and was able to repay Booth's great-hearted loan. Shortly after this the minority stockholder sold his share to the boy editor.

Harry thus became sole owner of the crusading *Mirror*, and his first act as proprietor was to start a campaign for an American equivalent of the Actors' Benevolent Fund of England.

The *Mirror's* drive coincided with the hard times of the winter of 1881–1882. There was acute unemployment and suffering in the theatrical profession. One of the sufferers was Harry Bascom, stranded in New York without a cent in his pocket. The actor had relatives in Boston, and he started the 250-mile walk over the Boston Post Road in the dead of winter. A week later he was found in a haymow, unconscious and badly frozen; at the hospital one of his legs had to be amputated.

The *Mirror* carried the story of Bascom's journey with all its drama and heartbreak. Harry Fiske sent telegrams to successful actors and received thousand-dollar checks in response. Benefit performances replenished the funds as an emergency committee apportioned them, and after months of brilliant service the Actors' Fund of America received its charter on June 8, 1882.

That year Harry saw Minnie Maddern for the second time. She was eighteen, starring as the ragged, winsome Clip in *Fogg's Ferry*—the imitation of Lotta Crabtree's trashy melodramas. The star, too, imitated the great Lotta, whose fame and fortune dazzled young actresses and managers out of recognizing that she was not an actress but a variety performer, brilliant in her specialty, but with nothing to offer those who imitated her. Along with other New York critics, Harry panned *Fogg's Ferry;* and in the girl actress he saw something finer than her idol.

Two years later Harry saw Minnie again—this time in *Caprice*, with her Lotta phase outgrown and with promise of a finer and deeper art. Next season she appeared in *In Spite of All*, still unfinished, still growing. During this performance he met her for the first time, and presently she became for him "the one and early star we see, and lose, and see again."

CHAPTER 6

The only times when something hadn't gone wrong with Minnie's costumes on the stage were those when one of her aunts was acting as her dresser.

At her wedding, both Aunt Emma and Aunt Mary were on hand to hook and button her into her wedding gown; Mrs. Shepard appeared at intervals to bestow advice and admiration, and little Cousin Emily raced in and out—a swirl of white lace and spun-gold hair. Her too eager concern was for the bouquets, especially the maid-of-honor's, which was her own. The bouquets were keeping fresh in the chilly conservatory, and wasn't it time to bring them in?

For the first time in her life Minnie had a presentiment of stage fright—although she was about to appear before the smallest and most affectionate of audiences.

Harrison Fiske's father had died that winter, and the plans for the wedding at the Shepards' villa had been reduced to the simplest ceremony, with only members of the two families present. Minnie would have only a few brief lines, with the minister prompting her. But in a moment of panic it seemed to her that she had forgotten to find the meaning of her lines. It was too late now. Little Emily was clamoring to thrust the bouquet into the bride's hands; her young brother wanted to know when the wedding was going to start: children in league with marriage. Harry, with whom she had forgotten to discuss the important things, had been taken directly to a room upstairs lest he have an unlucky glimpse of his bride before the ceremony.

When they had set their wedding date for March 19, 1890, Harry and Minnie had talked hopefully of spring, with green buds and blossoms beginning to unfold. This was the day—and from the chilly upstairs study Harry looked out through falling snow at trees sheathed in ice; when a gust of white wind swept through their branches he

43

could hear the groan of their icy joints; the ground was buried under two feet of snow that was beginning to drift.

His father's life had come to its end, and now it was Harry's turn to be the head of a household. At the moment, he confessed afterward, he felt nothing but oppression. His gloomy thoughts were interrupted by Otis, his younger brother and best man, who came to say that it was time. Was he feeling nervous, old man, and did he have the parson's fee where he could find it?

The ceremony went gracefully, even to the innovation of omitting the bride's promise to obey. There was a gay wedding breakfast with a three-tiered wedding cake, iced as white as the world outside; then the two were tucked into the waiting sleigh, and they started off for the railroad station to the accompaniment of good wishes and jingling sleigh bells, and a shower of rice, cream-colored through white snowflakes.

On the train going south with his bride, Harry wondered that he had ever thought of running away from the ceremony. When he confessed to Minnie, she told him that she had had the same impulse, and they laughed together at their foolishness.

From the train window they looked for signs of spring, but the New Jersey countryside was deep in winter, and Philadelphia was half-buried under snowdrifts. But they were sure of comfortable accommodations. Harry had written to the Bellevue Hotel for a suite, and George Boldt's secretary had replied, telling him that the hotel magnate and friend of the elder Fiskes was attending to the reservation personally.

George Boldt had done his utmost. When the Fiskes saw the accommodations they decided he had done too much. They had a vast and gloomy suite—a kind of combination furniture warehouse and museum of Victorian knickknacks. There were fussy sofas and fragile, cumbersome chairs—enough for their combined acquaintances to sit at one time in expensive discomfort. There was distance enough in which to go for a walk, but the way was narrow and far from straight, and it was obstructed by massive marble tables with gilded macaroni legs, and overloaded stands and whatnots. The touch of a hand could bring down an avalanche of photographs and seashells and statuettes and souvenirs; perhaps in anticipation of such a mishap, crayon portraits of Boldts and Boldts-in-law looked reproachfully from the walls.

The bedroom was as vast and crowded as the other rooms; the

dark walnut of the bed rose halfway to the distant ceiling, and the towering somber wardrobe seemed to duplicate the one that had terrified Minnie in childhood.

If Harry and Minnie had been madly in love, they would have been blind to their stuffy surroundings. But at the moment theirs was an ecstasy of admiration—Harry's for the elusive star and Minnie's for the suave intellectual giant. Their chief common interest was the theatre. Several times they fought their way through the storm to attend plays, Minnie judging the performance from one side of the footlights, Harry from the other. The experience did little to enrich their honeymoon; so the young couple decided to wait indoors for the storm to abate. Harry picked up a Bible concordance and studied it with a skepticism sharpened by association with his friend Bob Ingersoll, and Minnie became absorbed in a book she had bought. Sometimes Harry paused to touch Minnie's hand or put an arm about her. But the delicate wisp of a girl who looked so fragile and in need of protection was in fact staunch and independent. Life had dealt with her in the terms of the theatre, giving her applause instead of love and affection. She did not melt into Harry's arms as he expected, and instead of being at ease with his lovely wife, he became shy and awkward.

For two days they lived thus, Harry with his concordance, Minnie with her book, in surroundings that gave them the feeling of being buried under a pyramid among the trappings of some bad period of Egyptian art. For relief they looked from a high narrow window at the sleet lashing the snow-drifted city.

"It looks as if winter would never be over," Harry said.

Minnie was silent—then she asked impulsively, "Harry, why don't we go home?"

He embraced her enthusiastically. "Why don't we? The weather can't be any worse in New York, and you have never seen our new home!"

Plans that had taken days to arrange were canceled in minutes, and that same afternoon they were on the train.

Home was on East Seventy-first Street, rather far uptown, but convenient to Central Park on one side and on the other the elevated railroad, where steam trains could rush Harry to and from the *Mirror* office.

Harry had selected the house and furnished it with impeccable taste. His mother had breathed generous life into it. When the young couple arrived, the house was warm and gay with flowers, and the elder Mrs. Fiske's cook was installed in the basement kitchen.

After twenty years of the hazards and travel of the theatre, Minnie had come home to peace and security. She was almost childishly delighted with the new furniture, the superb Aubusson rug in the drawing room, the well-stocked library, the oil paintings on the walls, and the velvet draperies that moved like new-style theatre curtains at the pull of a cord, covering the gossamer glass curtains and shutting out the wintry scene. Minnie had never had anything to do with houses except to stay in them briefly, and she was entranced by a beautiful home of her own.

Dinner was announced by William, the West Indian who also served as Mr. Fiske's office boy. Everything was perfect: the monogrammed silver, the ice clinking in crystal goblets, the Spode platter with its shining silver dome concealing the roast that Harry was preparing to carve.

Mother Fiske was a good manager; she left such explicit directions with her trusty cook and with the house boy that for several days the house seemed to run itself, without help from Minnie. But it didn't last. The cook needed new instructions and fresh supplies of food. William had to go back to the office for a part of each day, and that left Minnie to deal with tradespeople and settle a host of matters she had never even thought about.

Housekeeping was a complicated task, and Minnie set out to master it. She ordered from Brentano's a set of books covering every phase of household management, and studied the volumes diligently, but they only confused things. While she concentrated on planning a meal, that mealtime passed and it was time to serve the next. She was bewildered by the discovery that she was expected to know more about the laundry than the washerwoman, who waited for instructions. And the household accounts! Her arithmetic was all wrong—the same columns of figures added up differently each time.

Harry gallantly took over the management of the house until his wife learned the routine, and things ran smoothly again. When they entertained, which was often, Minnie was able to forget her failure as a housekeeper.

Minnie had company in such miseries as there were in retirement. The same year that she left the stage, Lotta Crabtree retired. Minnie had long since graduated from imitating Lotta, but much of her childhood idolatry remained, and she was thrilled when Lotta called one

Sunday afternoon. They were neighbors, the famous caller explained; it was just a pleasant drive across town from her house on Riverside Drive—and she at last had time for the friendships which she had always wanted.

Lotta Crabtree was then in her forties, and she radiated a youthful charm which she had never possessed off stage in her sulky, cigar-smoking teens. In full daylight she looked like a woman in her twenties; when Minnie told her she could pass for eighteen, Lotta was delighted.

The call was the beginning of a strangely-assorted lifelong friendship. But the groundwork for Minnie's admiration had been laid in impressionable years, and to some degree the woman she always saw was the Lotta of her childhood dreams.

Among the Fiskes' first dinner guests were Madame Helena Modjeska and her manager-husband, Count Bozenta Chlapowski. Once the teen-age Minnie had traveled from Cincinnati to St. Louis in Madame Modjeska's private theatrical car. As she recalled the happy experience:

> The men were like older brothers, and the women were wonderfully kind. Among those whom I remember meeting in the company were Georgie Drew, a pretty, fair woman with golden curly hair, and her husband, Maurice Barrymore.
>
> During the trip Madame Modjeska sent for me. What a thrill it was to enter her presence! She was smoking, and as it was the first time I had seen a woman smoke I must have shown my surprise, for she said smilingly, "It is the custom of my country."
>
> We talked for a long time, and later we became close friends.

Off stage Modjeska was all gentleness and charm; she left temperament to Charlee, as she called her husband.

In contrast to his tall serene wife, Count Bozenta was a high-strung little man, scarred from dueling and forever under the excitement of ideas. He carried one pocket full of loose tobacco and another stuffed with cigarette papers and matches; while he talked, he rolled cigarettes. The act did not interfere with his talk, but when a cigarette was finished there began for his hosts the ordeal by fire. Bozenta would strike a match and move it toward the cigarette; then his mounting ideas would hypnotize his hand and it would remain immobile until the flame had reached his fingers. He would drop the burning match and strike another. Repeatedly the match flame touched off new ideas, but never the cigarette, and at the end of the evening the Fiskes' prized Aubusson rug was pock-marked with little black spots.

47

Modjeska listened to her husband with serene attention and let the burning matches fall where they would. If she noticed Charlee's habit, she never commented on it directly, though she told of her first meeting with him in a Warsaw drawing room, where he spilled his cup of coffee inside a grand piano. No harm was done, however, Madame finished happily; it was a rented instrument.

Another of Count Bozenta's habits was absent-mindedly to collect all the matches left about the room and add them to the jumble in his pocket. Once when Harry could not find a light for his cigar, Modjeska had her apologetic husband disgorge some of his collection. Madame thought the habit came from the time he was in prison, where smoking materials were precious.

Count Bozenta had fought for Polish freedom in an unsuccessful revolt against the Russians, and had spent months in prison. On one occasion he and another leader were sentenced to be shot, and were reprieved at the last moment. Such a thing was dramatic on the stage, but in real life it was trying; Bozenta's companion had gone insane, and Madame thought the experience was responsible for her husband's nervousness. When the Fiskes complimented her own serenity, she told them:

"I am the most nervous woman in the world; but when Charlee and I were married, I knew we could not both lose control. He was not able to restrain himself; I had the power. That is all."

Another favorite visitor was Madame Janauschek, the Bohemian tragic actress. Janauschek's vitality and great, many-colored voice had withstood the years, but new methods and new stars had crowded her from the stage. She lived from the sale of jewels given her by the rulers of Europe in recognition of her great roles: Medea, Brunnehilde, Lady Macbeth, Queen Katherine, and Mary Stuart. The royal patrons were dead or old—while Janauschek lived on vigorously, writing impossible plays which she thundered forth in the Fiskes' library, or rocking majestically in a chair on the veranda.

When the guests were gone the house resumed the quiet of a storm center—a conflict electric enough to be felt in every room. Mrs. Fiske had undertaken a role for which she was unsuited, and the realization met head on with her Maddern sense of honesty.

In addition to his full-time work at the *Mirror* office, Harry managed the house cheerfully and efficiently, but that only sharpened Minnie's conviction that she was contributing nothing to their life.

More disturbing than her failure at everyday things was the discovery that her husband took it for granted they would have children. It was one of the vital things they had failed to discuss before marriage. To Harry and to herself, Minnie pointed out her domestic incompetence, protesting that she was not qualified to have children. Deeper introspection would have disclosed other things—emotional immaturity, the scars of her fatherless and insecure childhood, and the memory of her own mother's killing struggle. Underlying all would be found the theatre. Minnie had renounced it, but its door remained open. If she became involved in the responsibilities of motherhood, she might never find the door again.

By nature Minnie was more spiritual than physical. She accepted the fact that men were the reverse, but she loved Harry and was willing to compromise if it did not involve having children. Harry declined the compromise, and his singleness of purpose was proof to her of how deeply she had failed him.

While Minnie battled with her conscience, Harry Fiske was singularly patient and self-effacing. He concealed the fact that she was worrying him as much as she was herself, and he sought in every way to make her happy; one of the things he did was to engage the artist M. Colin to paint her portrait.

Week after week Colin made no progress; he drove Minnie wild by complaining that she was never quiet long enough for him to arrive at any one expression. That—when she often sat for half an hour without moving a muscle!

From the artist's standpoint, the trouble was that one minute Mrs. Fiske was as still as a mouse making up its mind, and the next as still as a young tigress unreconciled to captivity. Even her eyes kept changing—from deepest blue to violet, and sometimes they had a bronze or greenish hue, with opalescent lights. The only thing about her that didn't change was the flame of her hair.

The portrait took a long time and it was wearing on both subject and painter, but it was completed at last. In it the youthful Mrs. Fiske, life-size, sits with her small feet on a cushion, one arm on the arm of the chair, and one restless hand holding a yellow rose in her lap. She leans back, not relaxed, but rather as if drawing away from some struggle seen by her great deep-blue eyes that look past the spectator into turbulent space. It might be a portrait of Annabel Lee, torn between the angels above and the demons down under the sea—or between the irreconcilable forces of home and stage.

CHAPTER 7

In her marriage to Harrison Grey Fiske, Minnie Maddern was regarded as a supremely fortunate young woman. She shared the view, but was nevertheless miserable and plagued by a sense of inferiority. From earliest childhood all her potentialities had been directed toward the stage, and when she turned her back on it, she was handicapped in every remaining direction.

Minnie did not look for excuses, however. Relieved of her household duties, she retreated to the library to piece out her shreds of education. She could at least make herself more worthy of her brilliant husband.

Reading was followed by writing, and that led naturally to playwriting. It proved to be an exciting adventure, and she was exhilarated by her own intuitive skill in shaping the materials she had been accustomed to use all her life.

Minnie's first attempt was a one-act play, *The Rose*, using the New Orleans of her childhood as a background. When she showed it to Harry, he was delighted. *The Rose*, he said, was sure to be produced. He urged her enthusiastically to go on.

In the next few years Minnie wrote sixteen one-act plays. Most of them were produced, and three of them—*The Rose*, *The Eyes of the Heart* and *A Light from St. Agnes*—became classics. *A Light from St. Agnes* was later made into an opera.

One day there came to the house on Seventy-first Street a soft-spoken young Irishman who looked like a Catholic priest. He was James O'Neill, the romantic actor and father of Eugene O'Neill, the playwright.

The actor had come to induce Harry to rescue him from prison. According to Dumas' *The Count of Monte Cristo*, the prisoner of the Chateau d'If was Edmond Dante, a Frenchman; but actually the pris-

50

oner was one James O'Neill, born in Kilkenny, Ireland. He had made such a success of the role that the play owned him, and the public owned the play. When he sickened of it and tried other roles, the public stayed away, or shouted, "Monte Cristo!" and he had to go back to the Chateau d'If. Man and boy, for ten years he had been chained nightly in the dungeon. He was in danger of losing his memory as people do in solitary confinement, or when they have to say the same words over and over.

Harry yielded to Irish eloquence and began concocting a play of daring exploits in the reign of Louis XV. He called on Minnie for advice, and presently made her a full-fledged collaborator. The play, *Fontenelle*, had an unmistakable Dumas flavor. It resembled *The Three Musketeers* rather than *Monte Cristo*—and it had no dungeon.

Before *Fontenelle* was completed, another star appealed for help. Madame Modjeska had three acts of a play written by Paul Kester, but the fourth act would not come out right.

Minnie turned from *Fontenelle* of eighteenth-century France to *The Countess Roudine*, a romantic melodrama of Nihilists and secret police in Russia, by and for Americans who had never been there.

Evenings in the Fiskes' library were exciting times. Modjeska and Count Bozenta would drop in after the theatre to see how Minnie was faring among the Russian princes and Nihilists; Harry sought advice in guiding his hero through the perils of a Breton smugglers' den or the slums of Paris. Occasionally the prisoner of the Chateau d'If appeared to inquire about the progress of his liberation or to declaim some of the dramatic lines he found in the manuscript:

"Curse her! Horse or no horse, I'll follow her!"

"If before midnight one week hence the diamond is not placed in your hands, denounce me!"

In late November, 1891, Harry and Minnie traveled to Chillicothe, Ohio, for the successful premiere of *Fontenelle*. O'Neill had found temporary escape from the Chateau d'If; everyone in Chillicothe agreed that it was a great drama—everyone except the authors. They knew it for old theatrical claptrap and were depressed by its emptiness.

Two weeks after Chillicothe, the Fiskes were at the Tremont Theatre in Boston to see Minnie's first play on the stage. The popular English actress Rosina Vokes, supported by Felix Morris and the London Comedy Company, was presenting three one-act plays; first on the bill was Mrs. Fiske's *The Rose*.

The little play was as graceful as an old song, and it had dramatic

51

power. Boston critics devoted three quarters of their space to praising *The Rose*, and the rest to the two other plays. Miss Vokes made the play her chief offering in a tour as far west as Portland, Oregon.

In New York *The Rose* got notices worthy of a full-length play. The *Herald* declared that the piece did for the one-act play what Bret Harte had done for the short story. *The Rose* remained the chief offering of the London Comedy Company for three years, and when the company returned to England, Miss Vokes's leading man stayed with it for his fourth year.

Shortly after the premiere of *The Rose, The Countess Roudine* opened in Philadelphia. It played there for three weeks, and disappeared from Modjeska's repertory. The only good thing the critics saw in the play was Minnie's fourth act.

On evenings when the Fiskes did not entertain or work, they went to the theatre—a luxury for Minnie, who had seen most of her acting from behind the footlights. Once in a January blizzard they went to the Fifth Avenue to see an Italian company present the old tearjerker, *Camille*.

Camille was a frail, tired little woman, without make-up and in dowdy costumes. To balance things, Armand's getup was resplendent; at his entrance Harry whispered, "He looks like an Italian barber on a holiday!"

It did not matter greatly; the house was only a quarter full, and not everyone stayed. In front of the Fiskes two criticis yawned through half the performance; then, deciding that they had "seen enough of the Wops," they went to kill the rest of the evening at the Gilsey bar.

The Fiskes stayed, watching the dowdy star use triumphantly the methods which Minnie had worked out in her teens. The actress seemed to live through experiences for the first time, reacting to them poignantly and with heart-breaking restraint.

The end of the play was greeted by a handful of applause, and Harry asked his wife what she thought of the actress.

Minnie answered, "I must see her in other plays, but I suspect that Eleonora Duse is the greatest actress in the world!"

In 1893, Sir Henry Irving and Ellen Terry opened their third American tour in New York.

As a struggling young actress, Minnie had worshiped Miss Terry from afar. Harry, in his confident and prosperous youth, had done better. In London, hobnobbing with the Davenports and Sotherns, he had met Ellen Terry. Later, as the editor of the *Dramatic Mirror*, he had renewed the acquaintance when Miss Terry and Sir Henry came to America. Harry now invited the actress to Sunday dinner at the house on Seventy-first Street.

Ellen Terry arrived: a big, carelessly-dressed Englishwoman, carrying an outrageous-looking handbag so bulging that Minnie wondered what all was in it. She found out immediately. Looking for the address of someone who had sent greetings to Harry, Miss Terry dumped the contents of the bag on the library table: letters, crumpled handkerchiefs, keys, a biscuit, gloves, photographs, sealing wax, an apple, a corset lace, American small change, large English pennies, and innumerable other odds and ends.

"What, no slingshot?" Harry asked.

"No slingshot," Miss Terry said with regret, pawing through the collection with man-sized hands.

At forty-five, Ellen Terry had put on weight, but her big-boned frame still suggested the ranginess of her earlier years. As then, she was tow-headed, with pale eyes, nondescript features and a freckled skin. None of which had anything to do with Miss Terry as theatregoers saw her. To innumerable men and women alike, she was all loveliness and all grace, shot through and through with poignancy. G. B. Shaw, who rarely took notice of the fact of love and then almost always with discomfort, observed that every famous theatregoing man of the last quarter of the nineteenth century was in love with Ellen Terry.

Miss Terry, who evoked so much more than could be said or written, was more than a charming dinner guest. Like Minnie, she saw acting as a science and she brought to it a mind brilliant with insight. The friendship that began that evening lasted until the older actress' death.

But when Minnie wrote of Ellen Terry's acting, it was not in the terms of science but in terms of the effect it produced:

"I can think of her only as the quality that was Ellen Terry, the indescribable iridescence of her, the brilliance that was like sunshine shimmering on the waters of a fountain . . . I think of light, light, radiance, radiance, always moving, moving, moving, always motion."

From the beginning of Minnie's retirement, producers had made offers and presented arguments for her return to the stage. Most persistent of them was the courtly, side-whiskered A. M. Palmer. He and Augustin Daly were the survivors of the triumvirate of great New York producers that had included Lester Wallack until his then-recent bankruptcy. Palmer was a special friend of the Fiskes and a privileged

53

character; as such, he was able to go on urging Minnie not to hide her light under a bushel. Her success as a playwright did not silence him. He continued for more than three years before receiving a spark of encouragement.

One evening in the spring of 1893 when Mr. Palmer asked, as usual, when the public would again see the electric Minnie Maddern on the stage, she answered,

"There is no Minnie Maddern; she retired to become Mrs. Fiske."

"And when may we hope to see Mrs. Fiske on the stage?"

"Never, unless it is a benefit performance, or a play written by Mr. Fiske."

Nothing more was said to Minnie, but the two men got together and the following evening Harry Fiske began writing a play. After it was done, Palmer counseled him to rewrite the last act—and he arranged for a fall production. Then Minnie was called on to make good her promise to appear in her husband's play.

Hester Crewe opened at the Tremont Theatre in Boston November 20, 1893, with Mrs. Fiske as Hester. The advance publicity stressed Minnie's early misdirection in Lotta roles and predicted that at last she had a play worthy of her talents. But the combined solicitude of playwright and producer had hatched another blunder.

Intent on giving his wife a dramatic role, Harry had written a somber piece which reached its climax with the wronged Hester wandering in a snowstorm and tossing the frozen body of her baby over a cliff into the sea. The drama was headed for tragedy—but Mr. Palmer objected that audiences did not like unhappy endings—and it wound up in farce that bewildered the tearful spectators and jolted the critical ones.

Hester was quickly withdrawn and Minnie returned to private life; but she had left ajar another door to the stage, and a foot was already in that door.

The evening after their return, the Fiskes had a call from their family physician. Like Mr. Palmer, Dr. Gurnsey was a privileged character and he came to ask a favor. The maternity department of Hannemann Hospital was in need of funds. Would Mrs. Fiske give a benefit performance of *Hester Crewe?*

Not *Hester Crewe;* but Mrs. Fiske would undertake the benefit and she agreed to find a suitable play. Her choice was influenced by the ghost of Lawrence Barrett.

When Minnie was an infant, the solemn young actor had blessed her in her champagne basket; seventeen years later, when he was the

Eminent Tragedian and she was touring in *Fogg's Ferry*, he had sent her a copy of Ibsen's *A Doll's House*, as an antidote to her misdirected career. Six years after that she and Barrett met in the wings of the Metropolitan Opera House, at Wallack's benefit performance of *Hamlet*. Barrett, made up as the Ghost, spoke of *A Doll's House* again and was visibly disappointed by Minnie's lack of enthusiasm.

That was the last time Minnie ever spoke with Lawrence Barrett. After his sudden death, a critic wrote that one of the regrets of the actor's life had been his failure to interest any American actress in the great role of Nora. To Minnie this sounded like a personal rebuke. She saw the ghost of Hamlet's father looking at her reproachfully.

She had been reading the aging copy of *A Doll's House* at intervals ever since, and with each reading she found new meanings and new dimensions. Now she chose Ibsen's play for the hospital benefit.

Mrs. Fiske gave a single performance of *A Doll's House* at the Empire Theatre on February 15, 1894. In the twenty years since Ibsen had written it, this was its second performance in English on the New York stage.

Henrik Ibsen was deeply grateful. From Christiania he sent Mrs. Fiske a laurel wreath bound with the Norwegian colors, together with a letter wishing her success.

The Norwegian laurels marked a turning point in theatre history. Mrs. Fiske's matinee cracked the solid front of American opposition to Ibsen, and it cracked the solemn faces of some of the Ibsen cultists. In the first act Mrs. Fiske played Nora as the doll-wife of her upbringing—frivolous and lovable and irresponsible—romping with her children and lying with the engaging naturalness of a child. Waves of laughter swept the theatre. The majority of the audience were women who had heard that Ibsen was a glacier of gloom—and they were enchanted by the actress' sunny performance and the playwright's unerring knowledge of feminine traits. At the end of the first act they began to grow up with Nora. As the curtain started to fall they read in her face the unmistakable beginning of her change from a child-wife to a thoughtful woman. There was a burst of applause—partly for the magic of the actress, and partly for what the audience felt to be its newly-found psychic power of knowing from Nora's face what was happening in her mind.

During the second act the audience was Nora's enthusiastic ally. The third act was played in electric silence—the audience identified with Nora and intent on losing not a gesture or inflection.

Discerning members of the audience saw more than a good show;

they saw every depth and angle of Ibsen's play illuminated by the clear light of genius, and they felt that they had witnessed a miracle: they had seen Minnie Maddern, the winsome and the capricious, suddenly loom up as a great actress.

William Gillette scooped all the critics with the first written acclaim. After Mrs. Fiske had received Ibsen's wreath and taken her last curtain call, Gillette, the Sherlock Holmes of the stage, borrowed writing materials at the theatre office and sent her a message: *BY JOVE!!* The two words, printed large on a sheet of notepaper, had a look of stunned surprise.

The single Ibsen matinee became world news. For the next three weeks excited accounts of the performance appeared in papers as far west as San Francisco, and as far east as London and Christiania; and in the New York press more kind things were said of Ibsen in one day than had been said in the previous two decades.

> *A Doll's House* was really good and understandable . . . Ibsen had been cold-shouldered in America for twenty years—yet all his plays needed to make them popular was an actress like Mrs. Fiske. . . . Mrs. Fiske was very near to being the American Duse. . . . It was doubtful if Duse would have done as well in the role of Nora. . . . The best Nora on the English stage was hollow and artificial in comparison with Mrs. Fiske . . . Mrs. Fiske had suddenly become a great actress. . . . Mrs. Fiske had been a great actress for years, but the ridiculous blunderheads who write theatrical criticism had failed to see it. . . . The American stage needed Mrs. Fiske.

In their library, among opened newspapers, letters and telegrams, with Ibsen's laurels on the mantelpiece, the Fiskes considered the implications of Minnie's triumph.

Harry had wanted a home and children. He had thought his wife would fit into the pattern which he had planned and be his helpmeet. Now he saw that her career was more important than his, and his life would have to be changed to fit hers. He put down the last newspaper, with its glowing tribute to Mrs. Fiske's Nora, and his voice was an animated rumble:

"Nothing quite like this has ever happened before, my dearest; it is a mandate for you to return to the stage!"

For a minute Mrs. Fiske was very still in her favorite chair. Then she looked at him radiantly.

"Harry, I want to go back—if you approve!"

He got up and went over to her.

"With all my heart! It is the right decision, my dear."

"Darling, it will be so wonderful—and so lonely." There were tears in Minnie's voice.

Harry took both her hands and drew her to him, and she responded to his embrace.

They were closer to each other than they had ever been before, but they were no longer alone; the world was there in the form of opened newspapers, letters, telegrams, and Ibsen's laurels on the mantelpiece—and the world had spoken.

CHAPTER 8

Mrs. Fiske returned to the stage in a different world from the one in which Minnie Maddern had made her first appearance. The thirty years of her life corresponded with the emergence of American power and wealth. With its explosive growth after the Civil War, the United States had become the leading manufacturing nation of the world. Most of the country's natural resources passed from the public domain into private hands, and great companies pushed into being to exploit them.

Business and the theatre breathed the same exciting air. Oil had its Rockefeller, steel its Carnegie, and the theatre its Charles Frohman, who sat in his office at the Empire Theatre under a bust of Bonaparte and basked in the title of "Little Napoleon." As others cornered commodities, Frohman cornered the foreign play market and a large slice of the domestic market. Less grasping producers took the useful remainder, and the Fiskes, seeking a role for Minnie, picked over the leavings.

They were still picking when Harry got a glimpse into the future. From the thousand *Dramatic Mirror* correspondents all over the United States came a stream of reports about theatres signing up with an unidentified New York booking agency. The methods and secrecy used in the signing suggested that in every case it was the same agency.

At that time, booking was a highly individualistic procedure. Between seasons, theatre managers from out of town took desk space in the dramatic agencies around Union Square. Brokers for small-town theatres bargained in the street, where lesser actors paraded up and down and made a brave show of being successful.

A national booking agency could be an improvement on the catch-
58

as-catch-can system, but in a decade of monopolies, an organization taking shape in secret had ominous forebodings.

In the face of these warnings the Fiskes made their plans. With Harry as a silent partner, Minnie was to appear under the management of Henry Greenwall in a repertory consisting of *The Queen of Liars*, Harry's adaptation of Alphonse Daudet's *La Menteuse*, and Ibsen's *A Doll's House*. Later they added Dumas *fils*' *La Femme de Claude*, rechristened *Cesarine*, and two one-act plays by Mrs. Fiske. It was an interim repertory designed to carry Minnie until she and Harry found the play of their dreams.

The stage had won out over the hearth, and for years to come Minnie was to spend most of her time on the road. In recognition of that fact she and Harry gave up the house on Seventy-first Street and made the Fifth Avenue Hotel their headquarters. Later, they moved to the Brevoort.

Minnie Maddern had made her farewell appearance on the stage of the Toronto Grand Opera House in the depths of a Canadian winter; Mrs. Fiske began her professional career at Lancaster, with a harvest moon shining on the autumn fields and laden orchards of a Pennsylvania-Dutch countryside. The audience at the Fulton Opera House was small, but it gave *The Queen of Liars* generous applause, and next day the *Examiner* hailed the occasion as Mrs. Fiske's "first step in a triumphal march back to the high place she formerly held in the theatrical firmament." The march, however, was to a different high place.

At Pittsburgh Harry was on hand to witness his wife's success, of which the *Commercial Gazette* said:

"One thing that strikes the observer at the very beginning is the entire absence of the appearance of acting. The audience forgets that it is in a theatre witnessing an impersonation."

On the fourth of October Mrs. Fiske presented *A Doll's House* for the first time since the historic benefit matinee, and the Pittsburgh press reacted as had the New York press on that earlier occasion. Under the heading A PLAY THAT WAS A REVELATION, the Pittsburgh *Times* hugged the likable Mr. Ibsen for his realism, his simplicity and his humanity. The reviewer congratulated the actress on succeeding in a role where Modjeska, Réjane and others had failed.

But the play was ahead of the times. Some people stayed away under the impression that *A Doll's House* was a children's play; and many who attended were puzzled and dissatisfied. The play ended with the

59

slamming of the street door as Nora left her outgrown "doll's" house
—and the audience settled down to wait for a fourth act and the
penitent return of the wife. The house lights went up, and down, and
up—and still they failed to take the hint. Finally the stage manager
announced bluntly that the play was over, and the audience went home
grumbling at being done out of a fourth act and a happy ending.

From Pittsburgh Harry returned to his multiple duties in New York,
and the company went on to Cleveland. There again Mrs. Fiske played
to small audiences and a full force of delighted critics, among them
the Cleveland reviewer who wrote:

> Five years ago, when Minnie Maddern married and ceased to act,
> I threw up my hands in dismay. What would become of the Ameri-
> can stage if she, its pride and hope, deserted it? And yet, I dreaded
> to witness her return on Thursday night. Fears were foolish, how-
> ever. Mrs. Fiske's first words revealed her wisdom; her first act re-
> established her dominion. She had improved—not by inches, but by
> leagues. I doubt if the world can produce her equal.

The same reviewer voiced the general dissatisfaction with *The
Queen of Liars*.

Harry Fiske kept sending his wife manuscripts of plays which
showed promise, but none of them appealed to her until she saw
Hardy's dramatization of his novel *Tess of the D'Urbervilles*. It had
already been rejected by all the important New York producers, and
Mrs. Fiske saw why: Hardy had tried to crowd the whole of his soul-
stirring novel onto the stage. If only he would consent to a playwright
doing the dramatization!

He did on the odd condition that the Fiskes technically accept his
play, after which they were permitted to discard it and write their own.

Now they had the material for their big play—they needed only a
playwright. But all the established playwrights were bound by contract. So they chose Lorimer Stoddard, son of the poet, Richard
Stoddard; he had written a pageant about Napoleon.

Harry started young Stoddard on the dramatization by hiding
Hardy's manuscript. As Stoddard finished each act of the new play it
was sent to Minnie, who read it and returned it with her suggestions.
The dramatization took shape as its manuscript acts shuttled back and
forth over the road which they were to traverse later as the "big play."

Mrs. Fiske and her company continued west to Chicago, where her
appearance was hailed as the most important event since Duse's visit

during the World's Fair. From Chicago they turned east, then south. In New Orleans Mrs. Fiske was greeted affectionately as "Our Minnie"; she relaxed her rule against interviews, and reporters from the *Picayune* and *Times-Democrat* called on her at the Grand Opera House.

Breathlessly the *Picayune* reporter gave his impressions:

> Such a pretty star she is! Such a winsome, wistfully sweet, un-affected little lady! No wonder that weird, eerie, lovely little face caught the heart of one of the cleverest newspapermen and the-atrical writers in the country—and no wonder that to the newsboys of New Orleans she is "Our Minnie!"

The winsome star had definite ideas: she discouraged "personal" interviews as intensely stupid; and she had no sympathy for the current move to bar children from the stage.

> For anyone who intends to make the stage his career, I think it is of incalculable benefit to go on as a child—to be raised on it, almost. Children absorb a wonderful amount of the practical side; and when they are older and their artistic thoughts begin to develop, it is of the greatest assistance in interpreting what they wish to say.

Minnie made no shocked denial when asked if she believed in prob-lem plays.

> I believe in all good plays, whatever their genre. The trouble is that in America and England there are so few good plays. I consider that the most vicious influence of the day is the chamber-maid-society dramas that have had such a run of late. We are far behind Italy, or France, or Spain. In Italy there are daily presented in the second-class theatres comedies that would be considered above the taste of the most select audiences of this country.

The *Times-Democrat* man risked a personal question: "How do you like the stage, Mrs. Fiske?"

"An actress must give up everything," she told him. "All one's strength must be saved for the night's performance; social life is fore-sworn, and one becomes a hermit, a crank, and boorish in everything."

It was time for rehearsal, but the encouraged reporter tried a final personal question.

"Will you tell me, Mrs. Fiske, what you did during the years you were off the stage?"

The question stirred clear depths of laughter.

"I got older."

There were many steps to "Our Minnie's" homecoming. The one she saved for last was her visit to the house on Baronne Street, near the aging St. Charles Theatre where her mother had once been leading lady for John Wilkes Booth, and where the youthful Lotta had danced and sung while Minnie slept in a dressing room. Minnie didn't recall the number of the house, but she would know it by its white galleries and its old slave quarters sleeping in the shadows of great trees.

Mrs. Fiske was accompanied by three privileged ladies of New Orleans, who were excited over the honor of being present when "Our Minnie" returned to the house of her birth. Their carriage turned into Baronne Street and Minnie looked ahead, puzzled; the quiet street of her childhood was cluttered with stores and rooming-house signs. The rambling tree-shaded house was gone. Then she saw it—a shrunken caricature of the great place of memory. The trees had been cut down and the old house was naked in the glaring sunshine of the unlovely street. Minnie gave no sign of recognition as the carriage rolled by, and when they had gone some distance farther, she told her expectant companions, "I don't seem able to find it, after all." On later visits she avoided Baronne Street.

In the heat of New Orleans Minnie had said she had no prejudice against problem plays; in Toronto in February she proved it by giving *Cesarine* its first English performance. In the years since the tearful *Camille*, Dumas had gone modern. *Cesarine* was a problem play written with a heavy hand, but it had historical significance: it had helped bring a divorce law to France.

In March the long tour brought the company to New York City.

New Yorkers had applauded Minnie Maddern as a child actress, and later as a young star. But only one audience had seen her as Mrs. Fiske, and that at a benefit performance. On the evening of St. Patrick's Day, theatregoers made their way through wind and rain to pack the Garden Theatre, where Minnie was making her first professional appearance as Mrs. Fiske, in *The Queen of Liars*, rechristened *Marie Deloche*. The occasion bore a resemblance to her long-ago debut in *Fogg's Ferry:* fifteen New York newspapers praised the actress and panned her play.

The following week Mrs. Fiske gave *Cesarine* its first English performance in New York. The play had once shocked Paris, and the English version shocked New York.

But the critics applauded the actress. Alan Dale of the *American* declared that if Mrs. Fiske had been heralded by a European reputation New York would have raved about her Cesarine. The *Home Journal* and the *World* agreed that she was the only forward-looking actress on the American stage.

While Mrs. Fiske was being saluted as the champion of progress, the enemy, which had already cast its shadow on the theatre, emerged from the twilight of anonymity and secret deals—a full-fledged theatrical syndicate. Its aim was to control the bookings of all first-class theatres, and of all touring attractions, in the United States and Canada, and eventually in Europe and Australia. Behind the dream of world conquest were Charles Frohman, self-styled "Napoleon of the Theatre," with his partners Abraham Lincoln Erlanger and Marc Klaw, and Samuel Nixon Nirdlinger and J. F. Zimmerman of Philadelphia.

While disclaiming any connection with the syndicate, Charles Frohman assured the public that it would do nothing to interfere with the freedom of the theatre. But the Fiskes, struggling under Frohman's monopoly of plays, were skeptical. While Mrs. Fiske was appearing at the Garden Theatre, a group of leading managers met in worried session in A. M. Palmer's office. There it was testified that weaker theatre managers were under pressure from the combine; some of them had signed over a third of their profits for "booking charges," and those who resisted were threatened with being driven out of business.

After the New York engagement the company toured west again, ending the season at Chicago in April with a trial presentation of Sardou's *Divorçons*.

The next step was the "big play."

The morning Lorimer Stoddard completed his dramatization of *Tess of the D'Urbervilles*, Harry gave a copy to Greenwall, Mrs. Fiske's manager. He got it back the same day with a vigorous note: if the Fiskes really meant to produce that rank piece, Mr. Greenwall preferred to part company with them.

They parted, and the Fiskes' old friend and adviser, A. M. Palmer, came to the rescue.

The "big play" was scheduled for spring production, and for the interim Mr. Palmer offered the translation of a modern German play, *The Right to Happiness*, which he would produce for Mrs. Fiske with Harry as a silent partner. When Harry confided the plans for *Tess*, the ministerial-looking producer winced, observing that he was one of those who had rejected Hardy's play—not for its form, but for its moral content.

63

Harry went home to find Aunt Emma Stevens imploring Minnie not to appear as Hardy's "pure" woman who bore an illegitimate child and died on the gallows for the murder of her paramour.

After the session with her aunt, Minnie was doubly distressed over Mr. Palmer's reaction.

"Doesn't anyone believe in poor Tess?"

"I do," Harry assured her; "and I believe it will be your great role." But the two appeared to be alone in their opinion.

A few days later Mr. Palmer's interest in the Fiskes' welfare overcame his restraint, and he wrote to Harry: "Tess is an utterly unsympathetic character; Mrs. Fiske would be playing against the audience from beginning to end. I implore you to abandon the idea."

Aunt Emma renewed her protest against what she considered a fatal blunder, and well-meaning friends joined in. The pressure became so heavy from so many directions that Minnie was almost bowed down.

"Maybe I should give up *Tess*," she told Harry. "It is my artistic judgment against the world, and those are terrible odds!"

Harry asked, "Who is going to play the role, you or the world?"

"I am," Minnie said. "If I am worth anything as an artist, I'll follow my own instincts." Having made up her mind, she went on with the plans for *Tess* and did not look back again.

Harry had steadfastly encouraged Minnie in her trials with *Tess*, but the decision was essentially hers; even if the play failed it would not come too hard on him—he was only a limited partner in the venture.

Then late one evening Harry came home, grave-faced, from a long session with Mr. Palmer.

"How was the conference?" Minnie asked.

"Behind locked doors," he told her grimly.

"Is something wrong, Harry?"

"With dear old A. M. He expects his bankruptcy to be declared in a few days. He advised me to dissolve our partnership before I become entangled in his ruin. He is losing his theatres, theatrical interests—everything!"

To Minnie it seemed the Twilight of the Gods. In her youth there had been three of them; Wallack, Daly and Palmer. Lesser producers came and went, but the great three seemed as enduring as the theatre itself. Since then Minnie had appeared at Wallack's benefit which had been called a "testimonial" because it seemed too preposterous that the great Wallack was penniless. Now Palmer had announced his own doom.

"Isn't there anything we can do to help him?" Minnie asked.

Harry told her, "I have asked him to stay as our manager. That will help him without involving us. As far as your plays are concerned, the chief difference will be that I shall be producer instead of a partner."

It was an item of difference that could change their lives. As a partial backer, Harry could gamble only what he could afford to lose; but Palmer's bankruptcy committed him to all the risks in a game where old masters were inexorably broken.

For the young editor and his actress wife the future never appeared blacker, or more exciting. They were pledged to gamble more than they had ever intended on a play everyone warned them against; and they were gambling in a swiftly-changing world, in the shadow of a theatrical trust whose full proportions had not yet been revealed.

CHAPTER 9

In the fall and winter of 1896 Mrs. Fiske toured with *The Right to Happiness* while Harry worked on *Tess of the D'Urbervilles*.

That winter there appeared in the New York *Sun* a long interview with Lotta Crabtree; in it Ellen Terry was represented as being envious of Lotta's look of perpetual adolescence. Lotta then contrasted herself with a younger, unnamed actress:

> Everybody told me that she was great; actors in particular have praised her talents to me. I always asked people who told me this: "Well, if she is great, why doesn't she make money? Why doesn't she succeed? Because the amount of money an actor makes is the real test of whether or not he is great."

The formula led to the inescapable conclusion that as the richest actress in the world, Lotta was also the greatest. Mrs. Fiske was persuaded that Lotta's jibe about the actress who couldn't make money was directed at her. She wrote asking Lotta if this were so, and expressing regret over the comment about Ellen Terry. In a few days she had Lotta's answer:

> My dear Talented Friend:
> In regard to yourself I deny the article in every way. . . . I have been ill over what it said about Miss Terry she has always been so very kind to me. I did not say that she looked old and tore her hair. . . . Let us hope that it will soon die a natural death. Wishing you all happiness Friend
> Lotta.

Meanwhile Mrs. Fiske's tour flickered unevenly. It reached its highest point on December 4 when she opened the new theatre of the vast Tampa Bay Hotel in Florida, midst a riot of tropical flora and booster

66

spirit, with all of the two thousand seats filled and people standing in the aisles. Two months later it expired at Goshen, Indiana, and Mrs. Fiske hurried back to New York, where she called the first rehearsal of *Tess of the D'Urbervilles*.

The cast of *Tess* included Charles Coghlan, masterful villain of the English stage; the engaging and gifted Edward M. Bell; the veteran character acter John Jack, who had witnessed Tom Davey's marriage to Lizzie Maddern; Mary E. Barker, another accomplished old trouper; the vital young English actress Annie Irish; and Bijou Fernandes, who had grown up on the stage of Augustin Daly's theatre.

In the casting of *Tess* there were gambles within the main gamble of the play, the greatest of them being on the two key actors, Charles Coghlan and Edward Bell.

Coghlan, the ideal Alec, had disappeared mysteriously from a play that was enjoying a huge success in London, and from inside sources the Fiskes had it that this was because of his disregard for responsibility —he felt he was doing well when he showed up for three performances out of four. The Fiskes were also reminded that on Coghlan's last American tour he had been hissed from a western stage. But despite all warnings the actor was engaged, by cable, at a salary in keeping with his abilities. Harry planned to deal with his shortcomings when they appeared.

Edward Bell was a once-popular juvenile actor who had become so alcoholic that he could no longer get a job in New York. Mr. Fiske was urged to have nothing to do with him. But Bell was the ideal Angel Clare, and he was engaged on his own solemn promise not to touch liquor during the run.

Minnie reached New York on Saturday, and for the first time in months she and Harry were able to relax in their suite at the Fifth Avenue. Sunday, over a late breakfast, they talked hopefully of the big production and congratulated each other on the passing of a milestone: Charles Coghlan's ship had docked that morning and the cast of *Tess* were all within reach of the Fifth Avenue Theatre and tomorrow's rehearsal.

"Suppose Mr. Coghlan falls into his habit of missing performances?" Minnie wondered.

"He won't have the chance," Harry assured her. "We're paying him for his best, and that's what we shall expect of him."

"You know how to bring out the best in people," Minnie agreed. But she thought of the debonair, black-haired Coghlan and the winning stage manner that made him attractive even as a villain, and some of her doubt returned. "I imagine Mr. Coghlan can be very persuasive, even in real life!"

"Leave that to me, dearest; his first sign of irresponsibility will be nipped in the bud!"

They were interrupted by an impressive knock, and Harry opened the door to a white-haired gentleman.

"Mr. Fiske? And Mrs. Fiske?" He bowed elegantly, his hat in his hand. "I am Charles Coghlan."

Harry was speechless; he gave Minnie a sideways glance, but she appeared to notice nothing unusual and she welcomed the caller cordially.

As they talked about the play and the role of Alec, the actor became more recognizable, and when he was about to leave he turned to Harry with something of the old Coghlan sprightliness.

"By the bye, I'll be much obliged if you'll excuse me from rehearsal tomorrow."

Harry started to agree; then, remembering his vow to nip irresponsibility in the bud, he reminded the actor of the importance of the first rehearsal.

Coghlan was sweetly apologetic.

"It is not that I want to" he explained; "it's my hair; been this way for years, but you wouldn't know it if I hadn't had to cross the Atlantic. I have a dye that's perfect except on salt water, when it turns a bright green. So I had to come this way. The dye is in one of my boxes at the dock and won't be delivered till evening. If you will excuse me tomorrow, I'll have time to make two applications before rehearsal Tuesday, and my hair will be dark enough not to start gossip in my dear profession. On opening night it will be the ebon black familiar to my audiences."

"Well, in that case—" Harry agreed.

After Coghlan had bowed himself out, Harry chuckled ruefully, "And I was going to nip irresponsibility in the bud!"

"You did the right thing," Minnie insisted. "You treated him as a responsible person."

It turned out that way. Charles Coghlan was present at all subsequent rehearsals, and during the long run of the play he never missed a performance.

Tess of the D'Urbervilles had its world premiere at the Fifth Avenue Theatre, Broadway and Twenty-eighth Street, on the evening of

March 2, 1897. The ancient house was the only one that had withstood the sweep of the Theatrical Trust, and it added one more hazard to the gamble.

At eight o'clock the curtain rose on the play everyone had warned the Fiskes against.

Hours later, in the hushed daybreak over Stonehenge, the curtain fell on one of the greatest triumphs in American stage history. The five-minute ovation was followed by many curtain calls, with latecomers joining in—actors and actresses who had rushed to the Fifth Avenue at the end of their own performances. "Elsie de Wolfe sat there with tears streaming down her face; Ida Conquest, fresh from her own triumph of the day before, was drinking in reverently the methods of a greater artist. Maurice Barrymore, Joseph Wheelock, and Frank Worthington just back from his trip to Honolulu stood in the rear of the orchestra, perfectly enthralled."

During the play, the consciousness of being in a theatre faded so completely for many of the spectators that they went out walking on air, with their heads in the clouds of the wide Wessex countryside.

To the critics, *Tess of the D'Urbervilles* had come like a glorious windfall near the end of a dull theatrical season. Young James Huneker of the New York *Advertiser* stumbled home, haunted by the memory of Tess—"The Wessex pagan, Tess, saluting the god of day as the law closes in about her. The scene is Wagnerian; it is superb, and is a final stroke of genius, for it sums up Tess's character, her love of nature, of light, of love. It gives us in a breathless moment what the rest of the play does not, the atmosphere of that half wild, unsullied sweethearted creature, Tess of the D'Urbervilles."

In the theatre lobby Alan Dale, brilliant hyper-critic of the New York *American*, waved aside questions about the portrayal of Tess. "Mrs. Fiske doesn't need any abstruse analysis just now. She won't need it until we have recovered from our ecstasy. That won't be today, or tomorrow, or the day after." He hurried away to be alone with the spell of the great event, and afterward he recalled his slow return to New York from the enchantment of Wessex. "When I left the Fifth Avenue Theatre on that eventful night, Broadway looked to me like a coarse and lurid dream; the peacock theatregoers struck me as people fantastic and unreal. The atmosphere was heavy with the prose of everyday life. Poetry and truth and pleasure lurked in that darkened Fifth Avenue Theatre."

New York critics were unanimous in their acclaim of Mrs. Fiske;

69

it was the first time an American actress had won such a victory. Her Tess was hailed as a work of genius, and she was compared favorably with Duse and Bernhardt.

That freshet of excited reviews was only the first splash of a flood of print. Sunday newspapers from New York to San Francisco carried full-page illustrated stories of the event, their motif being that the American theatre had come of age and America had her great actress: Minnie Maddern Fiske. After that, magazine stories and illustrations made the characters of the play as familiar to the American public as the newly inaugurated President McKinley and his family, and Harpers rushed a seventh edition of the novel. William Dean Howells, ruler of the literary roost, became a hero of blissful ignorance by announcing that he had seen the play without having read Hardy's famous novel.

Howells' eagerly-awaited opinion filled both columns of his Life and Letters department in *Harper's Weekly*. Of Mrs. Fiske's impersonation he said:

> Tess does not rise above her origin and environment; she is bound to them, as we all are in our several cases, by ties that are ultimately insoluble, though they loose her for a while to the semblance of free will. In her life the inevitable rules; she is fated to fall, and she is fated to sink back into her ruin, and to end her guilt in murder; that is what this fine actress makes you believe, though she does it with no insistence upon a continuous destiny, and only by her almost invariable truth in the successive incidents and events. She does it so perfectly that even her betrayer seems under the same law of fate, and he plays the devil's part so clearly because he must that you are obliged in honesty to keep your blame in your pocket since you really do not know where to bestow it.

The criticism showed how well playwright and players had translated the essence of the novel. It had been predicted that audiences would depart crushed under gloom—and instead they went away walking on air, in an ecstasy inspired by Hardy's irony and pity that seemed to include all human beings in a common destiny and on a common earth.

CHAPTER 10

The ticket seller said, "No seats for tonight."

"Tomorrow night, then."

"None for tomorrow night, either; the house is sold out for the next three weeks."

The man, who had nicked his chin in shaving, was disappointed. "I counted on seeing *Tess*—" He was interrupted by a customer who fumed out of the auditorium and slapped a ticket stub down at the window.

"I want my money back! I'm not going to look at a post for three hours!"

"I'll take that ticket," the man with the nicked chin said. "I don't mind . . ."

The ticket seller ignored the offer while he put down a silver dollar and took the stub from the angry man.

"Please let me have that ticket." The first man put down his dollar.

"You can't even see the stage from that seat," the irate customer warned him.

"It doesn't matter." He felt for the stub. "I am blind." His cane tapped the way into the auditorium before his abashed discourager could offer help.

The story was relayed behind scenes, and when the blind man was leaving after the last of many curtain calls, he felt a hand on his arm.

"Are you the gentleman who bought a ticket that was returned?"

"Yes."

"I am Mrs. Fiske's stage manager. Mrs. Fiske would like to speak to you."

It was too good to believe, but he let himself be led backstage and through the crowd waiting outside the actress' dressing room. For him there was no waiting.

Mrs. Fiske chatted with her visitor without making any reference to his handicap, but he could sense regret in her many-colored voice. "My brother is going to see the play next," he told her. "He will tell me what he saw."

"Good! Then you will have all of it."

"And I will describe what I heard."

"Oh, then your brother is—"

"Stone deaf," the blind man said, "but each of us will know half the play. We will compare notes and have all of it."

"Splendid!" Mrs. Fiske said. "But you must see it together, as my guests. We'll find seats where there isn't any post to interfere with precious sight and hearing."

There were other incidents, major and minor, on both sides of the curtain. Once, just before the murder scene, Alec's burst of insulting laughter from the bedroom did not materialize; there was only a gentle snoring. So Mrs. Fiske took up the carving knife and went through the door to the wings, where Charles Coghlan had fallen asleep waiting for his cue. Although her stage betrayer had damaged her climax, he looked so peaceful that Mrs. Fiske neither murdered nor woke him. Instead, she gave orders for no one to disturb him. Coghlan slept like a child until the final curtain, when he woke and rushed to Mrs. Fiske. The actor who was reputed to have a cynical disregard for obligations was so overwhelmed with remorse and self-accusation that the actress had to comfort him.

Body and soul, *Tess of the D'Urbervilles* was an impressive success; it was the finest and most thoughtful production of the year. The play also made money for the Fiskes, who had shared each other's faith in its merit. Important from their standpoint was the fact that Minnie had triumphed as Tess in the company of actors as able as herself. Nearly every critic wrote in detail about the work of at least ten members of the cast, and a few rated Charles Coghlan's Alec and Annie Irish's Marian above the star's Tess.

Several critics observed that Coghlan, Bell and Irish did their best work to date in *Tess of the D'Urbervilles*. It seemed a remarkable coincidence that there should be such a flowering of talent in a single cast. Actually, it was prophetic. In subsequent years it was noted with surprising regularity that actors did the best work of their careers with Mrs. Fiske.

Well-intentioned friends had pleaded with the Fiskes to abandon the play, which turned out to be the foundation of Minnie's subsequent career. The same friends had warned the Fiskes against their two chief actors, who were certain to wreck the production if it did not die of public indignation—and like a second miracle, the actors shone brilliantly to the end of the season without missing a performance.

If the friends had been able to watch the Fiskes and their cast more closely, they would have seen the miracle receiving judicious assistance. When Coghlan slept in the wings and missed his cue, he had already had a series of nights troubled by insomnia and all the devils of restlessness. A few evenings later he came to Mr. Fiske in his office in the theatre and told him that trouble was on the way. Like London, New York had a disturbing effect on him, and the disturbance was building up. He had already read all the French novels in stock at Brentano's, and he felt himself inclining toward more substantial diversions. If he let himself go, he would be lost as far as *Tess* was concerned; once he really started enjoying himself, he never remembered to return to a play. Ordinarily, indeed, he didn't bother to warn the producer, but the Fiskes had been so generous that they deserved perfect frankness.

Listening to the childlike candor of the actor of cynical repute, Harry saw that something had already been accomplished. He complimented the actor on knowing himself and observed that out of his self-knowledge Coghlan might be able to suggest something to avert a blow-up.

Yes, there was one remedy. If Mrs. Coghlan could sail immediately to New York and join him, Coghlan would be able to go on to the end of the engagement.

"An excellent idea," Harry agreed. "By all means cable Mrs. Coghlan."

The actor was overjoyed. "That saves the day!" His troubles were over, almost. As he was about to go back to his dressing room he remembered a minor point. "Perhaps you should cable her, Mr. Fiske. And, by the bye, would you cable her a hundred pounds for the trip? I haven't a *sou marque* to my name!"

Charles Coghlan had been a successful and highly paid actor for most of twenty years, but, as Harry told Minnie later that night, a man can spend a great deal of money if he enters into the spirit of it. Harry cabled the hundred pounds, and ten days later Coghlan's adoring wife arrived. The black-haired stage villain became as beatific as a child reunited with its mother.

The man whom the Fiskes had been most earnestly warned against was the handsome and talented dipsomaniac, Edward Bell. Night after night, to the end of the season, Bell confounded the warning voices by appearing as a sober Angel Clare, and he finished with a perfect record.

There was a miracle if there ever was one! If the mystified advisers had been able to look in on Bell's quarters at the Gilsey House during the last two weeks of *Tess* they would have seen some of the drama that went into the miracle.

The scene is Edward Bell's room in the Gilsey House, about ten in the morning. Bell, dressed but haggard and unshaven, slumps in a chair; only his eyes are alert. There is a knock at the door. Bell springs up to answer it. A second man appears and reaches the door at almost the same instant. He is Guy Smith, the Fiskes' treasurer.

Bell:

Never mind, Guy; just some flowers.

Smith:

I'll hold them for you. *(He examines the flowers while Bell whistles casually; reaches in his pocket for a tip. The boy exits. Smith puts the flowers in Bell's arms, goes to the wash basin, knocks the neck off a whiskey flask.)* Too bad. But you agreed to a bodyguard. And think of the record we're making for yourself!

Bell:

I'd rather it was my blood going down the drain!

Another scene:

The same room, at night. It is after another thrilling performance of Tess, *with every seat filled and people on chairs in the aisles. Bell sleeps peacefully, with the covers drawn up to his handsome chin, breathing with a deep even rhythm. In the half dark he opens first one eye, then the other. He draws back the covers and slips out of bed, fully dressed except for his shoes. He locates his shoes and moves stealthily to the door. Other unshod feet thump on the floor, and Smith, also dressed, bars the way.*

Smith:

Going somewhere?

Bell:

Just remembered I have to telegraph my Aunt Mabel. I didn't want to wake you.

Smith:

I was awake. Let me get my shoes and I'll go with you.

Bell *(hurt):*

Guy, if you don't trust me, I'll write out the telegram and you can take it—

Smith:

While you slip into Gilsey's Bar.

Bell *(with a sigh):*

I'm going back to bed.

Smith:

You might as well undress; you'll sleep better.

Bell *(from his bed):*

How many more nights of this?

Smith:

Ten.

Bell:

God! Ten nights without a barroom!

Smith:

With this record, you'll be able to get another job on Broadway next season.

Bell:

But a man can't stop drinking all at once—

Smith:

The agreement was "not a drop during the engagement." You said you'd die rather than let Mrs. Fiske down.

Bell:

This is worse than dying! Look, Guy, I'll give you ten dollars for a pint.

Smith:

Don't insult me.

Bell:

Twenty-five.

Smith:

I said, don't insult me.

Bell:

Fifty.

Smith:

Would you sell the Fiskes out for fifty dollars?

Bell:

No—but I'd sell my soul for a pint!

Smith:

You're not going to get a pint, so go to sleep.

For ten days and nights the actor thought up ingenious ruses, but Guy Smith was never caught napping.

At the end of the last performance of the season, the curtain descended with Angel Clare and Tess at the ruins of Stonehenge: Tess standing on the Druid altar, facing the rising sun, with the officers of the law closing about her—representatives of the implacable gods— and Angel Clare kneeling beside her, one hand covering his face to hide real tears.

Kneeling at the feet of the woman who had helped redeem his reputation and had inspired the best acting of his career, Edward M. Bell was seen for the last time on any stage. That same night, in his Angel clothes, he started on a week-long spree that led to a labyrinth of sanitariums and hospitals and ended in an institution for inebriates.

With Charles Coghlan the magic touch of *Tess* had a more lasting effect, and indirectly the Fiskes had a part in his continued success.

Five years earlier Harry and Minnie had traveled to Chillicothe for the premiere of *Fontenelle*. In the Ohio town they met the ambitious young George C. Tyler, who yearned to enter the theatrical business in New York. The Fiskes were favorably impressed, and later Harry made it possible for Tyler to come to New York by giving him a position on the *Dramatic Mirror*.

Charles Coghlan's brilliant and sustained work in *Tess of the D'Urbervilles* inspired Tyler to become a theatrical producer, starring Coghlan in his own play *The Royal Box*. The play was a tremendous success and it brought Coghlan more *sous marques* than he could immediately spend. It also encouraged Tyler in a second venture—Hall Caine's *The Christian*, starring Viola Allen. It was one of the popular hits of the decade, bringing him a fortune and establishing him as one of the most successful producers on Broadway.

Charles Coghlan starred in *The Royal Box* for two years. His second long tour ended at Galveston, Texas, where Coghlan died after a brief illness. The event seemed to discredit a crystal-gazer who had once professed to see the actor washed up, dead, on the Irish coast in front of the cottage where he was born.

The body of Coghlan, who had been disturbed by the prophecy, was placed in the receiving vault of a local cemetery to await burial. While it was there, Galveston was swept by the great hurricane and tidal wave of 1899, and Coghlan's coffin was carried out to sea. Thereafter there were reports of its making a landfall in various places. According to one, the coffin was cast up on the Irish coast a few miles from Coghlan's birthplace. Factually, it never reached any known shore.

CHAPTER 11

In Boston, cradle of American liberty, a handsome athletic actor stood before the call board of the Hollis Street Theatre and adjusted his monocle to read a freshly posted document:

NOTICE IS HEREBY GIVEN THAT, UNDER PAIN OF DISMISSAL, MEMBERS OF THE CAST ARE FORBIDDEN TO ADVERTISE IN, BUY OR READ THE NEW YORK *DRAMATIC MIRROR.*

The notice was signed by the business manager of the Klaw and Erlanger Traveling Company.

The actor swore vividly and strode out into the November sleet for a copy of the *Dramatic Mirror.* While he was out he telegraphed Harrison Grey Fiske:

HAVE RARELY READ A DRAMATIC NEWSPAPER BUT WILL READ THE MIRROR REGULARLY HEREAFTER
MAURICE BARRYMORE

Displaying a copy of the banned publication, Barrymore returned to what he hoped would be a fray, but he was disappointed. The manager had learned that the notice constituted a breach of criminal law, and it had been removed.

By the autumn of 1897 the Syndicate had gone far in its drive to control the theatrical business of the nation, and on the eastern seaboard it waged open warfare on those who would not come to heel. On November 14 the Washington, D. C., *Post* said of the Trust:

That this organization is beginning to adopt a high-handed style of dealing with opposition is proved by its treatment of the New York *Dramatic Mirror.* In Philadelphia this paper has been barred from all hotel news-stands that sell tickets to Syndicate theatres, and for some time past the *Mirror* has been forbidden even to mention the firm name of Klaw and Erlanger on penalty of exclusion from the news companies. Moreover, a reputable theatrical manager told the *Post* yesterday that he had been ordered to take his advertisement out of the *Mirror* if he wished to book his attractions in Syndicate houses. . .

Mr. Fiske announces that he will print a supplement devoted exclusively to "fighting the Trust," to which the Syndicate magnates retort by threatening to jail Mr. Fiske for malicious libel. Evidently there is to be a fight to the death between them.

The shooting had begun while Harry Fiske was preserving a neutral policy. The *Dramatic Mirror* had refrained from editorial comment, merely publishing facts along with the opinions of people prominent in the theatre, including Charles Frohman and Al Hayman. The two were key members of the Trust, and their Empire Theatre at Fortieth Street and Broadway was doubly next-door neighbor of the *Mirror*, having been built to surround the small old *Mirror* building on three sides. According to the way one looked at it, the *Mirror* had its head in the lion's mouth, or it was a thorn in the side of the Theatrical Trust.

Frohman disclaimed any active part in the Syndicate, but he assured the public that it was not a trust or combine and that managers would continue to control their own theatres.

Hayman insisted that the Syndicate would promote healthy competition which would benefit actors, managers and public alike.

The reassuring picture changed rapidly as the Syndicate gained control of nearly all the first-class houses in America. And there were incidents which seemed to contradict the promise not to change the terms of established actors unless to better them. One was the announcement that for the following season the terms of Madame Modjeska and Fanny Davenport would be reduced.

Harry Fiske inquired about this, and Hayman explained that the Syndicate was a business organization; Modjeska and Davenport were getting old and losing their box-office appeal, and the Syndicate would not cart old women about the country unless it could do so at a profit.

Another case was that of Francis Wilson. Early in March the popular comedian announced the cancellation of all his contracts made through the Syndicate and said he would appear thereafter only in independent houses. Hayman countered with the boast that the break had come from the Syndicate, not the actor. They had found that Wilson was

78

holding time in two Washington theatres, and they had decided to make an example of him as a warning to lesser culprits who booked time in independent theatres.

This attempt to break a well-known actor did not jibe with the Trust's announced intentions, but the *Mirror* continued to withhold editorial comment, while publishing the views of individuals affected by the combine. Those who dared to speak out were Augustin Daly, Joseph Jefferson, Richard Mansfield, Mrs. Fiske, James O'Neill, Francis Wilson and James A. Hearne. They unanimously condemned the Trust.

One afternoon the door to Mr. Fiske's private office flew open and Al Hayman stormed in with an ultimatum:

"Fiske, I order you not to make another mention of the Theatrical Syndicate in your paper! What the Syndicate does is my private business and no concern of the theatrical profession or the public!"

"On the contrary," Harry told him, "actors and managers have a right to opinions about their profession, and everyone concerned has obligations to the public. The *Dramatic Mirror* will continue to report matters of general interest, without fear or favor."

Hayman shook his finger under the editor's nose. "You go and do that and I'll kill the *Mirror*, break you, and drive Mrs. Fiske from the stage!"

Harry rose from his chair and went to the door, which he held open. "Good day, Mr. Hayman. Carry your threats out elsewhere."

That was the beginning of the Fiskes' twelve-year war with the Theatrical Trust.

The *Mirror* now trained its editorial guns on the Trust, and out-of-town newspapers responded by stepping up their attacks on the combine. In New York the Trust had silenced several newspapers with threats of libel suit. It now threatened to sue the American News Company if it distributed copies of the *Mirror* which mentioned the Syndicate.

The news company declined to be a battleground; so Harry Fiske launched a Theatrical Trust Supplement, which was distributed independently of the news company. The first supplement appeared on November 13, 1897, loaded with anti-trust dynamite. Two days later the Trust members started a $100,000 libel suit against the *Dramatic Mirror*.

The most prominent member of the combine was Charles Frohman; he was also the one most concerned with keeping the good will of the public. Frohman had disclaimed any active part in the Trust, but his name appeared as one of the plaintiffs in the action against the *Mirror,* and thereafter he became the chief target of anti-Trust newspapers.

Five days after the *Mirror's* first supplement, Joseph Pulitzer's New York *World* entered the battle with an editorial beginning:

> The Theatre Trust is a peculiar abomination. It aims not only to compel the public to pay what price the Trust pleases for its entertainment, but to decide arbitrarily what plays and what actors the public shall see. . .

John Norris, fighting editor of the *World,* came in with the assurance that a group of outstanding actors would unite in opposition to the Trust and stick by their guns.

The fight was on. Early in January of 1898 the newspaper carried a front-page spread entitled:

THE *WORLD'S* TRUST CATECHISM

> In letters to the *World* and in false publications in other newspapers the men composing the Theatre Trust have strongly protested their innocence of any wrongdoing.
>
> The *World* therefore asks the members of the Theatre Trust a few questions:
>
> Have you not systematically and persistently practiced fraud and deceit on the public?
>
> Have you not repeatedly sent out inferior companies, falsely representing them as the original casts of New York successes?
>
> Have you not repeatedly advertised actors as playing in these companies who in fact at that time were playing in other and distant cities? . . .
>
> Is it not true that the following advertisement appeared in the Boston *Post* on November 2 last:
>
> "Boston Museum—after two hundred nights of New York laughter, Charles Frohman presents, first time here, his funniest and most successful comedy, *Never Again,* with the same remarkable cast as at the Garrick Theatre, New York, during a six months' run."
>
> Was not all this falsehood?
>
> Is it not true that at that very time Ferdinand Gottschalk and Agnes Miller, who made the success of the play in New York, were playing at the Vaudeville Theatre in London. . .
>
> This is but the beginning.
>
> The *World* has other questions to ask, some of which may be even more interesting than these—both to the public and to the Trust.

While Trust methods were being exposed, a group of leading actors carried out their promise to the New York *World*. Early in December they organized The Association for the Promotion and Protection of an Independent Stage in the United States. The title was unwieldy, but the aim was clear. Unanimously the members signed an agreement to appear only in theatres whose managers would make contracts without middlemen; the arrangement permitted a member to book in a Trust theatre if the manager acted independently. Richard Mansfield was elected president of the new Association.

At that time Mansfield was appearing in Philadelphia at the Chestnut Theatre owned by Nirdlinger and Zimmerman. Each night he made fiery curtain speeches denouncing the Trust and warning the people of Philadelphia that the engagement would be his last in their city unless an independent theatre was established. The actor was warned repeatedly that if he attempted another curtain speech the orchestra would drown him out, but he persisted. On one occasion the asbestos curtain was dropped to cut him off, but the management was frightened by the resulting fury of the audience and they did not try it again. On another occasion Mansfield was arrested, but the move backfired, putting the actor in the role of a martyr and arousing new indignation against the Trust.

In other cities and from other stages, James O'Neill was blasting the Trust, which, he declared, was ruining his profession. At the same time Francis Wilson was making a triumphant anti-Trust tour of New England. He traveled on a special train, accompanied by hundreds of citizens and the Second Regimental Band. Wherever he went there were parades through crowded streets, and anti-Trust speeches in the atmosphere of a second American Revolution.

In New York the *Dramatic Mirror* blasted away at the Frohman and Hayman empire. Harry Fiske and his Trust neighbors were no longer on speaking terms, and on Mrs. Fiske's brief visits to New York she felt the mounting tension which finally broke into physical conflict. She and her husband were strolling on Broadway one evening when Mr. Erlanger overtook them and made an insulting comment. Harry turned and knocked him down. He then gave Mrs. Fiske his hat, cane and gloves to hold while he and Erlanger fought until a patrol wagon arrived and clanged them away to the police station.

Later that same year Mrs. Fiske dashed home from her hampered tour with *Tess* for the incorporation of the Independent Stage Associa-

81

tion. Richard Mansfield, president, had chosen a time when most of the members were playing in or near New York; he himself was appearing in *The Devil's Disciple* at the Harlem Opera House. They were to meet at his office on Twenty-eighth Street.

On the way uptown from their headquarters at the Brevoort, the Fiskes' carriage passed the Madison Square Theatre, which faced the park where one of the dramatic events of Richard Mansfield's life had been played. There was snow on the park bench under the sycamore tree.

When the Fiskes arrived at Mansfield's princely office, most of the other independents were already there; and the Fiskes' old friend, Judge Dittenhoefer, was reviewing the papers of incorporation with the stately A. M. Palmer, who was now Mansfield's manager. Mr. Mansfield was expected momentarily, Palmer said.

At ten minutes past the hour set for the meeting, he said it was not like Mr. Mansfield to be late.

At twenty minutes past, no one said anything.

At half past the appointed hour, a messenger brought a letter for Mr. Fiske and hurried away as if he had been instructed not to wait for an answer.

The letter was from Richard Mansfield, and after reading it carefully, Fiske summarized to the waiting actors: Mr. Mansfield regretted that he could not attend or preside over the meeting because of conflicting duties in connection with *The Devil's Disciple*.

Mr. Mansfield did not set any date for a future gathering.

The meeting was adjourned indefinitely. Judge Dittenhoefer went away with the articles of incorporation unsigned, and the actors drifted silently out of the oppressive atmosphere of Mansfield's splendid office.

In the carriage on the way back to the Brevoort, Minnie said quietly, "That was a short summary of a long letter."

"And an incomplete one," her husband told her. "I was ashamed to tell the rest."

"So Mr. Mansfield has gone over to the Trust."

"Body and soul," Harry said. "He was the biggest prize in either camp, and they offered him a fortune for joining them. In his letter he questioned the sincerity of the other independents, and he advises you not to bother any more about the Trust."

"How thoughtful of Mr. Mansfield!" Then she asked, "Why did he address the letter to you and not to the meeting?"

"That is a complete mystery," Harry said, "unless he thought you were the one most likely to carry on the fight and he wanted to dissuade you."

She did not think much of that. "Mr. Mansfield should have known that as long as I live I will fight for what I believe in—with or without his advice!"

The change that had enriched Mansfield had left the other independents much poorer.

"It will be a long fight now," Harry said, "but I am with you if it takes the rest of our lives." As their carriage rocked through the slush on Broadway, he said, "I still can't see why he did it. He has a princely income, and the Trust couldn't have dented it. Even if he played in barns, the public would flock to see him."

Again they came in sight of Madison Square, and the park bench under the sycamore tree where Richard Mansfield, comic opera comedian, had died in agony and Richard Mansfield, dramatic actor, had been born.

The young Englishman was broke, with a torn ankle that would never dance again. As a last hope he dragged himself to the stage door of the Madison Square Theatre, gritting back the pain, and walked blithely in for a tryout. The great A. M. Palmer gave him a hearing, and his first chance on the American legitimate stage. After the interview the young actor hobbled out and fainted on the park bench.

Two years later Mansfield was broke again. A grandiose tour under his own management had collapsed and left him starving in a luxurious hotel room. He was trying to conjure his way back to England when young Minnie Maddern breezed in and engaged him to play Antonius Kraft in *In Spite of All*. The role was another turning point of his life; he remained to become the greatest American actor of his time—and one of the wealthiest. Now the Trust war that had united the Fiskes and Richard Mansfield in a common cause had separated them decisively.

As Madison Square was falling behind them, Minnie spoke. "I think I understand why Mansfield did it."

Harry looked at her, and his grimness softened in answer to her smile. "Have you been studying him from the inside, as you do your roles?"

She nodded. "He did it because he died in agony on a park bench, because he starved to death in a hotel room."

83

"He seems very much alive to me."

"Only in a ghostly way," she insisted. "His vanity can never accept what happened on the park bench, in the hotel room. He will destroy himself piling up money and honors he doesn't need—trying to bury the suffering and humiliation, trying to deny what has already happened."

Nine years later, when Richard Mansfield died of driving ambition, and of stomach trouble dating from his starvation days, Harry agreed that his wife had been right. But at the time he was concerned with the results of the actor's desertion. When he reported it to John Norris, the *World's* attack on the Theatrical Trust stopped with a deafening silence. The Independent Stage Association never held another meeting, and one after another its members went over to the Trust—all except Madame Modjeska, who was driven into retirement never to reappear; and Minnie Maddern Fiske, who believed that fighting for one's principles is the reason for living.

CHAPTER 12

Tess of the D'Urbervilles appeared on the American scene at the beginning of a new era. President McKinley came into office with a giant young country of seventy-five millions awakening to its strength and thinking of empire; the New York *World's* front-page attacks on the Theatrical Trust were jostled by bellicose columns in which Pulitzer competed with Hearst in blasting at Spain, and that fall and winter *Tess* toured through a country being prepared for war.

Late in March, 1898, Mrs. Fiske ended a triumphal Chicago engagement. The Trust barred her from theatres farther west, but New York welcomed her return and *Tess* reopened at the Fifth Avenue Theatre to a packed house. There were changes in the cast: Belgian-born Frederic de Belleville now played Alec; Forrest Robinson replaced the lost Edward Bell as Angel Clare and Mary Shaw played Marian. Most critics felt that the new players were not the equals of the ones they replaced, but they were unanimous in agreeing that the production as a whole was more perfect.

In a year of playing, Mrs. Fiske's Tess had gained in power and poignancy. The *World's* critic devoted a third of his column to the way the actress spoke two words. One was the cry "Marian!" when Tess learned that she had been deceived about Angel's death. The other came after the murder, when Angel spoke to her, and Tess, deafened by the turmoil in her mind, answered, "What?" To the critic this was "a psychological exhibition so clean cut, so definite, that an expert in mental disorders could make his diagnosis from it."

It was a tribute to the actress that in a world resounding with war-like oratory, so much space should be given to her speaking of two words. Perhaps the only cry of the hour that outlived them was the slogan, "Remember the Maine!"

After two weeks of *Tess*, Mrs. Fiske presented a change of bill— *Love Finds the Way*, the Fiskes' new name for *The Right to Happiness*.

85

On the national scene there were developments rather than any change of bill. Spain had offered the equivalent of unconditional surrender, minus a small amount of face-saving, but President McKinley chose to overlook the conciliatory move; on the day that Mrs. Fiske presented *Love Finds the Way*, he asked Congress for a declaration of war.

Mrs. Fiske's engagement had been extended a second time, and love was still finding the way at the Fifth Avenue Theatre when Commodore Dewey destroyed the Spanish fleet in Manila Bay—giving the United States the islands from which the Acapulco galleons had brought their treasure and conferring the name of "Dewey" on great numbers of American boys born that year.

In that season of miracles everything seemed possible, and the Fiskes had a play suited to the times. *Love Finds the Way* is the story of a pampered young woman who was cured of hysterical lameness by a self-forgetful act.

New York critics found the German play cumbersome, but enthusiastic audiences accepted the cure of the crippled girl as a reality. The teachings of Mary Baker Eddy had not begun to spread until after the play was written, and the Fiskes were startled by their discovery that a large percentage of their audiences were members of the new faith. So many crippled persons were brought to see the play that the Fiskes' business manager proposed a special checkroom for crutches and wheel chairs.

After *Love Finds the Way*, Minnie's season got its third wind with a brilliant revival of Sardou's *Divorçons*. The actress ended her season at the Fifth Avenue in July, long after other theatres had closed. In spite of the Trust, which had hampered her everywhere, she had toured and played profitably for eight solid months.

The foundation of success was *Tess of the D'Urbervilles*. In the season of 1898 she and Harry agreed with the same mutual enthusiasm on another "big" play.

To innumerable people on both sides of the Atlantic, the scandalous heroine of *Vanity Fair* was a real and vital person. Thackeray had discovered that early in Becky's creation. He had planned her as a minor character, but the ambitious little governess with her sharp practices and her loaded dice had almost immediately snubbed the other female characters and made herself the heroine of the novel. Readers did not even try to resist her, and they were firmly convinced that along with her vices she had great dramatic talent. For two generations they had been asking, "Who will play Becky Sharp?"

86

During those leisurely decades there were many attempts to crowd *Vanity Fair* onto the stage, but those resounding failures did not interrupt the discussion. Nor were the Fiskes disturbed by the fact that they were on a course strewn with shipwrecks. However, they did examine and analyze the failures.

"This is a case where the layman sees more clearly than the experts," Minnie decided. "The public talks of Becky Sharp, and the dramatists try to give them all of *Vanity Fair*."

"Precisely," Harry agreed. "On the stage, Becky is superbly possible. *Vanity Fair* is impossible."

When they had agreed on that, the next step was to have the play written. Again the Trust monopoly on playwrights obliged the Fiskes to put a great project in the hands of an amateur. They finally chose young Langdon Mitchell, son of the famous Dr. S. Weir Mitchell. While studying in Europe Langdon had developed a passion for the stage, and he had returned to New York with a beautiful actress wife and a one-act play to his credit.

The Fiskes and Langdon Mitchell agreed on a play founded on *Vanity Fair*, not buried under it. There would not be any more of the novel than fitted conveniently into a play in which Becky Sharp was on the stage almost continuously.

In *Vanity Fair* Becky had reduced the other female characters to unimportance; in the play she got rid of most of the novel, and the conscienceless Becky was pleased. There was not gratitude in her, but the playwright and the actress and producer were rewarded by the way in which the little adventuress came to reckless life and sparkled in the acts which Langdon wrote so slowly and painstakingly but that seemed to have been dashed off without effort.

In the fall of 1898, while Becky Sharp was being reincarnated, Mrs. Fiske took her company on the road. The first engagement was in Buffalo, at the Lyceum. The theatre was given to vaudeville and melodrama, and the regular patrons were puzzled by the billing of *Tess of the D'Urbervilles* at double the usual rates. The program stated, *Mrs. Fiske does not play in theatres controlled by the Trust.* That line was to become the trademark of a valiant actress.

The company went on to the midwest, and when *Tess* opened in Chicago there was a new character in the cast. The role was a slight one, newly written in, and it was played by Tyrone Power, who had starred in Daly's company.

Why waste one of America's ablest actors in a walk-on part? In one of her rare interviews, Mrs. Fiske gave the clue—three acts of *Becky*

Sharp were written, and she was in love with the role. Tyrone Power was being kept on hand for the big production.

Beyond the Mississippi lay solid Trust territory; from Chicago Minnie turned back east. Most of the large cities were closed to her, but wherever the Trust was unable to bar her, she was a success. In Cincinnati, the *Times-Star* hailed her appearance as "a triumph for what is noble, human, real in stage art." Louisville saluted her as "an actress great, not as a fad, nor for a day or year, but for as long as she chooses to grace her country's stage." And while Minnie was in that hospitable city, the manager of the Baltimore Lyceum kicked over the Trust traces and wired that his theatre was open to her. The engagement was one of the most profitable of her tour.

From Baltimore, in mid-December, Minnie turned north to Jersey City and the comforts of the Brevoort across the Hudson. On Christmas she did not even have to take the ferry to Jersey; for the first time in many months she and Harry had a day to themselves, uninterrupted by a stage appearance. But the shadow of the theatre was upon them.

Under normal conditions, Minnie could have toured with *Tess* for a year without visiting all the cities that were clamoring for the play. But she was bottled up in the eastern third of the country, with many areas of that region closed to her; in her shuttlings back and forth, she had to keep adding new plays to her repertory, none of them as good as *Tess*. Harry's part was equally difficult—securing bookings in the Trust-riddled third of the country and working hours every day on the jigsaw puzzle of tours.

In moments of exhaustion and exasperation, the Fiskes buoyed each other up with, "Wait till we do *Becky*!" The production loomed ahead like an enchanted mountain.

But Langdon Mitchell had not finished the play, and the mountain was still a long way off. Minnie would need another play for the interim, and from the assortment available they chose *Magda*—a play which had tempted only the greatest actresses, with disputed results.

In January, Minnie began an engagement at Gilmore's Auditorium in Philadelphia. Aunt Emma Maddern was living in Philadelphia at the time and acting with the Girard Avenue Stock Company while her daughter, Emily Stevens, attended convent school.

Aunt Emma retained the flavor of childhood days on Baronne Street. With unbroken continuity she devoted herself to theatre and church in the vigorous tradition of Grandmother Maddern. Her daughter Emily, the flower girl of the Fiskes' wedding, was now a young woman

88

of seventeen, with clear-cut features, fair hair, dark eyes and eyebrows, and a mind of her own. The dead hand of Grandmother Maddern, which still guided Emma and restrained Minnie, produced in Emily only revolt. The girl was sad-faced in repose, and witty beyond her years, and those who opposed her she snagged with phrases as neatly turned as fishhooks. Along with her beauty and sharp wit, Emily had an ardent spirit; she was a favorite with Minnie, and the worldly-wise Harrison Fiske was her hero. The visit ended with Emily, the young woman, drawn closer to the Fiskes than she had been in Larchmont days.

After Philadelphia came a four-week engagement in Boston; then Montreal, where Mrs. Fiske was praised for standing alone against the Trust and for her strenuous, undismayed spirit; and Harry arrived to direct the tryout of *Magda*, which they had selected for an interim play. Minnie and he were hailed as "the leading American actress and the editor of the most complete and widely read dramatic paper in the world." Two weeks later in Toronto, Hector Charlesworth of the *Mail and Empire* led off with a quotation from Kipling's recently published *Stalky & Co.* " '*Je vais gloater, je vais gloater tout le* blessed afternoon.' I also gloat all the blessed afternoon because I have something worth writing about. . . ."

The same blessed week Mrs. Fiske gave Charlesworth one of her rare interviews, talking freely about her problems and her future plans. *Becky Sharp* was the biggest news: Langdon Mitchell had just finished the dramatization. It would be ready for fall production—a new play by an unknown writer—and Mrs. Fiske had such confidence in it that she was not even bothering to have another play ready.

The thirty-two-year-old woman who was winning artistic battles with one hand and fighting for existence with the other was a contradictory personality—a shy little being with a plain face and dumpy figure and a voice that many found harsh and unpleasant. On the stage she could persuade her audiences that she was beautiful; she could use her voice to break their hearts, drench them in tears with a sudden inflection, or leave them haunted by a word or cry; and she inspired other actors to do their best work.

Away from the theatre Minnie avoided people as much as possible and hardly seemed to have a life of her own. Off stage it always appeared to be Sunday for her—the Sunday of Grandmother Maddern who ruled her daughters with the iron hand of God.

Minnie's long interview with the critic of the *Mail and Empire* was neither typical nor impulsive. Three years before, when Hector Charlesworth tried to interview Mrs. Fiske for the first time, she had discouraged him to the core. As he was leaving, the unhappy critic blurted, "I knew your father when I was a little boy."

Mrs. Fiske's frigidity melted as he told her that his family and Tom Davey's had been neighbors in Hamilton. From the house next door, young Charlesworth had watched the party Davey had given for little Minnie Maddern, touring with McCullough's company.

It was a simple fragment of the past, but the door it opened was never closed again, and it was the beginning of a lifelong friendship. It was also a clue to the personality of Minnie Maddern Fiske. Her conscious thoughts were turned toward the future, but the key to her nature was in her childhood past. Tom Davey had clashed with Maddern strictness and piety, and gone his way, while she stayed to have those things ingrained into her. For that reason there was a touchstone quality about her lost father. By direct succession, she was the heir to his Bohemian spirit. The fact that she was never able to claim her inheritance did not prevent her from having dreams.

There was good reason for the meeting with Tom Davey to stand out sharply in his daughter's memory. He had left home in Minnie's infancy, and in a way it was the first time she had seen him. It was also the last. Tom Davey died a few months after Lizzie Maddern—Bohemianism and patient piety coming to the same end in the same year.

From Toronto Mrs. Fiske and her company went on to present *Magda* in New York.

Sudermann's drama was a lumpy affair of talk, with a strong dash of sound and fury, but what it signified was doubtful.

Modjeska had once given a confused and unsatisfactory performance of *Magda;* Bernhardt played it "like a gilded cockatoo who has strayed by mistake into a mothers' meeting," and afterward she termed it her one abject failure. Duse had flinched from Magda as she was, and distorted her into a sympathetic character. Mrs. Pat Campbell had paraded through the role like an elegant clotheshorse.

Magda at the Fifth Avenue Theatre was Magda as Sudermann had written her, a cynical and cruel egotist, too self-centered to give or want sympathy. For the first time a non-German Magda had given her audience something into which they could sink their teeth. They hated her for four acts and went away satisfied. But not even Mrs. Fiske could make them fond of Sudermann's drama. It was followed by the trivial and shopworn *Frou Frou.* Minnie had been opposed to the play, but

90

she was swayed into it by her husband's enthusiasm. *Frou Frou* failed and was withdrawn after ten costly performances, and Harry vowed he would leave the final decision on plays to his wife. He broke that vow once—long afterward— with disastrous results.

After the shelving of *Frou Frou*, *Little Italy* was presented along with *Divorçons*. The one-act tragedy of New York's East Side was carefully staged and splendidly cast with Frederic de Belleville, Tyrone Power and Mrs. Fiske.

Little Italy, "shining out from the general run of theatrical performances like some great white star," was played for three thrilling performances, then dropped.

The immediate reason was a protest from a group of New York Italians who saw in the play a travesty on Italian womanhood. Behind it was the fact that for generations American writers had used Italians, Irish, Negroes and Jews for stock comedy characters. Some change of climate—perhaps the advance winds of the twentieth century—was stirring minorities to protest, and it was inevitable that their bruised feelings would be over-sensitive. Mrs. Fiske did not share in the protesters' opinion of *Little Italy*, but she respected it and withdrew the play, thereby cutting short her New York engagement.

It was an abrupt and disappointing ending; but soon afterward *Harper's Weekly* pronounced Mrs. Fiske's season the most significant of any American actor's. *Harper's* said in part:

> Mrs. Fiske's season of repertory plays—*Magda, Frou Frou, Divorçons,* and *Tess of the D'Urbervilles*—has a merit of its own outside the merits of the various performances. The best of American actors, with very few exceptions, have fallen under the sway of the theatrical trust. . . It has one vital defect. Whenever one of its actor-servants makes a popular success, he is bound to it, hand and foot. As far as their freedom of artistic growth in concerned, such actors as Mr. Drew and Miss Maude Adams might as well be galley slaves. Mrs. Fiske has foregone the heralding of a more or less suborned press; she has been forced at times to play in theatres that a barn-stormer would pause before. But she plays what she chooses and what she chooses is the best that offers.

The sensation of the season had been Richard Mansfield as Cyrano de Bergerac, and *Harper's* went on to observe that while he played the hero of freedom under Trust auspices, Mrs. Fiske lived the role on her lonely crusade.

CHAPTER 13

In Langdon Mitchell's *Becky Sharp*, a thousand incidents of *Vanity Fair* were omitted, but all of Becky was there: her unprincipled resourcefulness, her hypocrisy—which she never used on herself—and her subversive appeal to spectators tired of identifying themselves with too-noble characters.

Harry Fiske's aim was a production worthy of his wife's talents, and he had spent a year and a small fortune in the effort. Each of the four stage-sets was done to authentic perfection, and one was a masterpiece. The second act takes place at the Duchess of Richmond's ball in Brussels, on the eve of Waterloo. For this, Harry Fiske planned a magnificently arched entrance hall and grand staircase that gave the illusion of being larger than the theatre itself, and brought a gasp of wonder from each successive audience.

The costuming of *Becky Sharp* was a correction on Thackeray. The author of *Vanity Fair* had clothed his characters in the dress of 1845, and in the play they were authentic 1815. The costumes were done from colored plates provided by the English artist, Percy Anderson, and they were complete to the smallest accessories.

Becky had thirty-two speaking parts and a flock of supernumeraries, and the cast was selected with a magnificent disregard of cost.

Mrs. Fiske's leading man was Maurice Barrymore. She had first met him in Modjeska's private theatrical car on the journey to St. Louis. At the time, Barrymore was known as a natural actor so gifted that he was only a few steps away from greatness. In twenty years he had not bothered to take those last few steps, but he was the ideal Rawdon Crawley, more in tune with the dashing Napoleonic age than with the Victorian one in which he found himself miscast in life.

Tyrone Power was the sinister Marquis of Steyne, and the rest of the cast was carefully chosen, down to Briggs, played by Aunt Mary Maddern, who had been on the stage for over fifty years.

The great production was launched at Montreal—a place where the English classic seemed sure of a welcome.

Becky Sharp had its premiere at the Montreal Academy of Music on September 4, 1899. The audience was silent as the curtain rose on Miss Crawley's sitting room in London, and almost as silent when the curtain fell at the end of the scene. As the play progressed there was only an occasional embarrassed laugh, and faint applause like the pattering of sleet. The audience never warmed up. The players were acutely aware of the fact that their audience was not amused; and the play needed cutting. It was near morning when the final curtain fell on Becky's room in Pumpernickle, and the auditorium began emptying in chilling silence. Backstage the silence was finally broken by the Fiskes' manager, who asked with brutal helpfulness, "What are we going to substitute for *Becky*?"

It was like asking the Fiskes what plans they had for the future, now that their death sentence had been passed.

Mrs. Fiske said nothing. They had no substitute. Harry was grim, but undaunted. "*Becky* isn't dead yet," he informed the manager.

Next day the press dealt *Becky Sharp* more blows. The Montreal *Herald* said the comedy was a tragic riot of evil, and Becky the most wicked woman the stage had ever seen. In its listing of entertainments, the paper classed *Becky Sharp* as unwholesome, and followed with an editorial that babbled of hospitals and morgues and cesspools. Currently, Lily Langtry was appearing in the sensational *The Degenerates*, and the editor lamented that: "It must be said of her (Mrs. Fiske) as of an English actress with whom she has little in common, that she has thrown her talents into the role of a 'degenerate.' "

Mrs. Fiske was already bowed under responsibility for the production; while she was still off balance, the *Herald's* attack was reprinted in the New York *American*. She sent the *American* a heated telegram, beginning:

"The malicious and abusive article in the Montreal *Herald*, and its dissemination, can be safely attributed to the industrious mercenaries of the Theatrical Trust. . ."

It was the first, and last, reply Mrs. Fiske ever made to a bad notice. The Trust had done her many bad turns, and was to do many more, but on quieter thought Mrs. Fiske concluded that the *Herald* had done no more than reflect the sentiment of her audience; and she shouldered the blame for what she considered her own shockingly bad first-night performance. But that was not all. Queen Victoria was solidly on the throne, trying to erase the memory of a bawdy period of English history that had preceded her reign. New York would be different. The Fiskes' faith in *Becky* remained unshaken.

Becky made her first curtsy to Broadway on September 12 at the old Fifth Avenue Theatre, the only place the Fiskes could get. The house was packed from pit to dome, and there were hundreds of standees in the aisles.

On that first night there were among the spectators some who had more than the usual stake in the performance. One of them was Dr. S. Weir Mitchell, who had made a surprise visit to New York to discover what kind of play his son had written. Another was the eighteen-year-old Ethel Barrymore, the bearer of family responsibilities, who was there to see how her father prospered as Rawdon Crawley. Still another was Harry Fiske. He had done all he could to the last moment—and he faded into the farthest reach of the audience to view the performance as a disinterested spectator.

The first act, in Miss Crawley's London house, was undramatic but colorful.

The second-act curtain rose on the Duchess of Richmond's ball at Brussels, "the sound of revelry by night," and the magnificent architectural stage set. The interruption of jealousies and gambling and flirtations by the booming of Napoleon's cannon was vastly effective, but the act was more pageant than drama.

The crucial third act, with only a few characters, held the audience more tensely than the magnificent pageantry of Brussels. The first scene ended with Becky seated at the harpsichord and, with an untroubled conscience, playing and singing demurely.

Jealous of the falling curtain, the audience was silent until the last tinkling note had been shut away. Then their applause broke out and swelled to an ovation. It was still roaring when Harry hurried backstage.

"Becky has conquered!" he told Minnie. "Not often in a lifetime do you hear such applause, my dear!"

The next scene belonged exclusively to the three great actors in the cast: Mrs. Fiske, Maurice Barrymore and Tyrone Power. It was Becky's *tete-a-tete* supper with the Marquis of Steyne, interrupted by the appearance of Rawdon.

The immediate product of those minutes was twelve vociferous curtain calls, and in memory they diffused the whole play with dramatic action.

The fourth act was quiet: Becky in poverty, living a Bohemian life in Pumpernickle, but on the upswing again, with the fatuous Joseph Sedley hooked and young Sir Pitt Crawley praying over her with an appraising eye; Becky as unrepentant as ever.

A sample of New York had seen Becky Sharp in the flesh, and she had flashed beyond the power of the critics to harm her, though most of them tried. The one exception was William Winter of the *Tribune*, who alone gave the production adequate space, praising Mitchell's play and the work of Mrs. Fiske, Maurice Barrymore, Tyrone Power and William Owen.

The Trust-friendly *Sun* expressed sorrow that Mrs. Fiske had embarked on an adventure which could hardly reward her with any gain in fame or money; and Mr. Towse of the *Evening Post* sadly misjudged the greatest dramatic success of the decade:

In dealing with such a theatrical monstrosity as *Becky Sharp* exhibited at the Fifth Avenue Theatre last night, before an audience which was packed, in more ways than one, there is a natural conflict between a sense of duty to the public at large and a feeling of compassion for the persons unfortunate enough to be interested or concerned in it. To tell the whole truth, briefly and baldly, might seem malicious, while to disguise it would plainly be a breach of faith. One way out of the difficulty would be to treat the whole thing as a rather poor joke, by which a feeble travesty was offered in the place of the rational entertainment which was expected. . . .

Mrs. Fiske was able to chuckle over the whole thing. Tickets were sold out a month in advance, and standing room was in demand at every performance. And a week later Mr. Towse reversed himself:

The management of the Fifth Avenue Theatre reports that *Becky Sharp* is being played to the largest audiences that the theatre has ever known. This fact, if it be a fact, justifies the opinion already expressed that there are certain features in the performance likely to please the average audience. . . .

The success of *Becky Sharp* had only begun. As had been the case with *Tess,* but to a greater degree, magazine pages were filled with *Becky* text and pictures that made the stage characters household figures throughout the English-speaking world. From all over the United States, newspapers and magazines blasted the New York press for its shabby treatment of *Becky*, and the Toronto *Mail and Empire* retold the story of the prejudiced New York critic who left before the end of the play and wrote disparagingly of Mrs. Fiske's acting in Becky's death scene—Becky Sharp, who never died!

Becky had never been more alive than she was in the last months of the eighteen hundreds. With the tide of her popularity still rising, Harper's brought out a "Becky Sharp" edition of *Vanity Fair*, with forty-eight illustrations from the play, and the edition sold out before it was off the press.

Mrs. Fiske had turned all her energies to making *Becky* a great production, but when the play brought her the ultimate of recognition, she was distressed. "Fame" meant endless hours at Sarony's posing for portraits to keep up with the demand, hours which to her were a painful ordeal. "Fame" meant being stared at by strangers wherever she went. It also meant that everyone who spoke to her felt called upon to talk about her "greatness."

During her formative days at Larchmont, wandering in the fields and woods, Minnie had desired to pass through the natural world unseen and unheard, without missing a sight or sound or scent, and without disturbing a living thing. Fame brought her the opposite, and her natural shyness increased. With her friends she still talked like untroubled lightning; but in public she winced when strangers recognized her, and she was uncomfortable and tongue-tied when half-strangers treated her like a celebrity.

At the Fifth Avenue, Becky went her triumphant way, gaining in richness and sparkle and subtlety. On December 11, the management handed out beautifully-illustrated booklets to celebrate the hundred and first performance of *Becky Sharp*.

The supply of audiences was inexhaustible—but the Theatrical Trust was in control of the situation. On Christmas Eve, with spectators crowding the aisles, the New York run of *Becky Sharp* came to an abrupt end. Manager Knowles of the Fifth Avenue had twice extended the engagement while the next attraction waited, and he had come to the limit of extensions. There were empty theatres in New York, but they were controlled by the Trust, and closed to Mrs. Fiske.

There was no room in New York for *Becky Sharp*, but the Fiskes secured a week's engagement at the Academy of Music in Brooklyn, opening there on Christmas night to a house as packed as the Fifth Avenue had been.

Becky's next stop was Boston; at the box office of the Tremont, theatregoers stood in line for hours in the snow, and before the end of the queue had reached the window, the last ticket for the three-week engagement had been sold.

From Boston *Becky* went on to Washington and Baltimore, playing to audiences that were limited only by the capacity of the theatres. Then the company turned north to Canada, where *Becky* had begun in failure. This time, however, the destination was Toronto and that city welcomed Becky like a queen who could do no wrong—or rather, a queen who did wrong in a soul-satisfying manner. With one voice the Toronto press greeted the play as the dramatic event of the season, and Mrs. Fiske as the greatest American actress. Hector Charlesworth of the *Mail and Empire* went farther, calling her "the most brilliant English-speaking actress." He went on:

> The impersonation of Becky by Mrs. Fiske not only conserves all the memories of Becky that the readers of Thackeray carry through life with them, but it contains elements of femininity that neither Thackeray nor any other man could describe. It will certainly be famous in the annals of the stage when all of us are dead and gone, and it is to be hoped that Mrs. Fiske will one day go to London, where the memory of such things is more jealously guarded, in order that the record of this impersonation may be more preciously preserved.

In Chicago, Sir Henry Irving and Ellen Terry were playing to capacity houses on their sixth American tour, but *Becky* received as brilliant a reception as the one that had been accorded them, and for the next two weeks the rival companies played to packed houses, with the exchange of more than surface courtesies.

When Mrs. Fiske called on Ellen Terry, her old friend urged her to bring *Becky Sharp* to London, where she was sure to triumph, and where Miss Terry could return the hospitality which Mrs. Fiske had so often shown her in New York. In London Mrs. Fiske would find herself in the midst of friends. *"Mes amis et les amis de mes amis sont vos amis,"* said Ellen Terry.

Miss Terry also had an inspiration about a suitable play for her friend. The season before she had appeared in George Bernard Shaw's *Captain Brassbound* in London. Mrs. Fiske's modern spirit was admirably suited to the Shaw play. Miss Terry had no definite plan to produce it in America, and her uncertain health made it doubtful that she would. She proposed to help Mrs. Fiske secure the American rights, if she was interested.

Mrs. Fiske was, and the following day she received Miss Terry's personal copy of the play, together with a note in the English actress' generous, irregular hand:

My Dear Mrs. Fiske
Here is the M.S.S.,—I do wonder if you will like it as much as I do? —If you like it, and want it, you might cable to Shaw—"Socialist—London"—If you don't want it, send it back to me & merely say "No"—

Your friend E. T.

After sealing the envelope, Miss Terry wrote a postscript on a narrow slip of paper and inserted it under the flap:

What about this for a cable to Shaw—
"Keep Brassbound for Minnie—Ellen Terry"—or anything you would like to say to him.

Mrs. Fiske approved the play; she telegraphed and wrote to Harry, and to her agent, Miss Alice Kauser; and Ellen Terry cabled Mr. Shaw.

When Sir Henry and Miss Terry moved on to Canada a week later, there had been no reply from London. Two weeks later, when her company was scheduled to open in New York, Ellen Terry was still in Toronto, where she had been taken ill. Mrs. Fiske wrote to her that there was still no word on *Captain Brassbound*. Miss Terry replied, enclosing a letter from Mr. Shaw, and a printed schedule of the Lyceum Company tour, on which she had scrawled, "a wild and whirling tour I think."

Miss Terry's letter read:

13–March
–Toronto

My Dear Mrs. Fiske
I was just going to write to you when yr. letter to me arrived—I was going to enclose you Mr. Shaw's letter, from which I gather he thinks you have heard of his play from Miss Marbury!!—as you have not had it from her I suppose you can waive a commission to her—& so save yr. pocket I hope! Please treat Mr. Shaw's letter as private, because it is a nonsensical letter, & return it to me. . . . Mr. Shaw is entirely open and fair in all his dealings, & I don't think it wd. vex him to know what I have done—
I hope you will have the play—if you don't, please let me know at once—& if you do conclude terms with him will you also let me know at once—
I've told no one—not even dear Norman Hapgood!

Thank you I'm almost well now, & I hope to be back at work in New York next Monday—I'd like to know your whereabouts—Queens Hotel—Toronto—

Plaza Hotel—Monday 19th.

Soon afterward, Mrs. Fiske heard from her husband, who had heard from Mr. Shaw after a series of misunderstandings. The playwright's financial terms were fair, but Shaw had apparently secured a railroad map of the United States, and he stipulated that *Captain Brassbound* be played in every town on the map. Harry had cabled that many of the "towns" were railroad sidings; he explained that the Trust prevented Mrs. Fiske from appearing in various cities; and he would not deal through Miss Marbury because she represented the monopoly.

Harry counted heavily on Shaw, the socialist. He did not know Shaw, the paradoxical.

When Harry Fiske wrote again, the *Brassbound* negotiations were off. Mr. Shaw had replied that Mr. Fiske had convinced him that it would be to his advantage to deal with the Theatrical Trust—and Harry had written a reply which flayed the socialist for disregarding his own principles.

During Mrs. Fiske's Philadelphia engagement, she received a letter from Mr. Shaw:

10 Adelphi Terrace W.C.

5th May 1900
Dear Madam

I greatly regret that the negociations opened in your behalf by Miss Kauser with me, and strongly recommended to me by Miss Ellen Terry should have failed. I had better explain to you that a bewildering miscarriage of letters, owing to Miss Kauser mistaking my registered telegraphic address for my postal address, led me to receiving, first, a cable message referring to you, and then, apparently by way of explanation a letter from Miss Kauser simply enclosing another letter from Mr. Langdon Mitchell, not referring to you, but suggesting that I should appoint Miss Kauser as my agent, and introducing her to me in such cordial and intimate terms that I was able to correspond with her at once without any sort of ceremony. Letters, however, take a long time to cross the Atlantic; and for some time we were all at cross purposes. Mr. Langdon Mitchell evidently supposing that Miss Kauser wanted to become my agent, whilst Miss Kauser herself supposed that I had received the lost letters.

To make the confusion worse, certain cable messages came from

Mr. Fiske. As they gave no address I took them to be from Miss Kauser, and I interpreted the name at the end as meaning "on behalf of Mrs. Fiske." One of them declined all dealing through Miss Marbury because of her connexion with the theatrical trust. I being by that time quite distracted by the bombardment of incomprehensible messages and letters, relieved my feelings by scolding Miss Kauser as she would have deserved if the refusal to deal with Miss Marbury had been hers. Finally, to save you further delay, I sent Miss Marbury a proposal, which I made as convenient to you in its terms as possible, to be submitted first to you, with further instructions that nobody else was to have more favorable terms, or any chance of anticipating you. Miss Marbury immediately placed this proposal before Miss Kauser. No complaint was made of the terms. Presently, however, Miss Kauser sent word that you did not care to take the play; and Miss Marbury accordingly sent it to its original destination, whence it had been diverted by Miss Ellen Terry on your behalf.

I should have accepted this without comment but for a letter I have just received from Mr. Harrison Grey Fiske, who informs me that the terms I proposed were satisfactory, but that he (on your behalf, I presume) refused to enter into a contract with an author of my odious personal character. That is a sufficient and unanswerable reason; and I do not at all resent it; but I am anxious that you should understand clearly that I have not disregarded your business interests or your convenience in the matter, and that the play was finally placed effectively at your disposal. As to the Trust, I made no stipulation concerning that. Through your attitude toward it, I should, if our negociation had ended happily, have been the loser. I was being pressed at the time to give the first offer of the play to Mr. Charles Frohman and Miss Rehan, from whom I could have had the benefit of the Trust organization. I reserved the first offer for you because you were the first in the field, and because a treaty with an artist of your distinction is not merely a matter of commerce. More than this I could not do.

I may add that I have had no difficulty with Miss Kauser, who is quite able to take care of herself, and perfectly understands my way of doing business. She has no doubt already conveyed my apologies to Mr. Fiske for my mistake about the cable messages. I regret that it was impossible for me to have a personal interview with him; it would probably have softened the strong indignation which finds expression in his letter.

Yours sincerely
G. Bernard Shaw.

Mrs. Fiske passed the news of *Brassbound's* fate on to her friend. Ellen Terry was then in St. Paul, where she and Henry Irving were three weeks behind schedule. Miss Terry wrote:

My Dear Mrs. Fiske—I am so entirely disconcerted by your tidings of "Brassbound" & Mr. Shaw that I can say nothing about how I feel in regard to the affair—

I am vexed—vexed—vexed! (That you don't have the play I mean—) Thanks for your lovely letter—you are a dear if you don't mind my saying so—When you come to London I shall be grateful if you will let me know where you are staying. Soon—before you get into the whirl of the place—

If you care to read a one-act play, the one I am sending you is I think clever and "fetching"—It is called "A Missed Connection"— the author has written me two or three one-act plays. This one I was to have played in America & didn't because I was not well enough all along to rehearse even so slight a thing as this—I am sick at the thought of going home and starting in with a young part, tired as I am, & unfit for publication! Think of it! "Olivia" at 52—I mean 502!!

With every fond wish

Yours most sincerely
Ellen Terry

No answer

In a postscript, Miss Terry forgot her own weariness in prescribing for her friend:

I'm interested to hear that you can't sleep. (I've been there!!) Think of it as a phase. It will pass I think when one brings oneself to think of it not as unusual—not as an extraordinary thing—A little food by one's bedside (milk and a crust?) if one awakes as I used to do, about 3 or 4 o'clock, gives tone to the stomach I found—It is just exhaustion—but you'll find the misfortunate calamity of sleeplessness will pass.

Madame Sarah I see by the London paper, is nowhere by the side of Mrs. Waller & "Tess." Poor Madame Sarah.

The comedy of errors which began in Chicago ended in a major loss for the stage. Mrs. Fiske with her modern spirit and methods was qualified above any other American actress to interpret Shaw's plays, and she never appeared in one of them.

During the Chicago engagement, the actress suffered another minor frustration by being a little ahead of her time. One afternoon she was leaving the Auditorium with her maid and pet poodle, Fifi, when a loud chugging and a reek of gasoline called her attention to one of Chicago's first taxicabs. Mrs. Fiske climbed in with her poodle and reminded her protesting maid that they were coming into the twentieth century. The driver let in the clutch and the taxi spurted across the street, where it knocked down a lamppost. The driver hurried into reverse, shuttling back across the street and repeating the performance on the other side. Mrs. Fiske left the driver untangling his vehicle from its second lamppost, and drove away in a horse-drawn brougham.

Becky Sharp played against strong Trust attractions in every city, a circumstance which led the Washington *Post* to observe that there hadn't been such a riot of talent since the first three-ring circus came to town. In St. Louis she played against Lily Langtry in *The Degenerates*, and the old popular favorite James O'Neill in *The Three Musketeers*. Moreover, *Becky Sharp* had been relegated to the old Grand Opera House, which had descended to a place of popular-priced melodrama; and the Theatrical Trust had just announced that it was going to bring out its own production of *Becky Sharp*.

It was an imposing array of obstacles, but Becky's was an enchanted tour and the obstacles blew away like smoke. On the opening night nearly all the St. Louis theatre managers deserted their own theatres to see what Becky had that they didn't have. For one thing, Becky had—and continued to have—the crowds while *The Degenerates* played to half-empty houses, and the public, tired at last of Dumas' heroics, left *The Three Musketeers* to console one another. The déclassé old Grand Opera House had no effect on *Becky*. As the newspapers gracefully put it, "Wherever Mrs. Fiske sits is the head of the table," and "For genius all places are temples."

A romantic touch of the St. Louis engagement was a delegation of theatregoers from Omaha, Nebraska. The Trust did not allow Mrs. Fiske to appear in Omaha, and the delegation had made the six-hundred-mile round trip to see *Becky Sharp*.

That season was one of the most profitable ever enjoyed by an American actress. It was also strenuous: on the stages of second- and third-rate theatres a four-act drama; and off stage the conflict with her resourceful enemies—a drama of unknown length and outcome. In the five years since her return to the stage, Mrs. Fiske had not missed a performance, and she showed no fatigue during her *Becky Sharp* season. It was about that time that she developed a concern for stray dogs and cats, which she rehabilitated and presented to her friends.

During the St. Louis engagement, Mrs. Fiske had a driver arrested for working a team of harness-galled horses. It was the first time she had figured in such an episode; in the years that followed she devoted an increasing amount of time to the relief of abused animals. But the ultimate rescuer of the horse was the automobile which Mrs. Fiske had left untangling itself from a lamppost.

From St. Louis *Becky Sharp* went to Cincinnati on the same train with *The Degenerates*. After that, Pittsburgh; then on to Philadelphia for the last engagement of the tour.

Mrs. Fiske had often been indifferently received in Philadelphia, but on *Becky's* opening night at the unfashionable Gilmore Auditorium she was greeted by a capacity audience, which the Philadelphia *Press* described as the "most fashionable and distinguished ever assembled in the same theatre." The entire three-week engagement had the gala flavor of an old home week. Reviewers recalled the long list of English and American playwrights who had failed to make a play out of *Vanity Fair*, and they took pride in the fact that Langdon Mitchell, a Philadelphia boy, had succeeded.

A Philadelphian by adoption also triumphed in *Becky Sharp*—the wayward Maurice Barrymore. In Philadelphia Maurice had married Georgie Drew of the famous theatrical family, and in Mrs. Drew's home Lionel, Ethel and John had been born, and the place had remained Barrymore headquarters during the twenty years that Maurice rollicked this side of greatness. Prior to *Becky*, greatness had moved a little farther away, and he was often a careless actor. But as Rawdon Crawley, Barrymore was the only member of the *Becky Sharp* cast who received universal praise; several critics declared that the play was a Barrymore rather than a Fiske triumph, and that the actor, who had seemed to be losing his grip, had come back triumphantly.

The role also seemed to have a rejuvenating effect; St. Louis newspapers spoke of Mr. Barrymore who had drunk deep of the Fountain of Youth, and described him as looking thirty.

In Philadelphia, Barrymore still had that strange bloom of youth on whatever maturity time had brought him. There, his Rawdon Crawley was hailed as the living embodiment of Thackeray's character, and one of the great roles of his career.

It was the last role Maurice Barrymore ever played. During the tour there had been straws in the wind—a passing difficulty of enunciation, a brief lapse of memory, and once in the discovery scene at the end of act three, Barrymore's stage frenzy had so taken possession of him that the curtain had to be dropped while stagehands rescued the Marquis of Steyne.

Barrymore was struggling desperately against physical illness and a growing difficulty of distinguishing reality from illusion. The Fiskes watched over him anxiously, and at the end of the season they did not re-engage him because they feared he could not stand the strain of another tour. It seemed the best thing they could do; but presently Mr. Fiske received a startling note on Lambs' Club stationery—a challenge to a duel from Barrymore! Harry laid the note aside sadly. It was so unlike the gentle Barrymore that it verified the Fiskes' fear that his mental breakup had begun.

CHAPTER 14

The artistic success of *Becky Sharp* was history, and financially it was a victory. Cramped at every turn by the Theatrical Trust, the massive production netted a profit of $90,000 during a season in which many plays failed.

Financial success was more vital to the Fiskes than outsiders believed. Harry Fiske was referred to as a millionaire, but the label was misleading. Lyman Fiske had never lacked money for baronial estates with flocks of servants, fine horses and carriages, but when he died a few weeks before Harry's marriage to Minnie, his wealth seemed to die with him; Harry inherited nothing.

The Harrison Grey Fiskes lived on the earnings of the *Dramatic Mirror* and Mrs. Fiske's plays. But Harry remained wrapped in the aura of the millionaire he never was, and his style of living fostered the illusion.

In the early summer of 1900, Mrs. Fiske was busy with the responsibilities of success: photographs at Sarony's, and sittings for newspaper sketch artists and portrait painters. Minnie's favorite was Ernest Haskell, who had done a lithograph of Becky for the *Critic* on the opening night in New York—and set a record by getting it on the presses the following morning.

Haskell now made a poster drawing of Minnie's profile, lithographed in black and orange. The posters had Becky's dash and style, and they became such a rage that presently it was impossible to keep up with the demand.

While the profiles were being snapped up, Mrs. Fiske was on her way to Europe—her first time away from continental North America.

In Canada and England there was talk about Mrs. Fiske's presenting *Becky Sharp* in London, but she was bent on discovery, not conquest, and her itinerary did not include England.

As a reputed millionaire, Harry Fiske might have been expected to vacation in Europe with his famous wife—but he was a confirmed New Yorker who was never quite happy away from Manhattan, and no one was greatly surprised by his staying behind. Actually it was a matter of necessity. Harry moved to the Manhattan Club and battled out his wife's tour for the coming season. The old Fifth Avenue Theatre had finally passed to Trust hands, and now, with New York at her feet, Mrs. Fiske would not be allowed to appear in the city. If she were to act at all, it would have to be on the road; until fall Harry had a full-time job arranging bookings with scattered independent theatres and locating other theatres so run-down or old that the Trust had overlooked them.

Meanwhile Minnie explored Italy and Switzerland. She rested in the Alps for the renewal of the battle, and wrote frequent letters home—letters touched with the delight of new places, with moments of home-sickness and with solicitude for her husband.

August 4th, 1900

Darling, darling Boy,
We left Meggen yesterday and after a few hours in Lucerne we went to Meyringen where we remained last night—coming on here, to Interlaken today. The journey from Lucerne to Meyringen was beautiful beyond words—and I fell in love with the little village of Meyringen—I do not like this place. It is the regular crowded, noisy, fussy "resort" with everything done to distract the attention from the beautiful mountains that surround the place. Tomorrow we visit the places of interest nearabout and on Monday we return to dear little Meggen where we shall stay until we start our homeward way and won't I be glad to see you!
If it is a very hot day you must not try to meet me at the steamer, only if you can meet me comfortably, I need not say how happy I shall be. . . Did I tell you we came to Meggen (or I had better say Lucerne) through the Italian lakes? But I like the Swiss lakes far, far better. They, the Swiss lakes are like our lakes. . .

Meggen, Switzerland—August 8th, 1900

Darling, darling Boy
Your letter of the 20th July—the Mirror of July 29th & the 2nd act of the play reached me safely—I see you have started the new design on the Mirror front page. It is, I think, a great improvement. Later, I suppose, you will have the "sketches" of prominent actors from time to time. I am bringing you some copies of the Italian dramatic newspaper—a poor little sheet, I think.

We have returned to Meggen after the trip of which I wrote you from Interlaken—The place, Grindelwald, we went to from Interlaken is wonderfully beautiful.—I am absolutely in love with it, but it was dreadful not to have you there. I am looking forward to our next visit together to that wondrously lovely spot. I should love to spend the summer there. It is a village on the top of the mountains & so, so beautiful. I shall tell you everything about it. It made me positively ache to keep thinking "Harry is not here!"—Oh, it is a beautiful spot and such air! . . . . On Sunday we go to Milan—thence to Genoa sailing from Genoa on the 16th.—

* * *

We have got to be quite at home at Meggen. It has none of the wondrous beauty and grandeur of Grindelwald but it is a sweet, pretty quaint and quiet little place. I would have been glad to remain at Grindelwald but it was too cold there! We must go there together, darling Boy.

* * *

I have been working easily on the play—an hour now and an hour then. As to the 1st Act, I think I have got it into shape, somewhat, as that Miss Brown will see the way to strengthen and improve it. I have done the "thinking out" of what should and can be done & under direction I think she will be able to do it. I have written to her asking her to come to New York to go over what has to be done on September 5th. . . So I have not actually done all work myself because I wish Miss Brown to do as much of it possible, but I have got it laid out so clearly that I think she will be able to do it. The 2nd Act, as you say, shows better work & the dialogue is very good in spots. I think I have a genuine inspiration for the 2nd Act but I do not wish to tell you until a rough draft of what I mean can be written out to submit to you for I do not think I could make the telling of what I mean quite adequate. . .

I hope we can get Mr. Dodson to play Lord Pilkington—the father. It is a delightful part—by all odds the part. As I see the development of the part of Lady Pilkington I fear that Miss—(I cannot, to save me, recall her name) I fear that she will not be able to master the part. You remember that we had thought of casting her for it—Lady Pilkington requires an authoritative all around actress & if we ever do the play in New York I would suggest Rose Eytinge or someone like that for the part.—As it is I think we had better give it to Mrs. Barker for the Chicago production. . . . Mrs. Barker is a good old "reliable" and while she cannot display the possibilities of Lady Pilkington as an Agnes Booth or a Rose Eytinge could she would not lack the necessary force and authority and general comprehensiveness.

We find that we can go on a through express, a good train, direct to Genoa so we shall skip Milan on the way & remain here at Meggen one day longer,—leaving for Genoa Monday morning & arriving there Monday evening.

We came here & shall go back over the beautiful St. Goddard.—

The weather and the air are superb & I am in spendid fettle.—

Darling Boy, I hope you are well & long to hear that you had a good outing.—

Take all care of yourself & have all the good time you can!

Your own Bunner.

To each other the Fiskes were "Boy" and "Bunner." Harry's nickname had come from one of the many summer vacations in the Adirondacks, where he had climbed trees and pranked and clowned for the amusement of young Emily Stevens. Emily had had few playmates in her childhood, and to her Harry Fiske was what a boy should be.

The meaning and origin of "Bunner" were forgotten almost as soon as it was coined. However, Minnie had a predilection for names beginning with "B."

Early in September Minnie returned home to prepare for the fall season and to work on the play with Miss Brown—one of the many plays which ate up time and energy, and then came to nothing.

The Fiskes' newly-acquired apartment at the Brevoort lacked the cool silence of the Alps, but it was livable except during heat waves. Ordinarily the only outside sounds were the rhythmic beat of hoofs and the roll of carriage wheels along Fifth Avenue. At the moment there was also a persistent clatter from a block south, where the avenue disappeared into Washington Square, as workmen hammered on the scaffolds around the triumphal arch that was to be dedicated at the coming Dewey Day Parade. But the hammering was hardly noticed by people used to the sound of stage carpenters. In the Fiske household, there were two professional actresses, and a third was within a few weeks of her stage debut—without knowing it.

One of the professionals had been the cause of frequent arguments as to whether actresses really have the fine life they appear to have on the stage. Her name was Fifi, and in *Becky Sharp* she played the role of Fido, Miss Crawley's dog, and she made her stage exit accompanied by the butler on her way to a dish of cream. There was a cause for argument. Do stage dogs really get cream, or is it something only talked about?

108

Fifi could have answered that the cream was real, and while it was no novelty in her life, it was always smooth. She had coaxed a dish from the maid by pretending to be her dear friend. The cream was finished and Fifi trotted down the hall, a coal-black four-year-old French poodle who had traveled and acted over eastern United States and Canada.

Familiar voices sounded in the drawing room, but the door was closed. It did not respond to nudging, and Fifi stood on her hind legs and turned the knob with her forepaws. The door opened a little, and Fifi peeked in to see what kind of reception she was going to have—affectionate or merely cordial.

The conversation stopped and Mrs. Fiske's warm staccato voice called, "Come in, Fifi!"

Fifi dropped on all fours and pranced in, showing gleaming white teeth as she smiled infectiously, first at Harry Fiske, then at his mother—both good and influential friends. But it was Mrs. Fiske who had welcomed Fifi to the drawing room, and she pranced over to her and settled down beside the straight, high-backed chair. Mrs. Fiske reached down and caressed the curly head while she talked.

Tea was being served. On a little table drawn up in front of Mrs. Fiske, a cup and saucer neighbored with papers and the acts of a play under discussion. On the wall behind her an ornate little clock hung from a button of amethyst.

Time was precious in an age that was growing more competitive and hurried, and in moments of silence, above the ticking of the clock, there came the sound of hammering on the arch that recorded America's victory over Spain—and through the click of hoofs and roll of carriage wheels, the buzzing of an automobile coming down the avenue like a beetle drunk on the fumes of gasoline.

Minnie ignored the hysterical drone of the machine, and the fumes that came in the open window. She picked up a bound, typewritten manuscript. "Here is another play with a germ of an idea, only a germ—" She was again interrupted by the door. This time it flew open, and Emily Stevens rushed in—a swirl of summer muslin, gold hair and teen-age excitement.

"It happened again!" Emily proclaimed, and alternated explanation with greetings. "A young man spoke to me on the trolley car! The handsomest young man!"

The time before a young man had tipped his straw hat and asked if he hadn't met her somewhere. It was the old device of young mashers, and Mother Fiske had counseled Emily to be prepared next time to look at the masher coldly, and say, "Young man, you are mistaken!"

The round of kisses had now brought Emily to Mother Fiske, and the old lady said, "I hope you weren't too flustered this time to remember what I told you."

"I remembered," Emily assured her. "He tipped his hat, and said, 'It's a nice day, isn't it?' I looked at him haughtily, and said, 'Young man, you are mistaken!' "

Emily joined in the laughter that drowned out Mother Fiske's protests, but when she settled down to her belated tea, her face lost its animation, and the corners of her mouth drooped even more than usual. She had suffered a nervous breakdown, and because of it had been transferred to a quiet convent school at Fort Lee, across the Hudson, where the Fiskes kept an eye on her. With her mother's consent, they had just decided on a more complete change. Mrs. Fiske began by sounding her out.

"Emily, would you be interested in a job as a maid with light duties?"

"A maid, Co'Min? Whose? Where?"

"The Duchess of Sutherland's, in the ballroom scene."

"Oh, acting." The eagerness was gone from Emily's voice.

"It would be a change, and you would see America."

"But I don't like traveling, Co'Min; I'd rather stay here."

Harry Fiske, who also found New York enough, reminded her, "There would always be New York to come back to."

Minnie said, "Take time to think it over."

"I have thought it over," Emily announced. "I'll have to make my own living, and acting is better than running a typewriting machine, isn't it?"

With that decision, another of the Maddern clan started on her way to stage fame.

CHAPTER 15

The autumn of 1900 was the season of the two *Becky Sharps*, with Mrs. Fiske acting in one and Harry Fiske and his lawyer in pursuit of the other. The Trust version had its premiere in Syracuse, and that night Harry telephoned Minnie that it was essentially their play! The adapter must have assumed that Langdon Mitchell's lines were Thackeray's. All Harry needed was a copy of the play.

Next night Harry reported that his stenographer had been thrown out of the theatre early in the first act. Since then, Harry and his lawyer had been rushing to a hotel room during intermissions and writing down what they remembered of the play.

The following day a judge granted an injunction, but the Trust producers left for the next town before the papers could be served.

Other reports drifted back as the pursuit continued from town to town. One constable charged with serving the papers was thwarted by the producers' losing themselves in the audience. A later one was seized by the producers, disguised as stagehands, and thrown out into the alley.

The pursuit was rumbling in the distance when Mrs. Fiske opened with her *Becky* at Bridgeport on October 8. Outside the Park Theatre an equinoctial storm flooded streets and tore branches off trees. At the height of the storm, in the Brussels ballroom scene, Emily Stevens made her first stage appearance. It was in the part of a maid, but it was the beginning of a career that justified nature's demonstration outside.

New Haven, two days later, marked a new phase of Minnie's battle with the Syndicate; the October 10 issue of *Collier's* carried under her name a hard-hitting exposé of Trust methods.

As Mrs. Fiske toured on, Harry sent word that the papers had finally been served and the rival *Becky Sharp* suspended until the court had its say. At the first hearing the producers were unable to explain the startling similarity of the two plays, but they insisted that their version had been written by Charles Coghlan, who was dead before Langdon Mitchell began his. At the second hearing Mr. Fiske produced Mrs. Coghlan, who testified that her husband had never written a play based on *Vanity Fair*. The Trust *Becky* was judged a plagiarism and was now officially dead.

As yet Mrs. Fiske had no true gauge of the vitality of her *Becky Sharp*, but Boston was to be a test. The preceding season she had played *Becky* there for three weeks; on October 15 she began a week's return engagement. The week drew out to a month of packed houses.

By now Becky and Mrs. Fiske were joined inseparably. They drew strength from each other, with important results to the production. The roles created by Maurice Barrymore, Tyrone Power and Wilfred North were now filled by lesser actors—and the Boston critics agreed that the net result was at least the equal of the original production.

It was not the first time Mrs. Fiske had made good actors appear like great ones. She also continued to enrich her own role; after a year she did not consider that she had fully played the part. Typical of many minor touches which rounded out the portrait of Becky was her attention to her corset in the Pumpernickle scene. In the original production the garment had reposed brazenly on a chair, in full sight of all her male callers. Now it continued to repose there until the voice of Dobbin was heard outside—then Becky bundled it out of sight. The gesture let the audience look into one more cranny of her mind, which grew more complex with transparency; and it highlighted Dobbin as the one decent man of her acquaintance.

In those early days of the twentieth century Mrs. Fiske's most spectacular fight was with the Theatrical Trust. But with Becky, as with nearly all of her plays, she was pushing back a frontier of prejudices. At Lawrence, Massachusetts, the *Telegram* felt obliged to justify the play by finding in it a moral: "It does not pay to be bad." A less advanced paper failed to discover the moral; it classed *Becky* as vicious, along with Mrs. Leslie Carter's *Zaza* and Olga Nethersole's *Sappho*. But the review ended on a note of crumbling resistance: "It was fashionable to be on hand and that settles it. Fashion, by the way, has no more regard for the susceptibility of a virgin than it has for its slaves."

Since the beginning of the season, Trust press agents had been predicting that Mrs. Fiske's tour would fail before it reached Chicago. There was no sign of that when the company arrived in Rochester, the last town they were playing before the western journey.

At Rochester, as elsewhere, Minnie was barred from first-class houses, but twenty-four hours of heroic work converted the ancient Cook Opera House into a usable theatre. During the engagement it was packed with what the press described as the most brilliant audiences ever gathered in a Rochester theatre.

From the moldering Cook Opera House, *Becky* was taken to the Grand Opera House in Chicago, opening on November 16, less than a year since it had played there before. The opening lacked novelty, but Chicago was the edge of a dramatic frontier. In the region to the west theatregoers had waited for four years to see *Tess,* and Minnie proposed to give them that play as well as *Becky.*

During the first three weeks in Chicago the company played in Thackeray and rehearsed in Hardy. And Emily Stevens had her first speaking part as Tess's younger sister, Liza Lu.

She studied her new role vehemently. At one rehearsal, her cousin took time to instruct her on proper facial expression.

"Wrinkle your brow like this," Minnie said. "Hold your mouth like this, and cast your eyes down demurely as you are speaking the line—and for heaven's sake, Emily, keep your back turned to the audience!"

Business prevented Harry Fiske from coming to Chicago to rehearse the company in *Tess,* and the revival opened without him. In the uneven first performance, a minor character was singled out for special praise by the *Daily News:* "Emily Stevens especially added an enjoying item to the evening's pleasure by a quiet, easy debut scarcely recognizable as such because of the charm and simplicity and serene comprehension of the insignificance of her opportunity—something admirable in a first-nighter."

On Minnie's thirty-sixth birthday, illness forced her to miss a performance for the first time in her career. That same day the belated Harry arrived, and the day after, Minnie was on hand for rehearsal and the evening performance.

The Fiskes were together until after Christmas, when Harry returned to New York and the company went on to invade Trust territory: Davenport, Sioux City, Lincoln and St. Joseph. Kansas City was closed to Minnie; and at Topeka, for the first time in the tour, there were rows of empty seats—the work of a stranger who had posed as the company's advance agent and spread the word that Mrs. Fiske's role would be played by an understudy.

At Wichita the depot was crowded with citizens awaiting Minnie's arrival. Scores of them called on her at her hotel to reminisce about *Fogg's Ferry* and *Caprice;* and she lifted her usual ban on reporters.

All the way west across the snowy plains the ban on the past remained lifted. While Emily was having her first glimpse of the Rocky Mountains, Minnie recalled her own early trouping days, when she was as young as her cousin, sitting on open station platforms, or walking up and down to keep from freezing until the winter sun peeked over the Rockies and colored the smoke of the long-awaited train. But when Emily asked if she had ever played at the Denver Theatre, which was their next stand, Minnie laughed. "In *Fogg's Ferry* days it would have been beneath the dignity of my stardom!"

But the Denver Theatre represented a victory. Months before, Harry had heard of the theatre, so small and old that the Trust had not noticed it. Harry had gotten in touch with a friendly Denver lawyer, who rented the theatre for a week, but with every legal safeguard. Mrs. Fiske was then billed to appear—and the forgotten little house became a battleground. Furious emissaries of the Trust ordered the owner to cancel Mrs. Fiske's contract and to turn over his bookings and a share of his profits for the next five years. If he failed to do that, the Trust would break him by barring from Colorado theatres every attraction that appeared at the Denver.

Under the threat of ruin, the owner had attempted to break the contract. The Fiskes' lawyer applied for an injunction restraining the Trust from interfering, and the battle shifted to the courts. It had been settled a few days before Mrs. Fiske's arrival—with the court ruling that the people of Denver had the right to see *Becky Sharp* regardless of whether or not tribute was paid to New York speculators who had no claim on either theatre or production.

The theatre which had been such a bone of contention was a third-rate affair in the slums. The week before *Becky Sharp*, a minstrel troupe had played there, with seats at ten cents; and *Uncle Tom's Cabin* was billed for the week after at the same price. For the week of *Becky* and *Tess* the prices were $1.50 and $2.00. On the first night, small boys stood goggle-eyed in the cold, watching Denver society arrive by carriage in a street where it was more customary for humbler people to arrive on foot.

Cinderella had nothing on the Denver Theatre for the week of January 7, 1901. But no art could conceal the fact that the stage was small. In the first scene Becky observed, *sotto voce*, to the half-dozen characters who filled the stage, "For a woman with a large fortune, Miss Crawley has a very small drawing-room!" The audience noticed

114

it, too, and wondered about the second act and the famous ballroom scene at Brussels, with all the beauty and chivalry of Belgium's capital gathered on a two-by-four stage.

The curtain rose on the second act—and the audience gasped with unbelief at the vast architectural set: the onyx staircase, lined with bronze statues; the massive columns and lofty arched ceilings that suggested a ballroom twice the size of the whole Denver Theatre. They were still marveling when an arctic wind swept through the theatre; a sprinkle of snow fell over the fair women and brave men—and spectators reached for their overcoats and furs. The impossible in stage setting had been accomplished by removing the back of the theatre and annexing part of the outdoors!

The Theatrical Trust barred Mrs. Fiske from Los Angeles and most other California towns. But the old California Theatre in San Francisco had kept its independence, and on January 21, 1901, Mrs. Fiske opened there in *Becky Sharp*. Next day the *Post* summed up: "Mrs. Fiske has come and conquered."

The conquest included more than San Francisco. During the four-week engagement the Southern Pacific featured special "Anti-Trust Excursions" from San Jose and other towns where Mrs. Fiske was barred; the California Theatre was kept overflowing to the end of the engagement, and a *Post* editorial proclaimed: "San Francisco is big enough, chivalrous, generous enough to make up the profit of playing in all the syndicate theatres of the Pacific Coast."

San Francisco was chivalrous and generous beyond any other city where Mrs. Fiske had played, and if there were those who did not share in the general enthusiasm, they were silenced by a review in the *Examiner* which began: "Dull people do not like Mrs. Fiske's acting." Minnie chuckled over the unfairness of giving people the choice of liking her art or being dull; she was still chuckling when she met the reviewer, the brilliant young Ashton Stevens, and the resulting friendship was to endure to the end of her life.

At about this time Emily went to a local photographer and returned announcing that she had discovered a genius; Co'Min simply had to meet him!

Emily's find was an extraordinarily tall, long-legged gentleman with a leonine head, long wavy hair touched with gray, challenging kindly eyes, and thick lips which spoke with the enthusiasm of youth and the accent of Germany. Arnold Genthe was a Latin, Greek and

Hebrew scholar who had come to San Francisco as tutor to a German baron's son. He had fallen in love with the city and stayed, to become a photographer.

Emily had described Genthe as a genius, and Mrs. Fiske agreed. None of his subjects seemed to have been aware of the camera; they were people snapped in the act of living, not people having their pictures taken. At the same time, the photographs had depth and subtlety and light and shade that gave them the quality of paintings. In Arnold Genthe's studio for the first time Mrs. Fiske saw photography as an art.

Genthe gave San Francisco credit for the revolution—Chinatown, to be exact, and the Chinese superstitious fear of being photographed. He had been so thrilled by the subjects going to waste on the streets of Chinatown that in 1895 he had devised a candid camera with which he photographed unsuspecting citizens against the background of their daily lives. Later, in his studio, while other photographers were still clamping the sitter's head in an iron vise to keep him motionless, Genthe had taken unposed, informal portraits while his subjects were unconscious of the camera.

Mrs. Fiske stayed, and returned, for Arnold Genthe to take the most natural and truest of all her photographs. The artist, however, had one regret about them all: none of them showed the Titian color of her hair. His earliest recollection of childhood in Berlin, he said, was of a doll with red hair—something that had enchanted him ever since; it was scientifically possible to take color photographs, and he was working on the idea.

From an improbable-sounding find of Emily's, Arnold Genthe became a friend who called Mrs. Fiske "Cousin Minnie" and whom she called "Ginky." In their different arts they were pioneers in naturalism; their civilized minds agreed with each other, and as long as they both lived Mrs. Fiske treated "Ginky" as an understanding blood relation.

The San Francisco engagement became more and more tinged with the colors of a glorious holiday. With "Ginky," Mrs. Fiske and Emily explored the city. Often after the evening performance they were joined by Ashton Stevens and Mrs. Stevens, sister of the novelist Gertrude Atherton. They would drive out to the beach and have supper at the Casino or the Cliff House. Late at night they would drive back through Golden Gate Park, in moonlight or starlight or through swirling fog—sometimes with Mrs. Fiske and Emily singing "Silver Threads Among the Gold," the pet aversion of Genthe, whose long wavy hair was touched with gray although he was five years younger than Cousin Minnie.

Other Madderns had settled in the region which Minnie and Emily found so enchanting, and there were relatives to visit across the bay, among them their cousin Bessie Maddern London and her two robust little daughters.

Bessie, a schoolteacher, had married the turbulent young Jack London, patched out his education, smoothed his stories into salability, and borne him two daughters before losing him to another woman.

Mrs. Fiske's family tie with Jack London was the shadow of something already dissolved, but there was still the claim of art and the fact that he was helping break the molds of the nineteenth century to form the larger ones of the twentieth.

Jack London called on her in San Francisco, ostensibly to ask her if she would be interested in having him write a play for her, but more, she thought, to justify himself. She found it remarkable that anyone could believe that he could justify everything he had ever done. She laughed at him for his defensive attitude where no one had attacked him. She laughed a little also over his ideal of twentieth-century womanhood—a man's mate who bore his children and endured with him and shared in his dreams and labors—because he had left such a woman for a nineteenth-century coquette who gave him neither help nor children. But she did not laugh much, because she saw it as his tragedy.

From San Francisco Mrs. Fiske's anti-Trust tour swung north to Sacramento, Portland, Seattle and Tacoma; then it crossed the Canadian border to Victoria and Vancouver, where audiences voted on whether they wanted to see *Becky Sharp* or *Tess of the D'Urbervilles*. Both cities selected *Tess*. Then on to Spokane, Butte, Winnipeg and a string of other cities and towns stretching from the Pacific to the Atlantic. Wherever the company played, second- and third-class theatres were packed with first-class audiences, and the tour was magical with success.

It hardly seemed that anything more new could be added, but when Minnie reached Milwaukee, Harry was there to meet her, laden with good news: the Syndicate's criminal libel suit against him had been thrown out of court; he had found a perfect role for Minnie for next season; and, greatest news of all, Harry had acquired a theatre under the very eyes of the Trust. Mrs. Fiske would be able to open in New York in the fall and stay as long as she chose.

Together the Fiskes guarded the secret of their own theatre, but it colored their days in Milwaukee; and together they listened to praise of their efforts in the theatre. While Mrs. Fiske's Becky was being hailed as one of the great stage achievements of recent times, the press reviewed the achievements of Harrison Grey Fiske's *Dramatic Mirror* —from its first valiant work for the Actors' Fund to its recent securing of an amendment to the copyright law protecting playwrights against piracy.

In that expansive atmosphere of praise, the Fiskes continued to guard the secret of their New York theatre; but in an interview with the *Wisconsin Journal*, Harry gave an advance glimpse of the role he had selected for Mrs. Fiske for the following season:

> It is a most unusual and difficult thing to get a strong and good character for a woman to play. A woman, be she ever so strong and deep, must be bad to be unusual. And particularly strong characteristics in a woman when kept within the bounds fixed by social conventionalities show themselves only in their own circles. A strong character for an actress and at the same time an entirely wholesome character is indeed *rara avis* and that is what we have found for Mrs. Fiske next season.

Under other circumstances, the actress might have questioned the value of portraying an ideal of womanhood created by men of bad conscience, but there was a rosy light on everything. The tour continued east to upstate New York and south to Louisville, and Mrs. Fiske, who was soon going home to her own theatre in New York, played happily in vaudeville houses and in cramped old theatres.

CHAPTER 16

The theatre which Harry had snatched under the eagle eyes of the Trust was located at Sixth Avenue and Thirty-third Street, where Gimbel's department store now stands. It had been built as the Standard, and its General Grant rococo architecture and garish colors made it the flower of an era of atrocious taste. Time and soot had tamed its tawdry colors, leaving it a bedraggled old prostitute of a theatre.

In 1898 William A. Brady and Florenz Ziegfeld had taken over the Standard, with a promise of rehabilitation. They had renamed it the Manhattan, and Brady announced that it had been acquired to fight "the outrageous Theatrical Trust." Soon afterward the partners had joined in the stampede of managers to the Trust. Now the Fiskes proceeded to make good on Brady's dedication of the Manhattan, and Brady and Ziegfeld were held up to savage ridicule by their fellow Trust members for letting the theatre slip through a blind to the enemy.

For Harry Fiske the leasing of the Manhattan was the consummation of a theatre-struck life. The crowning event of his childhood had been the gift of a toy stage, and since that time he had never been out of touch with the theatre. Now he had a full-sized theatre to work with. As a further challenge, hostile forces had wrecked the interior of the Manhattan before the Fiskes took possession. Harry had the building gutted, and in the remaining shell he built the theatre of his dreams. It was characteristic of Minnie that she rarely if ever entered her husband's office. In the same spirit she remained away from the Manhattan Theatre during its rebuilding. That was a man's job, and any urge to see how it was progressing was sublimated in work on the play Harry had selected for her.

Miranda of the Balcony was tried out at Montreal and brought to the Manhattan for its New York premiere on September 24. It was a many-sided event: a new play in a new theatre; a new phase of the war against the Trust; and the beginning of a new era in theatregoing. To the crowd that filled every seat, the most immediately striking thing was the theatre itself. Out of the hideous old Standard had been created the most beautiful and comfortable theatre in New York, finished in restful dark green and bronze and gold, under soft lights, with chairs upholstered in dark red and spaced for comfort rather than maximum revenue. In place of the customary printed sheet with the cast of characters, ushers handed out programs in booklet form, which set the style forever after.

The new era reached outside the Manhattan. Mr. Fiske had announced that ticket speculators would not be allowed around the theatre. The first to hawk his wares near the box office was arrested and bundled off to jail, and others were discouraged.

In keeping with the perfection of the theatre, the new-style programs announced a superb cast of thirty-five. The production had five stage-sets, each as perfect and beautiful as any ever seen on a New York stage. Matching them were the three gowns which Mrs. Fiske wore in the course of the play. She made her first entrance wearing the famous "Wheat Dress" which had won first prize at the Paris Exposition: a white satin creation embroidered with pearls and gold thread in a flowing design of wheat heads and wheat plants. Admirers spoke of it as the most beautiful gown in the world, but with its overlay of pearls and gold it weighed something like forty pounds.

On that opening night it was Minnie's wish that theatre and play speak for themselves. The only touch of a ceremony was the playing of a composition of Ethelbert Nevin's which was dedicated to Mrs. Fiske, "An African Love Song," with words by Paul Lawrence Dunbar. The audience gave Mrs. Fiske an ovation and called for a speech, but she asked to be excused, saying that she never went home after a first night without a feeling of deep humiliation, and she begged the audience not to increase it by exacting a speech.

The only other minor note on that magnificent occasion was the play itself.

The Theatrical Trust had not happened out of a vacuum, nor were the Fiskes existing in one, and conditions which had created the one could hardly fail to affect the other. It was the twentieth century and Theodore Roosevelt was president; but the nineteenth century had been dead less than eight months, and President McKinley only ten days. The Theatrical Trust had come into being almost simultaneously with McKinley's inaugural, in the flowering season of great American corporations. Never before had New York society been so bolstered by ostentatious wealth, or seemed so impregnable. One proof of the Fiskes' dazzlement was the fabulously expensive gowns which impeded Minnie's acting; another was the life-size painting of Minnie by Alphonse Jongers that hung in the beautiful new lobby of the Manhattan.

Another proof of dazzlement was the play which Harry Fiske had selected for his wife and the new theatre—a play which forsook the pioneering of *Tess* and *Becky* for the moral fashions of the day.

The fashions were of a peculiar cut. At the moment it would have been highly inconvenient to apply morals to business. But the leadership of wealth and industry were pledged to Christian morality, and a place was found for it in the home, where it became peculiarly a woman's concern.

Miranda, as she was revealed to the first-night audience of the Manhattan, was a matron of fashion who had just completed seven years of mourning for the supposed death of a husband she had loathed. Near the end of the first act she learns that he is still alive and she sends the man she loves on a perilous mission to find the scoundrel and restore him to her side. In the last act the retrieved husband is murdered by an enemy.

By the rules, Miranda must go into mourning again, with romance seven years farther off than it was at the beginning of the play— but the authors boggled over so much lost ground, and it ends with a vague promise of happiness.

As Miranda, Minnie was allowed no action, and the role was further complicated by Harry's dictum that a good woman suppresses whatever unavoidable emotion she has. When he went backstage at the end of the first act, Minnie's first question was, "Boy, am I playing with just the right touch of suppression?"

Harry assured her that she was, and then added sternly, "But from now on, for God's sake, don't be too suppressed!" From the back of the theatre he had watched the almost faultless production hold a mirror up to the ideals in which the best people professed to believe— and he had observed that even the best people were not stirred by the reflected vacuum.

That same week Harry Fiske accepted another play of high ideals by another amateur woman-playwright.

The play was *The Unwelcome Mrs. Hatch*, by Mrs. Burton Harrison, a member of the four hundred and a successful writer of society stories.

A lavish production was ordered, a special cast assembled, and the play went into secret rehearsal in mid-October—secret to prevent the Trust from trumpeting it as an admission that *Miranda* was a failure. The secret was kept ten days, until it leaked to the press and the *Telegraph* announced Mrs. Fiske's new play in detail.

The same afternoon, in his office at the theatre, Harry had a call from David Belasco, accompanied by his business manager, Mr. Raeder. Mr. Belasco praised the Manhattan as the most perfect theatre he had seen in Europe or America. But when Harry confirmed the rumor that he was rehearsing *The Unwelcome Mrs. Hatch*, Belasco tore theatrically at his black mop of hair, already streaked with gray, declaring that Mrs. Harrison had sold his most valuable property—a play he had written and produced in California fifteen years before, and given her to rewrite.

Harry raised his eyebrows, "You are a famous playwright—and you hired an amateur to rewrite your play?"

Belasco reminded him, "*Mrs. Hatch* is a play of high society and mother love, and Mrs. Harrison is a society woman and a mother—"

"—and since you are neither," Harry supplied.

"Exactly. I hired her to work on the play. It is my property, and I can prove it in ten minutes in court."

"That will be unnecessary," Harry told him. "Show me the *Hatch* play you wrote in California and the record of its production, and I shall respect your claim."

Mr. Belasco left, promising to bring the proof, but it was never furnished. After a long exchange of letters and telephone calls, Belasco took the dispute to court.

It was an ominous fact that David Belasco had engaged in many lawsuits over the authorship of his plays and had always won.

But the Fiskes continued with their production and Harry, who had seen one of Belasco's plays ghost-written in the *Mirror* office by one of his staff, busied himself securing affidavits.

By the repressive standards of *Miranda*, its author, as a good woman, would never have called attention to herself by writing a play; and Mrs. Fiske, as another, would never have acted in it. During the run of the play, as a further contradiction of outmoded standards, the actress gave an hour-long address before the Nineteenth Century Club

—an attack on the Theatrical Trust. Mrs. Fiske reviewed the history of the combine, named the newspapers that had fallen under its power, and the critics it had attempted to have discharged for honest criticism. She traced its blighting effect on American playwrights and actors and managers, and finally on the public, and on American civilization:

> Every year new playgoers come into existence, as youth attains the age when playgoing begins. What is the influence of the drama as it is written and the acting as it is seen under Trust auspices? What standards are preserved, what opportunities for intelligent comparison are permitted to these young and impressionable minds whose experience does not extend to the time when ambition was free and art flourished on our stage? What refinement of taste, what improvement of morals is likely to follow in the wake of a theatre control that is solely commercial?
>
> The inevitable results of the present tendency are always foreseen. An appetite for the trivial and mediocre is being created. . . Another of these inevitable results is seen among the older generation —persons of settled taste have become disgusted with the mediocrity of much that is offered. This class, which should be the best support of the theatre, has virtually ceased to support it at all. . . .

The address was delivered on December 12, 1902. On the thirteenth, Harry had his day in court, where he and his lawyer, Mr. Lydecker, answered David Belasco's application for an injunction. The hearing was held before Justice Lawrence and an appreciative audience from the press and theatre. There were few surprises, but many laughs.

In Mrs. Harrison's affidavit, she denied that Mr. Belasco had given her more than minor assistance, and she stated that the central idea of *Mrs. Hatch* could not have been his because she had lifted it from Sardou. No representative of that playwright was there to charge her with piracy, and Belasco, who had also borrowed from the French, did not make an issue of it.

The hearing reached its climax during the argument against the injunction. Mr. Lydecker, gesturing with a sheaf of papers, declared, "Mr. Belasco never wrote a play in his life!"

"What?" Belasco's lawyer, Judge Dittenhoeffer, started up, gasping, "What, what?"

"Belasco never wrote a line of this play, and I don't believe—I have affidavits here to prove it—that he ever wrote a play in his life."

"Oh, my, my!" Dittenhoeffer gasped. "Belasco, the greatest playwright, never wrote a play! Oh, my, my—" The portrayal of surprise was punctuated by the crash of the gavel.

"I have heard enough," Justice Lawrence said. "In all my twenty-eight years on the bench there has never been brought before me an application for an injunction on such a weak case. If the plaintiff has any foundation for his claims, he should seek redress in a court of common law. This court will not stretch out the strong arm of the law to interfere with the projects of persons who are innocent parties. . . I am going to deny the application for an injunction."

The unfettered *Mrs. Hatch* had its premiere at the Manhattan on November 25, magnificently staged and cast.

The Belasco controversy alone had been enough to make it an event, and the Manhattan was packed with as brilliant an audience as the one that had greeted *Miranda*. And again the play was an anti-climax to its setting. Near the end of the third act, however, there was a scene which allowed Mrs. Fiske to climb out of the morass of words and tears to a few minutes of superb acting. It was followed by an ovation, and calls of "Author!" that went on until Mrs. Fiske came to the footlights and explained that the author was not in the house.

Actually, the real authors of the piece were dead. *The Unwelcome Mrs. Hatch* was a modernization of *East Lynne*, in which Matilda Heron had played at the St. Charles before Minnie was born. New York critics found it an inferior version of the old tear-jerker; and William Winter, the arch foe of new trends in drama, blasted the play as a stale and hollow presentation of the Female in Distress.

By the force of genius and the opportunity for five good minutes of acting, Mrs. Fiske kept *The Unwelcome Mrs. Hatch* going at the Manhattan until late January, when she left for a tour of the midwest, with several high-salaried members of the cast replaced by young unknowns. Under Mrs. Fiske's sympathetic coaching, two of the replacements revealed unusual promise. One of them was the young Claus Bogle, who was later to replace George Arliss in a star role; the other was an awkward Swedish girl from Minnesota, a stage-struck orphan with a long history of walk-on parts and failures in minor roles. On the tour she received the first good notice of her career; it was the beginning of Carlotta Nillson's rise to fame.

Mrs. Fiske even had a releasing effect on actors who were no longer in her company. It was now ten years since the newly-married Fiskes had written *Fontenelle* to save James O'Neill from the monotony of

The Count of Monte Cristo. While she was in Chicago, O'Neill arrived, like a Flying Dutchman of the stage, still playing the old Dumas hero. In his company was Frederic de Belleville, Mrs. Fiske's former leading man. It could have been a melancholy meeting for the brilliant team—she in stuffy society dramas, and he playing second fiddle in old theatrical claptrap. But Mrs. Fiske had arranged by telegraph for something better. She borrowed de Belleville from O'Neill, and for four nights they sparkled in a revival of *Divorçons.*

In Boston that April Minnie played *Miranda* for the last time, and she followed her society plays with a revival of *A Doll's House.*

Bostonians were prejudiced against Ibsen, and the first night's audience was small, but it became wildly enthusiastic. The Tremont rang with un-Bostonian shouts of "Bravo!" and Mrs. Fiske and Max Figman responded to twelve curtain calls.

Soon afterward, Frederic de Belleville returned to the company for a double bill of *Divorçons* and *Little Italy.* And the Boston engagement, which had begun doubtfully, ended in triumph.

In Philadelphia Minnie played Mrs. Hatch for the last time. Unimpressed by the society background of the play, the critics labeled it a "housemaid's classic." But Mrs. Fiske gave the play her best to the end, and it was not entirely wasted. The *Inquirer's* critic found in her work a quality which restored his faith in the future of the drama; and the *North American* saluted her for work that had been equaled only twice that year—once by Mrs. Pat Campbell in the best English play of the year, and once by Otis Skinner in *Paolo and Francesca* —and the critic had not seen such moving work since Sarah Bernhardt's *L'Aiglon.*

Next evening, *A Doll's House* drew an audience twice the size of the one that had seen the last of Mrs. Hatch.

With her society plays laid to rest, Mrs. Fiske telegraphed Harry to arrange for a revival of *Tess,* which she would play for a week while deciding on her next move. When she returned to New York the Manhattan Theatre was sold out solidly for weeks, with customers waiting for more tickets to be printed.

In her old role of Tess, Mrs. Fiske played her first happy engagement in her new theatre. It was doubly a homecoming with the cast she and Harry had assembled. Frederic de Belleville, who had succeeded Charles Coghlan in the original cast, was Alec; Emily Stevens, who had played in a revival, was Tess's younger sister, Liza Lu; and the supporting cast included three of the original production: John

Craig, Mary E. Barker and John Jack. That hearty veteran liked to remind Mrs. Fiske that he had drunk at her parents' wedding in the year of Lincoln's election to the White House; now, in the presidency of Theodore Roosevelt, with automobile horns tooting in the traffic on Sixth Avenue, he played her stage father and got drunk at her wedding.

Mrs. Fiske had left on tour in January, and when she returned to triumph in *Tess* it was May, and Harry had the lobby and stairways of the Manhattan half-smothered under sprays of apple blossoms. During his wife's absence he had tried to keep the Manhattan open with productions of his own. He had suffered two failures, and was doubly glad for her return.

The revival of *Tess* proved that the play had not won all its triumphs in earlier productions. On the opening night it was taken to the heart of one of the most brilliant society audiences of the year. And William Winter, who had damned the play in the original production as "crude, prolix and wearisome," bowed his shaggy white head to the power of *Tess*. He recommended the play as one of the opportunities of the season for those "who seek in the drama a quickened imagination and a few hours of larger life."

There was irony in the fact that in two plays calculated to please the morally correct Mrs. Fiske had failed—yet triumphed as Tess, whom circumstances had made an adulteress and murderess.

The "best people" were unpredictable, but they were real enough. A few days later hundreds of them again turned out for the matinee performance of *A Doll's House*. One of them was the unchallenged moral arbiter of a curious age: the protégé of J. P. Morgan and of the dead hand of Victorianism that rested heavily on American culture. The New York *News* observed him shaping opinion by remote control, with a smile or frown:

> Prominent among those in the audience was William Dean Howells, toward whom many glasses were leveled from time to time when there was any doubt about forgiving certain moral features of the play.
> Luckily for the play and for the players, the Dean of American Letters was disposed to be liberal.

Nora was permitted to live, but it was Tess whom the fashionable took to their hearts. In recognition, the critic of the New York *Commercial Advertiser* relinquished his column for a day to one of the elite of the four hundred, who wrote a review of *Tess*. The lady admittedly had never before taken time from the social whirl to see Mrs. Fiske on the stage, but she found it a rewarding experience. She wrote in part:

> Where there is so much to praise it is difficult to select, but perhaps Mrs. Fiske's chief distinction lies in her remarkable sobriety of method, in her marvelous skill in producing effects with the smallest expenditure of voice and gesture. In a part like that of Tess such a capacity for silence and immovability is invaluable. All through the play Mrs. Fiske is the passionate, inarticulate peasant, and not the clever actress in a peasant makeup. Her extraordinary realism never once oversteps the bounds of stage illusion. . . . And the result, last night, was a triumph for that much underrated faculty, the intelligence of the theatrical public. The audience vibrated to every one of Mrs. Fiske's touches. A breath of fresh air, an unwonted thrill of reality, permeated the stale atmosphere of the theatre . . . When, after the murder, she stood mechanically brushing her hair— when Angel Clare loosened the brush from her rigid fingers and said "come"—one felt through the whole packed and breathless house the sweep of that mighty force which "purges the emotions by pity and terror."
>
> Such talent, united to such art, cannot be too highly commended in these days of theatrical clap-trap and triviality. Let Mrs. Fiske give New York a few more such impersonations—if possible, in plays more worthy of her powers—and she will do more than all the managers and all the dramatic critics to raise the theatrical ideals of the public and restore the dignity of the drama.

EDITH WHARTON

In the role of a milkmaid Mrs. Fiske had won the highest approval of New York society—and of a woman whose literary judgments would endure longer than those of the Dean of American Letters.

CHAPTER 17

While still a child in dresses, Harry Fiske had been taken to his first play by one of those unthinking nursemaids who shape the future man. The performance of *Joseph and His Brethren* had aroused in Harry a passion for the theatre. It had also identified for him the Bible as a source of drama, and it gave exciting color to *Mary of Magdala,* which he read in the summer of 1900.

The play, by Paul Heyse, dean of German playwrights, centered around the Crucifixion. In it Harry saw a great role for his wife, against a background of oriental pageantry—not the Barnum spectacle, but the ultimate and eternal one which it suggested.

Minnie approved the play, which she, in turn, envisioned against a background of Wagner's *Parsifal* music.

The first step toward the production of *Mary of Magdala* was an English version that would preserve the literary quality of the original. The Fiskes agreed on William Winter as the one best qualified for the task; also the one most likely to refuse.

In the opinion of the shaggy old poet-critic of the *Tribune,* the American stage was cluttered by "sorry and unclean Magdalas." It seemed improbable that Winter would link his name with the original of all Magdalas. But Harry believed that at the right moment almost anyone can be persuaded to do almost anything.

He waited for an annual dinner engagement which he had with William Winter, and went to the meeting place in flawless evening clothes, primed with Biblical quotations, serpent arguments and a mental list of Winter's favorite drinks. With the good wishes of the doubting Minnie and Emily, he left the Brevoort at dusk—to return in daylight, unsteady but victorious.

Chapter and verse, Harry recounted, he had quoted the New Testament to prove that Mary of Magdala was not the woman taken in

128

adultery. To be sure, Heyse's play perpetuated the injustice, but hard-drinking logic proved that there was no harm in writing about a virtuous woman, even if she was presented as a sinful one. Logic triumphed, and in the dawn of a wonderful understanding, Harry had escorted the old poet to the Staten Island ferry. William Winter's only stipulation had been that his identity as the translator be kept a profound secret.

The production as Minnie saw it would be in the manner of a Wagnerian opera, combining the arts of acting, poetry, music and lighting with the magnificent stage mounting introduced by Wagner. The value of the acting would be diminished in the process, but she believed there would be a net gain. She also saw that while she had the title role, she did not have the star part—but that did not trouble her.

Harry had planned to re-create Jerusalem in the time of Christ, but when he started to work on the project he learned that he was trying to reconstruct a lost picture. Historians and archaeologists could show the look of things in Greece and Rome and Egypt centuries before Christ, but Palestine in the first century A.D. was all words and no pictures. The Jews had no architecture of their own and no pictorial art, and their costume was a matter of guesswork.

While Harry struggled with the forgotten face of an age, Minnie assigned parts to members of her cast and studied the role of Mary of Magdala. On day coaches between one-night stands, she was usually poring over the Gospel according to John or Matthew, or Renan's weighty *Life of Jesus.*

By the summer of 1902 archaeologists had reconstructed the most probable architecture for the interiors and street scenes; a photographer in Jerusalem had taken pictures of a ravine through which a trail from the city led to Calvary, and scenic artists had produced five massive sets. Percy Anderson, London costume designer, had searched the museums of Europe for clues before sending a buyer to the Orient for fabrics.

That summer the Fiskes and Emily managed a few weeks of camping in the Adirondacks, then returned to the heat of New York for rehearsals.

As Minnie visualized the production, there would be no clutter of supernumeraries; in the mob scenes each would have his own personality and special function. Each member of the cast of a hundred and fifty was engaged individually.

At the head of the list was Judas, who would carry away the honors. Minnie's only choice for the role was Tyrone Power, whose impersonation of the Marquis of Steyne had been one of the great traditions of *Becky Sharp*. When he quit the play at its height to start on a voyage to Australia, he left a gap that was never adequately filled. The selection left another costly production at the mercy of a temperamental Irishman's whim, but Minnie felt that if *Mary of Magdala* could not continue without Power, neither could it begin without him.

Flavius, Magdala's Roman suitor, was played by the matinee idol, Henry Woodruff, who had created the role of Ben Hur in that famous piece of Sunday horse racing in which Christianity won over paganism by a nose. Among the lesser characters, Rachel was Rose Eytinge, who had supported Edwin Booth, and had been Lester Wallack's leading actress.

The Old Testament had long been accepted dramatic material, but the use of the New had to wait for the turn of a more liberal century. Harry Fiske had accepted the slowly receding prejudice; once he had helped enforce it to the death.

The pioneer of New Testament drama had been an idealistic Jew who tried in 1884 to stage a Passion Play in New York. Harry, young editor of the *Dramatic Mirror*, had fought the attempt because be believed it would bring the theatrical profession into disrepute. He and others had fought so well that the Passion Play ended in financial ruin for the pioneer, who drowned himself in the East River.

Oposition to religious plays had ebbed a long way since then, allowing such productions as *Quo Vadis*, *The Sign of the Cross*, *Ben Hur*, *The Christian* and *The Eternal City*.

Mary of Magdala, rather than resembling any of the current spectacles, was closer in spirit to the ill-starred Passion Play of 1884. It did not present Christ on the stage, but He was never far off. A sincere thought-provoking play was certain to stir more opposition than a commercial melodrama, but the Fiskes took pains to minimize the potential criticism. Copies of the play were submitted to the New York clergy for their comments, and ministers, rabbis and priests were invited to a secret dress rehearsal.

The reaction of the group was encouraging. Some of them questioned the propriety of staging the New Testament, but the majority welcomed the play. The only one who hadn't given his opinion was the Reverend Percy S. Grant, rector of the fashionable Church of the Ascension; he left at the end of the fourth act. But a few days later he wrote Mr. Fiske:

I was astonished as the play went on to see that the stage was capable of teaching Christianity in a way that no other art, not even the pulpit, could rival. . . .

I consider, therefore, your production of *Mary of Magdala* is a great moral force and vivid picture of those truths that sermons so often vaguely strive to present.

Dr. Grant's letter was the first review of the play, and one of the most influential.

When *Mary of Magdala* was tried out at the Pabst Theatre in Milwaukee on October 23, the Milwaukee *Journal* found the play a combination of Oberammergau and Bayreuth. Other critics agreed that the production revealed Mrs. Fiske as a great stage manager, and that Tyrone Power's Judas was close to greatness.

Magdala was taken next to the Grand Opera House at Chicago, and after the final curtain the audience filed out like worshipers leaving a cathedral.

With repeated performances the huge production rolled still more smoothly, gaining momentum, and by popular demand the engagement was extended.

Two critics had objected that Mrs. Fiske's Magdala was neither oriental nor Jewish—and Rabbi Emil Hirsch of Sinai Congregation, Chicago, answered that the impersonation was above all true to Jewish character and history. He also found Judas superior to the psychologically incoherent New Testament character. Heyse's Judas was a patriot of the later Irgun school, pledged to the liberation of Palestine by direct action, and he was disillusioned by finding Christ a man of peace.

While *Magdala* was triumphing in the midwest, two productions intended to keep the Manhattan open during her absence failed, and Minnie returned to a theatre that had been dark for two weeks at the height of the season. The opening night *Magdala* packed the theatre to the doors, with tickets sold out far in advance. Again Mrs. Fiske had a bad first night, but the magnificent sweep of the production carried the evening.

At the beginning of the third act the curtain rose on one of the most perfect stage illusions ever seen in New York: a sun-drenched square in Jerusalem and the streets opening from it thronged with people, "not a mechanical stage mob, but living, animated merchants, Roman soldiers, priests, travelers, young men and old, sweethearts and wives, natural and unconventional and colorful with human interest." The hypnotic effect of the stage picture was attested by the fact that critics spoke of its continuing for several moments—and actually it was three minutes before anything happened that was a direct part of the play.

In that magic square Mrs. Fiske made her appearance as the penitent Magdalene: "She stands humbly motionless near the wings, while a long and violent scene is enacted in the center of the stage, holding in her hands the alabaster box of ointment. Motionless, mind you, and without change of expression, and with no friendly calcium shaft to single her out—and yet that silent, obscure figure holds a steady heart-to-heart talk with you and brings you to the verge of tears."

The closing scene of the fourth act was the Magdalene's soul struggle between following Christ's admonition to sin no more, and yielding to Flavius, who promised that she could thereby prevent the Crucifixion. Mrs. Fiske played the scene alone, in darkness except for a single gleam of light that touched her face at the moment of her deciding vision of Christ. The scene was one of her few moments in the play, but it brought twelve curtain calls.

Judas, however, was the role of roles, and Tyrone Power made the most of it. His sinister classic make-up was as sure a work of art as a Rembrandt painting, and his magnificent physique and voice completed his identification with the character.

At the New York premiere, magnificent talent and equipment met head on. The fifth act began in the ravine leading to Calvary, with the remorse-crazed Judas wandering at night in a wild storm. Harry Fiske had equipped the Manhattan with a storm machine that took twenty men to operate—chutes the full height of the theatre, down which bowling balls were rolled; guns fired into hollow cylinders; drums and whistles and saws. The noises were synchronized by signals to emphasize Judas' lines; but on the opening night nervous stagehands bungled the timing of the storm. Each time Judas opened his mouth the thunder rolled and the wind screeched. Of his thirty lines, the audience got only an occasional shouted word.

Faces were red when the elements were finally brought under control, but the audience, shrinking and ducking through the realistic storm, was unaware that anything had gone wrong.

For years the New York *Sun's* critic had disparaged everything Mrs. Fiske did. He now wrote of Magdala as a well-known figure of the Jerusalem tenderloin, and he likened Mrs. Fiske's portrayal to an address by a female Salvation Army major.

The same issue of the *Sun* carried a second, surprise review by the paper's new dramatic critic, the brilliant James Huneker who was

Edith Wharton's "breath of fresh air blowing through the stale atmosphere of the theatre."

Huneker saw *Magdala* not as a great play, but as the best religious play which had been given to the American public.

Like *Tess* and *Becky Sharp, Mary of Magdala* was seen vicariously by millions. In America and in Europe thousands of columns of print discussed the play in many languages, and photographs of the characters and scenes became familiar to people continents away. The vast publicity inspired the Fiskes to plan a European tour, in which Mrs. Fiske would also play Lady Macbeth to Tyrone Power's Macbeth.

Mrs. Fiske now had her own theatre and *Magdala* could not be forced out of New York, where it ran until the spring of 1903. During the long run the actress was almost wholly absorbed by the character of the penitent Magdala; under that influence she wrote an article for the Christmas number of *Theatre*, in which she turned against Ibsen's merciless surgery of the human soul. Although she admitted his tremendous and original dramatic power, she felt he had "all but banished beauty, nobility, picturesqueness, and poetry from the stage." And she concluded that his final influence was baneful.

As usual with a piece of doubtful judgment, Minnie's article brought her many congratulations for being on the right track at last. That arch conservative William Winter publicly rejoiced that America's most talented actress had forsworn "the unclean folly of the Ibsen fad."

The article which brought joy to William Winter saddened James Huneker and inspired him to a five-column essay which was one of the ablest commentaries on Ibsen ever to be written in America. In defending Ibsen he could not damn Mrs. Fiske, for he was still under the spell of the immortal matinee performance in which "she sounded every note on the keyboard of Nora Helmer's character." The sad thing, Huneker said, was that it had to be Mrs. Fiske who turned against Ibsen, "for with her clear brain and powers of adaptability she woud have been an ideal interpreter of the Scandinavian's feminine gallery."

As Winter had done earlier, Huneker consoled himself with the thought, "This too will pass." He concluded:

> And this brings us back to the defection of Mrs. Fiske. We refuse to take it seriously. She has won fame, wealth, in plays removed from well-worn paths—why should she turn her shapely shoulders on Ibsen, that Ibsen who was her greatest inspiration!

In the huge cast of *Magdala* only three women had speaking roles; Emily Stevens was reduced to appearing in a mob scene, acted in the dark. Meanwhile, in Philadelphia, her mother neared the end of a long career.

Emma Maddern had made her first public appearance in the 1850's, as a child drummer, and had been on the stage almost continuously ever since. She played on into January of 1903, when a cold took an ominous turn, and her daughter was summoned. Emily found her mother in a hospital fighting pneumonia, with a good chance of recovery. There was nothing useful Emily could do, and in the spirit of Grandmother Maddern, Emma exhorted her daughter to have faith in God and to see that the play went on—and she sent Emily back to her minute role.

Emily was to return to Philadelphia on the weekend, but after the performance on Friday night, she was summoned to her cousin's dressing room. She hurried in, still wearing the costume in which she had fled through the black ravine.

Co'Min was holding an open telegram; Emily knew what it meant without reading it. She broke down, sobbing, and Mrs. Fiske took her in her arms and comforted her, as Emily's mother had comforted her in a dressing room a quarter of a century earlier.

From that hour of grief enacted in the robes of Calvary, Emily Stevens belonged entirely to the Fiske household, and more than ever she was heir to the love of her cousin, who had already been her guardian and stage mother and older sister.

In the early spring Mrs. Fiske took *Mary of Magdala* on the road. The huge production made it impracticable to invade the Trust-held West, but the tour east of the Mississippi was an almost continuous triumph. There was a minor undercurrent of protest on religious grounds, but it did not reach the surface until the last days of the tour. At Rochester the Reverend Evan Martin preached a sermon against Heyse's defamation of the blameless Magdala, a sermon which was printed and widely discussed. There was justice in the criticism, and on May 17 Mrs. Fiske replied in the Rochester *Herald:*

> There is no line in the gospels which would lead us to suppose that the woman of Magdala was a sinful woman. Every student of the Bible must be aware that the Scriptures offer no foundation for the poets' and the painters' dream. But who shall deny that the spiritual world and the world of art are richer for the dream? The clergyman of Rochester condemns the German poet's "attack" upon the woman

of Magdala. What of the "attack" of the great masters? Should the canvases of Raphael and Michelangelo be destroyed? And the wondrous, uplifting Magdalene of Titian? . . . So far as we know, the real Lady Macbeth was a harmless and inoffensive person, yet are we grateful for the poet's monster. . . .

Emily Stevens read the masterful defense and raised an eyebrow, and question: "If bad women do more good than good ones, why are they called bad?"

Mrs. Fiske answered sternly, but with the hint of a twinkle deep in her blue eyes, "When you are old enough you will understand."

Emily would not be put off. "I want to know now. Why won't you tell me, Co'Min?"

The twinkle became unmistakable. "Because I am not old enough, either."

The end of the season overlapped with plans for a greater one in which the Fiskes would present *Mary of Magdala* and *Macbeth* in Europe.

Their preparations were well advanced when Tyrone Power notified Mr. Fiske that he was leaving the cast. His Judas had made him the most praised actor of the year, and Charles Frohman had offered to star him in Stephen Phillips' *Ulysses* if he would break his two-year contract with the Fiskes.

It was the second time Power had left them in the lurch, and Harry began legal action—more as a gesture of exasperation than of hope. With their plans tumbling about them, the Fiskes prepared to spend the summer in Europe as tourists instead of producers. Mrs. Fiske and Emily would sail immediately, and Harry would follow when he had readjusted their mauled affairs. As James Huneker had predicted, Mrs. Fiske's revulsion against Ibsen had passed with some clear thinking on the subject. She put Lady Macbeth aside and took up the role of Hedda Gabler for the coming, crippled season.

CHAPTER 18

For more than a year Mrs. Fiske had been under the influence of German art: Heyse's play and Wagner's music. The influence went on after the season ended, and late in May she and Emily Stevens sailed for the Germany of her dreams. What was more, she found it in that age of innocence in European history.

Emily was now a member of the Fiske household, even to having a family nickname—the Whiffet. The bond was so close that the cousins wrote to Harry on the same pieces of stationery, much in the same vein and often giving the same information.

Soon after landing in Hamburg, the two did their only theatregoing of the trip; they would not have been tempted then except for the fact that the play was *Magda*, in which Minnie had won honors the year before, and the star was Sarah Bernhardt. A decade earlier Bernhardt had called the role her one complete and abject failure, and Mrs. Fiske did not find that time had improved matters. It was, she wrote, the worst performance she had ever seen.

From Hamburg the cousins went to spend a day in Heidelberg. After a week they were still there, and on June 6 Minnie wrote to Harry:

Darling—Darling Boy
It has been so beautiful here that we have lingered—we wander about the lovely old streets each afternoon—taking a long walk from the woods on the hill where we live, to Heidelberg. Yesterday we went to the ruins of the old castle. . . . A little American boy is employed here at the hotel. Yesterday we saw the Stars and Stripes floating over the court from an inside window. This little boy had put out the American flag in our honor and it will wave over the old hotel until we go! It looks good! The Whiff and I salute it every day to the great delight of the servants. We dine out under the trees. . . . I study "Hedda Gabler" in the mornings —walking in the woods. . . .

Can you imagine—darling Boy—how we look forward to your coming? Our thoughts are with you every minute of the day.

Your devoted
Bunner

They went on to Rothenburg, and from the Hotel Goldenen Hirsch the two wrote to Harry on opposite sides of the same generous sheet of notepaper—about vineyards on sunny hills, and how not even time and the elements could prevail against the ancient city; when walls crumbled they were restored to last another thousand years.

The cousins continued to Switzerland by way of Munich, and from Lucerne Emily wrote Harry two important pieces of news: at Munich Paul Heyse had called on Co'Min, and in Switzerland their first find had been a picture postcard of Fifi. Emily devoted a page to the discovery of the black poodle's likeness in the railway station, and a line to the playwright's visit, merely saying that he had called on Co'Min and afterward sent flowers.

Mrs. Fiske added a note to Emily's letter, touching on the same item of news:

I wrote you by this mail.
Think of our Fifi on a postcard!
Mr. Heyse is a dear! He called on me & we had a lovely talk.

your
Bunner

Mrs. Fiske and Emily were waiting confidently for a cable telling them that Harry was sailing to join them. A cable arrived a few hours after the postscript about the poodle and the playwright, but its news was crushing: Harry had been detained in New York, where his suit against Tyrone Power was pending, and at best he would hardly have time for more than a "Hello" and "Good-bye" to Europe.

Minnie wrote her third communication that day:

Darling Boy,
Your cable has just been received. I will not speak of our disappointment, for above all it is hard to think of yours and of the hopes for a happy vacation we had planned having to be abandoned. . . . Do not fail to sail on the 7th if it is at all possible. . . . But if you come on the 7th why cannot you remain a week longer in Europe? It will be absolutely safe for me to return home alone and the Whiff could remain with you? . . . Shall we meet you at Paris, or would you prefer London? . . . I fear things have not gone too well so you are forced to remain. I shall not tell you how sad we are. We had laid such plans for your coming. . . .

137

Try hard to come for a week in Paris with the boys! . . . Lucerne will be our address until I tell you differently . . . I hasten this to catch the first mail.

Your devoted
Bunner.

She and Emily continued hoping for another three weeks—then Harry cabled that he would be unable to leave New York. As second best, he proposed that when Minnie and Emily returned, the three of them could spend some time at the Knollwood Country Club in Westchester.

Mrs. Fiske answered:

. . . Of course we believed that you would be able to come, else I need not say, we would not have dreamed of coming. I know what great benefit a vacation abroad would be to you. . . .

Well, darling Boy, you could not come, and it cannot be helped. We know how much you wished to come and know you would have come had there been any way for you to manage it.

Your devoted
Bunner

Later on the 9th

Darling Boy—

I have already written you today, expressing the hope that you will arrange a good two weeks' vacation—a complete change and rest. The Whiffet can go with you—easily as she will not be needed during the "Hedda Gabler" rehearsals and one week of the "Mary" rehearsal will be all she requires. You must have the vacation. Then we will have Knollwood and, if you like, a visit to the sea at some place convenient for going up and down to and from New York.

We spent, as you know, nearly a week at the beautiful little Swiss town—Meiringen. Such a tiny town nestling among the mountains. . . . We had a quiet little hotel and I could go across the fields to a beautiful shady walk and then I paced with "Hedda." For I love to walk and study. Often I study in the little churches because they are so quiet. In Meiringen there was the dearest little church (I thought I was locked in once, and got scared!) and the most gaily colored and happy looking graveyard. . . . We got to be quite like old habitants roaming about the streets at night. . . . Then to Interlaken. . . . We remained over only till train time— then up—up—up—we climbed on the train—away to Grindelwald— which is a village on the way to the great peaks of the Eiger, the Matterhorn and other giants of the Alps. It was a wondrous ride— cataracts—glaciers—precipices towering snow-capped mountains and

138

ever and anon at the turn of the road a vision of the glittering, matchlessly beautiful Jungfrau—the darling of the Alps. . . . Our hotel was considerably above the village. We had a balcony and the view from it was gorgeous. The towering Eiger cut the sky sharply almost directly in front of us. It looked so lovely and terrible—but bless you, while we contemplated its apparently awful "remoteness" at night a lot of fireworks suddenly set off at a point where we imagined no human being had ever planted foot. That is a very disconcerting thing about the Alps. . . . We went to the Grindelwald glacier the second day . . . The Whiffet enjoyed the experience of entering the glacier. . . . In the evening we walked along the great Alp highway to our hotel—a distance of about three miles (not much of a walk!). . . . Monday we descended to Interlaken again. I'll write of that tomorrow and also the Asche and other matters. Good-night my darling—darling boy—

Your Bunner

Mrs. Fiske had come to Europe under the spell of German art, and after intensive study of *Hedda Gabler* she was under the spell of Ibsen for the first time in twenty years of acquaintance with his plays. Her almost constant companion was the black-bound volume of his *Prose Dramas*. Throughout the idyllic vacation Ibsen was Emily's only rival for her cousin's companionship, and Ibsen could be a potent rival.

Once, at Meiringen, Mrs. Fiske locked herself in the parlor of the little hotel and paced the floor with *Hedda Gabler* for an hour while her cousin waited outside in the cold. Afterward Emily was chilly to Mrs. Fiske's enthusiasm over the revealing scene between Hedda and Lövborg through which she had just lived, and Emily was outraged when she discovered that the scene was not even in the play, having taken place years before the opening curtain.

"Think of it, Whiff," Minnie said to Emily's unresponsive ears, "on the stage the play begins thirty-six hours before Hedda's suicide. Ibsen shows us only the last hours. To portray them I must know everything that has gone before. Ibsen makes that necessary, and provides the keys that unlock the past. I must know all that Hedda ever was. When I do, the role will play itself."

In the intense study of the role, Mrs. Fiske could forget Emily. But at other times she was still the orphaned child-actress, longing to draw what remained of her family close about her. In the same month that Harry decided not to leave New York, she and Emily turned home, although summer was only half over.

C H A P T E R 19

Early in August Minnie and Emily returned to New York, where they carried Harry off to the Knollwood Country Club for a vacation.

The vacation was jostled by the demands of the theatre; in addition to a new production, there were changes to be made in the old. Harry had lost the suit against Tryone Power, and Charles Kent had been engaged for the role of Judas. Flavius was to be played by Hobart Bosworth, and Emily was promoted to the role of Miriam.

It was the second year of *Mary of Magdala*, but the opening night furnished a surprise for the audience. Macmillan was about to publish the translation of the play under Winter's name, and the Manhattan Theatre program now carried an extra line: "Adapted and written in English verse by William Winter."

A fair share of the evening's triumph belonged to the old poet. Critics were ruthless with one of their number who turned traitor and wrote a play; but they had already praised the work, and it was too late for a Roman holiday at the expense of "Willie Winter."

The translator, who had poetic insight, also had his merciless intolerances. One of the daughters of Laura Keene for most of her brief life had kept a horsewhip near her, hoping to use it on the critic for a slur on her tragic mother. There were also examples of Winter's courage and incorruptibility. There was the case of Jim Fisk, the stock-manipulator, no relation to Harry. Jim was a dabbler in the theatre, and he thought enough of Winter's power to offer him fifty thousand dollars a year for an occasional public-relations item. Winter had answered by snubbing him in public, and the only item he wrote about Jim Fisk was an unpaid reference to his "pig face."

William Winter could make life as difficult for friends as for his enemies. The Harrison Grey Fiskes had been almost constantly in his good graces, beginning with Harry as the boy editor and Minnie as a teen-age star. Winter had almost forgiven Mrs. Fiske for her appearance in *A Doll's House,* and he forgave her altogether after the Christmas number of *Theatre* in which she renounced Ibsen.

The Fiske-Winter friendship reached its height at the beginning of the second season of *Mary of Magdala,* with all three now sharing publicly in its success.

The glow continued for three blissful weeks, and then Mrs. Fiske temporarily put *Magdala* aside for *Hedda Gabler.* On the opening night William Winter stood like a white-topped rock in the lobby of the Manhattan, splitting the current of theatregoers, saying savage things about Ibsen and deriding the audience as "long-haired men and flat-chested she-goats of women."

It was essentially the same audience that had delighted Winter on the opening night of *Magdala,* and the critic of the New York *Times* took him to task:

> There is no doubt about it, they go to see Ibsen because they like it. It is a sight to bring disquiet to those reactionary folk who so long ago proclaimed that they had sealed the mausoleum of Ibsen, and have been engaged in resealing it ever since.

Apropos of the gibes about "long-haired men" and Winter's own poetic locks, the *Times* commented:

> The only man with long hair thus far noted is one who has longest been occupied in sealing and resealing that mausoleum.

In the *Tribune* William Winter wrote of *Hedda Gabler:*

> The play is a long-winded colloquial exposition of disease and its heroine is an insane cat . . .
> It is a waste of time to discuss Mr. Ibsen . . . It is a pity that Mrs. Fiske should lend her name to this crazy fad; but it is only for a moment, and "this too will pass."

Those who saw *Hedda* with open minds shared in the thrill of discovery. William B. Mack had never distinguished himself before, but under the magic of Ibsen and Minnie he *was* Tesman, and critics of thirteen metropolitan dailies agreed he had given a perfect performance.

The second revelation of the evening was Mrs. Elvsted, played by Carlotta Nillson, remembered, if at all, as a perennial failure in small parts. Her opportunity came near the end of the third act, in the scene with the intoxicated Lövborg.

During the scene Minnie's Hedda gave Mrs. Elvsted the center of the stage, as no Hedda had ever done before. Miss Nillson, unaccustomed to applause, was bewildered by the storm of approval. At the end of the act Minnie made Miss Nillson precede her to the center of the stage in answer to an ovation. The younger actress stood there overwhelmed, with Minnie close beside her, smiling encouragingly. Suddenly Miss Nillson took Mrs. Fiske's hand and kissed it, and the responding applause shook the theatre.

In the midst of deploring the "madhouse wickedness" of the play, William Winter took time to praise her. James Huneker opined that the contrast between Mrs. Elvsted and Hedda had never been portrayed more graphically than in this performance between Miss Nillson and Mrs. Fiske. The *Times* review ended: "Miss Nillson has appeared hitherto, it is said, most prominently in London, at the Criterion and the Garrick. It is to be hoped that she has come among us to stay."

Carlotta Nillson had come among us to stay long ago, not as a famous actress from London, but as an immigrant child—but the ugly duckling had never truly arrived until she met a discerning woman who had faith in her.

Mrs. Fiske's Hedda, in her catlike way, had led Miss Nillson's Thea on to her undoing; "bit by bit she wrenched from the big-hearted little creature the whole sad story of her love for Eilert; with diabolical cruelty she had wounded her, and watched for the wounds to bleed" —and on the same stage Mrs. Fiske, the woman and artist, had effaced herself to give Carlotta the opportunity of her life.

In one respect Minnie sided with Hedda against her creator. In Ibsen's play Hedda is six months pregnant, although the cowardly and finicky neurotic will not allow the fact to be mentioned. In Minnie's production—as Hedda would have wished it—the pregnancy did not exist. The actress, who had been accused of not being able to portray mother love, did not choose to depict maternity. Her icy and remote Hedda, lost in selfish daydreams, triumphed without the aid of nature. An occasional critic regretted the omission, but it was agreed that Hedda Gabler was one of Mrs. Fiske's great roles. It also inspired James Huneker to criticism that continues to be quoted half a century later—like his comment on Hedda: "She went through life with the chip of chastity on her shoulder; yet dare a man approach her and she is in the throes of mock virtue."

Huneker declared that Hedda could keep the Manhattan filled all winter. But Minnie's tour was arranged, and Harry was giving the final touches to his production of *Marta of the Lowlands*. It took over at the Manhattan in mid-October, and Minnie began a national tour.

After six years of warfare with the Theatrical Trust, Minnie was buoyed up by a new tang in the American air. Theodore Roosevelt in the White House was thundering against "malefactors of great wealth" and trusts in particular. More usefully for the stage, the Theatrical Trust was sagging in the middle. Theatre owners had flocked to it for protection, only to find that the Trust protected its own interests at the expense of its satellites. When new theatres were built, their owners kept clear of the Trust.

Mrs. Fiske had secured bookings in thirty large cities, including Cleveland and Kansas City, where she had not been allowed to act for years. Her tour began in Baltimore, at the new and independent Maryland Theatre.

From the home front at the Manhattan, Harry Fiske reported that his impetuous leading lady, Corona Riccardo, had proved unsatisfactory, and she was resisting efforts to replace her. After another week the New York press reported that the lady had sprained her ankle and would be unable to go on. Immediately after, it was reported that she had been shot—and Emily Stevens told her cousin proudly, "I knew our Boy would find a way to get rid of the woman!"

The conflicting reports were cleared up by a letter from Harry Fiske. The lady had attempted suicide with a blank pistol and a basin of stage blood. Harry had continued to insist that she must go, dead or alive, and she had agreed to settle for a sprained ankle and retirement. She was replaced, and the play failed with another leading lady.

In December Minnie presented her plays in Detroit, where she had been unable to appear since the Trust's formation. Her next engagement was in Chicago, but—inadvertently this time—the Trust disrupted her plans. During a holiday matinee of *Mr. Bluebeard* Klaw and Erlanger's Iroquois Theatre in Chicago caught fire, and 460 women and children were trapped and burned to death. Among the repercussions to the disaster, *Life* published a savage cartoon depicting mothers and children burning to death in a theatre with padlocked fire exits, with the caption, "Klaw and Erlanger present *Mr. Bluebeard*." In the libel suit that followed, the court declined to award damages because it found nothing in the cartoon contrary to fact.

In Chicago, where the tragedy weighed heavily, all theatres were closed for the two weeks which coincided with Minnie's engagement. Comparatively, it was a minor inconvenience, but for a production the size of *Magdala* it was disaster enough. Minnie ordered her company to remain in Detroit; she sent her manager, Mr. Griffith, to see what could be done in Chicago, and she rushed to New York. At the Manhattan Theatre four plays had failed in quick succession, and Harry was rehearsing a fifth—a dramatization of Owen Wister's *The Virginian,* with a young actor named Dustin Farnum in the title role, and Guy Bates Post as Steve.

Minnie hoped to exert influence in New York which would open a Chicago theatre, but she had no success, and Mr. Griffith reported that nothing could be accomplished in Chicago. Minnie telegraphed her company to remain where they were, and she wired Mr. Griffith:

PROCEED IMMEDIATELY TO DETROIT LOCK UP COMPANYS BAGGAGE LOSE KEY UNTIL FURTHER ORDERS REGARDS MINNIE MADDERN FISKE.

At the end of the week she returned to her company, which she found intact but restless, and she decided to give them a change of boredom by taking them to Cleveland for their second idle week.

The stopping of theatrical wheels in Chicago had stranded many companies. The train to Cleveland was jammed with actors and theatrical effects. The change of prisons was only a temporary diversion for the company, but Mrs. Fiske had saved them a good deal of trouble and money. They ended the two weeks with increased respect for their little red-headed general, and performed with spirit at the Cleveland opening.

Early in this tour a Trust agent found an old actress who confused Mrs. Fiske with her mother and claimed to have appeared with her in 1859—the year before Minnie's parents were married. On the basis of a stage debut at three, her first Trust-released age was 48. It increased alarmingly as she toured and in a few weeks had touched sixty. The resulting excitement reached its height in Kansas City, where Mrs. Fiske was met by a flock of reporters who demanded the facts.

For the first time Mrs. Fiske broke her silence on the annoying subject; she told the reporters:

"There is no use in an actress lying about her age—there are too many checks. I am just thirty-eight." It was a courageous piece of honesty from a woman of thirty-nine.

In San Francisco Minnie's annual engagement had been extended from two weeks to four, and still it was not enough for the audiences that crowded the theatre. Neither was it enough for Minnie and Emily.

144

Between exhilarating expeditions with the Ashton Stevenses and
Arnold Genthe, there were warm family gatherings in Oakland. At
the St. Francis Hotel Mrs. Fiske had a visit from Jack London, who
had decided to write something for her. He talked in large terms about
his play that would cut itself off from stage traditions, stereotyped
motives, heroes and heroines, and enter a field of dramatic art un-
dreamed of by stay-at-home minds.

Minnie, who pioneered daily, was not overawed. She advised London
to familiarize himself with stage tradition, the better to break it, and
gave the project her blessing.

Nothing could have been more welcome to Minnie, who was forced
to revive old plays or discover new playwrights. Among the many
hopeless manuscripts she read that season was one by C. M. S. McLellan.
Under the *nom de plume* of "Hugh Morton," he had written *The Belle
of New York, In Gay New York* and other musicals that had helped
give the last decade of a century the name of "The Gay Nineties."

McLellan's present work was *Into the Great White Light*, a humor-
less and pompous melodrama with a long history of rejections in New
York and London. Minnie saw in it what others had missed—the dark
soul of a girl thief illuminated by lightning flashes in her upward struggle to redemption. Minnie accepted the play on condition that Mc-
Lellan rewrite it as she directed, and work began on what was to be
Leah Kleschna.

The following year, when Minnie was again in San Francisco, Jack
London handed her his dramatic effort. As he had promised, the play
broke all the traditions of the theatre—but Mrs. Fiske commented that
it seemed more the result of awkwardness than of design; nevertheless
she waited until Harry pronounced the play unusable; then she returned it with a tactful letter of criticism. Jack London replied:

Dear Mrs. Fiske:

I hardly know what to say in reply to your letter of Tuesday.
That you do not understand me has certainly gone with the writing
of said letter. How possibly could you understand me? When I
speak a language that is unintelligible to a certain group of people,
and when my very thought-symbols are totally different from the
thought-symbols of such a group of people, how possibly can such
a group of people, having no understanding of me whatever, give
you any understanding of me?

I should be quite happy to talk the matter over with you some
time, if we ever chance to meet, but I am too dreadfully rushed for
time just now to be able to take a day off in order to talk it over.

I remember the first case I ever saw tried in a court of law. At the conclusion of the hearing of the evidence pro and con, in my childish mind I could not for the life of me decide whether the man was innocent or guilty. Then the prosecuting attorney arose and addressed the Jury. As I listened, the whole thing seemed to become clear as print. The man was guilty. The man was an abominable wretch. The man deserved the extreme penalty of the law. No punishment could be severe enough for such a man. He was a contemptible scoundrel, etc., etc. So I concluded while talked the attorney for the prosecution. The attorney for the defense arose and addressed the Jury. I underwent a reversal of feeling while I listened to him. This poor, innocent man; this muchly-wronged and maligned individual; this man who had been so vilely treated, so unjustly treated—why, no jury under the sun could convict such a man. I flamed with indignation, and thought of all the injustice he had suffered. All the while talked the attorney for the defense. Then arose again the attorney for the prosecution, who made his final address to the Jury. As he talked, I began to reconsider; possibly I was mistaken after all. The man did not seem so innocent as he had seemed when his own attorney was talking. Here certainly he was guilty, and there certainly he was guilty. And the attorney for the prosecution talked on. I began to grow indignant on the other side of the case. The man certainly merited the utmost punishment that could be given him. He was deserving of no mercy whatever. He was as contemptible and vile as I had thought him when the prosecuting attorney first talked. . . . And then I went home. And when I cooled down, I considered what a fool had been made of me. And from this little affair I drew one conclusion which lasted me through all my life, namely, that very little reliance can be placed in special pleaders. Later I learned that every individual, when he pleaded for himself, made an unusually excellent special pleader.

A final word, in an effort to give you a clew to my character: What acts I have performed in this world have been directly in line with my highest conceptions of right conduct.

Sincerely yours,
Jack London

Minnie penciled a comment:

Stuff!—
Stuffing!

After California Minnie toured the Northwest, where most of the enthusiasm of the capacity audiences was for *Hedda Gabler*. All they needed for their education in Ibsen was the opportunity to see his plays.

Late in May Minnie approached a cherished prospect of the tour—

the performance of *Hedda* at Ann Arbor before the student body of the University of Michigan.

Confident of an ideal audience, Minnie relaxed her usual vigilance; ushers were not instructed to quiet or eject anyone who created a disturbance, and for once Mr. Griffith did not have to buy off the peanut venders in the neighborhood.

Unlike the beginning of any other performance in the tour, the curtain rose in an undertone of conversation that went on as if the students had not noticed that the play had begun. Mrs. Fiske, as Hedda, made her entrance "as though she had just driven up to the stage door and had swept in, not from the dressing room, but out of the frosty night onto the stage."

The entrance was made to the accompanying rustle of paper bags and the crack of peanut shells. In one of the boxes students were munching and talking, and tossing shells onto the stage.

Minnie stopped in the middle of a speech and had the curtain rung down.

"Refund the audience their money!" she cried to Mr. Griffith. "Let them buy peanuts!"

Instead, the manager persuaded her to compromise. He went before the curtain and announced that the performance would not go on unless the eating and talking stopped. They stopped, and the play resumed.

When it was over, Mrs. Fiske told reporters she would never stop at Ann Arbor again; that the University might be training its students, but it was not educating them.

Afterward Minnie regretted the whole much-publicized affair. It would never have happened if she hadn't endowed college students with her own eager search for knowledge.

C H A P T E R 20

In June of 1904 Mrs. Fiske brought her company home from thirty-seven weeks of touring.

After so much of cities and people, Minnie longed for the Adirondacks, where she could renew herself in a natural world of woods and lakes and islands. Instead, she and Emily went to the Knollwood Country Club, where it was *de rigeur* to dress for dinner, and where a great deal of time was devoted to fashions that would be out of date before the end of summer, and to golf scores that would be forgotten the next day.

The country club was not Mrs. Fiske's ideal; but Harry was a member, and the club had its comforts in a summer when he could not take a vacation. And he and Minnie and Emily could be together at least evenings and weekends.

It was fortunate for Harry Fiske that he loved New York, when so many things conspired to keep him there. While Minnie had been touring America, the Independent Theatrical Managers' Association had been falling to pieces; the Fiskes were again left alone in their fight for a free theatre. They were also left with a theatre on their hands, and decisions to make for the coming season and years.

What the Fiskes evolved at Knollwood was nothing new, but rather the speeding up of an idea they had had for years: a permanent company of the best actors in America, the best plays to be had, and productions as perfect as money and skill could make them.

The plan for a permanent Manhattan Theatre Company was little more than the statement of an ideal when Minnie was left to carry it out alone. Near the end of the summer, Harry was stricken with typhoid fever. While his doctor was considering moving him from the Brevoort to Hannemann Hospital, Harry's condition became so desperate that he could not be moved. Day and night nurses cared

148

for him while Mrs. Fiske wrestled with arrangements and rehearsals, and did what she could for her husband's comfort.

At the height of Harry's fever and delirium, he was agonized by the ringing of bells from the church next door, and he fixed on the idea that when the bells tolled again, it would be for him. He was so near death that it seemed more than probable—but the bells fell silent and stayed asleep for days. They were still silent when the crisis of his illness passed, and a horse-drawn ambulance took him to the hospital. Minnie then notified the kindly rector that her husband was out of hearing of the bells; when they tolled again, it was for someone else.

Harry Fiske recuperated until he was able to take an interest in the theatre once more—and then he was plunged into the fever and delirium of a second attack of typhoid. At the beginning of the fall season his life was still wavering in the balance.

Since childhood Minnie had been shadowed by the fear of death— not for herself, but for those she loved. And she had clung to her family with an anxious devotion that was only equaled by her loyalty to the play. All during the preparations for the fall season she was haunted by her husband's illness and overloaded with work, but she never slackened her pace.

On schedule, the Manhattan Theatre opened on September 15 with a brilliant revival of *Becky Sharp*. The program announced the formation of a permanent company to occupy the theatre, and the cast of characters revealed the quality of that company. George Arliss appeared for the first time as the Marquis of Steyne, William B. Mack as Pitt Crawley, John Mason as Rawdon Crawley, and the cast continued almost flawless to the end, with Briggs played by the veteran Mary Maddern.

That season the National Art Theatre Society was becoming insistent that something be done to uplift the American stage. The day after the premiere of the *Becky* revival, the New York *Press* suggested: "Why not end all this pother about the National Art Theatre Society at once by having that excellent body awarding national distinction to Mrs. Fiske and her players, now permanently located at the actress's own theatre?"

But the Manhattan Company lacked the label of a movement—and the finely-balanced cast was not the perfect one of Minnie's ideal. John Mason, who now played Rawdon, had begun his career at the Manhattan twenty-six years earlier. The theatre was then in its garish heyday as the Standard, and Mason had appeared in a small singing

149

part with Maggie Mitchell. Since then he had developed into one of the ablest actors in America. But in Mrs. Fiske's "dream theatre" the great guardsman was still played by Maurice Barrymore. To the end of the *Becky* chapter, thirty years later, the gap Barrymore left remained unfilled.

In the original production, Tyrone Power's desertion created another gap. It had taken five years to find another Marquis of Steyne, but now the role was filled by a young English actor who had come to New York with Mrs. Pat Campbell, and stayed to appear in Long and Belasco's *Darling of the Gods*. George Arliss was unknown to stardom, but the first glimpse of him as the Marquis of Steyne electrified the Manhattan audience.

In the first edition of *Vanity Fair* Thackeray's drawings of Steyne had shown a stooping old aristocrat with a bald pate, thick side hair, and a hairy, ape-like face that was nonetheless aristocratic. The portrait was so like the current Marquis of Hertford that it was suppressed in all subsequent editions. Now George Arliss brought the original Thackeray drawings to life, with a face that combined the ape ancestry of man and the ultimate of aristocratic degeneration—a cynical history of the human race sketched in a few strokes of makeup.

In the second act, before the Battle of Waterloo, Arliss's Marquis of Steyne made his entrance on the high landing, and descended the great staircase. There were a hundred and fifty other characters on the stage; he moved unostentatiously, but his stealthy, upright creep hypnotized the audience to the farthest reaches of the second balcony. In Critics' Row, William Winter looked on like an eagle watching the approach of a deadly snake. Next day he wrote of Arliss's Steyne, "From his first entrance at the head of the stairway, before he had uttered one word, the man stood revealed."

The revelation of genius made George Arliss the star of the first half of the performance. In the supper scene in the third act, Mason had his opportunity, Mrs. Fiske belatedly hit her stride and the audience had a thrilling glimpse of the teamwork which was Minnie's ideal for the Manhattan Company.

The critic of the *New York Times* was still under the spell when he wrote next day that the United States now had a company whose productions equaled the best in Europe, and that the Art Theatre Society should recognize Mrs. Fiske's Manhattan Company as the National Theatre of which it dreamed.

There were other actresses who appeared in plays as worthy as Mrs.

Fiske's, sometimes with greater popular acclaim, but none of them was thought of as the leader of the American stage. That title belonged to the little red-headed actress who had a genius for bringing out the best in others. She did not always bring out the best in herself.

For years there had been complaints about Mrs. Fiske's too rapid and blurred speech. After the first performance of the *Becky* revival, there were the loudest cries ever heard on the subject. Almost without exception, the critics agreed that many of Mrs. Fiske's lines were lost to the audience. But Alan Dale, who complained most bitterly, admitted that he was delighted by Mrs. Fiske's dumb show; and the other critics agreed that she *was* Becky Sharp—a fact that made her indispensable as well as maddening in her inaudible passages.

Mrs. Fiske had a gift for falling on her feet—but why did she impose so recklessly on her audiences? The question was not answered until twenty years later, when George Arliss wrote his delightful, *Up the Years from Bloomsbury*. Arliss observed of his first season with Mrs. Fiske:

> Our greatest difficulty at this time was to prevent her from effacing herself. She was so interested in getting the best out of everybody else that she always seemed to regard herself as a negligible quantity in the play.
>
> I remember saying to her, "Are you going to speak all that with your back to the audience?"
>
> "Yes," she said, "I want them to see your face."
>
> "But," I remonstrated, "it's a very long speech for you to deliver in that position."
>
> "Yes, I know," she sighed. "It's such a long speech that I want to get through with it as quickly as I can."

Mrs. Fiske had expected to play *Becky* for a month, and it ran for nine weeks. She then presented *Hedda Gabler*, which had met with such enthusiasm when it was played for an experimental week the season before.

In the new production of *Hedda*, Tesman was again played by William B. Mack, who had been judged perfect in the role. The wayward and erratic Eilert Lövborg was played magnificently by the wayward and bohemian John Mason. Another strengthening of the cast was George Arliss's Assessor Brack. Emily Stevens, who later played Hedda Gabler in her own right, appeared in the play for the first time as Berta. For reasons which young Emily could not make clear, she found the play, or her servant role, a source of innocent merriment. Solemnly, she would bring in a lamp, or make up the fire, and then leave the stage at an accelerated pace which brought her to the distant wings in convulsed laughter.

With four of the five major roles filled by Mrs. Fiske, Arliss, Mason, and Mack, all that was needed was Carlotta Nillson's Mrs. Elvsted— but her success of the previous season had been too complete for that. Carlotta was now appearing in the title role of Pinero's *Lady Letty*, with William Faversham as her leading man. In Miss Nillson's place, Mrs. Elvsted was played more than adequately by Laura McGilvry.

The cast of four great actors and three able ones gave what was probably the finest Ibsen performance that had been seen in America— and the most thrilling. In the excitement, William Winter almost forgot to abuse Ibsen, praising Mr. Arliss's performance, "finely marked with velvet duplicity and stealthy elegance . . ." and "Mr. Mason vitalizing the manuscript and pistol scenes with a powerful and touching outburst of the delirium of passionate grief." And Mrs. Fiske's performance, "mordant with sarcasm, keen with irony, dreadful with the suggestion of subtle, watchful wickedness and vicious eccentricity."

For a month *Hedda* filled the Manhattan with enthusiastic audiences, while critics less prejudiced than Winter hailed the new era of Ibsen in America.

Neither *Becky Sharp* nor *Hedda Gabler* had been intended as Mrs. Fiske's chief offering for the season. Ever since Harry's illness had interrupted the first rehearsal of *Leah Kleschna*, Minnie had been managing and directing alone, bringing the play to perfection. It had progressed a long way since Minnie's first reading of the crude piece which had been rejected by nearly all the producers in the United States and England. McLellan had rewritten and reshaped it along the lines which she had suggested, and he came over from England for rehearsals. Oddly enough, for any actress but Mrs. Fiske, one proportion of the play had not been changed. In the original draft, the role of Leah Kleschna had been fifth in importance; in the finished play it was still fifth.

Minnie, who was modest about her own work, could teach modesty to others. McLellan's stilted melodrama had developed, with her collaboration, into a highly effective play. With five of the best American and British actors in the principal roles it appeared as something of a masterpiece. McLellan, who had come to rehearsals shy and grateful, saw himself as a playwright of importance; and his confidence and artistic temperament increased accordingly. Once, at the end

152

of the third act rehearsal, he came storming onto the stage, furious because Mr. Mason had slurred his great curtain line.

Minnie, who was responsible for so much of the play, answered the playwright quietly but sharply:

"Well, my dear sir, bear up. You did not write that line!"

Leah Kleschna had its premiere at the Manhattan Theatre on December 12, 1904, with one of the most perfect casts ever seen on a New York stage. Kleschna, the professional thief, was played by Charles Cartwright, rated the best villain of the English stage and imported for the play. His lieutenant, Schram, was played by William B. Mack of the flawless performances as Tesman in Hedda Gabler. As the young degenerate, Raoul Berton, George Arliss gave another of his polished brilliant impersonations. As Leah Kleschna Mrs. Fiske gave a transcendental performance, with overtones that suggested something far greater than the play itself. Paul Sylvaine was played by John Mason, whose instinct about the characters he played was unerring. There were others more famous on Broadway, but George Arliss, who acted with him, maintained that Mason was potentially the greatest actor in America.

Among the lesser characters, Valentin Favre was played by Etienne Girardot, who had played Antonio to Ellen Terry's Beatrice in *Much Ado about Nothing*. And Emily Stevens appeared in a single scene as Claire Breton, sister of the decadent Raoul and fiancée of the noble Paul Sylvaine. The role had a one-word opportunity, the moment when Claire learned of the good looks of the girl thief whom her fiancé had allowed to escape. Claire said "Ah!" It might have suggested nothing more than a throat examination, but Emily said it in a manner that suggested a flood of jealous light pouring into a mean little soul; it convulsed every audience.

New York theatre critics had complained about the dreariness of the fall and winter season of 1904. Fourteen new plays had been presented by Charles Frohman, each bearing the stamp of Frohman's factory methods, and each flattering a Frohman star. The dead level of neat mediocrity led Alan Dale to comment on "the truck that affects us today; the weak dishwater flimsiness that has almost routed the season." Other critics said the same thing in other words.

It was against such a drab background that *Leah Kleschna* flashed on the theatrical scene. On the evening of December 12 the curtain at the Manhattan rose on the lodgings in the Rue de Clichy. Kleschna, the professional thief, was blacking his boots; Schram, his doglike helper, was repairing the cage of his beloved canaries; and in the adjoining room Kleschna's daughter, Leah, was trying to beautify herself—inspired by the photograph of the unknown hero who had recently saved her life.

It was the first time an American audience had seen Charles Cartwright, the famous English stage villain, and novelty was added to his superb acting as Kleschna. Mack's Schram was as perfect in its way; and as Leah, Mrs. Fiske appeared in a new kind of role, with her usual mannerisms gone and all her speeches clear and telling. Externally she was the skilled thief, untroubled by her safe-cracking assignment—but under her professional manner was the ferment started by the photograph of the stranger who had saved her life; it shone through with subtle and telling transparency.

If England had a more accomplished stage villain than Cartwright it was George Arliss, and he was waiting in the wings. Presently he appeared as Raoul, in pursuit of Leah, and the cross-purposes of the scene revealed four great actors in teamwork in which the play was the star.

When Leah agreed to a rendezvous which she did not intend to keep, and went out, John Mason entered as Paul Sylvaine, the intended victim of the burglary, and it was revealed that he was Leah's unknown rescuer and idol.

As Deputy Sylvaine Mason was giving the finest performance in his career. Combined with the work of four other great actors it was a memorable experience for theatregoers. The first-act curtain fell on the most perfect stage work the audience had ever seen, leaving them stunned by its magnificent completeness. The general sentiment was expressed by Horace Traubel, who had come from Philadelphia for the opening. When the ovation had finally died down and his companion asked him what he thought of the first act, Traubel said, "It's so perfect in every way that a defect or two might help. Seeing such work shocks me. The shock is a pleasant one. I'd like to have it repeated, but it is a shock."

In the second act the play reached a tense climax: Leah, standing at the safe, jewels in hand, was surprised by Paul Sylvaine and recognized him as her idol.

In the scene which followed, Mason's superb acting carried Sylvaine's preachments about crime and reform; and Mrs. Fiske gave a stirring portrayal of the dark soul of the criminal, lit by lightning flashes of ideals and conscience. The scene was interrupted by the intrusion of Arliss as the intoxicated Raoul, who threatened to create a scandal for Sylvaine, and it brought forth Leah's most telling line: "Here we are—three of us—a gentleman, a thief, and a blackguard. I'm the thief."

For two more breathless acts the acting and the play held the audience as Leah was saved from prison for the theft of the jewels which Raoul had finally stolen, and as she engaged in a desperate battle of courage and wits to free herself from her criminal associates.

After the play had run the gamut of suspense, thrills and soul-searching, the scene changed to a quiet epilogue in the market gardens of Neustadt, where Leah had returned to the peasant life of her mother. And here Sylvaine arrived to claim the reformed girl thief for his bride.

Not since *Tess of the D'Urbervilles* had a play so taken New York by storm, or created an illusion that persisted long after the final curtain. The critics were still under its spell when they wrote about it next day. After unanimously agreeing that Leah Kleschna was the triumph of the season and one of the finest productions in the memory of critics, they variously discovered that the play was a profound study in criminology, that McLellan was one of the great American playwrights; and two critics advanced the theory that *Leah* must have been adapted from a German or Scandinavian original because it was too great to have been written by an American! And the usually astute John Corbin of the *Sun* declared that the play had the simple and inevitable statement of character of Ibsen and the spiritual insight and moral propaganda of Tolstoi.

The reception of *Leah Kleschna* was a unique case of the mass hypnotism of critics by an inspired producer and an inspired cast of great actors. By the time the critics wrote their articles for the Sunday editions most of them had discovered that *Leah* was a melodrama whose meaning, if any, was confused. Alan Dale called it "Mrs. Fiske's dime-novel play," and John Corbin retracted most of his enthusiastic comparison with Ibsen and Tolstoi. They and other great writers, he observed, wrote of their own country and people. Mr. McLellan placed his story on the Continent, where improbable things seemed more plausible to Americans. And why, he asked, did the play have to deal with foreign criminals? What was the matter with American criminals? Were they not good enough for Americans?

The inevitable devaluation of the play detracted nothing from the production. It remained the most spectacular success of the theatre season, and for half a year it packed the Manhattan with enthusiastic audiences.

Soon after the fabulous *Leah* premiere, Harry Fiske returned to his office at the Manhattan Theatre. Illness had reduced him to a ninety-pound shadow of his former portly self, but his enthusiasms were beginning to kindle again.

While *Leah Kleschna* was in rehearsal, Minnie had asked Mr. Mc-Lellan for a month's option on the English rights of the play. Grateful for all that Mrs. Fiske had done for him, McLellan had said that she could have a year's option. The Fiskes now agreed it was time to arrange for Minnie's long-planned appearance on the English stage. They cabled McLellan that they were taking up their option, and they announced in the United States and England that Mrs. Fiske would take *Leah* to London.

After the announcement had been made, the Fiskes were jolted by McLellan's high-handed demand that they bring the play to England in the spring—which meant canceling engagements at home and throwing away most of the expected American profits. As the cables became more heated, Harry brought up—and McLellan denied—Mrs. Fiske's virtual collaboration on the play. Shortly afterward, they were informed that Mr. McLellan had sold the English rights to Charles Frohman.

In the shock of McLellan's ingratitude, Minnie decided that she would never appear on any stage but an American one—a resolve which she kept. Harry, with his valet, sailed for Europe to recuperate. Minnie, with one less dream, went on with *Leah Kleschna*, a success with an unpleasant aftertaste.

Near the end of the season there was a crisis with no opportunity for compromise. Minnie had been able to survive in the Eastern states by playing the second- and third-class Stair and Havlin theatres. Mr. Griffith now brought the news that the Trust had forced Stair and Havlin to bar her from their field by threatening to invade it.

"You're handcuffed, wired down, fenced in," he told her. "What are you going to do now?"

Minnie answered, "I am going to California for a vacation."

It was not a solution, but a necessity. Emily habitually felt that her more enduring cousin expected too much of her, and after the tensions and disappointments of the season she was barely speaking to Co'Min. If they became estranged Minnie would lose half her reason for being.

CHAPTER 21

Mrs. Fiske returned to the September heat of New York in robust health for her fall season—a season that had been made possible by the Trust's too-strenuous efforts to annihilate her. Concentrating on independent actors, the partners had ignored the efforts of the Shuberts to establish themselves—and the brothers had suddenly loomed up big, with newly-acquired theatres scattered over half the United States.

On a smaller scale, David Belasco repeated the pattern with theatres in New York, Washington and Pittsburgh. Minnie who had been forced out of the burlesque and vaudeville houses, suddenly had a score of first-class theatres open to her.

The sprawling hold of the Shuberts was precarious, and they had to count heavily on Mrs. Fiske's drawing power—but the theatres were there—a challenge to the Syndicate, and a different kind of challenge to the actress-manager.

While the Manhattan Company toured the East, the Manhattan Theatre would be kept open with productions Harry Fiske had in preparation. The season was to begin with a new comedy, *Mary and John,* followed by *Monna Vanna,* with Bertha Kalich, whom Harry was about to star.

The year before, the Fiskes had discovered Madame Kalich at the Yiddish Art Theatre on the Bowery—a woman of classical beauty with a magnificent voice and twenty years of experience in the Jewish theatres of Europe and New York. On short notice she could play any of a hundred and fifty roles, including the entire repertories of Duse and Bernhardt.

The Fiskes saw *Monna Vanna* as an important production—the first Maeterlinck play in America, and the Yiddish tragedienne's debut on the English-speaking stage.

With *Monna Vanna* and Minnie's tour more than a month away,

Harry presented *Mary and John,* which he expected to hit the popular taste. He had strengthened its special cast with John Mason and William Mack, borrowed from Minnie's company, and for a summer shower in the comedy he used the great storm machine left over from *Magdala.*

On the premiere evening of September 11, the hot weather broke with a violent thunderstorm that sent playgoers wading to the entrance of the Manhattan. The comedy was a weak, polite affair that the best actors could not save; its only excitement was a mimic storm, and the audience, with wet feet, was not amused.

Mary and John lingered for two unprofitable weeks—then Minnie jumped into the breach with *Leah Kleschna,* and the Manhattan was full to the doors again. At the end of three capacity weeks, the Manhattan Company boarded a special car and left on its eastern tour.

Since the season before, there had been only one change in the cast of *Leah.* Charles Cartwright had returned to England and Kleschna was played by Frederic de Belleville, who had spent loyal years in Mrs. Fiske's companies.

While *Leah Kleschna* filled the Lyric Theatre in Philadelphia for two weeks, Minnie led a quiet life off stage. She lived in the railway car and took long walks, veiled and alone, and sometimes she brought in food to prepare on board. One of her favorite concoctions was onions soaked overnight in milk—an invention of which she was very proud.

For the first time in eight years Minnie played in a real theatre in Pittsburgh. On October 30 *Leah* opened at the Belasco to an audience that filled all the standing room in the auditorium and extended into the foyer.

The review columns next day were almost as crowded with praise for the play—and for the little redheaded actress who gave the best opportunities to her fellow actors, and shone "not as a star, but in the greater light of a glowing production."

In Cincinnati *Leah* was presented at Robinson's Opera House—an ancient barn flitting with early memories. Even the star's dressing room which Minnie occupied was familiar with the intensity of a childhood impression. Her mother had once led her into that dressing room, into the presence of a young woman who had all the blonde beauty of a German fairy tale. The beautiful young woman looked Minnie over, decided she was "just the child," and explained the business of the play for which she had just been engaged. Then she took Minnie on her lap, and told her that she was a little red sunbeam who would some day be a great actress.

The beautiful star was Mary Anderson; the play, *Guy Mannering;*

and Minnie had been engaged for the role of the child who joined in the simple songs with which the cast enlivened their performance.

The memory of the dressing room was so vivid that Minnie told her manager of that early experience. In her nine years of association with Mr. Griffith it was her first mention of the "prehistoric past."

Cincinnati was woven thick with other memories. One afternoon Minnie invited a group of old friends to her hotel. A girl reporter found the girls of an earlier generation sitting all over the floor and on the bed where Minnie was resting. At the moment they were discussing events of old days at Madame Nesmith's School.

The reporter, on her way to a reception, was gotten up like Mrs. Astor's pet horse, and she felt called on to apologize for her clothes.

Minnie observed that she would prefer a life term in the penitentiary to a life in society; in the penitentiary, at least, she could catch up on her reading and thinking.

"Tell me," she said, "one worth-while thing you get out of society."

When the reporter could not think of one, Minnie asked, "Who ever heard of anyone saying anything at a reception that was worth remembering? Who ever got to know anyone better in that sort of abominable crush?"

The reporter presently tried to reestablish herself as the interviewer by asking the "girls" if they had ever thought when they were little that Minnie Maddern would become famous.

Minnie ruined the attempt with a burst of laughter, and a punch at the pillow under her head.

"These people have no opinion of what you describe as my 'greatness,' and they never at school treated me with a particle of respect!"

The girls then went back to discussing the algebra which they had suffered over when they were young. Minnie explained, "You know my education came by 'littles,' like Abraham Lincoln's."

In Boston, a few weeks later, the education which had come by "littles" was put to a strenuous test.

At one time or another during every engagement Mrs. Fiske had played in Boston, she had been greeted by a sad-faced gentleman who revealed a wide and scholarly knowledge of the theatre. He never discussed her acting, but his presence suggested that he found some value in it; and the meetings and talks ripened into an enduring friendship. The gentleman was Charles T. Copeland, lecturer on English literature at Harvard; a beloved schoolman known to countless Harvard men as "Copey."

At last, during Minnie's engagement in *Leah Kleschna*, she received indirect but unmistakable proof that the schoolman valued her work. It came in the form of a letter from Professor Copeland; in the name of the Harvard Ethical Society she was invited to deliver an address at Sanders Theatre, Harvard. Distinguished actors had spoken there, from Joseph Jefferson to Herbert Tree, but Mrs. Fiske was the second woman to be invited; the other was Eleonora Duse.

Her first reaction was incredulity, mixed with stage fright. The moment of panic passed when Minnie discovered that she had things to say, and she began preparing her speech. But there were minor details which loomed large to a woman who had never finished high school—or addressed the faculty and students of Harvard.

Years afterward, Henry M. Rideout gave Minnie the obverse picture of how one detail had been settled. He was in Copey's rooms when the telephone rang. Copey, slow and melancholy of mien, answered:

"How do you do, Mrs. Fiske?"

For five minutes Copey listened in silence to a sound from the telephone like the continuous play of distant lightning. At last Copey spoke:

"Eleonora Duse *sat*. Good-bye, Mrs. Fiske."

Minnie, too, sat as she delivered her hour-long talk.

Sanders Theatre was packed with faculty and students of Harvard and Radcliffe, and invited guests. Professor Copeland introduced Mrs. Fiske briefly. Her subject, he said, was "The Ethics of the Drama," on which she was qualified to speak. Mrs. Fiske was doing her best to free and elevate the stage; a student of the ethics of the drama; "one whom the trusts have interfered with but have not hindered."

Mrs. Fiske acknowledged the introduction with a few words on the stimulating effect of speaking in public. It was the first time, she said, that Mr. Copeland had ever paid her a compliment.

She began her talk by questioning the usefulness of art—and she answered with a quoted statement that the arts are man's successive attempts to express his highest ideals. As for the validity of men devoting themselves to art in a world where there was so much horror and injustice and suffering, she found that novelists like Tolstoi and Zola were chopping at the roots of those evils. The late Russian painter, Vereshchagin, had devoted his art to showing the inhumanity and terrors of war—and died in battle with his paintbrush in his hand.

In behalf of "our little brothers," the animals, Mrs. Fiske struck out at bullfighters in Spain and hunters at home. She found that the artist in any field was rarely a huntsman. And she was proud of her friendship with a great artist who went about, cold, in winter; he said he would never wear an overcoat until every man in the world who needed one was supplied.

From the ethics of the artist, Mrs. Fiske went on to the ethics of the audience. The theatre, she said, must count on intelligent playgoers to keep it within the bounds of sanity. She believed in no other censorship of the stage. . . .

Mrs. Fiske sketched the emergence and the nature of the modern drama, and its ethical position:

> Today we live in a practical age, and the spirit of the times is prone to question and analyze. From great general principles the drama is coming down to specific incidents in life, and there are rising masters of the craft who can make the details of existence, even the homely or sinister details, suggestive and instructive. From grand reaches and highly colored and heroic figures, we have been brought to the basis of everyday problems. . . I confess that my own interest is more definitely enlisted by the modern drama. . .

The actress noted the decline of violence on the stage, and she sounded the keynote of her suppressed, realistic acting and her own disciplined life:

> Have not many of our fiercest inward battles been fought quietly in our own solitary room at night? Have not the most dramatic moments of our lives been lived out in silence and secrecy? There may be no cries, no outbursts, no noise, but the great moments have been lived just the same.

Returning to the subject of immorality, Mrs. Fiske said of the "star" play:

> It debases the talent of the dramatist and subordinates all other personalities to the one purpose. It is a prostitution of dramatic art. . .

In Mrs. Fiske's view, Ibsen had done much for the actor as a thinking, creative artist.

> For example, take the plays *Rosmersholm*, *John Gabriel Borkman* and *Hedda Gabler*. In these plays we see the final moments in the lives of the principal characters. The whole mighty drama of *Rosmersholm* has been enacted before the curtain rises on the first act of the play. The actor must of necessity have studied all that has, in the past lives of the characters, led up to the final scene. . .

Mrs. Fiske spoke of the ideal play, ideally performed, and she ended:

I do not know where in the theatre this ideal may be found today, but I believe that if the public sets its standards high, something like the ideal may some day be evolved.

The audience that gave Mrs. Fiske its undivided attention and prolonged applause included Professor Baker of the Harvard Workshop course, William James, Dean Briggs, and E. H. Sothern and Julia Marlowe. It also included Mary Maddern, who had mothered Minnie's mother, and put Minnie to bed of nights. Aunt Mary shook her head over the unaccountable fact of genius.

"I declare, I don't know how you do it," she said. "There was nothing they taught you in those little convent schools that taught you to teach Harvard!"

On Christmas night, the Manhattan Company opened at the new Belasco Theatre in Washington, D. C. There *Leah* was saluted by the *Times* as the best play of the season, and the best production seen in Washington in many years.

At Harvard, Aunt Mary had been unable to trace the steps by which a scantily-educated girl had become the intellectual leader of the American stage. In Washington, the *Post* took the fact for granted:

Mrs. Fiske deserves this position because of her art and because she was the originator of the independent movement which has recently achieved all for which it has so long struggled.

Mrs. Fiske might be called the Jeanne d'Arc of the opposition to the theatrical trust, for she has suffered all sorts of privations, was deserted by her theatrical and business associates, one after another, and had she been sent to the stake in behalf of the cause there is no doubt that she would have gone without complaint. . .

The parallel between the maids of Orléans and New Orleans was inevitable. But the *Post* was mistaken in believing that the war of liberation was over. The Belasco Theatre in Washington represented one successful skirmish; there had been another nearer home.

In Brooklyn, on New Year's evening, the Manhattan Company began an engagement at the old Park Theatre, renamed the Shubert, with the "Welcome" sign out for independent companies.

The Brooklyn engagement reunited the Fiskes and let them take stock of their busy lives. *Leah* had triumphed everywhere; and Bertha Kalich had played a seven weeks' engagement at the Manhattan. She was now on tour, winning artistic recognition and losing only a mod-

162

erate amount of money for the Fiskes. Minnie, who had no artistic jealousy, was an advance agent for Mme. Kalich, praising her to managers and interviewers.

Certainly the year 1905 had been a great year for the Fiskes' partnership—and at the end of that year they decided to give up the Manhattan Theatre. Their lease would expire in April, and the building was to be torn down to make room for the New Hudson Tubes. Harry had planned a splendid new Manhattan Theatre farther uptown, but Minnie decided against it. The cost of the Manhattan had been high, and with the Shuberts and Belasco in the independent ranks, it was no longer needed. The theatre would have to go, but the Manhattan Company would remain intact.

From Brooklyn *Leah* was taken to Providence, where the Shuberts had refurbished the old Empire Theatre; Minnie was to inaugurate it as an independent playhouse.

Providence had never seen the twentieth-century Mrs. Fiske; the last they had seen of Minnie Maddern was in *Featherbrain*.

For the Rhode Island capital, *Leah Kleschna* was a double drama: the play of the year, and the triumphal entry of the theatre's Joan of Arc.

To the double drama, the weather added the melodrama of a blizzard that began early in the evening of January 8 and made the occasion memorable for the fourteen hundred who faced the storm.

The management went as far as it could to meet them, with a covered way through the snow from the curb to the entrance of the theatre. The covered way was flanked with American flags, and more flags decorated the walls and ceiling of the foyer—the manager's announcement that the theatre of Providence again belonged to the land of the free.

During the snowy week of celebration, Minnie took her company on a dash to Boston for a matinee performance of *Hedda* which represented another kind of triumph. Twelve years after she had first championed the unpopular Ibsen, Boston critics still resisted his plays—but there was a new generation of playgoers. Every seat in the Tremont was occupied; all standing room was sold; the orchestra was given the afternoon off, and their chairs were occupied by spectators, and *Hedda* was performed before the largest audience that had ever occupied the famous theatre.

A week later, in Montreal, *Leah Kleschna* was presented at the rickety and cavernous old Monument National, which Emily Stevens

163

nicknamed "Mausoleum National." The Montreal *Herald* observed of the event and of the Trust that had consigned the city to the theatrical backwaters:

> It is perhaps no great praise to say that a play is the best that has been sent us by any English-speaking writer in the past six years. We in Montreal have not seen the great plays of the period. We are indebted to the "independent" association of producers for giving us at a considerable risk, under great difficulties, and in an unsuitable theatre, the one really important play that has been seen here.

While the Shuberts and Belasco reopened some cities to Mrs. Fiske, others were closed to her through the Trust arrangement with Stair and Havlin. Toledo was lost, but she secured a booking in Findlay, fifty miles to the southeast.

Findlay was the center of an oil boom that was producing barrels of excitement and gallons of oil—but when it was announced that Mrs. Fiske was coming to town, things that Findlay had never dreamed of began to happen. They reached their climax on Thursday evening, with the two hotels and the railroad and interurban lines demoralized, and Findlay swamped with crowds from Toledo, Sandusky, Lima and a score of smaller towns. The crowds packed both sides of the wide and windy main street, with latecomers streaming into town in automobiles, carriages, buggies, farm wagons, and on horseback.

Most of that exciting day Minnie spent in her railroad car reading manuscript plays. In the afternoon she hired a livery rig and went for a drive, heavily veiled and unobserved except for a moment on Main Street. There she saw a shivering puppy limping on three legs, holding up a fourth, which appeared to be broken, its suffering unnoticed by the crowds.

Minnie told the driver to stop, swooped out of the carriage, and returned with the puppy in her arms. She then ordered the driver to head for a veterinarian—and she did not leave until she had seen the broken leg set and splinted.

Early that evening, at the front of the theatre, manager Griffith was visited by a relay of reporters and amateur sleuths, asking about a veiled lady and a kidnapped dog.

Later, behind the scenes, Minnie was confronted by an angry barkeeper, a lawyer, a detective and the sheriff, armed with a search warrant and a second warrant for the arrest of Mrs. Fiske on the charge of kidnaping a dog with the intent of taking it out of the state of Ohio.

164

Faced with jail, Minnie revealed that the puppy was resting comfortably at the vet's, with its bill paid until its owner could be found. The barkeeper became as sentimental as a barbershop ballad. While Messrs. de Belleville and Mack took their places for the first act, he knelt on the greenroom floor, asking forgiveness. Behind his kneeling figure stood the sheriff, detective and lawyer, moist-eyed, with hats in hand.

So the little drama ended as the curtain rose on the main event, in which Minnie won the hearts of a larger audience.

A month later, when the Findlay affair was becoming a legend, the Toledo *Blade* relived that glorious day:

> The crossroads for miles around advertised the great event, the trolley lines did a land office business, and the hotel clerks were swamped by an avalanche of telegrams from out-of-town people who, perhaps, had not known where Findlay was until the actress announced her intention of playing there . . . every city man or woman who had a friend or poor relation in Findlay waxed affectionate and paid him a visit on *Leah* day, which, by the way, turned out to be as big an occasion as circus day, Labor Day, Decoration Day, or the Fourth of July.

From starring at Findlay's crossroads, Minnie went on to Cleveland, where she played against the competition of Richard Mansfield. At the end of the week the Cleveland press voted it the most important in the city's history, and both theatres had broken their previous box-office records.

Dayton was closed to Mrs. Fiske, and the nearest available theatre was in Piqua—thirty-five miles to the north. The only one of the company who had ever seen Piqua was Minnie, who had played there in girlhood; she had favorable memories of the quiet little town on the Miami River.

When it was announced that the Manhattan Company would play at Piqua, Mr. May of the Opera House found himself in the big time. Orders for tickets to *Leah* poured in from surrounding towns until the Piqua *Call*, looking over Mr. May's shoulder, proclaimed that Dayton, Lima, Urbana, Greenville and Union City had become suburbs of Piqua.

Minnie arrived with her company to find the little town in a gold-rush excitement. One man had come all the way from Mississippi for the performance, and another had come from Mexico, giving Piqua international recognition; Mr. May was selling standing room and telegraphing the managers of Sarah Bernhardt and Mrs. Leslie Carter, offering them bookings—and the golden multitudes poured into town with every train. And old-timers were pointing out the post office, the former site of Conover's Opera House, where Minnie Maddern had played in *Caprice*.

Outside the turmoil, Minnie spent most of the day in her car on the Panhandle tracks; and in the afternoon she walked beside the river, out of hearing of the town's uproar.

That evening the Manhattan Company played before an audience more than twice the size of any that had ever gathered there previously. And the elated proprietor showered the crowd with hundreds of boxes of chocolates, and a thousand card-cases with a photograph of the Opera House on one side and a photograph of himself on the other.

From Piqua's circus day, the company was rushed to Columbus for a matinee and evening performance on Washington's Birthday. The event brought the press close to poetry, and the *State Journal* declared that the ecstasy would have been too complete without the exultation of a holiday.

No other actress had made such a tour, breaking records in cities and barnstorming at crossroads; fighting for survival with one hand, and the freedom of the theatre with the other.

With relentless self-discipline, Minnie played down the excitement of her tour by day and battled insomnia by night. When her mind began to race, she would control it by reading or studying; forgotten details and clear thoughts came to her in the late hours; she wrote them down on the scratch pad beside her, and pinned the memoranda to her nightgown.

At Columbus the little Maddern clan took a hotel suite, where old Aunt Mary and young Emily slept like the dead after the triumphal performance of *Leah*. Minnie was awake all night, with cities and towns and theatres bearing down on her out of the future and repeated with the endless procession of the years.

When Minnie had returned to the stage as a young woman, she thought she knew the conditions and she considered that her decision was final. Actually, she had not known how strenuous her career would be—and she had just realized how irrevocable *irrevocable* is. In her youth she had decided her future, and the decision had been granted its final decree.

In the next room Aunt Mary turned, muttering in her sleep; a trouper who had been touring America for sixty years, childless and homeless on the unending road. . . .

Resolutely, Minnie cleared her mind with reading and making notes. Still too terribly awake, she tried the bread and milk which Ellen Terry had recommended. Presently she covered her eyes from the early daylight, and lay down at last. Blessings on Ellen, and on sleep. . . .

The winter sun shone in on her, like a futuristic painter's dream: a little redheaded woman, with a black velvet mask over her eyes, sleeping, exhausted, on a big hotel bed, with scrawled messages pinned to the front of her flannel nightgown: *Buy two yards of blue veiling. Send Harry the check. Ask Mr. Griffith to put your age on the program. The nemesis of the adult is the youth that was himself. Ask Emily about her overuse of "the psychological moment." When is Janet's birthday? If society women want to do something useful, let them have children and live without an everlasting heartbreak.*

CHAPTER 22

In Columbus, at the height of a brilliant tour, Minnie had lost her zest for the life to which she was committed. But when she brought her company home after six months on the road, she was the only one who admitted to no fatigue—and she immediately plunged into her supplementary season.

With the Manhattan Theatre occupied by *Charlie's Aunt*, Minnie presented *Leah* at the Academy of Music, and rehearsed the company for a revival of *Becky Sharp*.

A dozen members of *Becky* casts were in the company, but a suitable Dobbin seemed unobtainable. Finally, when Minnie was hurrying in for a rehearsal, a stranger at the stage door raised his hat and said, "Mrs. Fiske, I understand you are looking for someone to play Dobbin."

She looked the actor over from head to foot—and suddenly clapped her hand on his arm and dragged him onto the stage without asking his name. The man, Corry Thomas, turned out to be the perfect Dobbin.

In her spare time Minnie worked with her husband on a daring tour for the following year. Harry was particularly elated by events: Minnie's triumphal second season in *Leah;* the artistic success of Bertha Kalich's tour, and the opening of the Shubert theatres. The fight against the Theatrical Trust had become fashionable; Sarah Bernhardt was touring the South as an independent, playing in a circus tent.

Minnie's plans for the fall season were building on a new comedy by Langdon Mitchell, and Mme. Kalich's on his adaptation of *The Kreutzer Sonata*.

In part, *Becky Sharp* had been revived to keep Mitchell's name fresh in the public mind. But the little adventuress needed no excuses. Becky was not revived; she was turned loose, and she packed the old Academy for the remainder of the New York engagement.

Under the skin of the buoyant and tireless Becky, Mrs. Fiske was tired to death and counting the days to the end of her season. For the summer she had rented a house in San Francisco, and for the first time in the sixteen years of their marriage, she and Harry were to have an extended vacation together. And they were to have it in San Francisco, which she loved and he had never seen.

On the morning of April 19, 1906, with vacation less than three weeks away, Mrs. Fiske was awakened by the shouting of newsboys who had suddenly lost all regard for the dignity of Fifth Avenue and the Brevoort; they were shouting, "Extra, Earthquake! San Francisco destroyed!"

While Mrs. Fiske was dressing, Emily Stevens dashed in with a newspaper. San Francisco had been leveled by an earthquake; the ruins, with hundreds of dead, were being swept by fire, and half a million citizens were in flight from the wrecked and burning city.

San Francisco had gone like a dream while Mrs. Fiske slept, and whatever replaced it would be something different—almost certainly nearer her ingrained ideas of propriety—and farther away from the carefree, pagan city which she had loved.

With the smoke of destruction hanging over the place where she had planned to rest, Minnie went on to the thirty-second and last week of her strenuous season. *Becky* opened in Brooklyn, with her buoyant and glittering comedy unabated.

Becky Sharp, which always seemed too short to the audience, was a long and exhausting play that ended after eleven-thirty, and it was only part of Mrs. Fiske's work. Three times during the week, she gave a special matinee at the Manhattan Theatre. The matinee consisted of her own *The Eyes of the Heart* and *A Light from St. Agnes*, and John Luther Long's one-act *Dolce*, a charming Cinderella bit she had played a few times on the road.

At the first special matinee, *Dolce* was performed before an audience that was almost entirely feminine, with a few notable exceptions. In one of the boxes, Mrs. Fiske saw the slight, gentlemanly figure of the author of *Madame Butterfly* and *Dolce*, and in his favorite seat back of Critics' Row, the bushy, snow-white head and the white suit of Mark Twain, who often attended her performances and greeted her as a friend—the young playwright applauding his own play, or the acting of it, and the old author making use of his handkerchief during moments of pathos.

The critics were there in full force, and they gave the matinee notices that were quoted all over America, the *Globe* declaring that it was a green oasis in the sterile desert of other New York attractions. Mrs. Fiske could not even mark time at the end of her season without making news.

The last special matinee was played on April 28 for a charity benefit. It was Mrs. Fiske's farewell to the Manhattan Theatre, which had brought together the greatest theatrical company of a generation and turned the tide against the Syndicate.

The Manhattan had served its purpose, and Mrs. Fiske was not overly-sentimental about giving it up. Only she and Harry knew what it had taken to keep the theatre open—and only she sensed the full significance of the cost.

Becky closed in Brooklyn on the same day as the last performance at the Manhattan, but Minnie was not quite through with stage appearances for the season. A few days later, instead of being in San Francisco as she had planned, she stood on the stage of the Metropolitan Opera House and read the requiem of the gay city, "San Francisco Desolate," written by Edwin Markham, and sent to her two days earlier. The occasion was a benefit performance that brought in a small fortune for the sufferers of the San Francisco disaster.

It was not the way Minnie had expected to show her affection for the city, but disaster did not change her plans; soon after, she and Emily boarded a train for California.

The Fiskes had planned to go together, and to have Mme. Kalich and her daughter Lillian as their guests for the summer. But Lillian was still in school, and Harry waited to accompany mother and daughter across the continent.

Ashton Stevens had rented a house in the Sierras for Minnie and Emily, and arranged to pool his vacation with the first two weeks of theirs. He described Minnie as she arrived, after the luxury of a transcontinental trip unbroken by one-night stands in makeshift theatres:

> Somehow she looked absurdly young that day; she was positively girlish in the slim lines of her simple black frock, in the freshness of her face against that thatch of uncompromisingly red hair. She seemed more like the Minnie Maddern of other days than the Mrs. Fiske of these. Laughter came from the depths of her eyes. . .

The young critic was in less blooming health, worn down by illness and six weeks of hectic days and nights in a wrecked city. Vacation hadn't arrived a day too soon, Mrs. Fiske said, but Ashton Stevens explained that he had one more interview ahead.

"With whom?" Mrs. Fiske asked. "And about what?"

"With you," he told her, "about Ibsen."

"Who am I?" she asked. "And what has Ibsen done to take your time when you should be asleep in a hammock under the trees?"

"You are Ibsen's keenest and most artistic interpreter, and Ibsen died yesterday at Christiania."

Mrs. Fiske had not opened a newspaper on the train, and the Master's death was news to her—but she felt no more grief than she did over the fact that there wasn't a sixth act to *Hamlet*.

She hated interviews, but this one was all that stood between a haggard young critic and rest. "If you must, I must."

She sat in a rustic chair in the living room, tapping the bare floor with one small foot while she answered questions. Ashton Stevens, who had been on his feet so many weeks that he could not rest, stood at the mantelpiece. He began asking Mrs. Fiske what the death of Ibsen would mean.

"Ibsen was one of those rare beings who live long enough and work long enough to walk the final steps side by side with their posterity. So it isn't so much what his death means as what his life means."

"And that?"

"Ibsen's life meant the revolution of the dramatic literature of every country. Think of all the honors that have been paid him by the dramatists of the world in their change of style, workmanship, even theme! Think how he enlarged the scope of every playwright, those that heretofore had literally been limited to the themes of love, jealousy, infidelity! In the bulk of Ibsen's work not one of those themes is used. He struck out, alone, for himself, found virgin forests and blazed new paths. . ."

At the mantelpiece, jotting furiously, Stevens said, "Go slower and, with your gift for dictation, I can take it down in longhand."

Minnie slowed her words to the speed of the pencil, and the critic smiled grim approval as he wrote on and on—his smile changed to a puzzled look; then his face went blank, and he slipped to the floor and lay still.

Emily came running at Minnie's call. Together, they got the unconscious interviewer to bed, and Minnie called the doctor.

When Ashton Stevens had slept off the effects of earthquake and fire, and regained full consciousness, he sat up in bed and asked, "What day is it?"

"Monday afternoon," Minnie told him.

Stevens groaned. "My God, our interview is two days late for the paper!"

Minnie laughed and handed him the Sunday *Examiner*, open to a special article:

MRS. FISKE TALKS OF IBSEN'S DEATH
To
ASHTON STEVENS

The interview was there, with what he had asked and would have asked, and what she had answered, and would have answered. Somewhere in the middle of it, he had gone out like a light—and Mrs. Fiske, who hated interviews, had finished it herself and telegraphed it to his paper. And she had kept it so perfectly in character that Ashton Stevens was never able to determine where his writing left off and hers began.

When Harry Fiske and the Kaliches arrived, Minnie welcomed them to a comfortable old-fashioned house she had rented in Oakland. Harry, with both his stars under one roof, made glowing plans for the season ahead, and Oakland Madderns gave the house the feelings of home. A frequent and favored visitor was Minnie's young second cousin Merle Maddern—a tall, graceful, dark-eyed girl with signs of the Maddern stage ability.

Another visitor was Bessie Maddern London. Transportation was difficult in the Bay area, but the resourceful Bessie contrived to rent a big touring car, and she devotedly drove the Fiskes' party about the country and through San Francisco streets which had been cleared of fallen masonry and twisted car tracks.

Harry Fiske, the confirmed New Yorker, found California uncomfortable. Wherever Bessie drove, clouds of dust rose along the unpaved roads, and what was left of San Francisco was miserably cold under the sea fogs of July. Oakland was less troubled by fog, but the heat of the day was turned off with the sun. His idea of a vacation included sitting out on a porch, and not indoors by a fire.

The Kaliches, too, were disappointed. They had heard San Francisco described as the Paris of America—and they could not visualize Paris in the ragged fringe of city which had survived, or in blackened ruins wrapped in fog.

For Minnie, California was matched only by the happiness of being there with her family around her. To her, San Francisco was still an enchanted city.

At the end of summer, Harry Fiske and his stars returned to New York to rehearse their productions, *The New York Idea* for Minnie, and *The Kreutzer Sonata* for Bertha Kalich.

The New York Idea was a satire on easy divorce—a subject made timely by the unprecedented number of divorces in the upper and lower brackets of society, with only the solid middle class resisting the oats of twentieth-century freedom.

The most powerful advance agent of Langdon Mitchell's play was President Theodore Roosevelt, whose ambitions for the American empire called for a large population. From the White House he was blasting at divorce and "race suicide," and calling on the American people to be fruitful and multiply; to "get the habit, be a rabbit."

England, too, had a stake in the upper-crust American scene, where marriage had become a plaything. The London *Fortnightly Review* had just published an ominous article with statistics showing that an American heiress was not worth an Englishman's title, which would bring more in Austria-Hungary. A hundred Austrian heiresses had borne their English husbands three hundred and fifty children, and in the same period a hundred American heiresses had borne their husbands only fifty-nine.

It had taken Langdon Mitchell seven years to toss off a new play for Mrs. Fiske—and it was so casual and sparkling that he was credited with having written it over a few weekends. Mrs. Fiske's only injunction to the playwright had been not to make it a star play. As a result, there were half a dozen roles of almost equal value, and they were filled with the best actors who could be found for the parts: John Mason, Mrs. Fiske, Charles Harbury, Dorothy Dorr, George Arliss and Dudley Clinton. The remaining roles were filled by William B. Mack, Dudley Digges, George Harcourt, Emily Stevens, Blanche Weaver and Ida Vernon—all stars by ordinary reckoning.

Mitchell's satire applied to every American city of wealth and "society," but the title tied it to New York, with an obvious hazard: if New York repudiated *The New York Idea*, it was not likely to go anywhere else. Accordingly, it was tried out in Milwaukee, where *Mary of Magdala* had had its successful premiere four years earlier.

The New York Idea opened at the crowded Shubert Theatre on October 9, 1906, and for four acts the audience, reflecting the play, scintillated with spontaneous laughter. While the performance was still going on, correspondents slipped away, reluctantly, to wire out-of-town papers that Mrs. Fiske had one of the most brilliant hits of her career. They would only have known how brilliant if they had observed the request on the program for spectators to remain seated until the final curtain. Each successive act topped the preceding one, and the play reached its surprise climax in the closing moments of the last act, when John and Cynthia Karslake discovered that they were still technically married—and in love.

In the ovation which followed, there were insistent and prolonged calls of "Author!" and Mrs. Fiske led the slight, nearsighted Langdon Mitchell onto the stage. Together they took six curtain calls, but the author of the wittiest play of the year was too diffident to speak. Mrs. Fiske then broke her lifelong rule against curtain speeches, and thanked the audience in Mr. Mitchell's behalf. The ovation continued, and for the first time in their association, Mrs. Fiske led her husband before the audience, where he made his most courtly bow but declined to speak.

Later, in a *New York Times* interview, Harry Fiske explained:

> Mrs. Fiske, so far as I know, is the only noted American actress who may truly be said to direct and supervise the plays in which she appears. She will doubtless tell you that I was myself mainly responsible for putting on *The New York Idea*, and I admit that this is the first instance in which I have perhaps borne the brunt of the labor. But my work, now as heretofore, has always been mainly concerned with the practical duties of preparing a play for the stage— with the arrangement of the scenery, the preparation of the prompt-book, the obtaining of the 'effects,' and similar details. Mrs. Fiske's work, on the contrary, has been essentially the psychological analysis and the rehearsal of the actors.

The New York Idea was lavishly staged, with Louis XV furniture, rare paintings, and silk fabrics so delicate that stagehands were not allowed to touch them without first donning fresh white gloves. And Minnie was to take that costly elegance on one of the roughest barnstorming tours since Joseph Jefferson followed the American Army into Mexico.

A week after the Milwaukee opening, *The New York Idea* was presented at the Chicago Grand Opera House before a small and doubting audience.

Chicagoans had packed the Opera House for *Hedda Gabler* and other plays of limited popularity, but the Milwaukee triumph of the new play left them cold. They sensed that the comedy was unworthy of their idol, and they did not want her to be in anything but the best.

The house was distressing to business manager Griffith, but the company was disciplined to play as if the stage had four walls instead of three, and to work for a perfect performance whether there were two people or two thousand in the audience.

It was *The New York Idea's* first bow before a metropolitan audience, but for once Mrs. Fiske was clear of her first-night jinx, and the Manhattan Company gave what even she considered a good performance. After the fall of the various act curtains, she kissed the foreheads of John Mason, George Arliss and Charles Harbury, saying, "You played beautifully tonight!"

On the other side of the imaginary fourth wall, the audience thawed quickly in what Amy Leslie called "the sun of Mrs. Fiske's great art," and was lost in enchantment. At the end of the first act, the critic James O'Donnell Bennett asked a seasoned and cynical theatre manager what he thought of it. The answer was: "This is the kind of thing that makes you proud of our stage!"

It was a sentiment that re-echoed through all the Chicago reviews.

The second performance filled every seat in the Opera House; the engagement went on to surpass all of Mrs. Fiske's records in Chicago, and the press devoted more space to her and *The New York Idea* than it had to any other actor and play in ten years.

The success of *The New York Idea* grew like a snowball, but as always Mrs. Fiske worked as strenuously as if the play were wavering on the brink of failure.

At Kansas City the morning after the great opening night, a reporter from the *Times* dropped in at the Shubert Theatre, where a squad of ushers was being drilled by a young woman in a short pink skirt, plaid reefer jacket and a scarlet tam-o'-shanter.

By stretching his imagination, the reporter recognized the schoolgirl figure as Mrs. Fiske, and he asked, "Isn't this rather unusual?"

She flashed a brilliant, elusive smile from her eyes. "It might be—for others, but I find that I can neglect nothing. I have to give much thought to the details of establishing the correct relationship between the stage and the auditorium. *En rapport* is the familiar term to express this condition but I detest the word. The American drama should have its own terminology. We shall find the exact word some day. I despair of nothing."

The woman who despaired of nothing in her search for perfection had assembled a cast that was almost, but not quite, perfect. In Dorothy Dorr, she had an example of success breeding failure. Miss Dorr had recently made a tremendous hit as the drunken wanton in Clyde Fitch's

175

The Woman in the Case, and she could not refrain from making her Vida Phillimore a repetition of the character that had won so much applause.

At rehearsals, Mrs. Fiske had several times taken Miss Dorr aside and reminded her that she was in Langdon Mitchell's play, but the actress was under the spell of her audiences and she could not be convinced.

The solution was provided by Langdon Mitchell. He was traveling with the play, accompanied by his beautiful actress wife, Marian Lea. Miss Lea knew her husband's play by heart, and when Miss Dorr left the company at St. Louis, she stepped into the role, playing it with a light, lackadaisical air that brought the satire close to perfection.

Pittsburgh claimed *The New York Idea* for its own, and the smart modern comedy played to full houses against the quaint counter attractions of *Bertha, The Sewing Machine Girl* and *Why Girls Leave Home.*

The New York Idea opened in New York on November 19, at the Shubert's Lyric Theatre. Then, the satire was tuned to concert pitch with an irresistible momentum of success. And the critics found no reason for resisting it; they delighted in the fact that Mrs. Fiske was sparkling in comedy again, in top form. Typically, Acton Davies of the *Evening Sun* recorded:

> It was almost a new Mrs. Fiske who, with her new play, swept into the Lyric last night and struck the target of success right in the bull's eye—a slight Mrs. Fiske with a wonderfully slim and stunning little figure and such an amount of good humor and animal spirits as she has not shown since she first played Cyprienne in Sardou's *Divorçons.*

Langdon Mitchell's play had already been compared favorably with the wittiest of W. S. Gilbert and George Bernard Shaw. It now received more of the same kind of comparison, and the *New York Times* found that its scintillating diamond dust of wit had almost blinded the sight to deep things in the play.

The twentieth century, which had loosened the marriage ties, had brought with it freer discussion of handier-seeming knots. New York journals overhauled "trial marriage"; "marriage on probation," recently advocated by Mrs. Parsons; and George Meredith's proposal that, instead of being for life, marriage should have a time limit, with an option for renewal. More conservatively, the *Times* interviewed Langdon Mitchell, Bishop Greer and Felix Adler on the cause and prevention of divorce. All three of them conceded that marriages were too lightly contracted and too lightly broken, but they disagreed as to the reason.

176

Mrs. Fiske, too, had been asked for words of wisdom but had declined, considering herself more bad example than authority.

An easier conscience would have dismissed her brief early marriage as a fantasy of what she called her "first time on earth"—but Mrs. Fiske's conscience never slept, or forgot. Twenty years after her divorce, she felt responsible for whatever disillusionment she had brought to Legrand White. She continued to keep up her friendship with his family all her life; helped them secure positions, and when Legrand died (in a mental institution about 1900), she insisted on paying his funeral expenses. Only then did she feel that her responsibility toward him had ended.

CHAPTER 23

The New York Idea played in its home city into the third week of January, 1907, when it was taken on tour.

In Boston the play stirred the familiar discussions of marriage and divorce, filling the Majestic Theatre and necessitating extra matinees. In late February it opened in Washington.

The year before, Washington had hailed Mrs. Fiske as the American Joan of Arc; this time the Belasco Theatre was crowded with as brilliant an audience as the capital could have mustered for a military hero. One of the stage boxes was occupied by President and Mrs. Roosevelt, Mrs. Nicholas Longworth, and Senator and Mrs. Lodge; another, by Secretary of War Taft and his family; other boxes and the parquet were filled by cabinet members, ambassadors, senators, congressmen, military men and Washington society.

In the enthusiastic audience the most obviously delighted member was Roosevelt, with approval flashing from his eyeglasses and teeth as he leaned forward in his box, applauding vigorously.

After the performance, manager Griffith relayed to Mrs. Fiske the President's congratulations on the wholesome message of her play and the great artistry with which it was presented.

Minnie admired Theodore Roosevelt for having begun conserving the natural resources of America, and opposing trusts. She told her manager that she particularly valued the message.

Mr. Griffith opined that the President would have been even more cordial if he could hunt on his vacations without a certain redheaded actress's sniping at him in the press for killing wild things.

Minnie chuckled. "Fallacious! A President can't take a vacation from being President. Every time he goes hunting, millions of American boys go hunting, or want to. He can't expect to set a bad example, and vacation in peace."

178

In Washington the satire had been the thing. In Philadelphia it was society. The beautiful Marian Lea had been a belle of Philadelphia, and her succesful role in *The New York Idea* gave society charter rights. The opening night of March 4 saw a hoof-to-bumper procession of 176 carriages and automobiles creeping up to the Lyric Theatre. An extra detail of police kept the old and new vehicles in line while they disembarked the old and new rich and the arbiters of society, Biddles and Cochrans and Draytons and Cadwaladers.

It was voted the greatest fashion parade of vehicles, and the most socially prominent first night in the history of the city; and for two weeks society filled the Lyric—regardless of the fact that the play was derisive of their class.

Three months later, the Manhattan Company paused at St. Joseph, Missouri, and considered the hostile territory beyond the river. For them, the only available theatre to the west was at Denver; the Pacific coast was closed to them, and no independent theatrical company had broken through the Trust lines since the San Francisco earthquake and fire.

Minnie accepted the imposing challenge, and on May 22, the Manhattan Company crossed the Missouri and headed west.

No more unlikely-appearing band of pioneers ever set out to blaze a trail through half a continent: led by a nunlike little actress who was timid about strangers, firearms, non-fireproof hotels, rear-end collisions, and the animals she befriended; there were Ida Vernon, the Southern *grande dame*, who had had her fortune confiscated after the burning of Richmond; George Arliss, the monocled English gentleman, and his pretty English wife; the luxury-loving John Mason, who had slippers waiting for him on eastern hearths; Marian Lea, the belle of Philadelphia; the flower-like Emily Stevens, who found the most comfortable tour exhausting; the stout and sedentary Charles Harbury, and the aging Robert Ferguson.

Matching the strange pioneers was their stock-in-trade—a sophisticated comedy and two baggage cars of elegant scenery and stage props, with the emphasis on white Louis XV furniture upholstered in pink silk.

The New York Idea was what it appeared to be, but the company was something more. Mrs. Fiske was timid about many things—but never about the odds against her; Ida Vernon had grown up in a day when ladies were expected to have superior qualities, including courage. During the Civil War, she had nursed in Confederate hospitals by day and acted at night, crossed the Potomac on a raft, run the blockade to

179

England and back to bring the South *Leah the Forsaken* and *East Lynne*. George Arliss either had rose-colored glass in his monocle or was such a thoroughbred gentleman that he was never ruffled by the draughtiest barn of a theatre, or the shabbiest hotel at a one-night stand; the hedonistic John Mason had never failed Mrs. Fiske in anything; the rest were worthy, if improbable-seeming, pioneers.

There was also business manager Frank Carlos Griffith. That Boston gentleman was qualified to represent a great actress in metropolitan centers—and ten years of campaigning with a Joan of Arc had given him other accomplishments.

Beyond the Missouri, the first stop was Sioux Falls, S. D. That divorce-mill town was a logical setting for *The New York Idea,* but its theatres were controlled by the Trust and Minnie compromised on Yankton, fifty miles to the south.

After the performance, resting his weary feet, Mr. Griffith made his report to Harry Fiske, in New York:

> Mrs. Fiske and the company did not reach Yankton until 4:15 P.M. of the day of the performance. At 7:30 P.M. the sky denoted a cyclone and a fierce storm of sleet, hail and rain set in. The house had been sold out, and some 220 persons had arranged to visit Yankton from points ranging from 25 to 75 miles distant by a special train starting at Platte.
>
> When the storm burst we had half the house in, and the theatre lobby was full when all the electric lights in town were extinguished by electric shocks. For three-quarters of an hour we were trying to handle the crowd by means of matches and two small candles discovered in a neighboring store. The men behind the scenes were trying to set the stage with the same means of illumination. At 8:30 o'clock the city lights came on, and the curtain was rung up on "The New York Idea" at about 9.
>
> The staff of a theatre in a town like Yankton is not large. I had to take tickets at the door. A woman came from some remote point with her husband and a nursing baby. She had put the baby to sleep on a pile of overcoats in the theatre office, which opened into the auditorium, and in the middle of the first act the baby began to cry. I put an usher at the door and "coochey-coochied" the infant for a time successfully. Before ringing up I had gone before the curtain and explained the delay; and after the first act I assisted the carpenters in setting the scenery, and made another speech informing the excursionists that their special train would be held despite the delay in the performance.

After Yankton, the company's last and only familiar stop was at Elitch's Gardens outside Denver. Fog and mud and an icy drizzle were at odds with the summer theatre, but Mrs. Fiske was too beloved a favorite for weather to make any difference.

The Denver audience that welcomed *The New York Idea* was as fashionable as any Eastern one—and as divorced. The press observed that the title could have been *The Denver Idea*, and that at least a third of the audience were legally emancipated from their spouses.

Late in May the Manhattan Company showed up in Raton, New Mexico Territory, where no first-class attraction had ever visited.

Raton had no theatre, but the roller-skating craze had brought it a large rink with a platform which served as a stage; in place of the usual carpeted passages to the right and left of the auditorium there were gravel paths; and a ticket office was approximated with a timekeeper's shack brought from a construction job. Most of the audience was expected to materialize out of the wide and barren countryside below Raton Pass.

It seemed like expecting figs from thistles. But at sunset the plateau roads and trails lifted plumes of dust that climbed toward Raton, bringing with them ranch wagons, buckboards, fringe-topped surreys and cow ponies carrying playgoers. The sombreroed theatre manager scanned the plumed horizon—and dispatched a wagon to the church annex for more folding chairs. He then formally opened the ticket office by laying a heavy-caliber revolver on the ticket-window shelf, and began taking in the currency of the country: two-, five- and ten-dollar gold pieces, and American and Mexican silver dollars.

All Raton was there except those who had to sit with the babies and the utilities; the countryside was drained for miles beyond the vast horizon; rough men and their women, who lived in sin back in a canyon, came to the play to hear about the folly of hasty marriage and divorce.

Before curtain time the town's supply of chairs had given out, and some had collapsed, but there was still sitting room in front of the front-most row. From the stage the company could hear the thud of holstered revolvers on maple as cowboys settled their haunches on the rink floor.

It was a colorful audience, dressed in frock coats, overalls and flannel shirts, and dress-up chaps—and one fabulous opera gown that might have just swept out of the Metropolitan. It was also a responsive, courteous audience that deepened Minnie's affection for the American scene.

The only skeptical note was sounded by the theatre magnate, who gave Mr. Griffith a heavy sack of gold and silver, and accompanied him through the desert starlight to the car on the siding. It was a great show, he said—but watch your step. There are men in town whimsying with the idea of asking their money back, along with everybody else's!

The following evening, Las Vegas saw its first real stage production. And while the artistry of Fiske, Arliss and Mason was being discussed in the excited town and around chuck wagons in the sagebrush, a Santa Fé train was carrying the Manhattan Company into the heart of the Southwest.

On May 30, Albuquerque filled the Elks' Opera House with an audience of metropolitan size and appreciativeness. There, as he was leaving, the *Journal's* amateur critic asked Mrs. Fiske if it would be all right if he didn't tell the story of the play. When she assured him that she preferred that kind of review, he explained, "There wouldn't be anyone to tell it to; everybody is here."

On the way south, with the Manhattan car on its tag end, the train ran for hours through desert country, and made a long stop at a silent station invisible from the rear car.

After the stop had drawn out interminably, Minnie heard members of her company leaving the car, then exclaiming and making witty remarks. She put aside her reading and followed them.

The Manhattan car was standing on the track in a desert that was broken only by giant cacti and distant, starved mountain peaks that prodded up into the sky where mirages were doing slow acrobatics. The train, from which they had become uncoupled, was somewhere beyond the horizon, racing toward Texas in a do-or-die effort to get the Manhattan Company to El Paso in time for their performance.

Minnie went back to her reading in the most blessed quiet she had known on the tour. It was not interrupted until hours later, when a locomotive came tearing up from the south and took the car in tow.

They arrived in El Paso in time after all, and their reception was worth a wild race through the desert. *The New York Idea* was presented in a huge old theatre before one of the largest audiences the company had ever seen, and one of the most delighted. It was an audience with an infusion of Spanish blood, and dark-eyed beauties; its warmth and color reminded Minnie of the New Orleans theatres of her childhood.

182

Ciudad Juárez, Mexico, and its bull ring were across the Rio Grande from El Paso, and Minnie came prepared.

The morning after the performance, she sent a note to Mr. Griffith, asking him to bring her the Juárez handbills. There were two bales of them, still in the wrappings of the New York printer. Mr. Griffith loaded them into a carriage—and Mrs. Fiske drove across the international bridge.

As a woman Minnie was shy of strangers and crowds, but as a crusader she never feared for herself. She spent hours on foot among the citizens of Ciudad Juárez, handing out black-and-orange handbills denouncing bullfighting in Spanish—returning to her carriage from time to time for a fresh supply. She handed them out in the busiest streets, on the plaza, in front of the cathedral, and at the gates of the Plaza de Toros, where bulls and picadors' horses died under the hot Mexican sun.

A bullfighter also died that day, but the little woman with the compassionate blue eyes had no regrets about him. Actors and acrobats and bullfighters took their chances—but cruelty to the helpless was inexcusable.

From El Paso the Manhattan Company crossed the desert into Arizona Territory. They were the first major company to appear at Bisbee and Tucson, where they played in the atmosphere of a frontier celebration.

After Tucson, the company jogged north on a narrow-gauge train. Their destination was the coppermining town of Globe, but the hour of their arrival passed while they were still a hundred miles away.

The toy train went more slowly, and stopped at every crossroad and siding to take on more passengers, or hook on another car loaded with passengers. All of them were bound for Globe to see *The New York Idea.*

Hundreds of other playgoers had traveled by stagecoach, buckboard and cow pony. They and the citizens of Globe were there beside the track to welcome the company.

It was night in the canyon, but the blazing starlight was answered by the lights of cabins, and of campfires in the sagebrush, and uplifted lanterns. The lantern light shone on cowboys in town regalia, miners and their families in their Sunday best, blanketed Indians, and a welcoming committee of mine officials in wrinkled evening clothes. Campfire smoke, the bitter scent of sagebrush and the smell of kerosene mingled with the odor of mothballs in the desert night.

This, too, was America—and the Manhattan Company had never been more honored by any welcome.

Curtain time was long past, but everyone crowded into the theatre in the heart of the canyon; and when Mr. Griffith announced that there would be a two-hour wait, the audience voted to stay.

Minnie had the curtain raised while the stage was set and the lighting effects arranged. The people out in front had earned the right to share in what went on behind the scenes.

The curtain was dipped and raised on the first act at ten o'clock, and the final curtain fell at two in the morning.

It was no ordinary audience, and the company gave no ordinary performance. In itself, *The New York Idea* was a brittle comedy without one sympathetic character—but in the canyon theatre there was warmth as well as brilliance, and it was answered by the most overwhelming response which the play had ever awakened.

At Los Angeles the Manhattan Company slipped through the Trust barricade into the Burbank Stock Company theatre, and played for a week while they rested from travel. There the play was greeted as a perfect production by the greatest American company.

Earthquake, and fire, and the Trust had deprived Mrs. Fiske of anything in San Francisco resembling a theatre, but she secured a week's booking at the Colonial motion-picture house. The Colonial was cramped of stage and located in a mélange of ruins and rebuilding—and Charles Frohman answered the actress's defiance by sending his star of stars, Maude Adams, across the continent to play against her in *Peter Pan*. Under difficulties *The New York Idea* played to crowded houses without being able to meet the demand for tickets.

Seattle had fallen to the Trust, but Minnie secured the old First Methodist Church on Third Avenue, improvised into a theatre. In that unlikely place, the comedy of the year was presented to paying congregations—and the palatial Grand Theatre was dark for want of a Trust attraction.

The pioneer theatre manager John Cort had made his bargain with the Syndicate, but there was nothing in his contract that forbade his musicians playing in church. When Cort heard that Mrs. Fiske was without music, he sent her the Grand orchestra as a token of his admiration.

The church was less cooperative. During the first act of the opening performance, Mr. Griffith sent Minnie a note on the peculiar acoustics of the place—the only actor who could be heard from the rear pews was Dudley Clinton as the Reverend Mathew Phillimore!

Thereafter everyone managed to make himself heard; and in the church where there had been much thundering against divorce, the Seattle *Star* found *The New York Idea* the best sermon ever preached there on the subject.

Bellingham was another Trust town, but Minnie secured a ghost of a theatre. Bellingham had resulted from the merging of two rival towns, with one theatre. During the stormy years of rivalry, the Fairhavenites had occupied the righthand side of the theatre and the Whatcomites the left. After the merger, the citizens buried the hatchet and built a new theatre, and the old one fell into disuse. When the Manhattan Company arrived, it had been closed for years and almost forgotten; its opening doors groaned like the gates of a disused cemetery, and bats flew out.

There were also better omens. The ghost theatre was the Bellingham—the name under which the rivals had united—and, for the first time, former enemies fraternized on their old battlefield.

During the second act, a disturbed bat short-circuited the switchboard and put the house in darkness. While they waited for lights, the actors ad-libbed lines which delighted their audience and established a warm bond across the darkened footlights.

In Vancouver, B. C., the stage carpenters learned the full meaning of their title when they had to build a stage in Dominion Hall—the nearest approach to a theatre that Minnie could engage. She was reminded of barnstorming with *Lucretia Borgia* under her father's management, when the company had made its own stages out of inn tables.

To the east of British Columbia, in the new provinces of Alberta and Saskatchewan, the last great fertile area in North America had been opened to homesteaders; and from Vancouver the Manhattan Company traveled to the "Last West" ahead of most of its pioneers.

At Calgary they found an efficient new theatre, and an audience that belied the illiterate pioneers of fiction. *The New York Idea* met with a swift and sensitive response, and cries of "Bravo!" and "Hear, hear!" in the accents of Oxford and Cambridge.

After the performance the company was surrounded by English younger sons, remittance men, and pioneering Canadians and Americans—all claiming the company as their own, and offering the hospitality of Calgary and the surrounding territory. The only fault they found with the company was its inexplicable haste. Why only one performance when the theatre could not hold everyone who wanted to see the play—when so many wanted to see it a second time?

Mrs. Fiske explained that they had an engagement at Edmonton the

185

following evening. Edmonton was at the end of the northern spur of the railroad; wouldn't the company return to Calgary? If Mrs. Fiske would say the word, a full theatre would be waiting for her.

In that democratic manner audience and actress arranged a return engagement.

Edmonton was three hundred miles above the United States border— the farthest-north point in America with railroad connection. Not even Minnie had been there in her "prehistoric days." There had been no Edmonton then.

On the way north, the train passed unbroken prairies, light forests of cottonwoods, and settlers' new cabins and barns in level fields of wheat. Hours late, the train stopped at the headwaters of the Saskatchewan at eight-thirty in the afternoon.

It was still broad daylight, but it was curtain time in the town across the river; the scenery was still in the baggage cars, and the theatre was an unknown quantity.

The theatre was the Thistle Rink, with refreshment counters along each side, and no dressing rooms. Properties were spread on the grass outside, and canvas screens were set up for outdoor dressing rooms. They went unused. Citizens living close to the rink opened their homes to the company, and the actors had more comfortable dressing rooms than most city theatres afforded.

It was eleven o'clock and growing dusk when the curtain rose on the first act of *The New York Idea*, with the white and pink Louis XV furniture of the second act standing in the green field outside. During the performance, citizens who were not in the rink came from across the field with hot coffee, cake and sandwiches for the actors and stagehands, and the brief Northern night was warm with the spirit of neighborliness.

When the final curtain fell at a little after two in the morning, the sun that had dipped below the prairie was rising again.

Mrs. Fiske declined a carriage, and she and the Arlisses and the weary Emily walked across the meadows and the bridge to their car in the delicious early morning.

It was years since Minnie had been able to sleep before daylight, and sometimes she felt as if she had been awake since the beginning of time. Here, where there was no night, she had a wonderful sense of well-being. She was touched with regret only when George Arliss observed that the performance in the rink had been up to their New York standard.

"That doesn't speak well for us," Minnie said. "After our year of experience with the play, it should be much better!"

On their return to Calgary, the Manhattan Company played to the full house which had been promised, then went on to the new province of Saskatchewan.

On the evening of the Fourth of July, the train pulled into Regina, hours late. It made less difference than usual because the baggage cars had gone astray and there was no scenery to delay the performance. And the provincial capital was entertaining itself with skyrockets and Roman candles and firecrackers set off by the bunch.

Minnie wondered what Canadians celebrated on that day, and she asked a citizen outside the station—a bearded Englishman who bore a striking resemblance to pictures of King Edward; he carried a lighted punk stick, and his tweed pockets bulged with firecrackers.

"We're celebrating the Fourth of July," he explained. "Independence Day, you know."

Minnie admitted that she had heard of that British holiday.

"Dancing on our own graves, what?" the Englishman said. "But so many of us up here are Yankees that history's a bit confused!"

In that genial corner of America where Yankees became Canadians and Englishmen celebrated the Fourth, *The New York Idea* was presented at the skating rink. One local stage-set, which resembled a country schoolroom, served as the drawing room of the Phillimore mansion on Washington Square, the boudoir of Vida Phillimore's Fifth Avenue home, and the library of John Karslake's house on Madison Avenue. The simple scene and local furniture gave zest to the acting, and Minnie asked herself how well art was served by lugging two carloads of stage-sets and furniture about the continent.

The following evening, with their scenery retrieved, the company pioneered at Brandon, Manitoba. The evening after, at Winnipeg, they ended the most remarkable tour in American theatre history: 18,000 miles, through Eastern blizzards and desert heat; from the Atlantic coast to the Pacific, and from the Mexican border to railroad's end in the Canadian North. On the long road, Minnie had discovered a dozen towns unknown to the theatrical world—and with a sophisticated satire she and her company had delighted every audience, from the President of the United States to the cowboys of the Southwest and the pioneers of Canada.

CHAPTER 24

The Fiskes' experience together in the theatre affected them in different ways. To the actress, born to the stage, ten years of unbroken success was a warning of trouble to come.

An external incident of the summer of 1907 had also left its impression on Minnie. On her way to California, the train made an abrupt stop on the west side of a Sierra height and did not go on. Investigating, Minnie discovered that four cars had jumped the track and were standing with their sides flush with a two-thousand-foot precipice. If the cars had gone a few inches farther, they would have taken the train with them into the depths of Blue Canyon.

The close call did not disturb Minnie at the time, but it continued to remind her that safety is an illusion.

Harry Fiske, a relative newcomer to the theatre, saw no reason why the fine weather of success should not last indefinitely, and he spread his wings just as his wife resolved to use hers with more care.

When Minnie returned from California, Harry was in a whirl of new enterprises. Inspired by the cracking of the Theatrical Trust in the East, he had organized second companies of *Tess* and *Leah* and was preparing to send them out to smaller towns. Minnie, whose instincts were against the large-scale haymaking, was the first to suffer. Her great Manhattan Company was scattered among four companies; in the shuffle she lost John Mason, who had been her mainstay as an artist and a human being. The only worry Mason had ever caused the Fiskes was his frequent borrowing on his next week's salary. The use he made of the money was revealing. George Arliss once found him putting new ten-dollar bills, fresh from the bank, into a series of envelopes. Mason explained that he was sending alimony to his ex-wives, and he couldn't bear to send them grubby-looking currency.

The Fiskes had responded to John Mason's loyalty in kind. Under

Minnie's influence, he had developed from a debonair matinee idol to the best straight actor in America—and Harry contributed usefully. Once when Mason tried to borrow on his salary for an ex-wife's alimony, Harry refused. As Mason was about to leave, crestfallen, Harry explained that there was no occasion to send the money; he had done some sleuthing and discovered that the ex-wife had remarried and had been collecting alimony fraudulently for over a year.

Shortly after Minnie returned from California she was followed by her second cousin Merle Maddern, who had decided on a stage career. Minnie welcomed the tall, dark-eyed girl into her family and her company, where she was rehearsed in the role of Izzy, the milkmaid, in the revival of *Tess*.

Minnie took pride in launching another Maddern on a stage career, but the coming of Merle had its bitter tang. The mother who brought Merle to New York had placed her in Harry Fiske's care. Harry had the warmer, more expansive personality, more leisure for listening to the problems of others, and throughout his life women of all ages were drawn to him. Merle, writing home to her mother, observed, "He is like a great warm fire. One goes to him shivering and cold and is quickly warmed and cheered."

Minnie, for all her love of family, was a stern realist about the theatre, and her sixth sense warned her against lingering in pleasant places where Harry grew expansive and saw no dangers.

The breaking of the Trust's monopoly in half the United States had opened new fields to Mrs. Fiske. Most of the Southern cities had missed her great triumphs from *Tess of the D'Urbervilles* on. Accordingly, her early fall tour was to be through the South, with *Tess* and *Leah Kleschna*.

The *Tess* revival had a great cast by ordinary standards but not by Minnie's. And the play itself was faintly dated, belonging more to the nineteenth century than the twentieth.

Neither did Minnie approve of the present *Leah* production. Three of the four giants of the original cast were scattered as leavening in Harry's other companies; only George Arliss remained.

The tour began uneasily and it did not warm up until Mobile, where Minnie was welcomed enthusiastically. The engagement was marred, however, by a strike of local stagehands, who were paid twenty-five cents an hour. It was the first labor trouble Minnie had ever encountered, and she wired the Shubert Theatre in New Orleans that she would cancel her engagement there unless a Union Stage Alliance crew could be provided.

The crew was produced, and on October 28 the Manhattan Company opened in New Orleans in *Tess of the D'Urbervilles*.

After an absence of nearly twelve years, Minnie returned to find that the city had almost forgotten her. When the curtain went up on the first act of *Tess*, she could feel the empty rows of seats. The audience that half-filled the theatre had been fed for a dozen years on stereotyped shows, and the suppressed realistic acting of the Manhattan Company left it cold. During the week of *Tess*, other audiences confirmed the impression that Minnie was a stranger, inconveniencing New Orleans playgoers with an unaccustomed variety of entertainment.

Leah Kleschna was better received, but the actress could not shake off her feeling of disillusionment. The New Orleans of her childhood was sacred ground—and she returned to the New Orleans of Charles Frohman, who had never lived there but had shaped the thinking of a generation of playgoers.

Spiritually, Minnie was closer to New York than to her birthplace, and still closer to Chicago and San Francisco. In the West, she had lifted her ban on interviews and talked with reporters about everything but herself. Here, when she tried to do the same thing, the interviews went flat. Least of all could she bring herself to speak of the New Orleans of memory. On one occasion a *Picayune* reporter answered her silence by saying carelessly, "I suppose one has to be born somewhere."

"Singular, isn't it?" Minnie said. She could not explain that her silence was due not to indifference, but to feeling too deeply.

West of New Orleans the Shubert theatres gave out, and the company barnstormed. At Houston they played a one-night stand at a wretched little vaudeville house from which half the would-be audience had to be turned away, frustrated and angry. At San Antonio a Texas norther whistled through a vast unheated barn called Beethoven Hall. The temperature inside was below freezing; Emily Stevens and Merle Maddern had to appear on the stage in low-cut evening gowns, and Minnie, numb with cold, was in an agony of apprehension lest the girls catch pneumonia.

The southern phase of the tour ended at Little Rock, where Minnie had made her first stage appearance forty years earlier—the company turned toward colder weather and warmer theatres.

At Waterloo, Iowa, the nightmare of San Antonio's Beethoven Hall was replaced by the luxury of the "Theatre Beautiful." The performance of *Leah* inaugurated the new theatre as an independent house, and the playgoers arrived from as far away as Minneapolis. For the first time in her years of daily letters to Harry, Minnie mentioned box-office receipts—nearly seven thousand dollars for a single performance. The Fiskes' morale needed it; Harry's road shows that had decimated the Manhattan Company had lost instead of made money.

Waterloo was a symbol of defeat as well as victory; from that town with the equivocal name Minnie wrote Harry:

Spring, 1908
Waterloo, Iowa

Darling Boy,

First I want to speak to you of this beautiful little theatre here. I met the owner and the manager last night. They are going to operate the theatre independently and they are building their hopes that you will speak of the theatre to Mr. Shubert and Mr. Belasco and influence them to send their attractions here when possible.

And now there is another thing I wish to speak of and I think I should speak of it now.

We must remember that the years are passing, Boy. After twelve years of hard and incessant work and considerable success we find ourselves with nothing. . . . We have earned enough to be placed beyond all stress and worry for the rest of our lives—This fortune has gone. . . . everything went in the effort to keep the (Manhattan) Theatre open. Now we see that it would have been wise to keep it closed except for my engagements.

Together we have built up a little following for me. . . not nearly so large or strong as the following possessed by Miss Maxine Elliott and others of the sort and it has to be carefully nourished. . . . "Tess" made a little fortune. "Becky Sharp" made a large one, "Mrs. Hatch" a fair one, "Mary Magdala" a little one, "Leah Kleschna" a goodly one and "The New York Idea" a little one. . . We must see the danger if we do not begin to accumulate *now*. We must put by money as soon as we are able. . . I am now nearly forty-two years of age. The little popularity I have may wane. . . I have a horror of an old age of financial distress and all the humiliation it brings. Let us determine to avoid it. . . There is danger in delay of this resolve— I do not speak in the slightest spirit of gloom or depression. Not in the least. It is only that we must devote ourselves to protecting the future.

Dearest and devoted love
Bunner.

CHAPTER 25

In the dressing room of the St. Charles Theatre, Grandmother Maddern had once discussed with the visiting Mrs. Crabtree ways and means by which stage people could avoid a penniless old age. The determined Mrs. Crabtree had attacked the problem so furiously that Lotta was spared both age and poverty—marooned for life on the sterile heights of perpetual girlhood, with her jealously-guarded millions.

Grandmother Maddern's daughters had been less successful, and her granddaughter, Minnie, found herself in middle age with nothing but her transient fame.

In her Waterloo letter, Mrs. Fiske emphasized the need to make money. The circumstances suggested a safe play that would hit the popular taste—but what was safe was a debatable question, and Mrs. Fiske, who credited American audiences with high intelligence, had succeeded more often than commercial producers who credited them with none.

She now decided on her long-deferred production of Ibsen's *Rosmersholm*.

The history of this tragedy in America was brief and ominous—in twenty years, two productions, both failures. But Minnie determined to produce it with the most perfect cast that could be found on the English-speaking stage—and one of the most expensive. She selected Forbes-Robertson for Rosmer, Fuller Mellish for Kroll, George Arliss for Mortensgard, and Tyrone Power for Ulric Brendel—regardless of the fact that Power had walked out on *Becky Sharp* and brought the costly production of *Magdala* to an untimely end by walking out again for a tempting offer from Charles Frohman.

The cast was perfect only in the actress's "dream theatre." Forbes-Robertson, the gentle traditional idealist, declined the part of Rosmer, who had the same qualities. Commenting on Forbes-Robertson's answer to her cable, Mrs. Fiske confided to Alexander Woollcott: "I suspect he thought I was quite mad. I suspect he had the British notion that Ibsen should be given only on Friday afternoons in January."

And Tyrone Power balked at the role of Ulric Brendel; even the offer of a fabulous salary could not induce him into what he looked on as a bit part.

Fuller Mellish accepted the part of Rector Kroll; George Arliss was in Mrs. Fiske's company—but one imperfection in the cast demanded another. Only Arliss could bring out all the complex ironies of Mortensgard, but any competent actor could play the role after a fashion. And with Tyrone Power out of the picture, Arliss was the only available actor who could play Ulric Brendel satisfactorily. So he was shifted from a role in which he would have been superb to one in which he was excellent.

For Rosmer, Mrs. Fiske compromised on Bruce McRae, the matinee idol. When his jaunty moustache was shaved off, he took on the saintly look which only Minnie had foreseen.

Mortensgard was played by Albert Bruning; and Madame Helseth by Florence Montgomery.

Rosmersholm was launched less than three weeks after Mrs. Fiske's return from her tour. The production was hastily assembled, but its parts had been long in preparation. Mrs. Fiske had been planning it and studying the role of Rebecca West for nearly five years, and on her tour she and George Arliss and Florence Montgomery, otherwise Mrs. Arliss, had rehearsed their roles. In the meantime, in New York, Harry Fiske had prepared the production and rehearsed the other members of the cast.

After a dress rehearsal of the assembled cast, *Rosmersholm* was tried out at New Haven on Christmas Day, 1907. The result was summed up by the correspondent of the New York *Telegram* who wired his paper that Mrs. Fiske had won a sweeping triumph; but Yale teachings abhorred pessimism and Ibsenism, and New Englanders disliked the play.

The *New York Times* dispatch noted that "Charles" Archer (William Archer, the translator) had dramatized Ibsen's book, and the *Tribune* credited Archer with having made the play *Rosmersholm* out of Ibsen's novel by the same name!

The play that was too profound and searching for Yale opened at the Lyric Theatre in New York on December 30. It was greeted by a full and enthusiastic house, and Mrs. Fiske won a personal triumph.

For reasons that would not have appealed to a vain actress, Mrs. Fiske had given years of study to a play in which she had limited opportunities and unusual burdens. One of the burdens was the fact that Rebecca's confession was precipitated by something like an algebraic equation completing itself in her mind and giving the answer of incest—something never put into words in the course of the play, or guessed by the other characters. Her confession and the final disaster followed inevitably for those who could "hear Mrs. Fiske think," as Bruce MacRae declared it was possible to do.

Younger, more modern critics, like Walter Prichard Eaton and Ashton Stevens, heard Mrs. Fiske think and understood the import of the scene; older critics, like Alan Dale and William Winter, who refused to bother their heads about unspoken meanings, missed the point and accepted Rebecca's ready explanation that she did not want to be known as illegitimate.

For those who got the full meaning and those who did not, Mrs. Fiske made Rebecca's scene with Kroll one of the most powerful they had witnessed on any stage, and she achieved it with the greatest economy of means, never rising from her chair, and almost without gesture.

In addition to giving actors and audience the inspiring benefits of teamwork, Mrs. Fiske's production helped rescue Ibsen from his cultists. *Rosmersholm* is a comedy as well as a tragedy; it contains a great deal of lively satire, and perhaps the only over-all moral that can be drawn from it is that neither radicals nor conservatives should take themselves too seriously. The humor and sanity that glinted through the dark play led the New York *Herald* to observe: "If Ibsen had been interpreted in the past as Mrs. Fiske and her company interpreted him last evening there would be less discussion and more appreciation of the Norwegian's writings."

The conflict of the overly-serious radicals and conservatives in *Rosmersholm* was prophetic of the tragi-comedy of Ibsen's reception in America. The man who had revolutionized the play-writing of the world was too vital to be done to death by his worshipers or detractors, but their combined efforts placed a tremendous burden on whoever produced his plays—and Mrs. Fiske had attempted his darkest work.

Rosmersholm played in New York for only three weeks, and its eastern tour began in Philadelphia on February 27.

Externally, the actress carried on buoyantly on her difficult tour with a play that forced audiences to think deeply, or rebel. There

194

was no outward sign of stress, but under the even assurance of her manner she was haunted by the inexorable things that constant touring were doing to her life, and to the lives of those she loved. The day before the Chicago opening, with the train rushing through falling snow over the prairies which she had been crossing and recrossing for nearly forty years, she wrote to Harry in New York:

> On train en route to
> Chicago, Feb. 16, 1908
>
> Darling Boy,
> . . . I shall be so glad if we can have our little home. It will make such a difference in our lives—and give Emily the healthy normal interests she needs. It will be the salvation of the child.
> So much of our little misunderstandings and friction and little unhappinesses have come from both Emily and I trying to live in a way that could never be good or happy for us. We both want a home more than anything else in the world. If you will take an interest and help us with your taste and ideas it can be beautiful with all the pretty things we have been accumulating. . . .
> Please come soon to lonely Bunner! My heart is full of love and devotion for you and Emily, who are all I have.
> Dearest dearest love darling Boy.
>
> Bunner

Harry was to join her farther west on the tour, but found he could not leave New York. As so often happened when they planned to be together, Minnie had to go alone.

The career to which the actress had wedded herself in youth had become the tyrant of her middle age, but it brought her certain rewards —never oftener or greater than in Chicago. There *Rosmersholm* drew the largest audiences in its history.

Other actresses checked on box-office receipts at least once during every performance. Minnie never checked at all. But the last Saturday matinee of the engagement was something that even Minnie could not take in her stride, and she treasured it as a triumph for Ibsen. Years afterward she recalled the event to Alexander Woollcott:

> When I listen to airily expressed opinions based on no real knowledge of Ibsen's history in this country, I am silent, but I like to recall a certain final matinée of "Rosmersholm" at the huge Grand Opera House in Chicago, when the audience crowded the theatre from pit to dome, when the stairways were literally packed with people standing, and when every space in the aisle was filled with chairs,

195

for at that time chairs were allowed in the aisles. And I like to remember the quality of that great audience. It was the sort of audience one would find at a symphony concert, an audience silent and
absorbed . . .

After the midwest, the Manhattan Company turned east to Boston,
where Mrs. Fiske was hailed as "the Mrs. Siddons of her generation."

The Boston public lagged behind the critics in appreciation, and
Rosmersholm played to meagre audiences. Minnie did not hold the
fact against Boston any more than she blamed one section of the country for having less rainfall than another. And the neighborhood held
some of her most enduring friends.

The doleful-mannered Copey was as dear to her as a member of
her own family—and the value of that great Harvard professor's approval was beyond calculation for a woman whose education had
come by "littles"—and who performed the most daring intellectual
feats of any actress in the history of the stage. And there was the
beautiful, fabulous Mrs. Jack Gardner who spent millions filling her
palace with art treasures from Europe—and hopefully tried to make
up for it by not owning a car, and begging rides with friends. And
there was Lotta Crabtree—Lotta, with hennaed hair and made-up
face, sitting in her rooms at the Brewster among a thousand photographs of herself and the gold nuggets which had been showered at
her feet by California miners half a century before.

So many years had passed since Minnie Maddern had tried to be
a second Lotta—and time had exaggerated the difference between the
two actresses until it was fantastic: the banjo-playing clown and mimic,
and the intellectual leader of the stage fighting the battle for Ibsen in
a reluctant country. They had nothing in common. But Minnie's
childhood dreams were stronger than reason. To her, the aging self-
centered Lotta was still touched with imperishable glamor.

From Boston, Mrs. Fiske took *Rosmersholm* to Toronto, where
she had been prevented from appearing for nearly five years. The
booking loosened one more tentacle of the Syndicate, but years of
contemporary drama from the Frohman factory had not helped
Toronto's reluctance. *Rosmersholm* opened to one of its smallest audiences, and the successive audiences diminished. Near the end of the
week's engagement, the *Telegram* observed that the small cast could
have engaged in a tug-of-war with the audience and made a good
gambling proposition of the outcome.

Since the New York premiere of *Rosmersholm*, the only change in the cast had been Mary Maddern's replacement of Florence Montgomery, but Bruce McRae's contract was nearing its end, and in New York Arthur Forrest was preparing for the role of Rosmer. Florence Montgomery, Arliss' wife, had given up the role of Madame Helseth, but she continued to travel with the company and presently she played a part in her husband's destiny.

In an interview with Mrs. Fiske, George Arliss reviewed his recent career. It was five years since he had agreed to stay in America a few months longer to play the Marquis of Steyne in *Becky Sharp*. The years in Mrs. Fiske's company had gone so pleasantly that Arliss had hardly noticed them slip by, but Florence paid more attention to such things than he did. She had just reminded him of the fact that he had been away from the English stage so long that he was almost forgotten there. He had, without noticing, become an American actor. Florence was ready to accept the fact, with recommendations. If he was going to continue on the American stage, it was time to think of his future career, and it was time for him to become a star.

In the company of the usual actress, there was room for only one star. With Mrs. Fiske the play came first; in her company there was no room for even one star. The conclusion was obvious, but Mrs. Fiske was no more anxious to lose George Arliss than he was to go, and she consulted with Harry in New York.

George Arliss' wife had raised the problem, and Mrs. Fiske's husband found the solution. Harry Fiske had recently acquired the American rights to Ferenc Molnár's play *The Devil*, and the title role might have been made to Arliss' order. It was agreed that Mr. Arliss would remain in Mrs. Fiske's company until June, and in the early fall he would be starred in *The Devil*, under Mr. Fiske's management. With his going, Mrs. Fiske would lose the last member of her great Manhattan Company, but Arliss would still be in the family.

After Toronto, *Rosmersholm* played a week at Cleveland, where Bruce McRae made his last appearance as Rosmer. At the Standard Oil capital, the audiences were of normal size again, and the press divided between praising the production and abusing Ibsen. As usual with an Ibsen play, the most potent weapon was ridicule of the fact that it made people think. The day after the opening, the Cleveland *Press* carried an article on the side-splitting fact that people who had seen *Rosmersholm* were discussing it and thinking, and others were reading the play. The article, widely copied through the Midwest, was to serve as the basis of a number of reviews.

In the same vein, Charles Frohman was advancing the creed that

197

the theatre was primarily for the amusement of the "tired business-man," and the creed was receiving wide newspaper attention. Minnie's tour continued to be harried by the twin concepts that provoking thought was un-American and that it was discourteous to the man who had put in a hard day at the office.

At Indianapolis, a *News* reporter asked the question of the hour: "What about the tired businessman and the other theatregoers who, after dinner, wish to be amused?"

The actress replied, "Everyone will continue to find his own level of performance in the theatre. The seriously inclined may find frequent inspiration and the complete imbecile will always be able to discover appropriate entertainment."

At Kokomo, George Arliss made his farewell appearance as Ulric Brendel before an unappreciative audience. The press was unappreciative, too. The *Dispatch* suggested that Kokomo had not got its money's worth because there were only six people in the cast—and it posthumously condemned *Tess of the D'Urbervilles* as a piece of "Derbyshire dirtiness."

In mid-June Minnie's hard-fought tour took her to El Paso, where *Rosmersholm* was presented before the largest audience ever collected in the Orpheum. Playgoers and press disputed over the merits of the play, with the *Times* declaring, "Honestly, it is no good. Of course it is rank heresy to say that Ibsen can write rot but *Rosmersholm* is rot."

The Southwest Territories had even fewer preconceived ideas about Ibsen. At Bisbee and Tucson and Phoenix, *Rosmersholm* enthralled its audiences of citizens and visiting cowboys and miners—and no one thought of its being too gloomy or obscure or highbrow. There, at last, Mrs. Fiske found audiences who saw and enjoyed the play as Ibsen had conceived it, "first and foremost a work of fiction, a story of human beings and human fates."

Los Angeles took kindly to *Rosmersholm*. San Francisco welcomed Mrs. Fiske but, for the most part, regretted her choice of a play. Among the critics, only Ralph Renaud of the *Bulletin* championed the play. The opening paragraph of his review told the over-all story of its reception in America:

> Those who went to see "Rosmersholm" at the Alcazar last night, expecting to be entertained or amused, were disappointed. Ibsen cultists who presume an esoteric meaning in the dramatist's plainest statements were also somewhat bewildered by the clarity and sanity of the performance. But those who desired an intellectual stimulus,

a chance to think, an opportunity to search their own hearts, were well rewarded.

From the huge New Alcazar, with an auditorium and stage too large for an intimate play with a cast of six, *Rosmersholm* went to Portland and the Lyric Theatre. There the stage was too small for the company's scenery, and local sets had to be used. It made little difference to the play, but that July 7 was the wrong day to be indoors in cramped quarters. In the words of the Portland *Telegram:*

> Every physical discomfort, resulting from the summer sultriness and the thermometer at 92, failed to distract attention from Mrs. Fiske in Ibsen's "Rosmersholm" at the Lyric yesterday, where she gave two performances. It was a tribute to Mrs. Fiske and her company that, while the audience sweltered and sighed for an ice cream cone between acts, they forgot perspiration, humidity and stickiness when the curtain was up. And also, it was a high compliment to the greatest of American actresses that the Portland show-shoppers could be tempted into a theatre on the hottest day of the year, to date. Few, if any other actresses in this country could have gathered such an audience in the Rose City yesterday.

When the curtain fell between the steaming auditorium and stage that night, the Manhattan Company had given its last performance of *Rosmersholm*—and friendly newspapers were regretting that Mrs. Fiske had lost money on an artistic success and six months of valiant effort. The loss was presumed as the automatic consequence of producing an Ibsen play.

Actually, to the woman born in the theatre, no play was any kind of a success unless it was seen by enough people to pay its way. *Rosmersholm* had paid its way and cleared $40,000 in addition. And that, Mrs. Fiske observed, did not exactly spell ruin.

CHAPTER 26

On her tour with *The New York Idea* Mrs. Fiske had been enchanted by her glimpse of the Canadian Rockies. She told the Arlisses, "I am going to see more of those mountains while I keep."

Mrs. Fiske made good her vow in the summer of 1908. She and her Negro maid spent a month in the wilds of the Selkirk Range, with guides and horses and dogs. She could have spent the rest of the summer there happily, but her conscience told her that she should be earning rather than spending. By mid-August Minnie was on her way to New York to prepare for her next season.

She arrived in time to see George Arliss' first appearance as a star, in Ferenc Molnár's *The Devil*, but she missed the melodrama which had gone before.

While Harry Fiske was working on the production of *The Devil*, he discovered that Col. H. W. Savage had also been sold the exclusive American rights to the play and was busy on his production. Also, Hungary was not in the international copyright agreement, and any producer could pirate the twice-sold play.

Whatever the courts might do, the winning producer would be the one who presented the play first. Harry rehearsed his cast secretly in a Tarrytown barn; George Arliss went about disguised and under his real name of Andrews; once, strolling on a Sleepy Hollow road, he saw a motoring dowager who was a friend of the colonel's, and he climbed a tree to avoid being recognized.

The first outside knowledge of Harry Fiske's production came when he announced on August 17 that the following evening he would present George Arliss in *The Devil* at the Belasco Theatre.

Colonel Savage had planned a September production, and his cast was vacationing as far away as Maine. But he summoned them by telegraph and announced his version of the play for the same evening as the Fiske production. After all night and all day rehearsing, the curtains rose simultaneously on the two *Devils*.

At the Belasco Theatre, George Arliss shone brilliantly; Florence Montgomery, who had decreed his stardom, gave him perfect support in the role of Vilma; and Emily Stevens, with her unusual beauty and freshness, added the right accent to the piece.

Both *Devils* were crippled by a duplication which only Molnár could have foreseen, but Harry's production settled down to a long Broadway run—and the Fiskes started work on a new production for Minnie.

Once more, in a crisis of her career, Mrs. Fiske was staking everything on the maiden play of an unknown. She had accepted it that spring, but it dated back to her Harvard address some three years before. When she had met Professor Baker of the Harvard Workshop in playwriting, she had agreed to read any of his students' work that he considered promising.

After three years of silence, Professor Baker sent her a student play. Mrs. Fiske read the manuscript at once and wired her acceptance an hour later. The play, about the Chicago slums, was called *Salvation Nell*, and it was by a Harvard senior, Edward Sheldon.

Harry was as thrilled by the play as was his wife, and he summoned the author to New York. Edward Sheldon was a tall, lean, bespectacled youth of twenty-two, with dark hair and a rosy cherub face, with an aura of boyish enthusiasm and modesty that never wore off.

The only major change which the Fiskes proposed for *Salvation Nell* was the setting. The play dealt with the Chicago slums, but since it was to be produced in New York, its chances would be better if it dealt with the slums of that city.

The willing young Sheldon studied the Cherry Hill district as the new locale of his play, and he did his work so well that a tenement house inspector could find nothing to add or take away from the portrayal of New York's Hell's Kitchen.

After the complex psychological study of Rebecca West, Minnie had the role of a downtrodden scrub woman and the challenge of bringing drama out of the humblest materials. For Harry there was the opportunity to present a facet of his beloved New York on the stage. In planning the production, he roved for days through the slums, getting the essence. When he hit on the typical locations and characters, he brought a cameraman to take photographs—and he immediately learned more about the slums: its inhabitants had pride, and they would not be photographed like wild animals. Harry made a mental note of the fact as he and his companion, with a smashed camera, ran up a Cherry Hill side street under a shower of rocks and broken brick.

On the next expedition, Harry waited until menacing toughs had gathered their forces and their bricks. He then explained to them that he was going to produce a play about the neighborhood; it could only be true and right if he had the help of people who lived there. Would they help him by posing for pictures and making suggestions?

The broken bricks were dropped, and Cherry Hill became a partner in the production of *Salvation Nell*.

On another expedition Harry attended an auction, and for the saloon scene in *Salvation Nell* he purchased a massive mahogany-and-brass bar which had seen life in Hell's Kitchen. Authentic bar mirrors, spittoons and swinging doors were acquired in the same way.

The casting of *Salvation Nell* was one with which the Fiskes struggled for weeks. They were determined on a perfect cast, and there were over fifty characters—not one of which was tailored to the style of the traditional actor. In an interview with Alexander Woollcott, Minnie confided: "I cannot *begin* to tell you how many times Mr. Fiske and I virtually dismissed an entire company; how over and over again we would start with an almost entirely new company, until every part, from Holbrook Blinn's down to the very tiniest, was perfectly realized; of the virtual opening of a dramatic conservatory; how much of the most exquisite care before *Salvation Nell* was ready."

The Fiskes tried out over twenty actresses in the role of Hallelujah Maggie. When they could think of no more possible candidates, Harry observed that the only woman he knew who fitted the character was Charlotte Thompson, a newspaper woman who had never been on the stage. Miss Thompson accepted the try-out as a lark, and proved to be the ideal Hallelujah Maggie. She played under the stage name, Mary Madison.

Another problem was that of the minor characters of the saloon and street scenes. Indifferent actors made indifferent loafers and humble citizens, and the atmosphere was thin and false. Harry dismissed the last lot of them, went to Cherry Hill, collected a fine mob of toughs and slum citizens. From them, the minor roles were filled to the last shade of authenticity, and the Fiskes learned still more about the slums. Never before had they had such loyal and reliable actors in minor parts. In the barroom scene, real money in generous amounts was used in the cash register, but none of it ever disappeared—and in the Fiskes' "dramatic conservatory" the men and women of Cherry Hill responded to direction with keener instinct than most professional minor actors.

It was late autumn when the production was as close to perfection as ingenuity and art could make it.

Salvation Nell was tried out in Providence on November 12. The Opera House was crowded with New Yorkers and Bostonians; a Harvard delegation surrounded Edward Sheldon near the back of the theatre, and Professor Baker's box party included the beloved "Copey."

The evening ended with Harvard rooting for Ned Sheldon and Mrs. Fiske, and coaxing them into brief curtain speeches. It was a victory for Harvard '08—but there was little general agreement on *Salvation Nell*, only that it was the most daring realism ever presented on the American stage, and Harry Fiske's sets the most perfect.

Salvation Nell had its New York premiere at the Hackett Theatre— some eight blocks from the setting of the first act at Tenth Avenue and Forty-eighth Street. Ordinarily it was a comfortable gulf that separated the Times Square neighborhood from Hell's Kitchen.

When the curtain rose the gulf was gone, and ladies conscious of their respectability drew back a little at finding themselves on the threshold of a Hell's Kitchen dive—not a stage presentment but the thing itself.

It was Christmas Eve in Sid McGovern's Empire Bar, with Christmas bells at the windows and snow outside, and MERRY CHRISTMAS printed large in soap on the ornate mirror behind the bar. In its way it was a splendid place, with paneled walls and glittering lights, and it had the solid comforts of a big brass rail, frequent spittoons, and towels for customers' hands, hanging from hooks at the front of the bar. The place also had its gesture of respectability, with tables for ladies and gents separated from the main barroom by a low partition and reached by a street door marked FAMILY ENTERANCE.

Bars like the Empire were the only touch of luxury in the lives of slum-dwellers, but the atmosphere of the place jarred genteel spectators with its loafers and thieves and prostitutes too real to be disbelieved; voices raised in real profanity and calling things by their real names; a one-legged fiddler, a little girl going out with a bucket of beer; and on the Family side, a dejected young streetwalker slumped at a table, and at another, a white-haired woman, sodden with drink; and a bedraggled scrubwoman on her knees, wiping up the barroom floor.

Virtuous sensibilities were further shocked by a police raid on the house of prostitution next door. The madam and nine of her girls were led past the window to the patrol wagon with a jeering crowd at their heels; the tenth, a brazen beauty by the name of Myrtle, escaped by ducking into the saloon, affronting comfortably virtuous ladies with her brazen imitation of their finery—and offending them still more by revealing a sense of humor.

Jim Platt enters, a drunkard with a heavy, brutal face, and manners to match. By an effort, the audience recognizes him as Holbrook Blinn.

The bedraggled scrubwoman leaves her bucket and rag, and taps Jim on the shoulder. She is his "girl," and he emphasizes the fact by forcing money from her, and getting drunker. With a further effort, the audience recognizes the scrubwoman, Nell, as Mrs. Fiske, but the act is almost half over before she has a line to say.

In defending Nell as his property, Jim Platt kills a man, and before the police arrive, Nell sits on the floor holding her drunken lover's head in her lap for fully ten minutes without a word, almost without a motion. The barroom was a scene of hurried activity but, "gradually one could watch nothing else; one became absorbed in the silent pathos of that dumb, sitting figure. Miss Mary Garden, herself a distinguished actress, said of this, 'Ah, to be able to *do nothing* like that!' " Walter Prichard Eaton recorded that summation of Mrs. Fiske's art and sent it echoing down the years.

The act ended with Myrtle, the prostitute, and Hallelujah Maggie contending for the outcast scrubwoman, and Nell casting her lot with the Salvation Army.

After many curtain calls, the audience poured into the lobby to exult or horrify over the starkest realism ever seen on a New York stage. Enthusiasts raved over the way Mrs. Fiske held her audience in the hollow of her motionless scrubwoman's hand; over the fact that Holbrook Blinn had revealed himself as one of the great of the stage, and over Hope Latham's brilliant flowering as Myrtle. Men who had accepted the conditions of Hell's Kitchen for a lifetime expostulated against those conditions being presented on the stage, predicting that "They (the public and the authorities) will never stand for this." And ladies said that no respectable person should see and hear such things, but all of them went back for more.

The previewers of *Salvation Nell* had declared that the production out-Belascoed Belasco. At the Hackett Theatre, David Belasco looked on from a stage box to see if such a thing were possible—and the setting of the third act justified the previewers' claim. The curtain rose, not on a stage, but on Cherry Street in the heart of the slums; on four-story tenements, complete with fire escapes and wash lines, and tenants at the windows of all the stories; a life-size Salvation Army headquarters on the corner, and the ground floors of the other buildings occupied by pawnshop, saloon, barbershop, and vegetable store, all stocked and equipped with real articles of trade. The crowds in the street were authentic, too; the tenement house inspector in the audience called attention to the fact. In the Hell's Kitchen scene there had been drunken women on the street, and that was true to Tenth Avenue. Here there were none, and that was true to the decent and domestic Cherry Hill.

Cherry Street, reconstructed on the Hackett stage and peopled with inhabitants of Cherry Street, out-Belascoed the little man in priest's garb—but, without knowing it, he had a vicarious hand in the premiere.

Near the close of the final act, Nell and Jim, returned from Sing Sing, reviewed their battered lives, and had their idyllic love scene seated on a box in front of the vegetable store.

As the scene had been rehearsed, Nell and Jim were in the tenement's shadow—as Mrs. Fiske observed, "a very proper light for two middle-aged lovers."

On the premiere night, however, an electrician who had worked for Belasco took over one of the lights in the last act. In the excitement he forgot everything but the instructions Belasco had drilled into him: "Find the star, and keep the spotlight on her."

As Mrs. Fiske and Holbrook Blinn took their places, the big spotlight burned away the dusk and blazed in their faces; its merciless glare continued to the falling of the curtain.

The performance ended with all the formalities of a success: the ovation, and the curtain calls, and the calls of "Author!" which continued until Mrs. Fiske took young Edward Sheldon by the hand and led him onto the stage—but the premiere was ruined for her. Under the terrible strain of a first night toward which she had been building for months, she felt nothing but the perfection that should have been, and the shattered thing that had come of it.

When the curtain was down, she turned on Harry for the first time in her life and upbraided him wildly for ruining the beautiful scene—the soul of the play! Time after time, Harry tried to interrupt her and explain. When she ended at last, he tried again—and was interrupted by the Belasco-trained electrician who explained that he alone was to blame. Mrs. Fiske asked her husband's forgiveness. He gallantly assured her that she had every right to be upset—and she never berated him again for anything.

Afterward, when Emily Stevens heard of the episode, she sided against her cousin and asked Harry, "Why do you put up with her? Why don't you divorce her?"

The little scene on the Hackett stage ended quietly, but it was a milestone on the pilgrimage of an actress who had nowhere to go but on—along a course that carried her farther away from warmth and love. She loved her gifted young cousin as much as ever and did what she could to mother her, but their ties were already strained by exhausting tours together. Minnie's outburst behind the lowered curtain strained them past healing. Emily had always been drawn to the warmer, more indulgent Harry, and she never forgave her cousin.

Merle Maddern was another part of the warm circle of Mrs. Fiske's dream—the family that would be close about her. She thought of Merle as her own daughter, and gave her extra mothering to offset any bad effects from her role as a streetwalker in *Salvation Nell*—but Merle's mother had put her in Harry's special care, which she preferred.

There was one more Maddern in the cast who should have been part of the close-knit circle—Aunt Mary, who had mothered Minnie in childhood, and whom Mrs. Fiske would care for as long as she lived. But Aunt Mary Maddern, who played the part of the drink-sodden old woman in the Hell's Kitchen saloon, had been on the stage longer than Mrs. Fiske; by now she was philosophically isolated in its loneliness, and she didn't feel that there was much left to say.

The New York press greeted the premiere of *Salvation Nell* with roses, and bricks. By general agreement, Holbrook Blinn as Jim Platt had joined the ranks of great actors, and Mrs. Fiske had added another enduring portrait to the national gallery.

But more than half the press deplored the play. As for the realism of the piece, William Winter wrote sneeringly: "Competition is not intended with the youthful Mr. Sheldon, in minute and particular knowledge of the customs of vile drinking dens, and the language and manners of prostitutes. Being, as it is understood, a recent graduate of a great institution of learning, his knowledge is, doubtless, ample and accurate."

At the other end of the scale, Charles Darnton of the *World* called *Salvation Nell* "A Divine Comedy of the Slums," a comment Mrs. Fiske added as a subtitle.

The controversy underlined the success of Sheldon's play. The young man woke up to find himself famous, and he wrote the woman who had lifted him from a university class into the rank of an established playwright:

Dear Mrs. Fiske,
You have done so much for me that I don't see how I can ever square things up. Thank you again. I think you must know by this time that you will always have my affection and gratitude.
Edward Sheldon
Wednesday

A few days later he wrote again:

Dear Mrs. Fiske,
Thank you for the book. It is interesting—I can't help telling you that one of my friends on Saturday said you were much prettier than Billie Burke and we all agreed.
Yours
Edward Sheldon

The Salvation Army was quick to cash in on the publicity given them by *Salvation Nell*. Army lassies shook their tambourines at the exits of the Hackett Theatre, and collected generously from spectators starry-eyed with the vision of Jim Platt dropping his last coin in Nell's tambourine.

Plays were forbidden to members of the organization, but in her dressing room after the first matinee Mrs. Fiske had a caller—a handsome and distinguished-looking young woman in a Salvation Army cloak and bonnet. The caller introduced herself as Commander Evangeline Booth and a devoted admirer of Mrs. Fiske.

Miss Booth came to thank the actress for *Salvation Nell*, which had proved a boon to her organization; she stayed to ask about life on the stage, and to experiment with the cosmetics on the dressing table. Make-up as well as playgoing was forbidden to the Army.

Often thereafter Evangeline slipped into Minnie's dressing room at the Hackett Theatre and made up beside her. When she had beautified herself, she would ask, "Now mightn't I pass for Salvation Nell?"

The two earnest women saw glamor in each other's lives. Minnie went with Evangeline to Salvation Army and public functions; once, on a platform, when they were seated behind the huge Governor of New York, Evangeline whispered: "We're girls hiding behind a vat barrel!"

While Commander Booth identified herself with Salvation Nell of the stage, Mrs. Fiske preached the Army's gospel of sin and redemption. Once, when Evangeline was making up at her dressing table, Mninie explained her own belief about such matters:

> Perhaps there is no escape from our sins, because we scarcely ever fail to do what we want to if we really want to do it very much. Of course there are people who refer with glaring virtue to supreme instances of resistance, but in the vortex of human experience, resistance is scarcely possible, though commonly assumed. I suspect it of being a fiction that has done a great deal of mischief in its day, Evangeline.
>
> There is an apotheosis in our lives, however, a divine precaution against the impetus of our sins—for we change, we move onward and upward—and our sins finally desert us, we leave them behind in the green valley of our first encounters. . . .

The two leaders found much in common and tried to share still more. Minnie talked up anti-cruelty work, for which Evangeline had no time, and Evangeline tried to interest her friend in prohibition—an idea Minnie considered unworkable.

In *Salvation Nell*, Edward Sheldon pictured the lives of human beings condemned to misery and squalor through no fault of their own, and his characters ended by proclaiming themselves sinners and turning to religion. Not everyone saw the logic of the solution, but *Salvation Nell* reached into many hearts, and many corners of New York; it even touched the lives of people in the slums.

Among the hundreds of letters which Mrs. Fiske received, there was one from J. G. Hallimond, Superintendent of the Bowery Mission. He wrote in part:

> During recent winters the Bowery Mission has given a breakfast every morning at one o'clock to homeless men, doomed to walk the streets all night . . . At present we provide for 1500 men, and, very often, we find this provision inadequate. . . .
>
> "The Bread Line," as it is called, is one of the most pathetic sights in our modern civilization, so-called. To think that in this prodigiously wealthy country there are thousands of American-born men, able and willing to work, but cannot, do what they will, obtain a chance to earn an honest living! Judge E. H. Gary, President of the United States Steel Corporation, inspected the "Line" himself a few nights ago, and unhesitatingly confirmed our view.
>
> You will therefore understand what a pathetic sight it is to see these men come in, ravenously hungry, gulp down the hasty meal,

and then pass out again into the tragic shadows of the winter night.

The incident to which I referred in my opening sentence was one which occurred the other night. A gentleman in elegant evening dress, accompanied by a lady, arrived in his automobile just when breakfast was in progress, and, after watching the scene with eager interest, he said, "My heart has never been stirred so deeply before. Here is $30, which is all the cash I have in my pocket. I will come again and bring an automobile load of young men, and I will insist upon each one of them giving you a handsome contribution for your noble work." He then went on to say, "You will wonder what caused me to come here tonight. A few hours ago I was sitting in the Hackett Theatre listening to Mrs. Fiske in 'Salvation Nell' when the impulse was created in my heart to go out at once and do something for my unfortunate fellow creatures in the underworld."

These were a few of the by-products of *Salvation Nell*. A twenty-two-year-old Harvard boy became famous for life; gilded gentlemen in evening dress visited the unfortunate in the underworld and contributed pocket money, and Judge Gary appeared on the bread line to acknowledge that in the world's richest city, the army of the starving marched all night to keep from freezing—because of the habitual slip between the cup of production and the lip for which it was intended. A slip for which he proposed no solution before going home in his limousine. Mrs. Fiske had produced a flurry that brought fame and fortune to some and coffee and rolls to others. On her account, as an actress, she had drawn the public closer to her heart; and as a woman who yearned for a loving family about her, she passed another milestone on the road to loneliness.

CHAPTER 27

The success of *Salvation Nell* was too big for its New York engagement. The crowds were still undiminished at the time the next attraction moved into the Hackett Theatre and the Manhattan Company
went on tour.

Salvation Nell opened at the Belasco in Washington on February 1.
The city had its wretched slums in the shadow of the capitol building,
but Sheldon's play was a strong dose of realism in the midst of preparations for Taft's inaugural. It was greeted by uneasy audiences and a
divided press. By one school of thought, *Salvation Nell* was an affront
to people who did not have to live in the slums; by another, Mrs.
Fiske was "a pioneering hero who brought society to the bar in
merciless arraignment."

Mrs. Fiske was Chicago's favorite actress; Chicago was Edward
Sheldon's home town. There the play filled the Grand Opera House
at every performance—but the Chicago press gave the actress most of
the credit for the success. Burns Mantle of the *Tribune* observed that
Sheldon's miniature of the slums had been set in a mighty frame that
dwarfed it by comparison, and Percy Hammond wrote of Mrs. Fiske
in the Evening *Post:* "Without the sincerity of her acting the play
would be nothing more than a full figured and exact photograph of
the underworld. . . . She is the filter through which its unpleasant-
ness is purified. . . ."

Mrs. Fiske, on the other hand, believed that young Sheldon deserved
credit for the emotions which his play suggested as well as for the
words.

During the Chicago engagement, Minnie stayed at the Virginia, led
her usual quiet, hard-working life, and avoided the press with a single
half-exception. Once, at the end of a rehearsal, her maid brought her
word that Forrest Arden of the *Examiner* was waiting to see her.

"No interviews," Mrs. Fiske said. "Tell Mr. Arden that I have nothing to say that would interest him." That would have been the end of it if her eyes hadn't caught the wistful look of one of the most minor members of the cast. The young Italian-born Gilda Varesi played the role of Mrs. Baxter in the third act—a Cherry Hill wife whose husband ran away with another woman. Her bit part amounted to one anguished outburst that was drowned almost immediately in the teeming medley of East-side noises—but it rang so true that critics dug her name out of forty others in the speaking cast, and commented on the perfection of her moment.

Gilda had sighed, apparently at the thought of an actress's snubbing helpful publicity, and Mrs. Fiske looked at her quizzically. "Well, Gilda, would *you* want to be interviewed?"

"I've never been asked," Gilda said, "but if I had something to say—"

"Wait, Letty," Mrs. Fiske ordered. Then she told Gilda, "You have something to talk about—the Three Arts Club. Letty, tell Mr. Arden that he will interview Miss Varesi!"

Forrest Arden, who had angled for an interview with a famous actress, settled down to interview one of the least of her company; and Minnie stayed to be an approving chorus.

Gilda Varesi was such a good subject that one question about something else brought forth two columns of *Examiner* copy about the Three Arts Club in New York—a club, Mrs. Fiske put in, in which Gilda was a shining light. The club was to take the place of the cheap and ghastly boardinghouse in which the girl drama or art or music student had to take shelter. It had been organized three years before, with a membership of five girls. Now the club occupied two large houses on West End Avenue and was completing plans for a home of its own to house its 240-odd members.

The club, Gilda explained, was a homelike place, with the best food that the market could afford, all at a nominal cost; if a girl was short of funds, she was carried until she made good—and not one girl had failed to meet her obligation.

Forrest Arden thought the millennium must have come to New York.

Gilda explained, "It's mostly Miss Hall, the manager, and her wonderful intuitive sense. She never makes a mistake in sizing up a girl."

"Remember, they are girls," Mrs. Fiske put in. "It would be dangerous to run a Home for Young Men of the Stage on those lines. Men have a deeper business sense of honor than women, but when it comes to moral obligations—but don't let me interrupt you, Gilda."

She interrupted again when Forrest Arden became convinced that the Three Arts Club had changed the world for hundreds of struggling art students. "What we want," Mrs. Fiske said, "is to have branches in every big city in America."

" 'We?' " Arden asked. "Are you in on this too, Mrs. Fiske?"

"Mrs. Fiske is one of the directors," Gilda said. "Without her—"

"Nonsense!" Mrs. Fiske said. "The club would be a failure if it depended on one person—and the girls must depend chiefly on themselves. In the final analysis of life our failure or success is in ourselves, but often there comes the need for a little lift. It's that lift each city should be prepared to give. And Chicago is the big field—but don't let me interrupt you, Gilda."

The interview prepared the ground for Chicago's Three Arts Club— and Forrest Arden realized how skillfully Mrs. Fiske had used Gilda Varesi as the symbol of the struggling girl artists of America to whom she was giving a lift.

Mrs. Fiske had plans for launching a Three Arts drive when she reached Philadelphia; in Boston a club was about to materialize, and Minnie had soaring plans for its future. With her encouragement, the moving spirit of the Boston branch was Mrs. Jack Gardner, whose art-filled palace Minnie had already earmarked as a home for art students.

Minnie's interest in struggling young artists did not diminish her humane activities. *The Devil* company was appearing in Milwaukee at the same time as *Salvation Nell*, and she drew on both companies for a benefit for the Wisconsin Humane Society.

The benefit performance began with the second act of *Hedda Gabler*, with Holbrook Blinn as Tesman, and George Arliss again playing Assessor Brack to Mrs. Fiske's Hedda. During the program, Mayor Rose of Milwaukee presented Mrs. Fiske with a certificate of life membership in the humane society; she, called on for a response, was overcome with stage fright.

In Philadelphia the young author of *Salvation Nell* was given more praise than he had received in his home town. The editor of the Evening *Star* asked what the police reporters of America had been doing while a college boy was seeing the slums with new eyes. The editorial was addressed to all newspapermen and it was headed, WE HAVE ALL BEEN SCOOPED BY A COLLEGE BOY.

At Boston Edward Sheldon again came into his own. On the night of April 6, Harvard men filled the stage boxes of the Majestic and sixteen rows of the orchestra; actress and playwright were called before the curtain and Minnie, with her arms full of roses, made the third curtain speech of her career and the second for Sheldon's play.

Backstage at the Lyric Theatre in Cincinnati the climax of Mrs. Fiske's twelve-year war with the Trust was enacted. Minnie was handed a telegram, which she read and handed to Mr. Griffith without comment. The middle-aged little woman in Salvation Army costume accepted her manager's congratulations with a nod of her bonnet—and went on with the rehearsal.

The telegram was from the New York office of Charles Frohman, and it offered Mrs. Fiske the use of any Syndicate house which she cared to occupy, on independent terms; all the theatres of America were open to her, and her days of barnstorming in churches and skating rinks were over.

The Trust that had surrendered to a woman had recently controlled all the theatres in America; it had a firm hold in England and Australia, and it reached tentacles into France and Germany. For years Mrs. Fiske had stood alone against the Trust, a pinpoint of resistance. But the pinpoint was diamond hard, and with the weight of the Shuberts and Belasco behind it, it had split the Trust.

Externally, the actress-manager had come through unscathed and victorious. But the twelve-year war had eaten up the fortune earned by her great successes; and long seasons of one-night stands had cracked her iron constitution.

There was a practical reason for the Trust's surrender to the independent actors. The Shuberts, whom Mrs. Fiske had helped establish, had built and acquired theatres in hundreds of Syndicate towns where there was room for only one first-class house, and they were engaging the Syndicate in a war to the death for the limited patronage. The original avowed aim of the Syndicate had been to end the duplication of booking agencies—and the final result was a ruinous duplication of theatres. Out of disorder it brought anarchy.

The war had revealed the bad points of Mrs. Fiske's enemies—and peace revealed the bad points of her allies. And the Shuberts with whom she ended were not the Shuberts with whom she had begun. Early in the conflict, the idealistic young Lee Shubert had been killed in a train wreck, and his tough-minded brothers carried on with methods which became increasingly like those of the enemy. By now there were, in effect, two trusts at war with each other; the Shuberts, confident in their growing power, were driving harder bargains with theatre managers than the weakening Syndicate which had shown them how.

The Syndicate declined, but Charles Frohman's methods lived after him, through the Shuberts, in the declining theatre; and they were to serve as the blueprint for motion pictures which replaced the legitimate theatre.

Early in the nineteen-hundreds, sensibilities were shocked when Charles Frohman boasted that he ran his theatres like department stores, and referred to the theatres of America as "my colossal business enterprise." By the time producers spoke of themselves as the "motion-picture industry," the public had forgotten that the theatre could be anything but an industry.

For years on her tours across the continent, Mrs. Fiske had checked on the condition of the humblest passengers that traveled by rail—cattle in transit to the stockyards. They traveled without food or water in open cars, where the weaker ones were frequently trampled or frozen to death before they arrived. Minnie's indignation was potent and catching. The agitation she sparked led to the building of comfortable enclosed cattle cars that saved animals a great deal of misery, and shippers millions of dollars.

The only class of travelers who had not received the actress's attention was the hobos. But on her tour with *Salvation Nell*, at a way station in the desert, she smiled at a dusty knight of the road and was rewarded by a start of recognition. The train moved on toward Salt Lake and the hobo disappeared, but was not left behind.

Minnie did not know at the time that the hobo was one of her fans, or that she had given him a purpose and a dream.

Six months later, in Dallas, a letter was forwarded to the actress:

Coalinga, Calif.
Dec. 18, 1909

My dear Mrs. Fiske,
Early last summer I rode into Salt Lake City on the deck (and several other places where they don't take tickets) on the same train that carried you. Back east I had seen you from a gallery seat at the theatre and remembered your face. The billboards about town proved I had not made a mistake.

I rustled an odd job next day moving furniture and spent a dollar the following night to see you play. Now I am not fond of packing other peoples stoves etc. up three flights of stairs. Never did I do it before or since to see anyone else on the stage but I would gladly

214

swing a sledge hammer for a week if by so doing I could see you act again. . . . I read all I could find to read about you and put you above the kind only interested in yourself and box office receipts. . . .

I haven't any home and working never got me much but a lame back, bum board and clothes and was such a stupid life that I went rambling.

I have rode the 20th Century Limited and hit every big city except Boston. I have been eighty miles from a railroad up in Montana to get to the cow-land. Been in Canada, Old Mexico and Japan. I have camped in the Yellow Stone and Yosemite Valleys. Rode for an exhibition troop in the southeast, picked oranges in California, worked in the mines in Butte and been from ocean to ocean and gulf to lakes inside of a year and didn't pay a cent of fare. . . .

The things I have seen and read have set me thinking and I want to do something worth while.

I have read all I could find and since Josiah Flint died and Jack London gave his attention to other things there has been no genuine writer of my class before the public. Neither of the above had the story to tell that I have. . . . Did you ever stop to think of the millions spent for higher education for reclaiming waste lands and almost every other purpose and not one cent to reclaim the waste youth—young homeless hoboes? Laws there are to punish him, millions are paid to watch and chase him. But I know of not one penny being spent to reclaim him. . . .

I have a big interesting story to tell and need help to get it properly prepared and placed before a magazine editor. Some skilled writer would have to correct my mistakes of grammar etc. . . .

I'll be mighty glad to get even a word of encouragement from you because you are the greatest actress I ever saw and I guess I have seen nearly all in America.

If you haven't time I still want to thank you for what I saw you do and wish you a Merry Christmas.

> Sincerely yours
> Joseph Miller
> Coalinga, Calif.
> Gen'l Del.

Mrs. Fiske corresponded with Miller over a period of years, encouraging him to write his story—it remained a dream, along with the dream books of hundreds of other hobos, businessmen and housewives.

At the first performance of *Salvation Nell* in San Francisco, it was part of a greater drama that extended out into the audience.

Hope Latham, who had won the praise of every critic for her portrayal of Myrtle, was a San Francisco girl; Merle Maddern, making her first impression as Sal, was from across the bay; and Holbrook Blinn, who was as close to being the star as anyone could be in a Fiske production, had grown up in San Francisco and been a pioneer student at nearby Stanford University. Since then he had acted successfully in London and been acknowledged as one of the few great American actors—and San Francisco had never seen him on the stage.

There was one more bond. Before the curtain rose at the Valencia Theatre, stretcher-bearers moved carefully into the right-hand stage box, carrying a frail gray-haired woman with the stamp of death and unaccountable joy on her wasted face.

The bearers put the stretcher down, and friends wrapped blankets around the woman, who lay still with her face turned toward the curtain, which was about to rise.

Mrs. Nellie Holbrook Blinn had fought valiantly to stay alive until her famous son came home. Mrs. Blinn had been an actress, and a dramatic coach in San Francisco for most of a lifetime. Among the scores she had helped, there was David Belasco, whom she had tutored and started on his way to fame; and she had given her son the groundwork for his career—but she had never seen him on the professional stage.

Sometimes the audience was aware of nothing but the play and their own pride in its great cast. Then their attention centered on the scene in the box: the anxious attendants, and the woman on the stretcher, in the reflected glow of light from the stage, her eyes shining and her face transfigured.

At the end of the first act there were eight curtain calls for Mrs. Fiske and Holbrook Blinn and Hope Latham, and as many more of the cast as they could bring to the footlights.

Even though it was the first time Nellie Holbrook Blinn had seen her son as a famous actor, for two acts she gave no token except for her intent eyes and smiling face. Then, at the end of the second act, after the great scene between Nell and Jim Platt in the tenement room, the dying woman raised herself on one elbow and tossed a bunch of carnations on the stage. They were taken to Mrs. Fiske, who gave one of them to Holbrook Blinn as the curtain rose and fell ten times in a mighty storm of applause.

The manager of the Valencia, too, had become a part of the drama that included actors and audience; the house remained dark during the intermission, and critic T. P. Magilligan cited the manager as a colossus of tact for not turning up the lights on an audience drenched in tears.

The play ended with the redeemed Jim dropping his last dime in Salvation Nell's tambourine and Nell, whom he thought he had lost, saying, "Wait fer me, Jim. I want ye to take me home."

The gesture, or the words—or the happy face of the woman on the stretcher—turned the audience into something that resembled "the Sacramento River at flood tide." Ten curtain calls did not entirely relieve their feelings, and the tactful manager gave the audience further time to compose itself before turning up the lights.

A few days later the teacher of Holbrook Blinn and David Belasco was dead.

The San Francisco *Call* regretted that Mrs. Fiske did not play *Salvation Nell* on Sunday because it would be the greatest sermon in town.

Mrs. Fiske had played in a church, but neither the building nor the day seemed important. The memory of the transfigured face of Nellie Holbrook Blinn reaffirmed her belief that the theatre, too, can be a holy place.

CHAPTER 28

The autumn season of 1909 began with the promise of a renaissance in the American theatre. Independents had forced the surrender of the Trust, and a national theatre was about to become an official reality.

A national theatre had been dreamed of and argued since the beginning of the nineties, with its advocates insisting that the American theatre would never be worth anything until it was led by a movement with a solemn title, and its opponents dismissing it as highbrow and visionary. More recently, Ashton Stevens and other alert critics had been pointing out that the United States already had a national theatre—the Manhattan Company, which produced the best available plays with the best actors of the English-speaking stage and took them to the American people.

The facts could not be disputed, but the solemn title and official aura were missing. Advocates of a national theatre found no comfort in having their dream realized in a practical manner while they talked. The big names of business and finance were missing from the project, and the Manhattan Company paid its own way, whereas a national theatre must show a deficit.

The comedy of the situation went unnoticed: Mrs. Fiske, the artist, assumed that a theatre must be run in a businesslike manner, and that if a production did not pay its own way it deserved extinction; in the opposing camp, hardheaded businessmen and financiers had rallied to the belief that art must be endowed up to its ears in wealth.

The national theatre project was named The New Theatre; its thrifty founders included John Jacob Astor, George F. Baker, August Belmont, Elbert H. Gary, George Gould, Archer M. Huntington, Otto Kahn, Clarence Mackay, J. Pierpont Morgan, Cornelius Vanderbilt, William K. Vanderbilt and Harry Payne Whitney.

Theatre dreamers believed the millennium was as good as purchased, but Mrs. Fiske was disappointed. When she looked over the array of names, she commented: "What absolute poverty! In the whole lot there isn't five cents' worth of theatre knowledge!"

The founders did not feel poor, and if they lacked knowledge of the theatre, they were confident of having something just as good—and they poured millions into the project.

For the site of the national theatre, the geographical center of the United States was located on Central Park West, New York City, between Sixty-second and Sixty-third streets. The building, of clear-gray Indiana limestone, was ready for the fall season of 1909. For those who could not travel to New York, it was described and pictured in a beautiful brochure, and some of its features contrasted entertainingly with theatres in which the Fiskes' unofficial national theatre company had played:

The architecture is classical in detail and proportions, and follows the precedent of the Italian Renaissance, suggesting the Sansovino Library in the Piazza di San Marco, Venice. The façade consists of a high base, containing the entrances, and a two-story colonnade crowned by a very rich cornice and balustrade. . . .

The architecture of the Raton skating rink had been desert-American, unpainted boards and tar paper. But there a thousand citizens of New Mexico Territory had seen *The New York Idea* with Mrs. Fiske, John Mason, George Arliss, William B. Mack and Marian Lea.

The relief, which has been studied to interpret the architectural design, is sometimes gray on a gold background and sometimes gold on a gray background. The proscenium arch is framed in a wide border of Connemara marble, and the curtain is made of red velvet embroidered in colors and gold . . .

At Sacramento's Clunie Opera House, the proscenium arch was tin, and the drop curtain canvas, with crudely-painted advertisements, and dropsical cupids afflicted with curvature of the spine and yellow jaundice, twanging away on impossible harps—but that dreadful curtain had risen on *Becky Sharp*, the most glittering comedy of a generation.

The boxes and foyer stalls are lined with red velvet, while the balustrades in front of the first tier of boxes are elevated on a Breche violet marble base, with marble dies and capping to the balustrades, the balustrades themselves being of gold bronze. . . .

In the rinks of the Southwest Territories and the "Last West" of the Canadian frontier, the choice seats were maple floors, polished by

219

roller skates, but from them miners and cowboys and English younger sons had seen the best company of a generation in the comedy of the year.

While the angels of The New Theatre donned their solid-gold wings for the rescue of American drama, Mrs. Fiske was preparing for her second season of *Salvation Nell*, and Harry Fiske rehearsed a dramatization of Locke's popular novel *Septimus*. George Arliss was in the title role, and co-starring with him was Emily Stevens as Emmy Oldrieve.

Emily Stevens had spent eight years of apprenticeship with her famous cousin, and a year in *The Devil* company. Emily was now an impatient twenty-seven—and Minnie still looked on her as a girl who had much to learn before she became an actress. It was Harry Fiske's idea to co-star Emily with George Arliss.

In Harry's quest for perfection, he was still rehearsing the *Septimus* company in the first act, with the opening date looming close ahead. Emily was letter-perfect in that act, and she despaired for her work in the rest of the play. Another actor close to perfection in the first act was Claus Bogel, who had also served a long apprenticeship with Mrs. Fiske. At Emily's suggestion, he rehearsed and coached her in the later acts.

Harry Fiske discovered the private rehearsals and rebuked the young actor for undertaking work for which he had not been engaged.

On the opening night, Emily Stevens gave a consistently fine performance, while other members of the cast were rough in the later acts. Next payday, Claus Bogel received an extra week's pay, with a notation in Harry Fiske's small handwriting: "For work for which you were not engaged."

Mrs. Fiske's tour opened at Bridgeport on October 11, with a red-letter performance. Afterward she told Alexander Woollcott, "I acted *Salvation Nell* steadily for two years, and in all that time I gave only one performance that I approved, only one that was really good. That solitary performance was given, by the way, in Bridgeport. Did you happen to be there?" she asked with mock concern.

Woollcott had not, and the local critics were unimpressed. According to the *Post:*

> Disappointment was written all over the faces of the big and classy audience which filled Jackson's Theatre last night after the final curtain of Mrs. Fiske's. The feeling of disappointment was keen, and it was almost universal. It was a feeling that centered not alone upon the vehicle, but also upon the actress.

A month later, while *Salvation Nell* was playing Grand Rapids, The New Theatre opened in New York, and its founders began learning their first—and last—lesson: an actress born in the theatre could make money out of Ibsen in the New Mexico desert—but the multimillionaires of America could pour money through the sieve of an endowed theatre in New York, and end with nothing but a sieve.

At Saginaw, on the night of November 22, Minnie had a jubilant long-distance call from Harry. He was at the Hackett Theatre in New York, after the premiere of *Septimus*, and he had an undoubted hit. Arliss had been superb, and Bunner would have been proud of Whiffet. She was established as an emotional actress, and during the final curtain calls the audience had shouted, "Emily Stevens, Stevens!"

A week later Minnie wrote Harry:

Whiffet writes me that she is working hard all the time to improve her performance. I am glad she is so interested and has this newly-awakened ambition. If she will correct some faults, acquire technical facility, and learn to control and develop her voice, I really think she will make a good substantial place for herself. There is really no "emotional ingenue" that I know of who could match her performance of "Emmy."

But *Septimus* was a weak play, and Harry Fiske had jeopardized the production by giving Emily Stevens her opportunity. Arliss had wanted the role of Emmy for his devoted wife, Florence; he had been dubious of the inexperienced Emily, and her success did not mend matters. It was the beginning of the end of Arliss' six-year association with the Fiskes.

Minnie's troubles that season were more personal. She was taken ill two days before the premiere of *Septimus*, and a doctor at Jackson, Michigan, advised her that she could not be well again without an operation. Minnie's trouper soul rebelled.

"Patch me up, somehow," she told the doctor, "and telephone ahead to a doctor at Saginaw. I have to play there tomorrow." At Saginaw she went through the same routine; and by the end of her tour she had been patched up by thirty-five doctors in thirteen states.

While touring and fighting illness, Minnie rehearsed her company in a new production. The play was Ibsen's *Pillars of Society*, in which she had cast Holbrook Blinn in the leading role of Karsten Bernick, and herself in the minor one of Lona Hessel.

Several years before, Minnie had laid *Pillars* aside as old-fashioned —to take it up again when some American pillars of society revealed old-fashioned weaknesses.

The casting of *Pillars* and the working out of the production were done while Minnie was on the road. Her daily letters to Harry were crowded with ideas and plans:

Sunday

Darling Boy,

In a very short time I shall send you the manuscript of the 1st, 3rd and 4th acts of "Pillars of Society." I sent you the 2nd act yesterday. Will you please go over the play at once—make all your corrections—then have the parts immediately copied and send those that I can use to me? It is necessary for me to begin rehearsals at the <u>earliest</u> moment. You see traveling as we do we are not able to <u>rehearse</u> <u>regularly</u> or everyday. We have to seize our time for rehearsals and use Sunday always, if possible. Altho February is still a way off there isn't an hour's too much time for the work we have to do—under the peculiar circumstances—so please send me the parts I need—as soon as you can. . . .

With the little handful of people we can safely keep from this company, I can proceed with "The Pillars" rehearsals very well and it will be of the greatest advantage to me. You know how slow I am! The new people can be perfect in their lines when we reach New York and fit in with us.

Dearest love
Bunner

I am writing you a description of the "Pillars" characters. I forgot to say that one of Hilmar's characteristics (as he lolls about the sofas and tables) is to stick his hands in his pockets—and he often has a cigarette—and occasionally turns his coat collar up (velvet lounging coat) in feeling a slight draught . . .

Springfield—Sunday

Hilmar Tonnesen is going to be the hardest part to cast in "Pillars of Society." It is a splendid part, and, in its perfection, demands the art of the most accomplished light comedian . . . Let us realize <u>now</u> the great difficulty of casting it and at once set about looking for actors.

Now today I had a rehearsal of the 1st act with Mr. Blinn and Mr. Tucker. Both of them can be completely relied upon to be silent as to the fact that we contemplate a production of the play. Later, when I have heard from you about the other members of the "Salvation Nell" company whom I have suggested, I shall add to the people attending rehearsals. Their presence helps me very much . . .

"Hilmar" is the part after "Bernick." Any actor reading the part would think it was a bad part!! They always do in these Ibsen plays. They never see them until they are shown. It's sickening. I could see today Mr. Tucker thought "Hilmar" was a poor part—and one that little could be made of. He was dumfounded when I rehearsed it for him and read the Ibsen parts to get the idea. Not one in ten thousand can. It is all so different from what they have been trained in. . . .

Dearest love
Bunner

December 14, 1909

Darling Boy,

Later I shall write you some suggestions about the three business associates of Bernick.

These parts also must be cast with infinite care. These men must carry a great deal of weight and impressiveness. THEY MUST LOOK THE PILLARS OF SOCIETY. In this there is the great irony of the play. The last act is helped greatly by the appearance and manner of these men. As the cast is to be perfect we shall have to consider every part in just this careful manner . . .

I have been thinking a great deal about the scene setting of "Pillars." As the scene sets throughout the entire play it should be charming, most attractive and cheerful . . . I once saw a room set by Mrs. Campbell which seemed to me the most perfect thing I had ever seen in a theatre. The illusion was perfect. The shape of the room, the furniture—everything seemed perfectly real. It looked as though people lived in it and had lived in it for years . . .

It seems to me that we should make a great deal of the portico or veranda, with its bright striped awnings and of the garden beyond, and of the low garden and the little street beyond with its row of houses. These houses should be painted to look very real and the lights shoud appear in the windows of those houses in the last act . . . It will be well to have the night approaching towards the end of the third act. A capital effect will be the suggestion of the coming summer storm. The sky above the houses should be painted and manipulated in such a way as to show the scurrying clouds and suggest in every way the sudden stirring of the storm. . . .

You know the whole back of the room is a large window leading to the portico and revealing the garden and street and sky. This can really be made perfectly beautiful with the bright sun shining through the room . . . So far as the openings are concerned, I have held strictly to Ibsen's directions. They will make it easier for you and me to work in accord—you with your rehearsals in New York, I with mine in traveling. . . .

P.S. Since writing the letter here—I've had more ideas about the

223

"Pillars" set. It can be stunning! . . . I really think I have a fine scheme and idea—When the curtain goes up it must disclose the set of the season!

Montgomery, Ala.
Jan. 12, 1910

In the note I wrote you hastily last night I strongly urged the use of the cyclorama for "Pillars." The same sort of thing we used to have in "Leah Kleschna." The cyclorama will enable you to have the sky effects splendidly done. You can have afternoon glows, evening twilight, moonlight if you wish, then the darkening and gathering of the storm and rushing clouds. For all these the cyclorama is excellent. The gaily striped awning can be hoisted after the 1st and 2nd acts, revealing a good bit of the sky. . . .

Olaf has some charming scenes—scenes that need the really clever acting of a child actor. Olaf should look to be a fine boy of 12, 13, or 14 years of age—little Antrim is too young. There is something tragic in the beating of the older boy—a boy who is just beginning to verge on young manhood. I find in the rehearsals that this idea is an effective one. Will you please have a thorough search made for a fine boy actor? Please do not have a girl to play this boy—the illusion is never complete—we must have a fine manly, real boy boy.

Dearest love
Bunner

As a child Minnie had been cast as a boy oftener than a girl—her first impressive success had been as Prince Arthur—and in her *Tess* Abraham Durbeyfield had been placed by an actress, but she had since renounced the belief that even if actresses could never quite become men, they might at least succeed in being little boys.

In *Salvation Nell* one major part was played by a boy, and for the children in the street scenes Minnie insisted on juvenile actors of the specified ages and sexes.

While the actress was throwing off the shackles of tradition, society was overcorrecting abuses in employment. Louisiana had recently passed a child-labor law which banned children under sixteen from the stage as well as the factory.

At the Tulane Theatre in New Orleans, Mrs. Fiske was offered actresses for the boys' roles, but she refused them. It was her belief that stage children were the best cared for and most fortunate in the world—and she announced that she would cancel her engagement rather than have the production crippled.

224

The deadlock was solved by manager Campbell of the Tulane, who submitted to arrest after each performance, and paid a twenty-five dollar fine the following morning.

At Jacksonville *Salvation Nell* broke all records at the Duval Theatre, with the orchestra moved under the stage and the pit filled with spectators. It was the climax of a financially successful tour—but Minnie was unreconciled to the loss of the great Manhattan Company that had been scattered in unprofitable ventures. After the Jacksonville triumph, she wrote to Harry:

> I never want to face an audience again with an inferior company. It so humiliated me that I feel that I'll never survive it. The audiences applaud until it is embarrassing and I feel it is only because they feel they should. . . .

The tour ended at Trenton on February 12, and Minnie entered a hospital for her long-overdue operation. The same afternoon she wrote Harry:

> Darling—precious Boy,
> I am just out of the ether. . . . I was in good condition and came out fine—I am hungry! and that is a wonderful state. I was hardly sick at all but can't sit up. Am on back flat. Felt fine when went up to operating room and mad to spoil a beautiful day.
> When under the ether I said, "These doctors are sweet creatures!" Hilda heard it.
> Have as good a time as you can, Boy. Whiffet is coming. Dearest love darling, darling boy.
>
> Bunner

CHAPTER 29

Six weeks after Mrs. Fiske's tour had ended in surgery, the curtain rose smoothly on *Pillars of Society*. During her brief convalescence, the two halves of the production had been welded in rehearsals and the play tried out at Rochester. The New York premiere was at the Lyceum Theatre, with its shades of Minnie Maddern, Harrison Grey Fiske of the *Mirror*, young Richard Mansfield and Steele MacKaye.

In the years since the historic engagement of *In Spite of All* in 1885, Mansfield had achieved fame and wealth—and driven himself to death; and MacKaye, genius of theatre mechanics, had died in poverty. Minnie, at forty-five, remained a solvent idealist, but her ideals went hand in hand with shrewd theatre knowledge.

Ibsen was still spoken of as the most unpopular playwright in America, but Mrs. Fiske was relying on *Pillars* for most of her season, and she had three-sheet posters printed in the Scandinavian languages and German for cities with large northern European elements.

She also believed that *Pillars of Society*, with its timely exposure of the methods of capitalists, and its happy ending, would appeal to native Americans more than the sterner Ibsen plays.

Her calculations were correct; the play was welcomed, and *Life* observed of its theme:

> It might not be a bad idea in the way of uplift for Mrs. Fiske to take her company downtown and give a special performance of "Pillars of Society" somewhere in the neighborhood of Wall Street, so that the gentlemen who conduct the corporation affairs of America might have a chance to study Mr. Ibsen's analysis of their kind of doings.

In the cast of twenty characters, the best opportunities went to Holbrook Blinn, Cyril Chadwick and young Merle Maddern. Well down in the order of importance, Lona Hessel was played by Mrs. Fiske. But in the play the unconventional Lona returned from America to leaven a stuffy Norwegian community with fresh air and light—and by the same token Minnie was the leaven of the production. In the great scene of Bernick's confession, Lona was only a spectator who made one inarticulate sound, but its effect on the play was sheer magic. Walter Prichard Eaton recorded:

> Mrs. Fiske, as Lona, sat quiet, one of the crowd; but gradually, as she saw the man she loved throwing off his yoke of hypocrisy, the light of a great joy radiated from her face, ending in a stifled cry, half sob, half laugh of triumph, of indescribable poignancy. To one beholder, at least, it brought the rush of tears, and made the emotional as well as the intellectual drift of the play suddenly completely clear, completely fused and compelling.

More than any other role in her career, Minnie's Lona Hessel radiated warmth and sanity. The glow touched the Ibsen-hating Alan Dale, who began his review: "How good and how immensely nourishing it did seem to sit in the Lyceum last night and watch Mrs. Fiske in 'Pillars of Society,' after a season of shredded stars, half-shell luminaries, and experimental ladies. . . ." He went on to approve of everything about Mrs. Fiske, even her diction, which she had "manicured so successfully that it leaped triumphantly over the footlights."

Oddly, the same performance inspired a poem which immortalized the mannerisms of speech which Minnie had almost conquered. The day after Alan Dale's review, New York and the actress chuckled over a bit of "deathless" rhyme by Franklin P. Adams in the *Evening Mail*:

FOOTLIGHT MOTIFS

I

Mrs. Fiske

(Note: Once a week upon this page
Shall come some verses on The Stage.)

Staccato,hurried,nervous,brisk,
  Cascading, intermittent,choppy.
The brittle voice of Mrs. Fiske
  Shall serve me now as copy.

Time was, when first that voice I heard,
  Despite my close and tense endeavor,
When many an important word
  Was lost and gone forever

Though unlike others at the play,
I never whispered: *"Wha'd 'd she say?"*

Somewords she runstogetherso;
   Some others are distinctly stated
Somecometoofast and   s o m e t o o s l o w
   And some are syncopated,
And yet no voice—I am sincere—
Exists that I prefer to hear.

For what is called "intelligence"
   By every Mrs. Fiskeian critic
As usual is just a sense
   Of humor, analytic.
So anytime I'm glad to frisk
Two bones to witness Mrs. Fiske.

The comparative reform of Minnie's diction, and the bracing role of Lona following the drab Salvation Nell were part of a conscious change in her relation to the public. Originally she had scheduled Hauptmann's *Hannele* ahead of *Pillars*, but she reversed the order and she gave her reasons in a letter to Harry. As Hannele she would again have a role of rags and misery and beatings. The critics, she said, would observe the similarity to Nell and complain.

Minnie was still doing what she wanted to do, but with a difference: she could no longer afford to ignore criticism, and she avoided it with over-all strategy.

Pillars was followed by *Hannele*, the story of a beggar girl dying in an almshouse, with a wish-fulfillment dream of ascending to Heaven in music and lights and the singing of angels—much as little Minnie Maddern as Eva had ascended in a soapbox in the long-ago production of *Uncle Tom's Cabin.*

Unconsciously, the middle-aged actress was drawn to the role in which she returned to childhood, with the exhausting experiences of life falling away from her. During most of the action she lay in an almshouse bed, and in the crystal peace of a glass coffin, surrounded by the reassuring religious symbols of childhood. After years of soul-searching roles, it had its comforts.

In producing *Hannele* with its literal angels, the vision of Christ, a golden stairway to Heaven, and the fact that Minnie was appearing as a girl of fourteen, there were many technical problems. In part the dream atmosphere was achieved by a mesh between stage and audience.

Music was important in establishing the mood of the play, and the score had been especially composed by Max Marschalk. Harry Fiske provided a symphonic orchestra and he engaged the visiting conductor, Alexander Birnbaum, who had run afoul of the musicians' union in his attempt to appear in the United States. Marschalk's prelude, composed for German audiences, was far too long for American patience, and Minnie cut it to a third of its original length.

On the night of *Hannele's* premiere, with the auditorium in darkness, the orchestra struck up in fine style—but Minnie noticed that Birnbaum had restored the first cut in the score. When he restored the second, she sent the stage manager with a reminder, but nothing could distract Birnbaum's attention from the full score. He went through the endless prelude with the audience writhing in their seats and applauding impatiently for the play to begin. When the prelude finally ended, with the audience verging on mutiny and hysteria, Birnbaum had made his American debut—and marred the premiere.

Just sixteen years before, the first American production of *Hannele* had rocked a New York ready to find blasphemy in the play. The S.P.C.C. had forced the producers to replace the sixteen-year-old girl in the title role with an elderly woman; a Tammany mayor banned the play; and the visiting Gerhart·Hauptmann was threatened with mobbing and arrest.

The New York of 1910 took *Hannele* in its stride without being too much impressed. Some critics saw beauty in it, others only gruesomeness; and the majority agreed that Mrs. Fiske had put the American stage in her debt with the first adequate production of the German classic.

On Central Park West, The New Theatre was performing similar services, at vast expense. The directors now recognized the Fiskes by inviting them to bring *Hannele* to The New Theatre. It was an opportunity to present the play on the most complete stage in America— but the Fiskes had been left out of the project for so long that they proudly declined. Afterward they regretted it, although Minnie had been convinced from the beginning that The New Theatre was doomed to failure under its lavish and impractical management.

Hannele was temporarily shelved at the end of the New York engagement, and Minnie took the company on the road. They played in *Pillars*, and on Sundays she rehearsed them in *Becky Sharp*.

The *Becky* production got its finishing touches in St. Louis. The regular theatre season was over, but necessity forced the actress to explore new territories in place and time, and she began a tour that lasted the year round. And presently she wrote Harry:

Darling Boysie,

I think it may be well for us to begin to lay out some general plan for next season's route. I have the following suggestion to offer:—

If Mr. Mitchell's play is satisfactory let us prepare it and present it for the last two weeks of our Chicago engagement in October. We can cast Mr. Mitchell's play very well with people in our present company. . . .

After the production of Mr. Mitchell's play in Chicago we should put it aside, no matter what its success. After the Chicago engagement let us begin the southern tour with nothing but "Becky Sharp" and the company should be revised and changed to the best advantage to ourselves for this tour of "Becky Sharp. . . ."

Of course everything has to be held off until we have finished reading Mr. Mitchell's play. I am delighted with my part in the first act. I shouldn't be at all surprised if we accepted the play, and then directly we can make our plans. . . .

The principal import of this letter is to say that I believe we shall find Becky a tower of strength. The play is not nearly exhausted and now that we have revived it, we should squeeze the lemon dry and make perfect use of it.

Early in the history of *Becky*, Mrs. Fiske had refused newspaper interviews for three years because a reporter had quoted her as saying the play was a hit. Behind her present tough-minded sentiment was the compelling reason of necessity.

The Trust war had done its worst, but in their different ways both the Fiskes had taken their own steps toward financial ruin. Minnie spent little on herself, but she belonged, and contributed, to nearly every humanitarian society in the world. Harry had grown up as the son of a reputed millionaire, and while he had inherited nothing, the millionaire aura clung to his manner of living—and he made stars and helped men and women in various walks of life precisely as if he had millions to draw on. In the theatre, he worked himself to exhaustion producing popular plays that were to earn money and give his wife greater freedom—but the popular plays often failed and cut into the profits earned by Minnie's artistic successes.

Septimus had established Emily Stevens as a star, but it had lost money, and Harry's production of *None So Blind* had lost more. Late in June Harry wrote his wife, contrasting his failures with the success of commercial producers.

The letter was delivered at the Mason Opera House in Los Angeles, just before a *Pillars* matinee. Minnie, in costume, wearing the fantastic hat Lona Hessel had brought from America, and in her bracing Lona frame of mind, dashed off a note to Harry:

Precious—darling Boysie:

All your dear letters are here. Today there is a matinee but I shall answer carefully tomorrow.

You haven't anything to be discouraged about—precious Boy. The theatrical profession is not a profession where brains & high intelligence & superior ability are needed. You and I are not of it and we shall succeed in concentrating upon the only sort of dramatic production we know & understand. These managers you speak of are many of them on the verge of ruin. One frequently threatens suicide! It's a queer business but we have our safe road in it!—a heartful of dearest love—Bunner.

After the matinee, she wrote:

Darling Boy

You have no idea how splendidly "Pillars of Society" goes. We can safely revive it in New York some time when we can get the ideal "Bernick" & then, I'll bet you'll see I was right about the play! It's good to have in one's repertoire—& some day we'll do it beautifully.

With her unending urgent seasons, Minnie seldom had time to think of herself, but in her third letter from Los Angeles she wrote:

For the first time California doesn't seem so dear! I am longing so much every minute for you & Whiffet—& Lake Pleasant & I am often very homesick (terribly so.) & lonely for my own ones. But things will be fine after this summer & we can have vacations together.

I'll write properly tomorrow. . . .

At San Francisco, with shrewd inverted showmanship, Mrs. Fiske made the public clamor for Ibsen. She managed it by announcing *Becky* for her engagement, with no mention of *Pillars*. The *Post* observed of the omission: "We felt that our culture had been challenged. . . The West is confoundedly sensitive concerning its culture."

Pillars was presented, and in mid-July drew large audiences in a San Francisco as cool as the Norwegian coast in summer. In the interior the climate was more like Africa. On the eighteenth, at Sacramento, the curtain of Clunie's Opera House—with drugstore and horse-doctor advertisements, and dropsical cupids—rose on the six-hundredth performance of *Becky Sharp*.

It was over 100 degrees in the theatre, but Mrs. Fiske never slackened

231

the furious tempo of the play. After the wilted audience and cast had scattered to their homes and hotels, she sent Harry a message, suggesting that she play *Pillars* at one-night stands. After three typed pages of intricate plans, she wrote in pen, as an afterthought, "Terribly hot here! Too hot for good house."

Demonstratedly, it was not too hot for the enduring little actress, but Emily Stevens had joined the company and in an interview she observed, "Mrs. Fiske is made of iron; she never tires, and she doesn't understand that other people can tire."

Portland's reception of *Pillars* justified Minnie's faith in playing it in the West. After the first performance, the *Journal* summed up: "It was in the nature of a complete triumph. The audience was lost in tumults of admiration. . . ."

Through superb management, and going without vacation, and her own genius, Mrs. Fiske was making her tour pay while she searched for her next attraction. She still had hopes of Langdon Mitchell's unfinished comedy, but it was progressing too slowly for her to feel at ease. During the year she had read nearly three hundred manuscript plays, and she had found only one with promise—an unfinished suffragette play by Gertrude Atherton.

Mrs. Fiske read plays all over America, without ever knowing in what town the lightning of a produceable play would strike. Most of the plays came through agents and friends of friends, but on an average of once a week, some unknown sent her a manuscript by registered mail. Occasionally, the postmaster refused to let Mrs. Fiske's manager sign for the offering, and she had to appear at the post office in person for some shopgirl's dream of high society, or a society matron's dream of the perils of shopgirls.

At Vancouver, B. C., Mrs. Fiske received something like her three-hundredth play for the year—a comedy by a man named Smith, with the suspiciously pompous title of *Mrs. Bumpstead-Leigh*. She began it dutifully and chuckled through it at one sitting.

Mrs. Bumpstead-Leigh was an artless homespun farce that would not have received a second thought from Mrs. Fiske's admirers. But the actress had a sense of humor which some of her followers lacked, and she had done nothing to encourage the traditions about her superior mind.

The preceding season, after a *Salvation Nell* matinee, Mrs. Fiske had laughed William Sage of the Cleveland *Leader* out of her dressing room for taking her intellect too seriously. A few days later, Sage avenged himself by sending her a Cincinnati review in which the great Montgomery Phister spoke of "Mrs. Fiske, the most intellectual of American actresses." Sage added a note, "What are you going to do with Phister? Read him out of the ranks, also?"

In reply, the actress sent Sage a picture postcard with a one-line message, "Isn't it awful, Mabel?"

With an "Isn't it awful, Mabel?" for the solemn-minded of her following, Minnie wired her acceptance of *Mrs. Bumpstead-Leigh*. It was the second time in two years that she had accepted a play by an unknown young Harvard man after an hour's consideration.

A few days later she wrote Harry:

Tacoma, Wash.
August 7, 1910

Darling—darling Boy,

I am sending you the manuscript of the new comedy of which I wrote you. I think it is immensely clever. But what impresses me most is the fact that "Adelaide"—Mrs. Bumpstead-Leigh—is simply stunning for me. . . .

The play has faults, but these, I am sure, can be easily and quickly corrected. I strongly urge that the author, Mr. Smith, prepare this play for production in Chicago. We could easily have it ready for the last week of the Chicago engagement.

I think the play will be a great success, simply because of the peculiar fitness of my part. We can at least give it a week's trial in Chicago and then put it aside, no matter how great its success may be, for later use.

On September 28, *Pillars* ended the Detroit engagement in what the press described as a blaze of glory. The same sleepless night, Minnie wrote her husband:

Darling Boy

When you come back—& after the bother of our new productions is over & we have a breathing space—we can talk over ideas in the aim to plan the next five years in such a way as to make them yield us a larger profit than we can make—going along in the usual way. . . I think we have reached a point now when we can hit upon some idea that will mean an immense profit to us in a short space of time—& to this thought & its practical consummation we will devote ourselves. My deep wish is to put enough by in securities during the next five years—so that the future will be safe. Then I should dearly love a small but comfortable little home—very near New York—

233

where I could live when I am in N. Y. A place nearby—like Mt.
St. Vincent—for example (only about 10 minutes from New York
by automobile.) The place would not be at all a rival of the place I
hope we shall one day have at Lake Pleasant—Not at all—I would
like a modest little place—that would be so little expense that we
could lock it up at any time we wished. . . An automobile would
make it perfectly practicable. . .

With enough money invested in good securities—& enough of it—
we should be able to travel—if we wished—& to have a little leisure
and pleasure.

I want to work like a beaver for the next five years to help bring
this about!! . . .

In October of her vacationless year, Minnie brought her company to
Chicago for a two-week engagement. As a good omen, she was wel-
comed by Ashton Stevens, who had recently been transferred to the
Chicago *Examiner.*

After the opening night, Stevens expressed the hope that the new
plays he missed were one-tenth as interesting as the revival of *Becky
Sharp;* and most of the other critics joined him in finding Mrs. Fiske
secure in the highest niche of the American theatre.

Minnie thanked them all—and refused to be interviewed on theatre
matters; Sunday feature-stories had to be concocted out of her evasions
and Humane Society handouts.

Ashton Stevens fared better personally than the other critics, accompanying Mrs. Fiske on her theatregoing expeditions—usually to vaudeville shows since her own performances ruled out legitimate attractions.
Mr. Stevens recalled that her applause was usually for the acrobats; the
good ones reminded her of the certitude she enjoyed in the acting of
Duse and Réjane. Acrobats, she said, had to be good or break their
necks. And once, smiling through her veil, she observed that it might be
a good thing for the legitimate stage if actors broke their necks when
they failed to follow the code of honest teamwork.

Externally, Mrs. Fiske was still the remote artist, hewing to the line
and ignoring the chips of box-office receipts. In actuality, her Chicago
success was so complete that no interviews could add to it, and she was
encouraging the drums to be beaten elsewhere. The seemingly aloof
artist was writing long letters to editor Waldron of the *Dramatic
Mirror,* urging him to squeeze the last drop of publicity out of her
Chicago triumph.

CHAPTER 30

Mrs. Fiske was beginning to see her career in perspective, with her great creative efforts behind her, and *Becky Sharp* the greatest of them all. From Montgomery, Alabama, on November 30, she wrote Harry a long letter in which she urged that her New York engagement begin with the revival of *Becky Sharp*. She argued:

> I somehow feel that I owe it to myself, and to the work I have put into the part to give it this opportunity, if there is any possible way in the world to do so. I have worked on the part, rounded it, developed it, and elaborated it tremendously. I have, I think, corrected all the old faults, and I know that it is quite a different thing from seven years ago; in some respects it is perhaps the best and most important part that I shall ever have. . . .

A few days afterwards her exclusive hold was shaken. The New Theatre announced that in January it would present Marie Tempest as Becky Sharp in a dramatization of *Vanity Fair* by Cosmo Gordon Lennox, husband of the actress.

Years before, the Lennox-Tempest *Becky* had been presented in London in the wake of Mrs. Fiske's history-making success in the role in America. It had been one of a series of events that prevented Minnie forever from appearing on the English stage.

The new blow came in a hard-pressed year, with Mrs. Fiske touring in the role and counting heavily on it. She wrote to Harry:

Darling Boy—
It was a shock to me to hear that The New Theatre was to present "Becky."

Frankly, this had been quite a serious blow to me. Now that I have rounded out the part, and developed it, as far as I can ever develop it, I feel that at the moment, old as it is, it is the most valuable thing

235

we possess artistically. Coming after all the dullness of the year I felt it would make a stronger effect than anything we have ever done. I know, in my heart, that it is now an entirely different thing from what it was six years ago. I do not think that what is to be presented at The New Theatre will have anything like its real value. I do not see what can be done, but perhaps you will think wisely on the subject and see if something cannot be done to advance my interests in this matter. Even if we were to cancel some of the one-night stands and arrange a New York engagement in the near future, such a procedure would scarcely be dignified. . . .

Whatever we do, or whatever our plans are to be, I think it is most advisable to announce "Becky Sharp" at once, as to be part of our New York repertoire. . . . The announcement could be simply to the effect that the plays we are to produce in New York are Becky Sharp, Julia France, and Mrs. Bumpstead-Leigh. I really believe that if we had announced Becky before this The New Theatre would not have considered its present plan. . . .

I repeat the thing has been a great disappointment to me. . . . I think "Becky" would have stirred old New York—as it is now. I did not play it well in the past. Oh! I am so disappointed! I had counted so much on the opportunity!

At the top of the letter, she wrote in pencil: "Please regard this letter as absolutely private between us."

A little later, Minnie wrote buoyantly and generously:

We must do our Becky exquisitely and beautifully for a week—when we come!

Do not let the Mirror be uncomplimentary to The New Theatre production. If the Mirror critic does not like it—make him soften his criticism!

The New Theatre production of *Vanity Fair* was scheduled for early January, 1911. On December 28, from Reading, Mrs. Fiske wrote her final injunction about the rival production:

Darling Boy

When Vanity Fair is produced at The New Theatre will you please instruct Mr. Waldron to see that no comparison of Miss Tempest's "Becky" with mine be made in the Mirror? The Mirror critic might think he ought to say something detrimental to Miss Tempest's "Becky" in comparison & that would be bad taste in your paper.

Dearest love
Bunnikin

236

Mrs. Fiske returned to New York in March of 1911. She returned, to match her travel-worn *Becky* with the one that had played in the marble-and-gold palace of The New Theatre.

The verdict was almost entirely in favor of the Fiske production. The New Theatre version was classed as less significant in the writing and the acting; and less true to the novel and its times—a graceful comedy lacking the depths which made Mrs. Fiske's Becky a lifelong memory for a generation of theatregoers.

The contest for which she had steeled herself was nothing, but there was another contest for which she was not prepared: she was playing against her own production of better times, and against time itself.

The Fiskes could no longer afford a prodigal cast of stars; the best they could do was a new Marquis of Steyne for the production. Mrs. Fiske had written Harry, "We could try to get old Tyrone Power for the part." But Power had deserted them twice, and Harry would have nothing more to do with him.

They compromised on Henry E. Dixey, who was an accomplished actor, but handicapped by having to play against spectators' memories of Tyrone Power's great Steyne, and George Arliss' still greater and more recent impersonation.

Playing against her own earlier productions, Mrs. Fiske's *Becky* revival did not make the stir in New York that she had hoped for, but the press noted that her Becky was more real and alive than ever. The revival filled the Lyceum for two weeks, while Minnie held daily rehearsals of her next offering.

Before the brief tryout of *Mrs. Bumpstead-Leigh* in Chicago, the author, Harry James Smith, had been summoned to work on the play. He was a shy and frail young New Englander, far finer than his rowdy farce suggested. In Chicago he had worked on the play with unfailing patience and good humor. Writing to a friend during those strenuous days, he gave a glimpse of the labor, and the rewards of working with Mrs. Fiske:

> Everybody is working like a dray-horse to do his best. And the situations and lines still remain so amusing to us, despite our deep-furrowed familiarity with them that over and over again the rehearsal is held up while we shake with mirth. Mrs. Fiske's sense of humor is delicious. She is a taskmistress, if ever there was one; but even when most exacting, you are only too glad to serve her. Her genius is so indubitable, so compelling, that you sweat blood, and thank her for the privilege. . .

Since Chicago, Mr. Smith had lengthened and improved the play in line with the actress's suggestions. In New York he was on hand again for two weeks of doctoring and rehearsing.

Hard necessity had required economies in the production, and the saga of the patent-medicine heiresses had just missed being enacted in the room from which Ibsen's Rosmer and Rebecca had gone to their deaths in the millrace. At the last minute Mrs. Fiske had changed her mind in favor of a repainted set from *The Devil*.

Henry Dixey was not one of the economies of *Bumpstead-Leigh*. Mrs. Fiske had accepted the high-salaried actor as a passable Marquis of Steyne because she saw him as the ideal Peter Swallow. His superb light-comedy manner took most of the curse from the heavy humor of the tombstone salesman.

The plot of *Mrs. Bumpstead-Leigh* was built around the family of the late Jim Sayles, patent-medicine king of Missionary Loop, Indiana. Inheriting a fortune, Ma Sayles and her two daughters went social-climbing in Washington, D. C. The idea and the generalship were supplied by the indomitable Della, who became Adelaide. Ollie, the appealing younger sister, became Violet. Ma remained hopelessly Hoosier, but she was taught to keep her mouth shut, which served almost as well as wit. And the family name was changed from Sayles to De Salle.

In Washington, Adelaide stormed an English clergyman of the lesser nobility and became Mrs. Bumpstead-Leigh. In England, she cultivated a stupendous British accent and got her sister engaged to Anthony Rawson, scion of a wealthy old American family.

The play begins with the three climbers visiting the Rawsons on Long Island, Adelaide dripping with culture in public, and easing into Hoosier vernacular when she is alone with Ma and Violet.

Enter Peter Swallow, tombstone salesman from Hoboken. Peter, formerly of Missionary Loop, has known the Sayleses in their patent-medicine days and been jilted by Adelaide. Hearing of the De Salles through the Rawsons, Peter suspects that they are none other than the Sayleses. He is about to confront them.

Forewarned, Adelaide sends Ma to bed with a sick headache and marshals her forces for the battle of her life. Violet remains passive.

Peter Swallow arrives, with much heavy humor, and opines that Adelaide is Della Sayles.

Adelaide looks through her lorgnette at what she declares to be an American type unknown to her, and deluges Peter with pretentious English and French until he is no longer sure who he is himself, let alone who this geyser of culture may be. He retreats, dumbfounded.

The battle is won—but Violet throws it away by proclaiming the truth, and the impostors are invited to leave.

When all seems lost, Adelaide discovers that Violet and Geoffrey, the youngest Rawson son, are in love and about to elope. She marshals her forces again, confronts the elder Rawsons with a scandal garnered from the servants, and offers them a choice.

The Rawsons announce to a waiting reporter the engagement of Violet and Geoffrey. True love, and blackmail, triumph.

The hit of the piece was Minnie's Mrs. Bumpstead-Leigh. It was observed that the audience positively kicked up its heels with delight at the prospect of her being left in privacy with her mother and sister. Her change from drawing room English and French phrases to Hoosier dialect was as exciting as dramatic action, and more hilarious.

Next day most of the critics hailed *Mrs. Bumpstead-Leigh* as a new home-grown *Becky Sharp*, the drollest role Mrs. Fiske had played since *Featherbrain*, and a revelation in modern comedy. A few others, who had previously complained of Mrs. Fiske's intellectuality and her somber roles, now objected to her playing a vulgarian in a crudely written farce. The public came to the Lyceum in droves, and *Mrs. Bumpstead-Leigh* settled down to the longest New York run which Mrs. Fiske had had in years; and the Fiskes' precarious fortunes steadied.

While newspapers argued the merits of Mrs. Fiske's plunge into light comedy, the current issue of *Century Magazine* featured an article by Walter Prichard Eaton entitled, "Mrs. Fiske and Her Influence on the American Stage." The article began with a statement made in Paris by Mme. Réjane: "As a producer of plays, Mrs. Fiske has no superior in Europe." And it ended: "Acting like this which sees the character steadily and sees it whole, which sees it in its setting and holds it there, of course cannot be mere intuition of the emotions; it must 'come from the head.' But it must come from the heart, too, or how could it move so many of us to tears? . . . Mannerisms and limitations Mrs. Fiske has; but her combined talents of intellectual judgment in selecting plays, imaginative skill in stage management, and nervous intensity and spiritual insight in acting, make her, though she be a woman, the leader of the American stage to-day."

A practical example of Mrs. Fiske's influence was on view at the Astor Theatre, on Broadway, less than a block from the Lyceum. It was one of the popular hits of the year: *The Boss*, written by Edward Sheldon whom Mrs. Fiske had helped from the classroom to the front rank of successful playwrights. Sheldon's play was the first starring vehicle of Holbrook Blinn, who had come into his own in the great production of *Salvation Nell,* and Blinn's leading lady was Emily Stevens, about whom *Life* observed: "Miss Emily Stevens is harvesting the fruits of her considerable apprenticeship with Mrs. Fiske. Her teaching is shown a little by imitation of mannerisms of speech, but more creditably in freedom from conventional pose and movement. . . ."

The author of *The Boss* and its stars owed a good deal to Mrs. Fiske, but she was not entirely satisfied with their performance. *The Boss,* Edward Sheldon's third play in three years, did not live up to the promise he had shown in *Salvation Nell* and *The Nigger,* and its popular success did not blind Mrs. Fiske to the fact that it was a melodrama made up of stock situations. Sheldon, she thought, should have done better; and while he was now a firmly established playwright, he had still to prove that he was a good one. Neither was Mrs. Fiske satisfied with Holbrook Blinn as the Boss. Notwithstanding his great performance as Jim Platt, and Mrs. Fiske's personal liking for him, she had since decided that he was lacking as an actor. An actor, she believed, could be no bigger than his imagination, and she found the generous and able Blinn lacking in that quality. As the Boss's wife, Emily Stevens fared better in Mrs. Fiske's judgment, making a good deal out of a vague and inconsistent part. It was also true that Minnie, by habit, still looked on her younger cousin as a girl and made allowances for imperfections in her work.

The doubts Mrs. Fiske sometimes had about Edward Sheldon's stamina as an artist did not keep her from encouraging him to write another play for her—and they did not extend to him personally. Financial success had not changed the open-hearted, boyish playwright. Chivalry was making its last stand in some of the young men who had come of age early in the century, and Edward Sheldon was the beau ideal of the last of the knights. An apocryphal story about him concerned his falling in love with an actress who appeared in one of his plays. Sheldon, on bended knee, implored the young woman to be his bride.

The actress was fond of him, but reluctant. "But Ned," she told him, "how do you know it would work? We might be perfectly miserable. Why don't we live together for a while, and see how we get along?"

Sheldon, according to the story, rose from his knees and proclaimed with all the solemnity of his twenty-few years, "Lips that have not spoken the marriage vow shall never touch mine!"

Mrs. Fiske's second Harvard playwright was an idealist of a different sort. The difference between them was suggested by the ways in which they spent their money. After *Salvation Nell*, Mrs. Fiske received letters from Ned Sheldon written in Berlin and Vienna and Paris, and after the success of *The Nigger*, letters written in a gondola on the Grand Canal at Venice.

After the successful tryout of *Mrs. Bumpstead-Leigh* in Chicago, Harry James Smith had gone into northern Connecticut to spend all his money on a beautiful black saddle horse, and he spent three days riding home through snow squalls and rain flurries across the wild Litchfields, which he called, "my own heart's country." With the more substantial success of his comedy, he began looking for a farmhouse on the Gaspé peninsula in Quebec.

Mrs. Fiske had found the young playwright reserved, even for a New Englander, but in early June when she was about to begin her western tour, she received a revealing letter:

Berlin, Connecticut
31 May.

Dear Mrs. Fiske—

I suspect that I shall not have a better chance than the present moment to tell you what I have long wished I could tell you and what I would have told you, too, only for the half morbid fear I have of seeming to use the implements so readily used by the self-seeking and untrue. Dreading to be classed with professional courtiers, I usually run to the opposite extreme and say nothing. But now that I have no longer (so far as I know) any favors to ask, I want to do myself the justice of telling you that the acquaintance I have had with you these past months has been the biggest inspiration of my life. You have done more for me than I could ever possibly acknowledge:—I can only hope that my work in the future will prove, in some sense, worthy of the discipline and uplift my association with you has brought me—I entertain, as you doubtless know, no very mean idea of my own work; I certainly hope to go far before I am done; but I shall retain all my life a deep and cherished sense of my indebtedness to you—the most wonderful woman I have ever known.

If the inclination takes you, some day, will you be so kind as to send me an inscribed photograph of yourself? I need not tell you, after what I have said, that I should prize it.

This letter, of course, requires no response. I write it chiefly for my own sake—because I owe it to myself; and I am sure you will accept it in the spirit in which it was written.

With all good wishes
Sincerely yours
Harry James Smith

241

As Harry Smith predicted in another letter, wherever Mrs. Fiske went, her *Mrs. Bumpstead-Leigh* was remembered with happy laughter. Her western tour lasted from early June to mid-August, and except for the heat, it was an easy tour. The role made few demands on her, and she was able to devote a good deal of her time to projects that were close to her heart. One of them was working up interest in a monument to her late friend, Mark Twain, who had died the year before. Typical of her speeches and interviews, she observed: "Mark Twain improved always. He never went backward. His soul grew finer and sweeter every year. That was because he remained alert and alive to contemporary life and kept his sympathies keen by exercising them."

Still more of her time was devoted to humanitarian causes, in which Twain had helped her valiantly by writing an anti-bullfighting story, *A Horse's Tale.* She gave interviews and talks against the wearing of furs and feathers, and the inhuman treatment of cattle on the range, and she continued to rebuke ex-President Roosevelt for his African hunt. In New York she had come across a Swedish humane document, the prayer of a horse to its master, which included excellent directions for the proper treatment of horses. At her own expense, Mrs. Fiske had "A Horse's Prayer to Mankind" translated into English and printed on linen-backed posters. In Wisconsin, she had many copies of the document posted in the northern lumber camps. Later, she distributed the posters wherever horses were used in large numbers, and to this day copies of the "Horse's Prayer" may be found in riding academies.

In Minnesota, the "traveling humane society," as Mrs. Fiske was called, heard of an armless marksman who was having remarkable success in shooting pigeons. Forthwith, she had a warrant sworn out for his arrest—only to discover that the pigeons were of clay. She offered her apologies and joined in the public laugh.

For Mrs. Fiske the high spot of the tour was reached in San Francisco. Through arrangements with the National Humane Alliance, of which Harry Fiske was president and Mrs. Fiske vice-president, a horses' drinking fountain had been erected at Mission and Thirteenth streets. The fountain was a five-ton affair of polished Maine granite, with bronze hardware, a circular drinking basin for horses and lower ones for dogs, and it was inaugurated on July Fourth.

San Francisco, as usual, was in the midst of civic contention, and some of the crosscurrents found their way into the dedication of the animals' drinking place. Also, it was Mrs. Fiske's practical view that the fountain was a place for horses to drink, and not for orators to spout. The *Bulletin* described the scene:

Wearing a coat suit of blue, and soft straw hat trimmed in lavender, set off by two veils, Mrs. Fiske arrived at 10:50 o'clock in a little Maxwell runabout, looking rather petite. Her Negro maid accompanied her.

With practically no preliminaries, she alighted from the car and, prancing up the steps leading to the platform, Mrs. Fiske quickly took her wooden seat in the front row.

The Mayor, as usual, was late in arriving, and halted the ceremonies for several minutes. His speech of acceptance to the presentation address of John Partridge, president of the San Francisco Society for the Prevention of Cruelty to Animals, contained more of the self-boosting principles of his administration.

He took special pride, he said, in the fact that the fountain is located "south of Market street."

Mrs. Fiske declined to remove either her white automobile veil or the black dotted one underneath, despite the apparent eagerness of the crowd to see her at a close glance without paying for it.

Neither did she seem particularly interested in the speeches, for several times during the Mayor's speech she rose to watch the sparrows and dogs which came to drink of the fountain's waters. . . .

Mrs. Fiske, eager to have the fountain put to its intended uses, made no speech, limiting herself to pulling the unveiling cord. The police then cleared a way through the crowd, and made a human chain to deflect traffic to the new drinking place.

The first vehicle to be caught in the net was an automobile. When teams of horses were driven up, they were too frightened by the crowd to drink. Later, when Minnie heard that fourteen hundred horses were drinking from the new fountain every day, she felt rewarded.

Earlier in her tour Minnie had written Harry that she was almost embarrassed with a richness of plays, with a new comedy on the way from Langdon Mitchell, and the renowned Gertrude Atherton writing her a play on women's suffrage, the most-discussed cause in America.

By now, however, she was troubled. In Paris, Langdon Mitchell's comedy was creeping at a snail's pace toward completion. And in San Francisco, Mrs. Atherton had just given an interview in which she observed that playwriting was so easy that she would have trouble going back to the labor of writing novels. It shocked Mrs. Fiske that anyone should believe that there was anything easy about a play.

The *Bumpstead-Leigh* tour ended in Minneapolis on August 10. Mrs. Fiske returned to New York, where she remained long enough to pack for a month's rest in the Adirondacks.

For three solid years she had been playing six days a week, and rehearsing on Sundays. It took her a week in the mountains to learn how to rest again, and during her entire vacation she had forebodings about the coming season.

At Camp Craig in the Adirondacks, Minnie received a letter from her non-producing hobo friend, whom she now thought of as Ulric Brendel sitting on an empty treasure chest. He wrote in part:

> The same night I saw you play in Minneapolis I caught a train for the west and as always on the road there was plenty of adventure before I reached Butte.
>
> This place is full of wonderful stories. Deep down in the mines it is wonderful. I would like to write so another would understand as I do the things I have seen when I worked as a miner here. . . Perhaps I may write the big story of the road yet.

Late that sleepless night, Minnie wrote a note and pinned it to her nightgown: "There are wonderful plays, too, deep down in the mines, but who will dig them out?"

CHAPTER 31

The Fiskes had accepted *The New Marriage* on the strength of an idea and a promising first act. But some jinx had hung over Langdon in Paris; the play crept at a snail's pace during the spring and summer, and when the later acts reached Mrs. Fiske, they were weak and disappointing—but she was committed to the play.

The Fiskes had been forced to economize on *Mrs. Bumpstead-Leigh* although it seemed certain of success—and now they were obliged to give Mitchell's doubtful play a production that would help make up for its weaknesses. Harry staged it elaborately, and it was presented with a splendid cast that included Joseph Kilgour and Hattie Russell (sister of Ada Rehan), Shelley Hull, Gilda Varesi, and T. Tamamoto.

When *The New Marriage* was tried out at Syracuse on October 19, it was apparent that everyone was trying too hard. It was called an overwrought play, done in an overwrought way, and Mrs. Fiske impressed one critic as being on the verge of hysteria.

Three days later, at Pittsburgh, all the critics praised every member of the cast; they found only one fault with the production—it lacked a play.

While Minnie struggled on the road with *The New Marriage*, Harry was preparing what was to be the greatest individual success of his career as a producer. It was also a production that came as close as anything could to his realizing the dream of theatre glamor which had been awakened in him as a child.

The new play was *Kismet*, by Edward Knobloch, an Arabian Nights piece which called for a cast of a hundred, gorgeous costuming and scenery, with a huge swimming pool on the stage where girls of the harem threw off their clothes in the moonlight, and plunged into the pool in flesh-colored tights.

Harry Fiske was in his element, working out the magnificent spec-

245

tacle. He had engaged Otis Skinner for the title role, and every one of the hundred other characters was selected with studied care.

On the road, tense as she was over her own play, Mrs. Fiske caught the excitement of the *Kismet* preparations, and felt an unexpected nostalgia. Her happiest memories of the stage were of riding through the air in the spectacle of *The Ice Witch* with a little French acrobat stowed away in her golden chariot.

Kismet was so far removed from her present work that she was able to enter into the spirit of it happily, and make suggestions based on her childhood experiences. In such a vast, circusy production, she wrote, the atmosphere of the stage must extend into the audience. Incense should be burned in the theatre to begin the enchantment as soon as the spectators entered the auditorium.

In Mrs. Fiske's own play, enchantment was more difficult. *The New Marriage* faced the acid test of Chicago on October 30, with Langdon Mitchell returned from Paris and on hand, but too late to be of help. It was still the burden of the cast to dazzle the audience which filled the Grand Opera House into seeing a play where one had not quite materialized.

Next day Ashton Stevens summed it up in the first, fateful line of his review: "It is brilliant, but it is all words."

Minnie continued to hope while she prepared for a revival of *Mrs. Bumpstead-Leigh.*

On Sunday she wrote to Harry:

> Please keep the little place for Aunt Mary in Kismet. I shall write her that she need not attend the Kismet rehearsals until the week I get back (the week in Brooklyn) when I can arrange about moving her downtown. I know you can excuse her from rehearsals until then.
>
> I telegraphed you last night asking if you would try Mr. Hull in the part of the Caliph. . . . Now that we are able to offer him Geoffrey it is all right and better than the Caliph idea. "The New Marriage" is all wrong but the part is there and material for a splendid comedy. . . . It should not be thrown away without some consideration—but we should not be bound in any way or pay Mr. Mitchell one dollar for any rewriting. We have lost enough on his foggy play. . .

Before the end of the week, the audience at the Grand Opera House had dwindled to near the vanishing point, and Mrs. Fiske was struggling to get clear of her first failure in a dozen years. She wrote to Harry:

246

Darling Boy:

I have just seen Mr. Askin. He is trying his best to fill the time for the Theatre so that we may go out of it on the 18th. . . . If it is possible to book time a good distance from Chicago it may be an advantage to do so. It would be well to get as far away as possible and out of the Chicago zone so that we will be out of the radius of any of the effects of our Chicago falling down. . . .

Mr. Askin says that people here think that Mrs. Bumpstead-Leigh is beneath my dignity. That it is wrong for me to play such plays. But I say where are plays to be had? We have got to do the best and only things we can do at the present moment. I shall read plays constantly. I am not at all ashamed of Mrs. Bumpstead-Leigh and shall be only grateful to it if it will take us at least through part of our season.

> Dearest, devoted love
> Bunner

When Mrs. Fiske scored her first smashing failure in a decade, it was two years to the week since The New Theatre had opened with Morgans and Astors and Vanderbilts combining to give New York the biggest and best theatre in America; they had overdone it, like ever so many rich uncles chipping in to buy a child a stuffed toy which turned out to be a full-size, uncuddlesome elephant.

The vast temple on Central Park had been found too large for plays; it was to be abandoned and a new New Theatre to be built in a more suitable size and a more convenient location.

The day after Minnie wrote of her efforts to get out of the area of her Chicago failure, she received a letter from Harry which changed the whole prospect of her life, and his. He wrote that he had just had a conference with Paul D. Cravath, the only active founder of The New Theatre. Mr. Cravath had represented that the enterprise needed not only a theatre of practical size, but practical, artistic direction which would produce the balance which the Manhattan Company had achieved. Mr. Cravath, in the name of the organization, asked Harry Fiske to take over the direction of The New Theatre and, if possible, persuade Mrs. Fiske to associate herself with the enterprise.

It offered security for herself and Harry, after years of heartbreaking effort which had left them empty-handed.

On Mrs. Fiske's flight from the region of her failure, she paused to present *The New Marriage* before an almost empty house at Rockford. There she wrote to Harry, sending one copy of her letter to the New York Athletic Club, and the other to his *Mirror* office:

Darling Boysie:

I received your long letter regarding the New Theatre proposal and it seemed too serious and important a matter that I thought it best to wait a day or two before writing you my thoughts about it.

I think it is a splendid opportunity and that such a position in the work of the theatre is far more suited to you than the regular theatre business of the theatrical manager.

I shall be happy indeed to be associated with you in the direction of the theatre. As a matter of fact I feel sure that we can succeed together in the work as neither of us could succeed alone. We each help the other wonderfully and each supplies what the other lacks. I really have no desire to force myself into the project—I have not the smallest desire for celebrity or selfish feelings of any sort. I only would be glad to see the plan a great and solid success for practical reasons and I believe that, working together—we could achieve that success. It would make a solid place for us. You say, Boy, that The New Theatre could not afford to compensate me for giving up my present activities. Darling Boy—my work in the Theatre has yielded me nothing. After stupendous activities of seventeen years it has re-paid me not a dollar. There is far more opportunity for me in such a proposal as The New Theatre makes. If we are given a proper share of the profits of the road tours we should make a great deal of money. Even with the awful blundering and mismanagement of the Ames New Theatre—the road tours were splendid except in a few places. . . The road tours should be managed with the fine sense of the right sort of advertisement—they should be so managed as to make the public know that they were the one supreme and important happening in the Theatre world. George Tyler is doing something of the sort in Chicago now—in heralding "The Garden of Allah". . . Neither you nor I have the smallest talent for that sort of thing, but you can hire it and it is essential in handling the business end of such an enterprise as The New Theatre, or so it seems to me. That is, essential if the very best and most practical results are to be obtained. . . Of course, the whole thing will be different under our management. We shall proceed in a workmanlike and professional manner.

. . . Personally, my whole feeling about the Theatre is an absolutely practical one. I have no desire to shine in any capacity—I have no atom of vanity about it or no wish for fame. I feel only that we should have one unceasing thought and aim—that is to protect our future and to win from the Theatre something to compensate us for a lifetime of unceasing service. I think you will win back a great deal with Kismet. I would never do anything I was ashamed of in the

Theatre—but from now on I would like to exact the pound of flesh from the queer, uncertain institution. I think there would be more chance for me if I gave up my individual activities for a season and worked with you in the New Theatre—but I don't know. I have no preference of any sort. My one desire is to do that which will be best for me practically—which will yield me the best returns and which will be best for the future.

Dearest, devoted love
Bunnikin

Two days later, Minnie wrote from Bloomington,

. . . I hope nothing will bungle to prevent your acceptance of The New Theatre offer. It is the finest opportunity ever offered anyone in this country—or perhaps any country. I should be sorry to have you lose it. It is a far greater opportunity than was offered to Mr. Ames. . . He was almost fatally handicapped by that hopelessly big Theatre—a place good only for spectacles. What is offered you is a different and practical proposition.

The directors are probably of the opinion that I make a great deal of money and that they could not afford, as you told them, to reimburse me for the temporary abandonment of my tours. It is better that they do think so. They might be willing to give me a third or fourth of the profits—the season's profit, for payment for my services. I feel so confident of the success of The New Theatre tours that I am willing to take the chance of profit in that way.

The new field of work may be an advantage to me. (Consider that aspect of it, Boy.) For six years—ever since the second season of Leah Kleschna—I have been utterly weary of this old way of going on. A new deal may wake me up again. You know, Boysie—I have none of the feeling for the theatre that you have. I am glad you have it as it is your work. I mean that I have no pleasure or intoxication in the preparing of plays. It is with me—just a business—a means of making money which I have always hoped would some day come, money that I might use in ways that did give me pleasure and interest me. I do not mean that I would not be devoted to my work in The New Theatre or in my work as we go along in this way. You know that I am always conscientious—but there is no pleasure in it for me. I hate the theatre business. I think it saps life and gives nothing in return. But this new work I think would stir me to more interest because it would, it seems to me, offer a chance of reward. I hope it may come to pass for that reason. And then I think it is the opportunity—the great chance of your career. . . .

A few days later, at Akron, *The New Marriage* was presented for the last time. In a letter to Harry, she wrote the epitaph of *The New Marriage:* "It trembled on the verge of a great success."

She brought her company home, and revived *Mrs. Bumpstead-Leigh* at the Broadway Theatre in Brooklyn. It was a new experience, being forced back to port, but it had its timely element. Harry had accepted the bid from The New Theatre, and in the turmoil of producing *Kismet,* he had presented his and Mrs. Fiske's plan for making it a self-supporting national theatre. Soon after Mrs. Fiske's return, they were summoned to a conference with Paul Cravath and Otto Kahn, treasurer of The New Theatre.

At the conference, however, she was too proud and honest to use any salesmanship, or paint any glowing picture; she proceeded on the basis of talking serious business with businessmen, and she promised nothing that she did not feel certain of being able to fulfill. On the way back to the Brevoort, she asked Harry if she hadn't been something of a wet blanket. But Otto Kahn, who had listened to so many rosy dreams about The New Theatre, was pleased with the practical, down-to-earth conference; Paul Cravath had already decided that the Fiskes were the right directors for the project, and he set about putting the cumbersome machinery of the organization into motion.

A few days later, Mrs. Fiske was honored by the Society of American Dramatists and Composers, which had selected her as the guest of honor at the annual dinner of the society. To meet the exigencies of the stage, the dinner was held at Delmonico's on Sunday evening, December 10. The meeting was presided over by Augustus Thomas, dean of American playwrights, and attended by nearly all the well-known writers for the stage.

Six years earlier, at Harvard, Minnie had spoken with quiet power and confidence. Now, worn and desperate for security, she chose the oblique method of having Mr. J. I. C. Clarke speak for her from notes which she had prepared. In them, Mrs. Fiske stated flatly that she was not an intellectual.

She gave credit to Harrison Grey Fiske, whose taste, skill and suggestions had brought success.

Mrs. Fiske had appeared in many foreign plays, but had drifted instinctively toward plays of American life which seemed the need of the American theatre. She had sought the American author, and an impressive list of American authors whose plays she had produced showed that her efforts had not been fruitless.

250

She observed that she had never approached the *great* American authors for plays. "I never really dared. For some reason they have not proffered their plays to me. I was left with the young, the maiden authors, as it were. . . I give courteous notice now that the veterans of triumphs will confer honor and bring pleasure to me in considering me as a desirable manager hereafter."

As to the plays the actress wanted: "I detest the star play, with everything distorted to make a part for one actor. If the theme is interesting, the story told dramatically. . . I do not care if the part that suits me has two lines or many hundreds."

As for the actor: "The man or woman who takes the part with the sole idea of doing his best for the play is the player for me. In thirty seconds I can tell the actor who approaches the play with the 'My Part' idea in his head. . ."

The notes, which had begun as terse jottings, branched out as they progressed; and they ended, clad in the living foliage of Mrs. Fiske's creed: "I am one with the modern American theatre in its fresh themes from our daily lives, freshly treated. I am one with the modern spirit, which is not all gloom, not all dramatic muck-raking. The art of the drama should never be subordinated to mere trick or prettiness, but for me the ideal play is rich with spiritual uplift and bearing a message of hope."

If Mrs. Fiske's plea to the older, established dramatists had been heeded, it would have corrected a very obvious hiatus in the American theatre—but the pattern had already been set. The woman who had blazed her own trail in acting and producing was left as before to the playwrights she had created, and the new ones she was still to discover.

December of 1911 was checkered with light and shadow for the Fiskes. Early in the month, *Kismet*, with Otis Skinner, had a triumphal premiere in Washington, and a week later a New York premiere that launched it as the most spectacular success of the year. Later in the same month, Harry Fiske sold the *Dramatic Mirror*, of which he had been the guiding spirit since he had become the "boy editor" in 1879, and which had fallen into neglect. Harry did not regret its going as much as Mrs. Fiske. She had no illusions about the stage and considered journalism a more worthy profession.

During several years at the height of her career, Mrs. Fiske had planned to play Lady Macbeth to Otis Skinner's Macbeth. He had never been available at the right time; and when the Fiskes finally secured Mr. Skinner it was for the role of Kismet. In their own way, however, the Fiskes had enacted part of the Macbeth story. Her stage ambitions had drawn her husband into the theatre. He had started reluctantly, but afterward he had waded in, deeper and deeper, without any thought of turning back—while the woman presently regretted the security they had lost, and was haunted by increasing fears.

Late in December Mrs. Fiske resumed her tour, with *Mrs. Bumpstead-Leigh,* hoping daily for word from The New Theatre. When it came, at last, it was a confidential report from Paul Cravath. He had submitted the Fiskes' plan to the founders of The New Theatre; nearly all of them approved and were willing to contribute more money, but he had been unable to get a majority of them to meet and vote on the project. The urge to uplift the American theatre had died in the multimillionaire hearts, and Mr. Cravath felt that there was nothing left to do but shelve the lifeless project.

At the beginning of the project, Mrs. Fiske had commented on the poverty of the founders, without five cents' worth of theatre knowledge among them. And after the debacle, she wrote Harry:

> The establishment of a Theatre (in the sense of something national and representative) does not require money so much as it requires expert, understanding projection—expert, understanding management. The New Theatre showed us that money is not the great essential. All those New Theatre millions might just as well have been thrown into a waste basket.
>
> Expert projection—expert management, expert carrying out of a clearly defined policy which shall be in perfect harmony with the spirit of the time. These are the essentials.

The Fiskes, who had the essentials, and The New Theatre founders, who had the less important but necessary money, passed each other like ships in the night and went their opposite directions—The New Theatre to its immediate foundering, and the Fiskes to staggering on, precariously, through the early years of another decade.

CHAPTER 32

After the failure of *The New Marriage* in Chicago, Mrs. Fiske's tour in the revival of *Mrs. Bumpstead-Leigh* had its inevitable aura of second-best, but it was a signal for recognition which had not been won by more important plays—the offer from The New Theatre, and the honors from the American Society of Dramatists and Composers.

During the Cincinnati engagement, the play was the thing, and Minnie's role of Mrs. Bumpstead-Leigh received a kind of recognition it had not been granted elsewhere. The dean of Cincinnati critics was Montgomery Phister, one of the most vital critics of the day, and the personal friend of every good actor who had toured America during his long tenure at the *Commercial Times-Star*. With Cincinnati in the grip of an unprecedented cold spell and deep snow that made theatregoing difficult, Phister preached the gospel of *Mrs. Bumpstead-Leigh*. Every other day, he filled columns of the *Commercial* with dynamic thoughts about the actress and the role. On January 14, he began his four-column review, his fourth that week:

> It is impossible to get Mrs. Fiske out of mind.
> Her "Mrs. Bumpstead-Leigh" seems such a happy stroke of genius that it clings to the memory, bobbing up and jogging thought at all and the most unexpected times. . . .
> Mrs. Bumpstead-Leigh is the soul of everything; she is the play, the character, the plot, the incidents and their life, the thought, the fiction, the denouement, the solution, the focus of all interest and desires. . . . Mrs. Bumpstead-Leigh will be associated with the Fiske name as long as any record of the drama exists. . . .

While Montgomery Phister was writing that, Mrs. Fiske was working heroically on a play to replace *Bumpstead-Leigh*. She had planned a tryout of *Julia France* in Cincinnati, and summoned Gertrude Atherton from South Carolina, where she was wintering. The novelist arrived, and there were daily rehearsals at the snow-shrouded Grand, where Minnie tried every known device to breathe life into a stillborn play.

Away from the theatre, Mrs. Atherton put up at the Burnet House, where she worked on making a novel out of her play, and she showed a confidence that the actress did not feel that she could afford. Minnie was in one of her periodic spells of granting no interviews to the press, while Mrs. Atherton talked freely about her work. She would like to write a book to show that Bacon, and not Shakespeare, wrote the plays, but she couldn't afford to be considered a freak. In San Francisco, she had observed that playwriting was so simple that she would find it hard going back to the novel, but she now confided to the press that she had nearly died writing *Julia France*. Someone advised her to study *Rosmersholm* for dramatic construction; she had tried, and found it very stupid. Someone else had recommended a book on playwriting; she had read it, but it had "gone in one ear and out the other." Personally, she got her pleasure out of writing, just as many women did out of having large families. The perfect woman, she stated, should contain the potentialities of both man and woman. If she can't find the necessary man she is able to stand alone. Colleges had already knocked out the idea of marriage as the ultimate and only goal.

Julia France was supposed to be a suffrage play, but it was beyond that; it pictured the approach of woman to the absolute poise where she would no longer be dependent on men.

Mrs. Atherton was glad that Mrs. Fiske was producing her play; she couldn't stand most actresses—and even then she had found it ghastly to have her stuff read aloud to her. . . .

Mrs. Fiske had set her heart on a play about woman's suffrage, and she had encouraged Mrs. Atherton to write *Julia France*, feeling that a treatment of the issue of the hour by a famous novelist would outweigh the dramatic shortcomings of the piece and fill theatres with women.

If Mrs. Atherton was the logical one to write a play on the emancipation of woman, it was equally logical that the leading role should go to Mrs. Fiske. The fact, however, did not prevent the novelist and the actress from being poles apart. Mrs. Fiske saw the timeliness of a woman's suffrage play, but it did not mean that her personal sympathies were involved. While the rehearsals of *Julia France* were going on, she wrote Harry that she had never given suffrage much thought and she didn't know whether she was in favor of it or not.

With other of Gertrude Atherton's views, she was definitely not in accord. The novelist believed that women should be able to stand alone and that an Amazonian society was in the offing; she found her work a thoroughly satisfactory substitute for a family, and although she had one daughter, whom she occasionally saw, she confessed to having no maternal instincts. Minnie, on the other hand, looked on Harry as the stabilizing influence in her artistic life; she regretted her early decision not to have children, and she considered her career a poor substitute for a large family about her.

The two women had little in common.

Because of the severe cold and its chilling effect on Cincinnati audiences, Minnie postponed the tryout of *Julia France*, and she and her company and Mrs. Atherton went on to Toronto. There she opened at the Princess Theatre in *Mrs. Bumpstead-Leigh* and announced *Julia France* for the end of her engagement.

Harry Fiske arrived in Toronto on the same day as his wife, and worked with her on the final rehearsals of the new play. Harry had been dubious of it from the beginning. After the dress rehearsal, he had no hope for the work, while Minnie gave it a slender chance of survival.

Julia France was presented on the evening of January 17, 1912, before an audience of moderate size, with the queenly Gertrude Atherton looking on from a stage box and Harry Fiske, after his first-night custom, sitting far back in the orchestra where he could observe the audience as well as the play.

The audience was polite and patient during the three acts, but the strain was palpable. It began soon after the rise of the curtain as one lesser character after another joined in outlining the position and character of Julia, possessed of all superior qualities and married to a lunatic from whom the English law would not grant her a divorce. The exposition lasted half an hour—so long that the *Star* critic observed that the audience suspected Mrs. Fiske had had a motor accident.

The play was almost over before words began to lead to action. Julia France was freed of her mad husband—and an elemental young niece fell in love with Julia's paragon admirer. There was promise of a spirited contest between the mature New Woman and the youthful Eve—but Julia disdained to compete; she presented the young man to her niece, and announced that she was dedicated to the emancipation of women.

Julia France was Mrs. Atherton, and it had taken her three acts to tell the audience what she had already told reporters in one sentence:

that her career was a quite satisfactory substitute for a husband and family. No one was inclined to argue her choice, but it did not make a play. After one perfunctory curtain call, the audience drifted out into the snowy street without calling for the author of the piece.

The Toronto papers next day pronunced *Julia France* a flat failure from every point of view, and the *News* declared that Mrs. Fiske had seriously damaged her reputation in Toronto by producing the dreary work of an ambitious amateur. Mrs. Fiske had already written the play off as a loss and decided against presenting it a second time. And Gertrude Atherton, with her poise unshaken, told reporters that nothing the press could say about *Julia France* could be worse than her own opinion of the piece. Its failure did not strain her diplomatic relations with Mrs. Fiske, although she felt that one performance was not an adequate trial. The actress, however, had tested the buzz saw of public disapproval with one finger, and she was not inclined to follow it with her hand.

After ten years of unbroken successes, Minnie had experienced her second failure in three months. Failure had been long overdue; Minnie was prepared for it mentally, but financially she was not, and she returned gratefully to *Mrs. Bumpstead-Leigh*, and rehearsed for her third new play that season.

The play was *Lady Patricia*. Rudolph Besier had written it for Mrs. Pat Campbell, who had had a great success in London in the title role, and Harry Fiske had secured the American rights from Charles Frohman.

The whirligig of time had brought the Fiskes closer to their old enemies than to the now highhanded Shuberts. Messrs. Klaw and Erlanger were Harry's financial backers in *Kismet*, which was touring America with spectacular success, and they now provided the Empire Theatre for the New York run of *Lady Patricia*. That and the fact that the production rights had been bought from Charles Frohman were the only connection which the Syndicate partners had with the play, but they were eager to make the most of it. On January 6, Minnie wrote Harry from Detroit:

Darling, darling Boy,
. . . I read an announcement of "Lady Patricia" in the New York Times, and I was rather upset about the manner in which the announcement was made. I don't suppose that there was any intentional idea of misleading anyone, but the announcement was worded in such a way as to suggest that there was some sort of change in our

256

management, and of course, such an impression must never be allowed to exist. I have been solely under your management ever since I returned to the stage and I wish the public always to know and feel that there never will be the slightest change in the way we have conducted our affairs. Will you please, in the future announcements, have everyone concerned be careful to give no false impression? We are producing "Lady Patricia" under our own management, exactly as we have produced everything since 1895, and just exactly as we shall continue to produce everything as long as we continue to be associated with the theatre. . . .

> Devoted love
> Bunnikin

In New York, Harry devoted himself to making *Lady Patricia* a perfect and beautiful production, and on the road, Minnie toured with *Mrs. Bumpstead-Leigh* through a savagely cold winter. She returned to New York in time for the premiere of *Lady Patricia*, which rounded out a phase of her life.

The Empire was Minnie's favorite New York theatre, and she returned to it after an exile of eighteen years. Her last appearance there had been as Nora in the famous matinee performance of *A Doll's House*, and she was welcomed back to the theatre like a queen.

It was over two years since the Theatre Trust had given in, but the premiere of *Lady Patricia* at the Empire gave the peace a graceful final touch.

On the opening night, in a dressing room full of flowers, Charles Frohman's card was brought in to Minnie. She had seen him last in the eighteen-eighties, when both of them were ambitious beginners, just out of their teens. Since then, she had helped wreck his dream of being dictator of the world's theatres, and he had been responsible for her financial troubles. But, for better or worse, when Charles Frohman hobbled into the dressing room, it was the meeting of the two most powerful figures in the American theatre: the body and the soul, somewhat battered by their long strife and by time. Frohman, in his early fifties, walked with difficulty with the aid of a cane, and behind his beaming smile there lurked the anguish of rheumatic years brought about by his diet of chocolate and pies, and by a fall.

Mrs. Fiske, at forty-seven, was as quick-moving as she had been as a girl, and as sparkling, but she was touched with the heaviness of middle age, and years of strenuous barnstorming had overstrained her heart.

They faced each other, the instruments of each other's defeat, and dismissed a quarter century with silent laughter. The ailing Napoleon's mind went back to the night in Boston when he and the youthful David Belasco fought in the alley outside the Tremont Theatre, while the vivid young Minnie Maddern looked on from the stage doorway. Charles Frohman had won and was the first to present his battered bouquet. Hobbling in, as if it had been yesterday, he asked, "Did you keep the flowers?"

Mrs. Fiske held out both her hands. "Oh, my dear Mr. Frohman, would that I could have!"

CHAPTER 33

Innumerable times on makeshift stages, Mrs. Fiske had triumphed against the opposition of the Theatrical Trust. Now, with her former enemies eager to make everything easy for her in their choicest New York theatre, she faltered short of success.

Lady Patricia had been written around Mrs. Pat Campbell, and that exotic if mature beauty had only to burlesque herself to make the thing a success.

Mrs. Fiske had a harder task. She was diminutive, with odd features that were plain except when they were illuminated by the inner radiance of her mind and spirit, and Mrs. Campbell's method was as foreign to her as her willowy figure. If Lady Patricia were to be anything to the little American actress, it would have to be a play and not an exploitation. From her earliest reading of the play, she had worked to bring out the human and comedy values of her role—things that had been sketched in lightly by the dramatist, and passed over with equal lightness by the English actress.

She brought out everything there was in the play, but it was like trying to make a painted backdrop come to life, and it was not enough. Critics complained that the play was thin and unworthy of Mrs. Fiske, and theatregoers who remembered the actress in her great roles were halfhearted in their applause.

For that season, at least, Minnie was no longer the favored one of her family. Harry's production of Kismet was still breaking box-office records, and even Emily Stevens, whom Minnie still thought of as a girl, did better.

During the second week of Lady Patricia, Emily opened at Rochester in Half a Husband. The farce had a life of only a few weeks but it added to Emily's reputation, and her co-star, John Barrymore, gave a performance in his first important role that made the slight play an historic event. A few days after the closing of *Half a Husband*, Emily Stevens took Chicago by storm with her portrayal of Mary Turner in *Within the Law*—and before the end of the engagement, which ran for a hundred nights, Emily was rated as famous.

Within the Law was "cheap" in Minnie's judgment, and yet it was unlikely that it would have triumphed, or ever have been written, except for her influence. It was one of the flood of melodramas turned loose by her daring production of *Leah Kleschna*, which introduced the crook melodrama to the American stage; and *Within the Law* was made memorable by the work of two actors who had first made their mark in *Leah Kleschna*—Emily Stevens, and William B. Mack, whose Schram had equaled the work of George Arliss.

Mrs. Fiske's influence on plays and players blazed up sensationally in Chicago, and in New York her own production wavered toward its end. *Lady Patricia* lingered four weeks at the Empire Theatre, and died there—the actress's third failure that season.

Previously, she had insisted on out-of-town tryouts for plays, and if the course had been followed with *Lady Patricia*, it might have had a degree of success, but her backers had been overconfident—and there was no resurrection for a play that died in New York.

Her third failure that season left Minnie without a play and with three months of the regular season ahead of her. She chose to spend the first of the enforced vacation with her mother-in-law.

Mother Fiske was then past eighty, and it was several years since she had accompanied her daughter-in-law on tours, but she was still brisk of mind and body, and good company. She was living at Brielle, New Jersey, near her oldest son, Willard; and at Brielle Minnie forgot insomnia and worries while she tasted the charms of what she called the "home life." In her first vacation letter to Boyleykeeno (otherwise Harry), she wrote that she had slept for thirteen solid hours without waking. In her second letter, addressed to Boggie, she informed Harry that a vegetable garden was perfectly thrilling, and you betsky she was going to have one some day.

Later, from the home of friends in Yonkers, Minnie wrote Boy that the Holbrook Blinns were beseeching her to visit their farm, and Sister Mary Sebastian had renewed her year-round invitation to Tarrytown, but Minnie was too enchanted by the home life at Yonkers to think of staying anywhere else. Early in May she wrote with little-girl pride that she had swept all the porches.

A few days afterwards she read Edward Sheldon's most recent play, and she wrote, with an overtone of foreboding:

Darling Boy:

Since reading Princess Zim-Zim I feel that we must not place absolute reliance on Mr. Sheldon. Do not misunderstand me, Boy. I have the greatest faith in his idea for our play and I have the greatest hopes for it. I really think it will be all right. But we must take care not to find ourselves in the position we found ourselves in when Mr. Mitchell's play failed. Indeed, if Mr. Sheldon's play failed we should not be in as good a position as we were when the Mitchell play went wrong. Then we did have old Bumpstead-Leigh to fall back on to at least carry us through decently.

The Princess Zim-Zim is a perfectly worthless play. I have read few that were worse. The first act had a charming idea and that act is good. The rest was utterly cheap and beneath contempt. How it ever got on the stage I cannot see. "The New Marriage" was a perfect gem compared to it. But I would not pay so much attention to the cheapness of a play. He may have been trying to write a cheap play. "The Boss" was a pretty bad play and very cheap but in "The Boss" Mr. Sheldon did reveal a sense of the Theatre. Always before he had that—the sense of the Theatre. What really scared me in The Princess Zim-Zim was the fact that after the first act the play absolutely lacked any sense of the Theatre. It was not a play. So Mr. Sheldon can go terribly wrong and it will be just as well for us to have a little eye open in case he should go wrong with our play. .

Aunt Mary Maddern had made her last stage appearance in a bit part in *Kismet* during the winter, and she died that spring. One after another, the children she had mothered had outgrown the need for her devotion. When it came her turn again to be mothered, she had tried to disguise the fact that Minnie was looking after her with an exaggerated show of independence. She also did a great deal of audible grumbling to herself about the inconveniences of the road, which she had started traveling with the Maddern Family Concert Company sixty years before. There was nothing in it but discomfort; she had never arrived anywhere except at the same towns year after year, and without any profit to herself, she had played in everything from *Toodles* and *A Kiss in the Dark* to Ibsen's *Rosmersholm*.

Aunt Mary's grumbling about the road had accompanied the rumble and gallop of train wheels all over America—but when she was too feeble to travel, she grumbled still more and felt lost. She died that May. There was nothing else for her to do.

On the eighteenth, soon after Mary Maddern's death, Mrs. Fiske sailed for Europe on the S.S. *Lapland*.

During most of the spring, at Brielle and at Yonkers, she had been within a few hours or a few miles of New York, without seeing Harry half a dozen times. The nearness and daily letters were almost enough, but she had forebodings of homesickness as soon as she decided on the voyage. While she was still in New York harbor, she wrote a note to be sent ashore with the pilot:

May 18, 1912
S.S. Lapland

Precious, precious Boy,

I have looked at you as long as I could—I kept the red flowers held way out as long as there was a chance of your seeing them. You arranged everything so happily and comfortably and beautifully for me. It's lovely. I shall now look for your basket. Thank you darling precious Boy for all your thoughtful care. Take all care of yourself. Keep your health perfect. <u>Get some golf!!</u> I shall hope for your coming.

Dearest, devoted love
Bunnikin

The *Lapland* docked at Antwerp, and from there Mrs. Fiske visited Paris, and went on to take the cure at Brides-les-Baines, in Savoie. From there she wrote Harry on June 10:

. . . Yesterday was Sunday & I went for a little while into the little Catholic church for morning service—as I wanted to see the peasants who come from away up in the remote mountains for mass. Some of the old peasant women were dressed in wonderful old dresses.—I sat outside the church after a while—and as it was some feast day—the priest and his altar boys—followed by the congregation—presently filed out from the church—& marched around it while the organ played inside. . . .

In the afternoon I took a twelve mile walk in company with a woman and her daughter—pleasant New York people. We climbed the mountain and ascended gradually through beautiful fields covered with brilliantly colored wild flowers. We finally reached a strange little village away—away up in the mountains—so far out of the world. The streets of the little place were crowded with the peasants in Sunday dress—The priest & the boys & the congregation from the church had marched through the streets before we came—& there were flowers strewn all along the way. . . .

On the nineteenth she wrote:

. . . I will confess that I have been suffering to the limit in homesickness. Nothing is to blame.—The voyage over was beautiful—the visit to Paris simply delightful—in every way,—this place is lovely and the cure is doing me loads of good—there have been kind, charming, pleasant people—but in spite of it all—I've been like the ghost of a person in homesickness. If I ever get my family back I'll never let them go again!

Minnie crossed over to England, and motored out from London in search of a pleasant place to stay in the country. From Chilham, in Kent, she wrote Harry on July 16:

Darling, precious boy:
. . . This place is simply beautiful—I know nothing of the country life of England save what I have got from books. But I cannot believe there is anything lovelier or more peaceful than this. The little village in soft rolling country. There is the church, the old inn, the castle. The people are gentle-voiced and kindly. At the back of the inn—there is an old fashioned garden. There my pretty little table is spread for breakfast and dinner—Yesterday—I went to Canterbury (only a few minutes away) and passed some time in the old Cathedral and wandering about the pleasant town. It is all doing me good. The twilight lasts until after nine and I go to bed in daylight. . . .

Wherever Minnie went, she found Europe peaceful in the serene summer of 1912, and everywhere—in the foot-worn streets of Antwerp, in flowering fields of the French mountains, and in the long summer twilight of the English countryside—she felt like a ghost and she felt that she must go home, or choke with tears.

She returned by the *Lapland* a month earlier than she had planned; and before sailing, she wrote Harry:

Please, when I arrive—do not in the presence of any third party mention the fact of my having been homesick or having altered the date of my return. These private matters I keep entirely to myself. I hope all goes as well as it can. Blessed darling Boy. How glad I shall be to see you.

Devoted love
Bunnikin

Before sailing for Europe, Minnie had had her first misgivings about Edward Sheldon's play on which she was depending for the coming season. In Paris she had seen Alice Kauser, who was Sheldon's agent, and Miss Kauser told her that part of the manuscript would be delayed. Just before sailing, Minnie had a letter from Harry, telling her that the play would not be completed until September first.

She returned vowing that she would never again depend on an unwritten play—but where were modern plays to be had?

The immediate fears of the harried actress were not realized. Edward Sheldon met the September-first deadline, and the play went into rehearsal soon afterward. It was referred to as "the play" because it defied the efforts of the author and the producers to give it a name.

But Minnie had at least known from the beginning what the play was about. It was an allegory of the evolution of a human being—the story of a woman's pilgrimage through life. In its intent, it was one of the most important things that Minnie had ever undertaken, but the Grecian allegory translated into modern terms had a strong flavor of Sheldon melodrama.

Still without a title, the play was subtitled "A Pilgrimage in Five Parts." In the first, Mary Page was a poor and ill-treated country girl of seventeen, clad in calico and a sunbonnet. Four parts and twenty years later, she was a labor leader and the wife of the governor of New York, who was about to become president of the United States.

In its drama, the allegory had a strong flavor of *The Boss*, which Mrs. Fiske had despised as cheap, but however crude, it was the logical successor to *A Doll's House*, *Tess of the D'Urbervilles*, *Magda* and the unsuccessful *Julia France*, a play that called for a showdown on woman's right to live and grow and learn by her mistakes. The original idea, which Mrs. Fiske had helped shape, was there, and she devoted herself to putting life into the disjointed, wooden scenes, and to reading into them values and overtones which they did not have of themselves.

After two weeks of doctoring and rehearsing, Sheldon's allegory began to take on the shape of a play, but it was still nameless in spite of many determined efforts.

None of the titles stuck, and the play remained nameless into the third week. At odd moments during rehearsals, Mrs. Fiske sang snatches of old songs, and on one occasion it was "Loch Lomond." She got as far as "Oh! ye'll take the high road—" when she stopped abruptly and burst out, "That's it! 'The High Road!' That's the name of our play!" Sheldon and Harry Fiske and everyone else agreed that it was the right name for the story of an aspiring woman's journey through life, and the play was *The High Road* from that moment on.

The Fiskes' experience with *Lady Patricia* had taught them beyond forgetting not to open an untried play in New York, where half a dozen critics could kill a play that might otherwise have succeeded

264

everywhere else. *The High Road*, with all that staging and casting and human skill and effort could put into it, had its premiere at Montreal on October 14, 1912.

So much had gone into the production and it was so well done that it could not quite be a failure, but the audience at His Majesty's Theatre was more respectful than enthusiastic. Audiences on the other side of the border responded in much the same way, and *The High Road* labored to Chicago. There it ran for three weeks that were not quite success or failure—and Mrs. Fiske turned toward Broadway and a desperate gamble with a play that had never come to life.

The High Road opened at the Hudson Theatre in New York on November 19, and it was greeted with more enthusiasm than it had won during a week of nights elsewhere. After the final curtain call, Mrs. Fiske was weak, and profoundly grateful for the miracle. Some of the tremendous effort that had gone into the production was beginning to pay dividends—or for once New York was easier to please than Chicago, or lesser towns.

The critics next day were almost unanimous in their praise of *The High Road*. Mrs. Fiske was saved from financial ruin, and *The High Road*, which had started so dubiously in the autumn of 1912, played and toured until the spring of 1914. That did not tell the whole story, however. The life and meaning of *The High Road* were in the actress, not in the wooden allegory, and its long run was uphill every step of the way.

CHAPTER 34

Once in an Ohio river town, the elder Junius Brutus Booth engaged an undertaker and a minister to perform the last rites for a mysterious deceased. The gentlemen were willing, but the eccentric actor was slow about giving them something to work on—and when the *corpus delecti* was produced, it was in the plural—a bushel of dead pigeons.

The story was repeated endlessly as a proof of Booth's insanity. Time and events, however, have made it a question of who was insane—the men who killed the pigeons, or the actor who gave them Christian burial. The birds were the fabulous passenger pigeons that flocked over America by the billion, sometimes darkening the sky in one of nature's most prodigal displays of bounty—and Booth's act was in protest against their insane slaughter. A generation later, there was a standing reward of fifteen hundred dollars for a nest of the birds that had sold, dead, for a few cents a bushel. The reward will stand until the end of time, unless exterminated things can be brought back into existence.

In the spring of 1913, another actor moved to the rescue of birds that were slated for extinction. The bird was the snowy heron, or egret, and its filmy plumes were the most prized ornaments in the millinery trade. A woman who did not possess at least one aigrette plume hid her hat for shame, and wealthy women collected them as they collected diamonds. The rage for aigrettes reached its height in the first decade of the century, and at the same time the source of supply inconsiderately diminished.

Ornithologists lamented the slaughter of the birds, but they saw no way of curbing feminine vanity. Typically, a leading ornithologist wrote in 1910 that no power on earth could save the egret from extinction at the hands of plume hunters.

There was one power that had done a good deal for the underprivileged animal kingdom, but Minnie Maddern Fiske was busy in

266

another field of humane activities. At the time she was calling attention to the senseless waste and cruelty of allowing millions of cattle to starve and freeze to death each winter on the western ranges—and she was wearing aigrette plumes on her hat.

In Chicago, she gave one of her innumerable interviews on the plight of range cattle. It was generally well received, but the next day one reporter commented on the fact that Mrs. Fiske pleaded for a humane cause while wearing aigrettes!

Until that time the actress had never stopped to consider whether aigrette plumes were animal, vegetable or mineral, but the reporter's sneer set her to finding out. She learned that aigrettes were the nuptial plumes of the female; that they reached their perfect beauty at nesting time; and plume hunters killed the female and left the young to starve in the nest. She also learned that plume hunters often staked up wounded birds as decoys for others, and that the red ants of the tropics ate out their eyes while they were held helpless within sound of their starving young.

When Mrs. Fiske had learned the facts, she burned her aigrette plumes and had her friends do the same. Thereafter the only feathers she ever wore were ostrich plumes, and she adopted them only after making certain that harvesting them was a process which the ostriches did not mind.

For some time, the actress's campaign against aigrette plumes was limited to her immediate contacts; she was harried by unsuccessful plays and finances, and she was going through one of her phases of avoiding all interviews with the press.

In December of 1912, however, she tackled the aigrette problem on a major scale. The Audubon Society and the New York Zoological Society had introduced a bill in Congress forbidding the importation of aigrette plumes, and Mrs. Fiske undertook to arouse the nation in favor of the bill. Suitably, the campaign coincided with her tour in *The High Road*, the play which underlined the twentieth-century rights and dignity of women, and the call for women to renounce a barbarous vanity.

The aigrette campaign was combined with an appeal to women not to wear furs. At first, in her interviews and speeches, Mrs. Fiske played up the cruel trade in female and foetal sealskins—but her humane work was being carried on in a rapidly changing world. In California, some of her statements about seals were challenged by Professor George A. Clark of Stanford University, who stated that the killing of female seals had been stopped in 1911 by the treaty on pelagic sealing. Professor Clark was the world's leading authority on fur seals, and he had played a major role in preventing their extermination. In the presence of such authority, Mrs. Fiske acknowledged in the press that her information was out of date, and revised her statements.

The opening gun of the campaign was fired on December 20, 1912, at a drawing-room lecture in New York, under the auspices of the Vivisection Investigation League. Papers read by Minnie Maddern Fiske and Poultney Bigelow opposed every type of cruelty to animals, but the meeting had its realistic elements. One of the officers of the league was the nature writer, Ernest Thompson Seton, who was starting one of the first fur farms, where animals were killed humanely.

Mrs. Fiske's paper called on women to give up furs procured by trapping, and aigrette plumes, which could only be procured inhumanely. The demands she made on herself were sterner; she had permanently given up furs of every kind and all feathers except ostrich plumes. She had also given up eating meat, less permanently, and was to waver a long time before deciding not to abstain.

When *The High Road* was playing in Boston in January, 1913, Mrs. Fiske appeared at a meeting of the Massachusetts S.P.C.A. and repeated her plea for women not to wear furs or aigrettes. She also declared that meat was unnecessary and wrong, but admitted that she ate it.

In Detroit, on February 12, Mrs. Fiske delivered her message to the members of the Chamber of Commerce and their guests. There were five hundred society women present, and the Flamingo Room of the Hotel Pontchartrain was a sea of furs and aigrette plumes.

At the speakers' table, Mrs. Abner Learned introduced Mrs. Fiske, and the actress began:

> Is it too fanciful a dream that many of us, shuddering at the unspeakable things done for woman's adornment, hope, from our souls, for the coming of a time when enlightened women of kind hearts will refuse to wear fur and aigrettes?
>
> Then this awful business of procuring them will end. Furs are quite unnecessary. Many of us have not worn them for years. I have not missed nor needed them in the coldest countries. Once we have learned how aigrettes are procured we must refuse to wear them. . . .

When she told of the agonies suffered by trapped animals, some of her listeners tried to conceal their furs; and when she pointed out that every aigrette plume represented a nestful of young birds starved to death, faces reddened and women removed their hats.

Like other meetings before it, and many afterward, it represented a trade. The actress who disliked being recognized off stage had sacrificed her privacy to strike a blow for hunted wild things; and society women had seen Mrs. Fiske in return for having their feelings harrowed.

The length of Mrs. Fiske's discomforting talk left no time for the reading of the Welfare League's report on legislation to stop the traffic in worn-out horses in Detroit—but, perversely, the answer to the problem was forecast by the lavish display of furs and aigrettes. They represented the fast growing wealth of the automobile industry, which in a generation would rescue the horse from ten thousand years of slavery—and banish it to limbo.

At the tea in Detroit, Mrs. Fiske had made hundreds of women blush for their prized aigrettes—and immediately afterward she laid plans to redden faces all over America. In the past, Mrs. Fiske had often sniped at Theodore Roosevelt for hunting—but Roosevelt had done more to conserve wildlife than all the presidents before him, and he now came out with the statement, "It is a disgrace to America that we should permit the sale of aigrettes." Mrs. Fiske gave the statement a prominent place in a letter which she was composing for the press. She also learned that when President Wilson had been Governor of New Jersey and an aigrette company had tried to establish itself there, Wilson had vetoed the bill which would have permitted it, commenting that New Jersey could do without blood money.

To the heavy ammunition supplied by the President and ex-President, Mrs. Fiske added a letter from a Latin American plume hunter, telling of the torture of female egrets used as decoys, and the death by starvation of their young.

Mindful of the fact that egrets were dwindling rapidly toward extinction, Mrs. Fiske wrote:

There is need for immediate action on the part of those interested in striving to put an end to this nefarious aigrette traffic in the United States. . . .

American women can help this movement by notifying milliners that they will withdraw patronage from any millinery establishment that permits the sale of aigrettes and other plumes barbarously obtained. . . .

There will undoubtedly be strong opposition to the proposed law

269

—opposition on the part of merchant milliners who encourage the aigrette atrocities as a source of revenue.

The matter is in the hands of the American women.

Her letter was written in Philadelphia, where she was appearing in *The High Road* against the formidable competition of George Arliss in *Disraeli*.

It was six years since Arliss had left the Manhattan Company to become a star, but Minnie confidently summoned him to the rescue of the egrets. Together they tuned up the letter to the press, and when it was mimeographed on the actress's New York letterheads, they spent two afternoons signing copies for every newspaper in the United States and Canada.

The letter landed in the New York press with a much larger splash than the usual humane appeal. It was a fighting letter and, typically, the *Evening Sun* gave it half a page, with pictures of Mrs. Fiske and the monocled George Arliss, under the headlines:

AMERICAN WOMEN URGED TO BOYCOTT MILLINERS WHO SELL AIGRETTES

Many women did; and by mid-June the sentiment was so overwhelming that plume importers and the millinery trade came out in favor of a bill that forbade the importation of aigrette plumes. It was not the Underwood bill for which the actress was fighting, but a counter-measure which permitted the importation of the feathers of game birds killed for food and as pests.

The industry, which had seemed invincible a few months before, settled for that small crumb, and Mrs. Fiske returned to New York at the end of her season with the battle more than half won.

In September, when she began her western tour, the law against the importation of aigrettes was about to go into effect. And individual states, in answer to her appeal, had banned the sale of plumes from any source. The chief unfinished problem was the women who still clung to their aigrette plumes as the right of wealth and social position. And every blow Minnie struck at them was multiplied by the press.

A generation before, only cranks and anarchists criticized the doings of people who made the United States and Europe their playground. But the Populists had had their say, and Theodore Roosevelt had thundered against "malefactors of great wealth," and the great and not so great fortunes had come to depend more on the goodwill of the average citizen.

In Boston, wealthy women with consciences put snob appeal into reverse by giving a fortune in aigrette plumes to their servants, and women who clung to them were humiliated by meeting some friend's cook or washerwoman under a white mist of plumes as fine as her own. In New York, leaders like Mrs. John D. Rockefeller, Jr., Mrs. Henry Fairfield Osborn and Mrs. Oliver Iselin let it be known that the wearing of aigrette plumes was neither civilized nor fashionable. Attacked from within and without, the aigrette craze collapsed. The plumes became definitely unfashionable and they disappeared even from the rusty hats of servants.

It was the most complete victory of any humane crusade in America, and the Audubon Society gave a public testimonial to Mrs. Fiske, who had made it possible.

The egrets, which ornithologists had written off as doomed, were rescued just short of extinction. After another nesting season, it was estimated that there were eight thousand more egrets in the Southern states than there had been the year before. Gilbert Pearson, of the Audubon Society, wrote Mrs. Fiske of revisiting a rookery in the Everglades. The year before, he had found only seventy-five living birds in the rookery, the swamp littered with the bodies of the recently-killed, and the nests full of dead and dying young. On his second visit, there were no dead birds; only nests of healthy young, and hundreds of parent egrets, untroubled by hunters.

In Minnie Maddern's young days, she had heard Lawrence Barrett lament the perishable nature of the actor's art. Every night, he said, he carved a statue in snow. Minnie had laughed at him then, and she laughed afterward when she was reminded of the actor's solemn lament. She was never troubled by such thoughts. And her 1913 season was written in the snow of birds of unearthly beauty that returned each year in increasing numbers—the females with their misty nuptial plumes.

CHAPTER 35

Ashton Stevens recalled afterward that sometimes in Chicago when he accompanied Mrs. Fiske on an afternoon jaunt, she suggested a nickelodeon instead of a vaudeville show, but they never went because he didn't believe she could be serious about wanting to see motion pictures. It was at a time, he observed, "when Percy Hammond and James Huneker and a fool named Stevens were making pompous fun of the first nickel shows."

Mrs. Fiske was serious, though, and she often went alone to picture shows to study the efforts of early producers, who were using a medium with undiscovered possibilities—much as cavemen might have pelted each other with chunks of uranium ore.

The possibilities of moving pictures were almost undiscovered, but once in San Francisco, Mrs. Fiske was startled into admiration by the technique of a minor actor in the role of a clown. She saw the film through twice, and went back the next day to study the technique of the unknown comedian, proclaiming that the motion pictures were harboring a genius. Her friends were puzzled or scandalized, but an actress was allowed her eccentricities—and Charlie Chaplin, whom she had discovered, quickly justified her opinion.

Minnie, who had been born and grown middle-aged in the theatre, had no intention of acting for the films herself, although Daniel Frohman had often suggested it. But he raised the question again in the spring of 1913. He had just launched the Famous Players, and the new company needed a film that would justify its name. Frohman urged Mrs. Fiske to appear in *Tess of the D'Urbervilles*, and offered her an advance of ten thousand dollars for the picture.

She wanted to refuse again, but ten thousand dollars was important to her shaky finances; besides, the picture could be made at a time that would not interfere with her stage appearances.

Tess of the D'Urbervilles was filmed in New Jersey after the close of Mrs. Fiske's midwestern tour. The years had been steadily widening the gap between the actress and Hardy's fateful milkmaid; but at forty-eight Minnie was still youthful and smooth-skinned; in all but the close-ups she might have been the spiritualized Tess who had written a great chapter of stage history at the old Fifth Avenue Theatre sixteen years earlier.

The repressed, realistic method of acting which Mrs. Fiske had used in *Tess of the D'Urbervilles* was ideal for the camera, which revealed every exaggeration and made overacting intolerable. The coincidence helped make *Tess* one of the best pictures of its time, but unfortunately it left Mrs. Fiske with the mistaken belief that the camera adapted itself to any method of acting—a misconception that two years later backfired when she played Becky Sharp in the Edison Company's film version of *Vanity Fair*. When Becky's mannerisms were exaggerated by projection on the screen, they became a cruel burlesque. It was a belated lesson in acting before the camera, and Minnie was too old to make use of it personally. She realized that the success of *Tess* had been due to a happy accident—and that made her think less of the picture. "As soon as I suspect a fine effect is being achieved by accident, I lose interest." She told Alexander Woollcott, "I am not interested, you see, in unskilled labor."

After the filming of *Tess of the D'Urbervilles*, Mrs. Fiske joined her husband and Emily Stevens for a vacation. They spent the precious little that was left of summer in the Adirondacks; and in September Mrs. Fiske began her western tour in *The High Road*. She had given the play its fine, swinging name, but the play itself had never swung along; in private, she had another name for it—*The Hard Road*.

On tour she sometimes played in cities where *Tess of the D'Urbervilles* was showing—symbolizing in her own work the growing rivalry between stage and screen.

Mrs. Fiske had been far ahead of most of her contemporaries in evaluating the new medium, and her first experience before the camera gave her a new vision. In Minneapolis, a reporter asked Mrs. Fiske her views on moving pictures. She answered with the most glowing and prophetic statement that had ever been made on the subject. In part, she said:

It is too late to question the importance of the motion picture in the life of today. Its development as a popular amusement has been

273

one of the marvels of our time. . . . The motion picture affords a unique opportunity to the actor to equip himself in the neglected but essential art of pantomime.

Although technically motion pictures were to go far beyond Mrs. Fiske's dream of a pantomime art, some of her vision is still unrealized. But the possibility remains, and the actress's miscalculation was only in the human element. It was something she might have foreseen in the advertising of *Tess*. The picture was ballyhooed as the "most pretentious and expensive film ever offered." American motion pictures were already on the way to becoming an industry.

CHAPTER 36

Near the end of Mrs. Fiske's western tour, on January 29, 1914, Harry telegraphed the news of his mother's death. It was not unexpected of a woman of eighty-three, but it left the actress with a feeling of desolation.

Only a few years before, the gallant old lady had accompanied her daughter-in-law on tour, showing all the qualities of a seasoned trouper. On the same tour, Aunt Mary and Emily Stevens had been in Minnie's little family. Now both the older women were dead, and Emily was an established actress, going her own way while Minnie went on alone. Her feeling of desolation was increased by the fact that, instead of touring the Pacific Coast in spring and summer as she usually did, she was seeing it in the rains of winter—and her play required constant and exhausting effort. She wrote Harry of *The High Road:* "It never once moved by itself. It has to be shouldered and the physical effort to make it hold together would tax Mr. Sandow to his limit."

But neither time nor the effort of *The High Road* could settle Minnie in a mental rut. On January 22, she wrote hopefully from Beaumont, Texas:

I am beginning to feel certain that we are getting to the end of the day when scenery and properties will be so important as we have thought them in the past—and that will be a good thing . . . twice this season we have had to practically cut out the scenery and properties in our present play. We showed only a tiny corner of the first act garden, and also a tiny corner of the second act room. It was really remarkable, but we all felt that the play had never gone so well! The absence of scenery and properties gave an added spur to the acting and they were never missed. It may be that these new German ideas are right, and if so, it will relieve us of a great deal . . .

In mid-February *The High Road* was pushed and pulled through its last performance—and Minnie turned gratefully to a revival of *Mrs. Bumpstead-Leigh.*

The effort of *The High Road* left the actress too exhausted for her usual humane work. But during her Cleveland engagement, at Easter, she fought an impassioned skirmish for the young of a common variety of fowl. Tradesmen in search of new ways to profit from the Resurrection had begun selling Easter chicks that were bought by sentimental women and mauled to death by well-meaning children. Minnie launched a campaign to stop their sale.

During the difficult tour, another Minnie was traveling and playing vicariously, without pain—the film of *Tess of the D'Urbervilles* playing to crowded movie houses everywhere.

Minnie was buoyed up by the thought of the profits it was earning for her and she wrote to Harry:

Darling Boy—has Mr. Frohman yet made the first payment of our share of the profits of the "Tess" picture? Will you let me know what they are? And when they are paid will you please invest them in the very safest government bonds in my name—so that we will not touch them—but keep them forever sacred! We must just imagine—Darling Boy—that we have not got them! We must keep them untouched and sacred & some day we shall be glad of this. And you must explain to me what a Government bond is—and what I have to show for it—for I do not know!!—Government bonds are absolutely safe—are they not? They could not fail—could they?

The pictures have been tremendously successful. They were repeated three times in Cincinnati—playing a week each time. In Salt Lake City they filled the enormous Auditorium—constantly—all day. —Will you let me know about the profits and the Government bonds investment—please—darling Boy?

It was a letter that might have been written by a child, but Harry's answer was hard for even a mature woman to take: The film of *Tess* has been mismanaged from the actress's standpoint—being shown at nickelodeon prices. It had established the Famous Players Film Company, but the most successful picture of the year had earned no profits for Mrs. Fiske; the statement showed that her share was less than the ten thousand dollars advance. She had been overpaid!

The Fiskes' hope for profits from that season were gone, and they put their faith in the next—Minnie in *Lady Betty Martingale*, a partly-written play by John Luther Long; and Harry in *The White Dove*, with a Russian dancer whom he planned to star as an actress.

276

They had never come to grief with a play in which they both believed, but this time each was dubious of the other's choice. Minnie
observed that *The White Dove* was a bit light, and suggested that it
be tried out by the Burbank Stock Company in Los Angeles—a procedure which would cost Harry nothing, and give him a perspective of the
play.

For his part, Harry found *Lady Betty Martingale* too light for an
actress of Minnie's standing. He expressed his first doubts in a letter
and she replied:

> . . . It is a sad and discouraging thing—but plays & actors do not
> succeed because they are good—the best plays & the best actors fail
> —often. There is only one success in the theatre—the success of mag-
> netism—the current that is established by the play or the actor. A
> wretched play may succeed wonderfully—if some actor in it has
> established that current. That is all the theatre is—& so it is a danger-
> ous profession! You cannot be certain of your electric current—with
> even the best plays—& the best actors. Of course I mean that is the
> way it is here—Not so in Germany—or countries where the theatre
> means a definite art. In this play I can establish the current with a
> refined audience.
>
> As I said in my earlier letter—do not risk anything further on
> the play—but if you could associate some one with it—I think it
> would develop worth while. . . .

In a later letter she elaborated further:

Precious Boy,

> In order to get something new and striking—get this thrill of
> novelty—do you not think it will be well for us to try everything
> possible in the way of novel effect? I do think there may be con-
> siderable value in presenting the play in such a manner as to show
> what an old fashioned entertainment was . . . The setting for the
> first act could, of course, be historically correct, but not made of the
> cumbersome scenery that I hope with all my heart is passing away.
> I mean all that solid stuff that Frank likes so much and which is
> ineffective and so utterly expensive both to build and to carry.
>
> Do you not think it would be very amusing to "close in" after
> the first scene just as we used to do in the theatre when I was a
> little girl? At the end of the first scene of the play a whistle blows.—
> The scene hands close in the two side flats, making the wood scene.
> There would, of course, be appropriate and mysterious music pre-
> cisely as they used to do in nearly every play in which I acted as a
> child. They used to call it "villain music." Lady Pat and Lady Fewitts
> would appear in this front scene masked and mysterious, making

their flight from prison. This would emphasize the old fashioned idea and lend color and novelty to the Act. At the end of the scene flats draw off and the prison scene is discovered.

. . . The jail, of course, would have to be a jail and the color of a jail . . .

Confidentially I don't think Miss Kauser has good ideas about scenery and costumes. I know she has the very best intentions and means to be helpful in every possible way, and I say it in absolute kindness and confidence. Take for example, the second act in "The High Road." All that great heavy, solid stuff that cost us a fortune to carry through the United States could easily have been dispensed with without losing one particle of effect. The only reason for having those enormous heavy Venetian doors was because there exists in the manuscript a brief mention of them two acts later. . . . If I were you I would just make a revolution in that work, and I am sure we will get the best sort of effects for about one third of the expense and with no necessity for carrying an extra car. (We have done so much for dramatists, authors and scene painters and carpenters!) . . .

If we have the old fashioned long program, gotten up in the old fashioned manner might we not have, as we used to, a little synopsis of the acts as they go?

With the incidental music and the two or three songs introduced, and I hope—a dance—it should all have an air of great novelty in the theatre today.

In a word, we should concentrate in making Lady Pat an evening of far away charm and delight; a bit of the old theatre, when there was no thought of being absolutely "true" and "real," but when the one idea was to allure with lightness and music and charm, and when the audience and stage directors helped themselves freely to every child-like trick from the whole bag of tricks.

I do think that this will be absolutely necessary to insure what we wish to insure—popular success.

Dearest—devoted love
Precious—darling boy
Bunnikin

Minnie Maddern Fiske had completed a cycle which brought her back to the theatre of her childhood. In the letter, she was not "America's most intellectual actress," who never mentioned her "prehistoric past," and who seldom referred to a date more ancient than to-morrow. She was a homesick child, or a tired woman who had begun to look back at last, after so many years of forced marches into the future.

278

My grandmamma was an English girl of "family" but the family's war-like feelings were outraged when she married the poor musician who subsequently became my grandpapa.

For a while the disgraceful pair lived along merrily enough under the haughty noses of the offended ~~family~~ aristocrats, and just about the time when a *facetiously* ~~particularly~~ spiteful cousin sent my grandmamma a shilling, the genial young couple sailed away to America with eleven sturdy young ones — and the shilling.

A page from Mrs. Fiske's unfinished autobiography.

Little Minnie Maddern. *Left*, 8 years old, as Little Eva. *Center*, about 6
years old, unidentified role. *Right*, portrait at about 4 years.

Thomas Davey, Mrs. Fiske's father.   Lizzie Maddern, Mrs. Fiske's mother

Left, Minnie Maddern at about 12 as Ralph Rackstraw in *Pinafore*. *Right*, a tintype of Minnie, about 13 years.

Photographs of Minnie at 16 and 17 years.

Two photographs of Minnie at about 20 and the famous Haskell drawing.

Upper left, Legrand White.
Upper right, Harrison Grey
Fiske.

Left, playbill of Mrs. Fiske's first
appearance in *A Doll's House*,
turning point in her career.

Left, Mrs. Fiske as Nora in *A Doll's House*, 1895. *Right*, Mrs. Fiske in *Marie Deloche*, 1895.

A scene from *Love Finds a Way*, 1896.

Mrs. Fiske and James Neill in *Marie Deloche*, 1896.

Divorçons, 1896.

Scenes from *Tess of the D'Urbervilles*, 1897.

Act III, *Tess of the D'Urbervilles.*

Act IV, *Tess of the D'Urbervilles.*

Scene from the motion picture, *Tess of the D'Urbervilles.*

Mrs. Fiske and Frederic de Belleville in *Little Italy*, 1898.

Left, Mrs. Fiske as Alexandra Victoria Belchamber in *A Bit of Old Chelsea,* 1898. *Right,* An Arnold Genthe portrait of Mrs. Fiske as she appeared in *Frou Frou,* 1899.

Mrs. Fiske in two 1899 roles: Becky Sharp (*left*) and Magda.

A scene from *Becky Sharp*.

The famous setting for *Becky Sharp*.

Mrs. Fiske as Mary of Magdala, 1902.

The Manhattan Theatre.

Emily Stevens.

Mrs. Fiske as Hedda Gabler, 1903.

Mrs. Fiske in *Hedda Gabler* at the Manhattan Theatre, 1903.

Mrs. Fiske as she appeared in *Leah Kleschna*, 1904 (*left*) and *The New York Idea*, 1906.

Two Arnold Genthe portraits of Mrs. Fiske, as Mrs. Karslak (*left*) in *The New York Idea* and as Dolce in *Dolce*.

Mrs. Fiske as Dolce, 1906.

Mrs. Fiske as Rebecca West in *Rosmersholm*, 1907.

Mrs. Fiske as Nell Sanders in
Salvation Nell, 1908.

Inside the Empire Bar, Act I, *Salvation Nell.*

Setting for Act III, *Salvation Nell.*

Scene from *Mrs. Bumpstead-Leigh*, 1911.

Scene from *The High Road*, 1912.

Scene from *Erstwhile Susan*, 1916.

Mrs. Fiske as Madame Sand, 1917.

Scene from *Mis' Nelly of N'Orleans*, 1919.

Mrs. Fiske in *Wake Up, Jonathan*, 1921.

Mrs. Fiske in the 1927 production of *Ghosts*.

Candid shots of Minnie and Harrison Fiske at Camp Veery.

Henrietta Crosman and Mrs. Fiske in *Merry Wives of Windsor*, 1928.

Mrs. Fiske as Mrs. Malaprop in *The Rivals*, 1925.

A special company assembled for a revival of *Mrs. Bumpstead-Leigh* in 1931.

Paradoxically, at that very moment of looking back, she was urging Harry to break with the stuffy traditions of the past; and she pointed the way for him to revolutionize stage design.

In her letter, Mrs. Fiske continually referred to *Lady Betty Martingale* as *Lady Pat*—the play in which she had failed at the Empire Theatre two years before. It could have been taken as a measure of her exhaustion, or as a bad omen. But she had set her heart on the play, and Harry plunged into the expense of producing an elaborate costume piece.

In the same season, Mrs. Fiske was cheered by the prospect of resuming her mothering of Emily Stevens. Ever since Emily's outburst against Minnie on the opening night of *Salvation Nell*, the girl had been closer to Harry than to her cousin. Since then she had also become an established actress, with her own circle of friends. She had continued to look on Harry as her guardian and guide, but Minnie saw little of her, except on occasional family vacations when Emily was present more because of Harry than because of her cousin.

That spring the situation changed, and on May 18, Mrs. Fiske wrote to Harry:

> Emily has shown a great disposition to spend the summer with me and I am delighted. . . . I think the sea and the sea bathing will be splendid for all of us. I suppose I shall get back to New York sometime on the 8th. I thought if I can get off with Emily by the 12th, that will give me three or four days in New York, and as soon as I have Emily settled, I can come to New York as often as you need me. . . .
>
> It will, of course, be necessary for us to arrange everything with regards to Mr. Long's play, and so I shall be close enough whenever you want me. I would rather not mention to Emily that I expect to go to New York occasionally. When I have her settled, I know it will be all right for me to do so, but please do not mention to her now that I shall be attending to business as well as to her. I want her to get all business out of her head and go with a very quiet spirit and feeling that she is going to take the very best sort of rest and vacation that will make her all over.

For the early part of her vacation with Emily, Minnie had selected a direction rather than a place. On June 12 they started up the New England coast, planning to go, and stay, wherever fancy suggested. A week later, Minnie wrote to Harry from Wauwient House, Nantucket:

Precious Boy:

I shall reserve for another letter this history of our adventures since leaving New York & how—by a wonderful fall of good fortune, we came upon this perfectly ideal place. First of all—tho'—can you manage to come & bring Baa-Baa? Can you & will you? If you can come—darling Boy—I think we would have a happier time if you came alone.—I mean I would love to ask you to bring Miss Lopocova—(she is a dear little thing) if we had more time—but I have not a very long vacation—(if we do a picture—) & I would so love & enjoy just to have a family time. I know you would not mind that. We can be free like children . . .

The productions of *The White Dove* and *Lady Betty Martingale* kept Harry Fiske in New York while the cousins kept each other company. Nothing came of plans for a film version of *Salvation Nell,* and Minnie did not make her excursions to New York, but she was content to mother Emily, far from the din of Broadway. That part of the vacation turned out even better than she had dared to hope.

Emily was now perhaps the most popular young actress in America, with the most brilliant promise—and faced with at least the usual hazards. Her more scientific training and wiser early management had prepared her to rise in the theatre more rapidly than her older cousin and to go at least as far, but there was no substitute for Minnie's iron stamina. Emily had suffered a nervous breakdown before her more enduring cousin had first taken charge of her; and since her rise to fame she had been burning the candle at both ends, gathering brilliant people around her and shining off stage as well as on. The first ominous signs of nervous exhaustion had prompted Minnie to plan the quiet vacation.

On the remote beach, Emily relaxed in the sunshine and forgot about being witty; her color and her appetite returned—and she and Minnie drew closer together as the golden June days passed.

Nothing of note happened in the half-forgotten outside world until near the end of their stay at Nantucket, when the Archduke of Austria was assassinated in Bosnia. Minnie and Emily read about it in a day-old newspaper—it did not seem an insuperable loss.

Unfortunately, that was not the end of it. Good lives were about to be thrown after a bad one. As the cousins traveled north, war was engulfing the Europe which Minnie had found so peaceful two summers earlier—Belgium and France and the dreaming English countryside. It took time for the fact to be revealed, but from the island of

Nantucket she and Emily never found their way back to the world they had left; it was gone in chaos.

The second half of the cousins' vacation was a month at Cape Breton, Nova Scotia, a place where neither of them had ever been before.

Harry James Smith had persuaded Minnie to make the visit, and he had rented a house for her and Emily at Arichat, where he spent his summers.

Cape Breton was to be the ultimate in remote peacefulness—but when Minnie and Emily arrived, they were in a country at least theoretically at war. Even so, Arichat was an infinitely restful and courteous village; Minnie commented that she had never seen such good manners in all her life, and she would have to mend her own so as not to appear boorish.

Harry James Smith had done all he could think of for the comfort of the visitors, and then retired into the background of unobtrusive villagers, but he remained alert and observant. In a letter to a friend, he wrote of Mrs. Fiske:

Arichat fairly adopted her. She talked to everyone she met, and always was followed about by a loyal contingent of boys and girls—the former chiefly barefoot and belonging to the more disreputable families. We saw rather little of her and Miss Stevens, for I felt that they were happier left to themselves to prowl and discover. But they made several brief visits to my house, and I took them out a number of times for little boating trips. Mrs. Fiske's inextinguishable enthusiasm was the trait in her that most struck me. It is adorable in a woman of her maturity and sophistication. An unreasoning energy of living, an eagerness that fairly sweeps one along with it . . .

Minnie had recuperated more rapidly than her younger cousin. While she helped Emily forget the theatre, she made notes for the costuming of *Lady Betty Martingale*, worked on the music plot and the revision of Act I, Scene I, which was all she had received of the play.

Among the many notes on her costumes for *Lady Betty* was this one: "This is only a rough measure as I have not here the proper corsets with which to make me smaller. My full height (without shoes) is 62 ¾ inches. Please reduce to feet."

Harry had planned to join the women at Arichat for most of July, but the fifteenth found him at Pittsfield, Massachusetts, rehearsing the cast of *The White Dove*. It was a now familiar pattern, and after three weeks at Arichat Minnie wrote:

Precious Boy:
You must not think us rattle brained for changing our plans—but we thought it wise to alter them.

We would have loved you to come here—but in talking it over—we felt sure you could not, knowing what business you had to attend to . . . And so—as we wish so much to have you with us for a little part of vacation—we thought it best for us to come near you—close enough for you to come to us.

We shall wander along for a week after leaving here—through the Evangeline country—& then get to New York for two days' stay (longer if you need me). . . .

Minnie wanted to hear about the premiere of *The White Dove*, but Harry had nothing good to report. It had taken Lydia Lopokova arduous years to become a dancer—and when she was tired of dancing, she convinced herself and others that she could be an actress by inspiration.

At Pittsfield it became evident that inspiration was not enough, and on the opening night in New York even the inspiration was missing. *The White Dove* fell flat.

CHAPTER 37

The failure of *The White Dove* added to the burden on *Lady Betty Martingale*, which was already weighted down with troubles.

Illness, and the procrastinations that writers are heir to, had delayed Mr. Long's manuscript to the point where it snarled the whole production, particularly the costumes. In London, Percy Anderson worked from an incomplete script and made wrong guesses, which exasperated Mrs. Fiske. When the costumes were finally completed, international complications set in. England was at war, and wartime laws forbade the exportation of trivial merchandise like actors' costumes. Eventually the costumes were sent under fictitious names as personal baggage—all of which multiplied the delays and the cost.

Even without a war *Lady Betty* would have been an expensive production: a costume piece with a large cast; incidental music specially composed by William Furst; and a chorus of male voices, which meant mouths to feed three times a day in return for a few snatches of song.

A little disheveled and breathless, *Lady Betty* opened on schedule at Buffalo on September 17, and went on to Pittsburgh, Detroit, Cleveland and Philadelphia. It moved under the pall of depression which war had brought to the theatre, and its gay, light spirit did not help.

Old-time critics and theatregoers mourned for Minnie Maddern of the days of *Caprice* and *Featherbrain;* but when she returned to the spirit of the still earlier theatre, some of the same critics were less satisfied than they had been with Ibsen—and the tender burlesque of the theatre in its age of innocence was lost on a younger generation that did not know what to make of a play which ended with the cast forgetting what they were about and dancing an eight-hand reel.

Minnie had felt rather than thought about the play, and produced it because she wanted to get back to the past—and she found what reasons she could afterward. In normal times it would have had a chance of succeeding, but normal times had evaporated from the world and dried up the theatre.

Harry was still trying to get on his feet after the failure of *The White Dove* and Mrs. Fiske was battling on, precariously, giving him what help she could.

From Pittsburgh she wrote:

Precious Boy

I know you must be under a terrible financial strain. Of course every penny I have in Jersey City is yours— Send me a check to sign whenever you wish.

But have I enough to meet this awful theatre depression? Can we make a turn?—I am in the dark & so am deeply worried.

Will you tell me the prospects you have of making a turn?

I think all will be well with you later but just now— I know your strain.

Please tell me—darling—precious Boy.

Bunner

The play seems really charming. Mr. Church was intensely enthusiastic but nothing seems to lift the theatre.

Have I enough to avert disaster & can we make a turn?

Dear—dear Boy, I am very well—& shall do my best.

Her best was not enough. *Lady Betty Martingale* expired in Philadelphia, and the mountain of debt made a molehill of *The White Dove* failure.

Critics were almost unanimous in the opinion that *Lady Betty* failed because it was a trivial play, unworthy of a great actress. Mrs. Fiske never agreed with the verdict. Three years afterward she wrote to Alexander Woollcott:

. . . One beautiful thing we did throw away. This was "Lady Betty Martingale" by John Luther Long. It had great faults, but they were the kind you could remedy in two days. Properly nursed, the play would have developed the priceless quality of delicate charm, and I think we owe it to Mr. Long to shout this from the housetops. All the long faces that hover close when success does not immediately perch upon one's banner gathered about "Lady Betty Martingale." All those who could not see, who could not instantly and instinctively reach the psychological root of the trouble, closed in upon the play and a beautiful thing was crushed to death and lost to the American theatre. . . .

At the time, Mrs. Fiske blamed only herself for an expensive failure at the moment when it was essential for her to succeed and rescue Harry from an entanglement of debts. She believed the play would have succeeded if she had been more diligent and enduring.

She was left in mid-season without a play, and she had to retire to the side lines like a vanquished athlete. There were many places where she could have gone, but she chose to stay with Harry's younger brother, Otis, and his lovely, understanding wife, Georgina. Young Otis had acted as best man at Harry and Minnie's wedding. Since that time he had made no demands on his famous brother and more famous sister-in-law, who rarely saw him; but when he could be of help he emerged from the background, and he and Georgina welcomed Minnie into their home.

The Otis Fiskes lived at Great Kills, Staten Island, diagonally across the lower bay from Brooklyn, and in sight of the towers of Manhattan. Minnie arrived there with mixed feelings of exile and homecoming in a confused world. Great Kills was restful after the road, and quiet after New York—but the visible tides of war moved by in sight of the town: ships with great neutral flags painted on their sides, and ships without flags steamed up the bay in grim triumph, or set out, more grimly, into the submarine zone.

In the midst of world drama the actress had become a spectator. She spent her temporary, enforced retirement much as she had her earlier, voluntary one—in writing and studying and taking long walks. Harry Fiske was only a few miles away, but she rarely saw him. Over the years their relationship had found its natural level: a business partnership with mutual affection between the actress whose emotions had been long trained in sublimation, and the ardent man who had filled a vacancy with many friendships. The exchange of letters was enough to keep Minnie from being lonely; and except when they were in the throes of financial harassment, they supplemented each other in harmony:

Darling Boy,
Again I come to you for help!
Will you write me a short article for this syndicate and say that while all religions possess much that is supremely beautiful I could never be impelled to join any one church because I know of no Christian religion that makes the consideration of the great dumb creation a part of its creed. The great creation of animals and birds is a part of the universal principle of life but the Christian Church

285

has for the most part ignored that creation and its claims upon us and our responsibility toward it.

Therefore to me the creeds or doctrines of the various religions have not seemed complete or comprehensive or satisfying because they are not founded on a philosophy that sees life as a whole—demanding justice towards every living thing whether human or animal. . . .

I shall be grateful to receive this as soon as can conveniently. Use this as a basis for article, Please!

Devoted love
Bunner

The letter revealed the basis of Mrs. Fiske's humane endeavors: a philosophy which saw life whole, in the spirit of her beloved St. Francis of Assisi, who had called the animals "our little brothers," and in the spirit of evolution which recognized no alien gulf between different forms of life.

New financial crises shook the Fiskes, and an old one rose up to plague them. On the brief tour with *Lady Betty*, when Harry was on the verge of bankruptcy, Minnie had made a desperate attempt to save the situation. George Tyler had repeatedly offered her three thousand dollars a week and a share of the profits if she would appear under his management, but she had always refused, saying that she would never appear under any management but her husband's. But with disaster just around the corner, she saw the arrangement as the last remaining hope, and she opened negotiations with Tyler. However, the theatre depression which had driven the Fiskes to the wall had had its effect on the younger producer, and nothing came of the attempt. Accidentally, months later, Harry learned of the negotiations. At the time, his creditors were pressing him from every side. Driven to the breaking point, he saw his wife's unsuccessful move as one more blow struck at him, and he dashed off a bitter letter, accusing her of attempting to desert him in his hour of need.

The letter reached her at Great Kills on the bleak nineteenth of November. She too had suffered, but she had had time for thinking, and rest enough to restore some of her vital buoyancy. She answered the letter almost calmly, but it wrung from her admissions that she had never made before, to anyone:

Darling Boy

. . . You are mistaken. The idea of any change in management was not evolved in Indianapolis.—When it was evolved—it came at a moment of what seemed a crisis—& my whole thought was for you.—It was not my idea alone—but that also of your most loyal—true & devoted friends. Rather it was evolved together. This I tell you—pledging you to the strictest confidence not to repeat my words. Every thought was for you. I thought—foolishly—that I might demand an immediate advance—which I planned to send you to help in a crisis.

Precious Boy—I have not been quite normal—hardly quite sane for many, many years.

You do not see—you seem not to be able to see—what an incredible tumult my life has been.—It has not been life. It has been tumult of one sort or another—&, at last, I seemed to go down under it—but I feel myself coming up—& when it all starts again—it will be on a better—firmer basis.—It will be all different and I have not been so hopeful in years.

You have been the strong one—& I the weak. You have not understood that. There have been a thousand things—great and small—that you do not even seem to have realized.

It does not matter because we have got to begin all over again.

Say and think what you will—I have been your best friend—Not your wisest friend—I should have been far wiser & stronger—& braver— But no friend has been so true in devotion.

I do feel hopeful for you and for myself.—I think everything will adjust itself. And the shocking disorder of my homeless life is at an end—for I could not live it any longer—I can make my home with Otie until things come right. And—I can have a place of my own—The other life would break & demoralize any human being who had labored so long for something else—& who would be left alone to brood.

It is all coming out right—I do believe—darling Boy.

A thousand times you have completely misunderstood me.

Devotedly, Bunnikin

The Harry Fiske of popular legend was one of the fortunate men of the earth—an hereditary millionaire, highlighted by the glamor of distinguished stage productions and a famous wife. Harry had clinched the legend by dressing as a gentleman, living magnificently at the New York Athletic Club, and giving lavish help to men and women in the theatre and out of it. In the winter of 1914, he reached the bitter end of his financial tether. While Minnie was living with the Otis Fiskes, Harry turned for help to his millionaire older brother, Willard Fisk. Willard had avoided all connection with the theatre, even to dropping the final "e" from the family name his brother and sister-in-law had made famous. But he was ready to give brotherly advice. He looked over Harry's books and advised him to go into bankruptcy.

Willard Fisk knew even less about the theatre than Harry Fiske knew about finances. Afterward, it appeared that Willard's advice was the worst that could have been given in the situation, and that Harry could have avoided bankruptcy by careful management. But the advice was given, and taken, in good faith.

Harry entered a petition of bankruptcy on December 30, 1914, and the sale of goods was set for February 16, 1915. It was the most humiliating situation of his life, and the fact that he was looked on as one of the mighty drew all the more attention to his fall.

At the hour when his creditors were to take over, Harry Fiske laid his keys on his desk and left his office, with its rare books and mementos and letters from the great. The only possession he had taken was his revolver.

From the office he went to the New York Athletic Club, where he made his final arrangements for leaving; then he went on to Central Park. He had six dollars in his pocket with which to start again at the age of fifty-five, and he had his revolver. From now on, he had decided, his life could only be a useless anticlimax; Bunner would be better off without him, and there was only one gentlemanly thing he could do.

He found a secluded park bench in the snow, sat down, and put the muzzle of the revolver to his temple. Then he asked himself whether he was doing this for Bunner's sake, or because he was a coward.

He lowered the revolver long enough to tell himself again that Bunner would be better off without him. Thinking of her made him ask how she would take the news that her bankrupt husband had blown out his brains on a park bench. It would only multiply the disgrace if he added cowardice to failure. Bunner had taken repeated blows valiantly. Right now, in exile at Great Kills, she was working confidently to make her comeback, and she needed his help more than ever.

Harry put the revolver back in his pocket.

He sat in the snowy park long enough to regain his composure, and then he hunted out a cheap room on the West Side. It was a decisive day, but not the one he had planned. Before he had spent the last of his six dollars, an old friend hunted him out. Soon afterward he received a letter from his friends at the New York Athletic Club, offering him a loan, and that same day his office staff sent word that they would continue without pay, gambling with him on his new endeavors.

On Monday, Harry was back at his office—the impeccable gentleman with the aura of a millionaire—but he had made a great change. He had moved the last of his personal belongings to the West Side rooming house, resigned from all his clubs, and was living austerely as he began the steep climb back toward solvency.

CHAPTER 38

The mighty had fallen—Harry Fiske to a West Side rooming house, and Minnie to exile on Staten Island; and in New York, Charles Frohman hobbled up the gangplank of the *Lusitania* for his farewell trip abroad.

The overseas colony of Frohman's fading empire was now only a shadow, but the Little Napoleon of the theatre had grown increasingly sentimental with time and suffering, and he sailed for England to have one more visit with James M. Barrie.

On May Day, from the garden at Great Kills, Minnie and Georgina Fiske watched the huge black-and-white four-stack *Lusitania* steam down the lower bay, drop her pilot off Sandy Hook, and fade swiftly toward Europe in the early afternoon sunshine on the Atlantic. The sailing was given dramatic interest by an Imperial German Embassy advertisement in the morning *Times*, warning travelers that Allied ships sailing for the war zone were liable to destruction.

Even from the distance of three miles the *Lusitania* had loomed enormous in the lower bay, a target no torpedo could have missed. The women discussed the possibility, and agreed with the press that it was only German bluster.

"It would be as easy as throwing a rock through the window of St. Patrick's," Minnie said, "but who would do it?"

Six days later the evening headlines carried the news that the *Lusitania* had been torpedoed off Queenstown with a loss of twelve hundred lives, among them Charles Frohman's. He had died quoting from *Peter Pan*, "Why fear death? It is the most beautiful adventure in life."

The manager had the dramatic exit, and the actress labored on, earning small sums from articles while she looked for a play in which she could return to the stage.

In playwriting, as in acting, one success does not always lead to another. Langdon Mitchell, Edward Sheldon and John Luther Long had failed her in various degrees in their latest attempts—and Harry James Smith had not written a successful play since *Bumpstead-Leigh*. But four years of rejected plays did not change Mrs. Fiske's estimate of Harry James Smith. Of all her playwrights, she felt most akin to the sensitive and idealistic young New Englander; she also thought him the most promising playwright on the American horizon.

Since *Bumpstead-Leigh*, Smith had been unable to suggest a theme which appealed to Mrs. Fiske, but early in 1915 she found one in his novel *Effie's Soul*—a gay satire-burlesque with a character which suited her, and an hilarious episode about a modern painting called "Intoxication from Kissing."

Work on the play, and correspondence with Mr. Smith buoyed her up for several months, and then she was shaken by doubts. The play, which they had named *Suki at Parnassus*, was charming, but it was airy and unrealistic—and she had had two recent, disastrous failures in plays that were too light for her; she could not risk another.

Early in May she wrote to Smith, telling him her doubts, and suggesting that he submit *Suki* to Marie Tempest. She loved the play but didn't dare produce it until she had had a definite success. "Don't don't be discouraged, my dear boy!" she wrote. "I know this is fiendish!"

Harry James Smith was not discouraged, and a few weeks later he wrote to Mrs. Fiske, buoyantly:

> Litchfield, Conn.
> 4 June, 1915
>
> Such a wonderful horseback ride of thirty-five miles as I had this morning, reaching this beautiful old town (how you would adore it!) at seven A.M. I leave my mare here for the summer.
> A thousand greetings from the hills of spring.
> H.J.S.

Minnie did not appear on the stage during 1915, but that summer the moving-picture division of the Edison Company asked her to appear as Becky Sharp in a film of *Vanity Fair*. The offer came with the same advance as she had received for the filming of *Tess of the D'Urbervilles*. Ten thousand dollars was little enough for acting her most famous role before the camera, but it would bring Harry that much nearer solvency, and she accepted.

Vanity Fair was filmed at the Edison studio in New Jersey in the early fall, under the direction of Eugene Knowland. None of Minnie's old company was in the cast, and the scenario was from an unfamiliar version of *Vanity Fair*. But Becky Sharp was still Becky, and Minnie played the character before the camera as she had played it on the stage over a period of sixteen years.

Minnie had viewed the *Vanity Fair* picture as a means of helping Harry up from financial disaster, but before the picture was completed, he had already accomplished the impossible—in less than a year he had cleared away a mountain of debt, paid his actors and office staff in full, and been released from bankruptcy.

On November 28, Mrs. Fiske wrote from Great Kills:

Darling Boy
 . . . The "Vanity Fair" picture is to be shown next Saturday night —at the Ritz-Carlton for the benefit of Flower Hospital. Mr. Farrell & others are doing it. I have promised to be present—so I shall be in next Saturday & I hope you can come to the picture. Please plan ahead so that you can—if possible.—I shall not need any more money until then so you need not send any. When I see you next Saturday it will do. I'll write all details re time of the performance—where to meet—etc.

It was the first time she had left the island in weeks, and they celebrated with dinner at Delmonico's—Harry in evening clothes and millionaire aura, and Minnie looking like a poor relative. In recent years she had become increasingly indifferent to her clothes off stage; she put on anything which came handy, and covered her face with a heavy veil—sometimes two.

Harry prided himself on being able to say anything to any woman without giving offense, and at dinner he criticized Minnie's getup. It reminded him, he said, of a certain engrosser's signature. The engrosser had been called on to prepare a testimonial for the distinguished guest of the Lotos Club; he illuminated the parchment after the best manner of the medieval monks, and without a moment's hesitation he duplicated the signatures of the officers of the club so perfectly that the gentlemen and their bankers would have sworn to the genuineness of the handwriting—and when the engrosser presented his bill, he signed his own name in a characterless scrawl that would have been a disgrace to a schoolboy.

"That is as it should be," Minnie said. "No one cares about an engrosser's personal handwriting, or what old Bunner wears off stage."

She was confident that Becky had been right before the camera, and that the showing of the film at the Ritz-Carlton would give the little adventuress a new lease on life. But the flickering film played unpleasant tricks on Becky. Her nervous and abrupt mannerisms, so effective on stage, made it appear on the screen that she was acting on the top of a hot stove.

Harry rumbled deep damnation of Edison's nickelodeon technique, and the grand ballroom full of New York society applauded politely when there was some recognizable token of Mrs. Fiske's stage character. But she saw it for the personal failure that it was, a cruel burlesque of her greatest role.

Harry saw her to the Staten Island ferry, talking reassuringly of successes to come—then she was alone with the recollection of her failure on the dark, rough voyage down the sleet-lashed harbor. Becky had given the worst performance in the film because she was the Becky of the stage. The new medium required a new technique—something close to the repressed, naturalistic acting which Minnie had introduced to the American stage and Duse to the European; like that, but lighter and more smoothly done.

She was not too old to learn—but at fifty-one she was too old to have another opportunity.

For months Minnie had been guiding an amateur playwright in work on the play which she planned to produce the following season. The playwright was Marian de Forest, and the play was *Erstwhile Susan,* a dramatization of Helen R. Martin's novel *Barnabetta.* It was the story of a lady elocutionist who married a narrow-minded Pennsylvania-Dutch farmer in order to rescue his gifted daughter from a life of drudgery. It was no great play, but it had good opportunities for comedy.

Except in the special case of *Leah Kleschna,* Minnie had accepted neither credit nor compensation for work on other people's plays. But hard times were beginning to put a limit on generosity; just before the showing of the *Vanity Fair* film, she wrote Harry:

> . . . I am—as usual—doing an immense amount of work on "Erstwhile Susan." The work practically amounts to collaboration —& will be of the greatest benefit to the play. I am asking nothing for this work—but—if the play should be largely successful—is it not fair that I should have a third interest in the profits of the road companies that would be sent out? If the new play succeeds it will be, owing in a great measure, to the work I am now putting on it. Should there not be something in the contract to the effect that I

have a third interest always in the profits of the play—whatever company is producing it? And also in the stock company productions? If I am to have no share in any of these productions (in the event of the play's success) it seems to me most unfair. . . .

The production of *Erstwhile Susan* was still nearly a year away, but early in 1916 Minnie began playing a new role in a new medium. The role was that of Mrs. Fiske; the medium was the spoken word, with Alexander Woollcott acting as the word camera and making a permanent record of the professional views of Mrs. Fiske.

Minnie refused to give interviews except on the rare occasions when they would be helpful to what she was doing at the moment, and her personal acquaintance with critics was limited. Only a few great souls like Montgomery Phister, Ashton Stevens and Norman Hapgood could claim her as a personal friend; and she had a nodding acquaintance with the new generation of alert young New York critics: George Jean Nathan, Alexander Woollcott, Heywood Broun and Robert Benchley.

Woollcott she had met, belatedly, through Emily Stevens. Emily, spoken of as the best young actress on the English-speaking stage, had moved from the Three Arts Club to the apartment at the Brevoort which the Fiskes could no longer afford. There her informal salons attracted some of the liveliest minds in New York. One of the liveliest was Alexander Woollcott's. He was also the most constant visitor because, it was said, Emily Stevens was the one person he knew who could keep up with his wit.

Minnie had never had time for salons, but she occasionally met Woollcott at her cousin's. At the time, her last successful play was several years behind her, but her position as first lady of the theatre was secure and Alexander Woollcott was duly worshipful of her. At a chance meeting early in 1916, he suggested that they meet from time to time and discuss stage matters. Nothing was said about her talking for publication, but there was the telltale gleam of a book in Woollcott's eyes.

Minnie pretended not to see the gleam as she innocently agreed to Woollcott's suggestion. She could use the bolstering of publicity, and she had ideas about the stage which might be worth recording.

The pact was the beginning of a brisk association extending over most of a year. During it, Woollcott was often seen accompanying the veiled lady to the theatre, or sitting with her in an out-of-the-way

294

restaurant, in animated conversation over a half-forgotten lunch. It was a Boswell and Johnson association, minus the heaviness; under creative questioning, Minnie aired her views on the science of acting and the functions of a director, all illustrated by examples from her own experience.

Woollcott never made notes while in Mrs. Fiske's company; ostensibly it was all for the joy of discussing a common enthusiasm. But the *Times* critic recorded everything in his remarkably retentive mind, and the actress saw to it that what she said was worth recording. She treated her part of the interviews as a role to which she gave her usual careful preparation, and her care to be in the right mood, striking the right note.

She was a definite success; the character that emerged in Woollcott's articles was the essence of Mrs. Fiske—the actress and producer with the brilliant mind that reached ahead of its time. The portrayal was stripped of non-essential details like the poverty of the present and the desperate uncertainty of the future. But the actress did not attempt to glamorize herself; when she spoke of herself at all, it was in relation to a battle for some ideal, or to one of her failures from which more could be learned than from success.

But in her long and amiable association with Alexander Woollcott, Minnie never trusted him. He was, she thought, a gossipy party, and in their talks, which sounded so delightfully spontaneous, she was forever on her guard against saying anything she would not have wanted quipped from the penthouse tops.

Woollcott did handsomely by her. The interviews appeared serially in *Century Magazine*, and were later collected in a volume: *MRS. FISKE: Her Views on the Stage*. It was the only book about herself of which Minnie ever approved, and by far the most valuable one. It was nearly all Mrs. Fiske, and very little Alexander Woollcott; it was unique among his books for its relative humility.

By coincidence, the day before Charles Frohman sank with the *Lusitania*, Mrs. Fiske helped bring recognition to another Charles. In *Harper's Weekly* of May 6, 1917, there appeared an article by her entitled "The Art of Charles Chaplin." The title was startling, but it was nothing to the revolutionary text:

. . . To the writer Charles Chaplin appears as a great comic artist, possessing inspirational powers and a technique as unfaltering as Réjane's. If it be treason to Art to say this, then let those exalted persons who allow culture to be defined only upon their own terms make the most of it. . . .

Chaplin already had his following among those who saw what they liked; for those who had to be told, it was now made clear that Charlie Chaplin was not only an artist but one of the very great. It became fashionable as well as popular to see him on the screen and discuss his art. But on his rise to unique success and fame, his most valued press clipping was the *Harper's Weekly* article in which Minnie Maddern Fiske had let fresh air and daylight into the petrified forest of art.

CHAPTER 39

In one of her interviews with Alexander Woollcott that year, Mrs. Fiske confided that she had retired from the stage.

Poverty made her physical retirement impossible, but she knew that her days of strenuous roles were over—the statement was partly a wish. Fifty years on the stage was enough, and she was in the shadow of the successor whom she had taught.

Emily Stevens was then in the midst of the dazzling three-year run of *The Unchastened Woman*, while Minnie struggled to regain a foothold on the stage. And like a further hint at her retirement, Minnie now became Emily's aunt instead of cousin. In earlier years Emily had repeatedly corrected interviewers who made the mistake in their relationship. Now she let it go uncorrected, and in the double-page interviews about her success, she always spoke of Mrs. Fiske as "my aunt."

Emily would always seem very young to Minnie, but she was thirty-four instead of the less than thirty that she claimed, and her fight against age was part of the same battle that Minnie had been fighting for years. Only the year before, she had directed Harry to remove her name from all *Who's Who* books because the facts were too revealing.

In one important respect, Minnie was happier as Emily's aunt than as her cousin; Emily's dazzling success in her own right eased her resentment against her famous relative. As Emily Stevens expressed it to interviewers, "Now Mrs. Fiske and I can be aunt and niece in perfect comfort."

While her famous "niece" was being hailed as America's greatest young emotional actress, Minnie returned to the stage. In the fall of 1916 she opened in Boston in *Erstwhile Susan*. It was a creaking, second-rate dramatic structure, but Minnie held it together and gave it life, and the play settled down to a successful run.

In *Erstwhile Susan*, Mrs. Fiske was presented by Madison Corey and Joseph Riter by arrangement with Harrison Grey Fiske. The change, which was a result of Harry's bankruptcy, was chiefly a matter of printing; he acted in his usual capacity.

On the opening night, Copey sent Minnie a bouquet of violets.

A few days later, her earliest idol of the theatre wrote from the Brewster:

My dear friend:
    May I have the courtesy of a box for Friday night and the pleasure of seeing you after the performance? If so, please place in the enclosed envelope, and greatly oblige
                                        Most sincerely and appreciatively
                                                Lotta
October Thirty-first, Nineteen Hundred and Sixteen.
P.S. Kindly pardon use of typewriter

It was twenty years since Lotta Crabtree had implied in print that Minnie was not a great actress because she had amassed no wealth. Minnie had even less money now, but years punctuated by calls and association in humane work had endeared Minnie to Lotta, as much as anyone was ever endeared to her—and Minnie would always seem young to the youth-struck Lotta, just as Emily would always seem a young girl to Minnie.

Erstwhile Susan moved to the Gaiety Theatre and the acid test of New York. In her collaboration Minnie had violated her own ideals of playwriting; she had made Juliet Miller a star part, and tailored the role to her showiest abilities. She had done the job so well that critics and playgoers were dazzled—and the play kept the Gaiety full into January, then toured successfully for the remainder of the season.

In the summer of 1917, in the peace of the Adirondacks, Minnie turned her attention to a play nearer her heart's desire.

The play grew out of a happy triumvirate: the brilliant young Philip Moeller to write it; Arthur Hopkins to direct, and Mrs. Fiske to play the title role. *Madame Sand* began with that fabulous romantic about to flee from Paris with Alfred de Musset; Heinrich Heine and Franz Liszt appeared along the way; and it ended with George Sand meeting Frederic Chopin at the Baron de Rothschild's reception and in her own words, "taking the poor, tired boy home to bed."

At various times in Minnie's career, she had averred that she could not play a love scene—and in *Madame Sand* she was to appear as the

298

great and busy lover who divided her torrent of energy between romantic novels and impassioned affairs. It seemed a contradictory role for an actress who was all mind and sublimation to her work— but in it Minnie saw comedy and pathos and tender irony, and many other things which to her added up to life itself. In her foreword to the published play, she wrote:

Only one man has had the wit to paint Aurore Dudevant in a few swift words—Matthew Arnold.

"She was like one of the early Gods," he said—or something like that. Only her own hundred odd books can give even a faint understanding of this amazing woman. Among all women—this creature of a thousand colors—grande dame and Bohemian—gamine and daughter of kings, soubrette and philosopher, pagan and religieuse, housefrau and mad lover, everyday hard worker and impassioned dreamer, simpleton and sage, poseuse and farm woman, tragedy queen and imp of mischief, Sibyl and "big child," everything that lives and burns and flames in man or woman, George Sand the generous, the kind, the simple. What she loved best in all the world was kindness.

Your incorrigibly brilliant and funny play, dear Mr. Moeller, reached me in the North Woods and I laughed and laughed and then when I had quite finished laughing I set out to learn something of George Sand—something that would give me a better understanding than my superficial knowledge of the earlier flamboyant novels —or the beautiful peasant stories. But to study your astonishing heroine is like swimming in the ocean. Gather into yourself all your knowledge of all men, women and children—unfold your entire "comedie humaine" and George Sand will play every part for you.

Something of all mankind is hers, and in splendor. George who could cut the hair from her head to offer it at the feet of her lover. George who could mend furniture at four in the morning. George who, cigar in hand, could "slip from the balcony window" and swagger along the darkened road for twenty miles in the summer storm. George who could wait with her kind eyes watching for "the little cat that comes to us over the roofs"—wonderful, wonderful George with the friendly smile almost always playing around her lips. The friendly smile that Heine loved—ridiculous, priceless George.

And as I came to know her more and love her more and more as the most flagrantly human creature in history, I began to feel that we, you and I, were party to an act of unforgivable impertinence in our conspiracy to reveal your Aurora as we have revealed her. But this feeling passed—and passed because I continued to know her more and more and love her more and more and in this ever increasing love and knowledge I know that in no other way can she be revealed.

Minnie Maddern Fiske

Minnie, too, had written successfully, harangued a nation, watched over "the little cat that comes to us over the roofs," and done many other things that gave her more in common with George Sand than appeared on the surface. True, she had never been the mad lover, and in countless letters to Harry she had implored him not to smoke cigars —but love affairs were only one phase of her George Sand, and stage business was stage business. Minnie began experimentally puffing at cigars, and she learned to smoke well enough for stage purposes.

She dreamed of casting *Madame Sand* as it would have been cast in the days of the Manhattan Theatre, when she had gathered the best actors of the English-speaking world about her. But now the Fiskes were poor, and the actors who might have played the roles of Heine, the de Musset brothers, Liszt and Chopin were in the trenches or doing war work. Minnie rehearsed valiantly with a second-best cast.

Madame Sand was tried out at the Academy of Music, Baltimore, on October 29, 1917. From there it was taken to a successful New York premiere at the Criterion Theatre, where it played until the end of December, when it was moved to the Knickerbocker.

As George Sand, Minnie had set herself as complex a task as she had had in any role in her career: to play the flamboyant part in utter seriousness while showing the audience its absurdity, and through both to project the essential loneliness of the character.

One who had never had any doubts about her suitability was Philip Moeller. In an interview, he said, "George Sand interests me as one of the most amazingly energetic women in the history of the world. It is because of this that Mrs. Fiske is inevitably the one woman in the theatre in America, if not in the entire world, most fittingly suited to play my glorious heroine. Mrs. Fiske has unerringly understood and most perfectly realized George Sand's dominant and indefatigable spirit . . ."

Under peacetime conditions, George Sand might have been one of the actress's memorable roles—but she took little pleasure in shining in an unsatisfactory production, and she was relieved when the play closed. She wrote Harry that many of the important roles were atrociously acted, and the play had been a trial to her.

It was a season when Minnie's spiritual children fared better than

300

she herself. Emily Stevens, at the end of her fabulous run in *The Un-chastened Woman*, won new honors as Clare in the first American production of Galsworthy's *The Fugitive*—and Harry James Smith had finally come into his own.

In the fall, Smith's *A Tailor-Made Man* took Broadway by storm. It was still breaking box-office records in February, 1918, when its author's *The Little Teacher* was produced at the Playhouse. *The Little Teacher* was an instantaneous hit.

During Harry James Smith's six years of failure and rejections, Mrs. Fiske had buoyed him up by declaring that he was the best writer of comedy in America, and that he should have five comedies playing simultaneously on Broadway. Her estimate was now two-fifths achieved, and it might have been more nearly fulfilled except for war.

Because of his frail health, Smith had been rejected by every branch of the armed services. When enlistment proved impossible, he studied with Dr. John Bonsall Porter, the Canadian pioneer in the use of sphagnum moss for surgical dressings.

Before long Smith was working on his own; the production of *The Little Teacher* was delayed six months because the playwright was in Nova Scotia—wading through bogs in fog and rain, and stalled on impassable roads, where a more robust and less dedicated man might have died of pneumonia.

After the belated premiere of *The Little Teacher*, Mrs. Fiske kissed her protégé on the forehead, with a flashing "I told you so!" But Smith's mind was no longer on playwriting. That same week he went to Washington, where he had been brevetted as chairman of a commission on sphagnum moss; later in the month he left for Seattle to carry on his work in the Pacific Northwest.

From *Madame Sand*, Minnie returned briefly to her husband's management, and the luxury of an experimental play, *Service*, by Henri Lavedan. Lavedan was one of the "Immortals" of the French Academy, and he appeared to have taken the title literally. He began his play of pacifism and war in the last decade of the nineteenth century—and finished it in time to have its run at the Theatre Sarah Bernhardt interrupted by the outbreak of World War I.

Harry Fiske had acquired the American rights of *Service* while the United States was a neutral country, but before he got the play into production, war had been declared on Germany. The circumstance relegated the "to fight or not to fight" question of the play to something less than an academic discussion.

Service was a short play for its long gestation, and it was presented with Dunsany's *A Night at an Inn*. With Minnie in the role of Madame Eulin, *Service* opened at the Tremont Theatre in Boston and fared indifferently for the month of March.

In *Service*, the pacifist Lieutenant Eulin had accidentally devised a new and terrible destructive force; the question was whether or not it should be turned loose on the world for the momentary advantage of his country. With the United States embarked on a "war to end all wars," the discussion was of no present help—and it seemed to have no application to the future.

While the Eulin family debated on the stage, the real war took its toll in Europe, and in devious ways at home.

One morning at breakfast, in the middle of the Boston run of *Service*, Mrs. Fiske's eye was caught by a headline: LEADING PLAYWRIGHT KILLED IN TRAIN-AUTOMOBILE CRASH. The account went on to say that Harry James Smith had died the day before. He had gone to British Columbia to supervise a shipment of sphagnum moss, and his errand of mercy had ended near Murrayville.

The lonely grade crossing where Smith was killed was only a few miles from Vancouver, where Minnie had read the first rough version of *Mrs. Bumpstead-Leigh* by a then unknown youth.

Service went from Boston to New York. *A Tailor-Made Man* and *The Little Teacher* were still hits on Broadway. For Minnie, the great hum of the crowds pouring out of the theatres after the final curtain had a lonely sound.

Service flickered out with April—just in time for Minnie to begin a nationwide tour with a more immediately useful war play. The play was *Out There*, by J. Hartley Manners, and it was presented with an all-star cast that included Laurette Taylor, George Arliss, Chauncey Olcott, George M. Cohan, James K. Hackett and H. B. Warner. The purpose of the production was to raise money for the Red Cross; Mrs. Fiske held the key position—delivering the Red Cross appeal at the end of the performance. Her lines had been especially written by President Wilson, and the response to them was remarkable; in some of the larger cities, the receipts amounted to more than $30,000 for a single performance.

For the length of its tour, *Out There* took in more than any other play in history. It was also the greatest contribution ever made by the theatrical profession—the members of the all-star cast played without compensation and paid their own expenses.

Service and *Out There* left Minnie financially poorer, and faced by the old problem of finding a suitable play. She and Harry were juggling with half a dozen possibilities, ranging from Sheridan's *The Rivals* to a play of Edward Sheldon's, still in scenario form. The idea of the Sheridan revival had originated with Minnie and it was scheduled for the next production, but she had learned by long and often bitter experience not to trust in a single play—and *The Rivals* would only postpone her need for a new play.

In the welter of uncertainty, Minnie decided once more to create a play for herself. She did not feel equal to the entire task, and she selected talented young Laurence Eyre to work with her; she provided the plot and characters and setting.

At fifty-four, Minnie was pioneering again—and at the same moment she was looking back. For her central character she selected Nellie Hazeltine, the glorious belle who had begun her reign in St. Louis about the time Minnie began in earnest to make her living on the stage. For the setting of the play she chose the New Orleans of her childhood—not the Baronne Street house, with its strict Sabbath observance ruled over by her Puritanical grandmother, but the gay Creole city, with all unhappinesses filtered out by time, touched with the magic atmosphere of Mardi Gras.

The collaboration prospered, and on August 6 she wrote to Harry:

Darling Boy,

I have some very pleasant news for you! The first act (the first rough draft) of the play that Mr. Eyre & I are doing together is finished & typed and I am sending it to you by parcel post. It's called—

"Mis' Nelly of N'Orleans"

I think it is going to be perfectly delightful—perhaps the most delightful & suitable part I have ever had. I hope you will like it! We both do! The first & third acts are to be all charm & buoyancy & in the second act—we get a thrill!

We are making no attempt at the Creole way—(the N'Orleans) way of speech—etc. as in the Cable novels. We are making no attempt at atmosphere.—When the play is finished we'll get some one to George Cable it for us from end to end. Perhaps Mr. Cable himself! It must reek with atmosphere. . . .

The buoyant and indefatigable spirit of the letter was worthy of a George Sand—even if Mrs. Fiske had given up trousers and black cigars with the role.

Before the end of August, Minnie and young Eyre had finished the first draft of *Mis' Nelly*, and she wrote Harry from the Adirondacks:

. . . That play—I promise—is going to be a very perfect work of art before it leaves our hands—if it takes us six months to perfect it. So bank on it. It's going to be Bully. (You are right about "Nelly's" age. We'll make her under fifty. Fifty is too old.)

Next to "The Rivals"—perhaps equal to it—"Mis' Nelly" is our strongest possession.

The sketch you sent me of Mr. Sheldon's play is vastly interesting. I shall be delighted to read it when you send me the completed act & the scenario of the remaining two. . . I hope Mr. Sheldon has written it as effectively as you tell it!

We had a sad tragedy here last night. A young man—a nice amiable fellow—a familiar figure in the little village—killed in his automobile—right here.

> Devoted love
> Bunner

That autumn Edward Sheldon's promising play was still unfinished; the Fiskes had been unable to secure some of the actors they needed for *The Rivals*, and flaws or difficulties had shown up in other plays. *Mis' Nelly*, on the other hand, had prospered, and Minnie's devoted friend, George Cable, had given the dialogue the authentic Creole touch.

For once, Minnie enjoyed the luxury of a new play finished well in advance of production. Laurence Eyre's enthusiasm had never lost its edge, and it now became an inconvenience. The young playwright winced as the first of his precious lines was cut at rehearsal, and he protested over the cutting of the tenth. During the next rehearsal, his protests were almost continuous; and at the next, his argument with the Fiskes stalled the rehearsal, which was dismissed early. Mrs. Fiske told him sternly that the success of the piece depended on his staying away while the inevitable surgery was going on.

Next day Laurence Eyre found the doors of the Henry Miller Theatre locked to him. All his beatings produced was to have one door open a crack while a burly doorman informed him; "Ya can't come in, Mr. Eyre." For days he haunted the outside of the theatre, trying to get in, but locked doors and the implacable doorman—and the even more implacable Fiskes—kept him out in the cold while he envisioned his beautiful play being hacked to death by butchers.

Mis' Nelly was a play on which the Fiskes' existence depended; they never relented until the end of rehearsals, when Mrs. Fiske invited Eyre to attend the opening night of *Mis' Nelly of N'Orleans* in Baltimore.

304

The premiere took place on January 6, 1919, at Ford's Opera House; Laurence Eyre sat moodily in a box waiting for the curtain to go up. His spirits rose a little when he looked at the program—*Mis' Nelly of N'Orleans*, "a Comedy of Moonshine, Madness and Make-Believe" by Laurence Eyre. Mrs. Fiske, who had provided the characters, the setting and the story, as well as much of the dialogue, was taking no credit for her part in the writing—or for the butchering of it afterward.

The single stage-set for *Mis' Nelly* was the front of a house, and a garden on St. Charles Street, New Orleans—a block or two from the Baronne Street house where Minnie was born, and a few doors from the St. Charles Theatre, where she had been cradled in her mother's dressing room. In front of the stage house were great trees like those that had been cut down long ago in front of the Baronne Street house; and flowering rose bushes climbed the walls toward the second-story balcony and the French windows of the room where the middle-aged Nelly Daventry slept at three in the afternoon, having just returned from Paris to the city where she had once reigned as a dashing and profane belle.

Stagehands with huge perfume atomizers sprayed the artificial flowers in the garden and retired—then the curtan rose.

Mis' Nelly was a new comedy, but it was also old—older than Minnie. It violated nearly all the rules of Mrs. Fiske, the uncompromising artist and realist. It was shamelessly a star piece, a Minnie Maddern play, or rather a showy and inconsequential play of the sort in which Lotta had cavorted her way to fame half a century before.

With *Mis' Nelly*, Mrs. Fiske had completed a cycle: from a soubrette imitator of Lotta, to the most significant work of her generation on the American stage, and back again. The play also completed a secondary cycle: from Minnie Maddern, the homesick child traveling the length of the Mississippi valley in search of the phantom of home and security; to Mrs. Fiske who never spoke of the "prehistoric past"; to the woman who placed her play within a few doors of her birthplace, and shaded her stage house with the great, remembered trees of childhood.

For three long acts Mrs. Fiske held her audience with "moonlight and madness and make-believe," feigning age and decrepitude, persuading her earlier-day suitor to shout absurdities into her ear trumpet, and revealing herself as a dazzling beauty.

After the dinning applause and the many curtain calls, Minnie planted a kiss on the forehead of Hamilton Revelle, her leading man, and told him, "You played beautifully tonight!"

Then Laurence Eyre, bewildered and starry-eyed, made his way to Mrs. Fiske and told her, "The play was utterly beautiful."—Could she forgive him for doubting her wisdom and fighting to retain lines which he never missed in the perfect production?

She took the young playwright's face between her hands and kissed him and promised eternal friendship. There was as much gratitude on her side as his.

CHAPTER 40

Minnie had observed that in hardhearted New York old comedy should wait until the season had mellowed. *Mis' Nelly of N'Orleans*, timed accordingly, had its Broadway premiere on February 4, 1920. By then there was hardly a trace of acid in the acid test of New York.

The audience which packed the Henry Miller Theatre greeted Minnie's first entrance with applause which stopped the play until she made a curtain speech. In the lordly times of the Manhattan Theatre, she had refused such concessions, which broke the spell of the play. But hard experience had taught her that the audience, too, was important, and she made a little speech, telling the audience that Mr. Eyre and she hoped they would find entertainment in a drowsy old garden in New Orleans.

The play went on; and the audience found Miss Nelly's garden anything but drowsy, accompanying almost every line with delighted laughter. At the end of the second act, the applause built up to an ovation, and there were calls of "Author!"

Again the actress came before the curtain. Mr. Eyre was not in the house, she explained.

"We don't want him!" a gallant shouted. "We want you!" The declaration was greeted with laughter and applause, and *Mis' Nelly* continued in an atmosphere that suggested she was the darling of "hardhearted" New York.

The press seconded the verdict of the audience. Alan Dale, who had quarreled with nearly every one of Mrs. Fiske's plays since *Tess of the D'Urbervilles* in 1897, began ecstatically: "It has been golden decades, blue moons, and countless tinted periods of time since Mrs. Fiske has charmed and fascinated us by the witchery of her unique personality."

Other critics and successive audiences verified the triumph of *Mis' Nelly*—and the Fiskes were living again after eight desperate years of failure.

In a way, it had been an easy triumph; Minnie had only to design her own star play and reveal herself as a master of showmanship. The revelation was less surprising than the fact that she had struggled so long before compromising her ideals.

Earlier that season Mrs. Fiske had lived cheaply in the country to save expenses. On Sunday, April 6, she dined at the Biltmore in style at a dinner given by the Society of Arts and Sciences in her honor, "in recognition of her contributions to the American Drama, and in appreciation of her Genius as an Artist."

At the speakers' table, Mrs. Fiske was in distinguished company. Otis Skinner was toastmaster, and the other speakers included John Drew, Henry Miller, William Gillette, Major General John F. O'Ryan, Geraldine Farrar, John Luther Long, David Belasco, Walter Prichard Eaton, Norman Hapgood, Otto Kahn, Mary Shaw and Harrison Grey Fiske. The names of the other diners were like a roll call of the great in the theatre: George Arliss, Maxine Elliott, William Faversham, Chauncey Olcott, Robert B. Mantell, David Warfield, Bertha Kalich, Ruth Chatterton, DeWolf Hopper, Raymond Hitchcock, Holbrook Blinn, George M. Cohan, Ethel Barrymore, Mme. Nazimova, Margaret Anglin, Rose Coghlan, Lionel Barrymore, Guy Bates Post, James K. Hackett, Joseph Jefferson, Jr. and William B. Mack.

At the height of her career, when she had come as close to pure art as anyone is likely to in the theatre, Minnie had scorned to glamorize herself; now that she had less youth and beauty and more necessity to appeal to the public, she withdrew her restrictions. The souvenir menu of the dinner bore a glamorous picture of Mrs. Fiske, looking up intensely with great, dark eyes, her hair like a halo of light. The photograph had been taken by Hamilton Revelle, Mrs. Fiske's leading man and an ardent amateur photographer. He had been exercised over the fact that none of Mrs. Fiske's recent portraits had done her justice, and the menu photograph represented his idea of how she should be portrayed.

Minnie's speech before the Society of Arts and Sciences was mellow and human:

I have never been among those who continually deplore the decadence of the stage and point regretfully to the past, as though the past alone comprised its better days. Fashions change in plays and acting of course, but after all the theatre remains the same. It is one of our most conservative institutions. . . .

After discussing some of the quaint stage customs of Shakespeare's and Garrick's time, she called up the theatre of her childhood—and the influence of Grandmother Maddern, who had marked her life with the imprint of the Puritan Sabbath:

I came upon the scene in what might be called the Twilight of the Palmy Days and my recollection of that period of apprenticeship is still vivid. The stage child then, as in my own case, was often reared in a strictly religious atmosphere. On Sunday night our mothers might be dancing in tarlatan skirts at the theatre, but on Sunday morning we were obliged to speak in hushed voices, wear starched skirts, listen to the reading of the Bible and if we sang, confine our repertory strictly to hymns. . . . I was virtually born on the stage. In my early days we used to be called upon to do things that would be very trying to the theatrical youngster of today. When I was twelve I had a large repertory of widely contrasting parts that I might be called upon to play with very little notice. Sometimes I would be cast for the Widow Melnotte in "The Lady of Lyons," and the next night Little Eva in "Uncle Tom's Cabin." . . . On another night I would be expected to comport myself as Little Mary Morgan in "Ten Nights in a Barroom," and sing, "Father, Dear Father, Come Home With Me Now"; the following night would find me as François, undertaking the momentous mission for Cardinal Richelieu. On successive evenings I would be Lucy Fairweather in "The Streets of New York" and Peanuts, the newsboy in "Under the Gaslight."

During that time it was my privilege to play children's parts with many of the illustrious actors of the period—the robust Barry Sullivan, the dynamic Lucille Western, the beautiful Mary Anderson, and many others who then wore the crown of fame. I remember them all so well—Edwin Booth, with his burning eyes and irresistible genius, John McCullough, the embodiment of Roman dignity, Lawrence Barrett, the artist and scholar, Helena Modjeska, the essence of grace and charm, and many other celebrated men and women.

In the audience, there were some of the most famous leading men of the day, who had become famous or done their best work in Mrs. Fiske's Manhattan Company: George Arliss, Holbrook Blinn, Bruce MacRae, Guy Bates Post and William B. Mack; Mrs. Fiske touched only lightly on a few:

Once upon a time, when I first began to twinkle feebly as a star, there appeared in the cast, as my leading man, Mr. Henry J. Miller. I note little change in him, not even his R's, which used to give him some concern. We were having a season of strenuous travel that year. I remember one evening Mr. Miller and I were playing a sentimental love scene, when the house fell upon us, burying us in a sea of canvas.

I cannot truthfully say that the house rose to us; I suppose it would be more accurate to claim that we brought down the house.

Then, once upon a time, at an earlier date, there was a very tall, a very serious young man with hungry histrionic ambitions. We were in Cincinnati I think. The play to be given on one occasion was entitled "A Mother's Secret." The elderly leading actor of the company was taken ill suddenly, with the result that Mr. William Gillette was catapulted into the character at a half hour's notice. I have never witnessed such a spectacle of abject fright as the tall young man presented. I have neglected to say that although a member of the company, I was, of course, a very small infant at the time, but possessed of a phenomenal memory.

Romance also has its place in this gathering tonight, for here is young Mr. David Belasco, whom I can recall as one of my most devoted and enterprising admirers in the long ago. He had an original idea in paying his court, and one that only a man of his resourceful mind could have hit upon. The favorite diversion that he offered was an invitation to "take a ride." The ride was always taken on an elevated railway train and consisted of journeying back and forth to the terminus at either end.

Mrs. Fiske told her favorite story of the duel fought over her by youthful David Belasco and Charles Frohman; and she went on to dispel legends about temperament and villainy in the theatre. As for managers being in a conspiracy to keep worthy plays from the public:

> I can say, after spending much time for many years in reading these manuscripts, that I am convinced that every one of the one hundred-and-ten-millions of people who populate this country is ambitious to be a playwright and that in spite of the alleged managerial conspiracy, there are few plays of worth that do not quickly find production.

She twitted Daniel Frohman for his part in the production of motion pictures, which competed with the stage:

> Mr. Frohman has lured me and many others from the straight and narrow path of the drama into the treacherous, echoless pandemonium of the movies and still he smiles, and still he is respected, and still he masquerades as a theatrical manager. . . . I should hate to have the thoughts which must come to him in his moments of solitude.
>
> . . . The public, like the manager, is frequently damned, and yet, speaking personally as well as from observation, I have admiration as well as respect for the public, for in spite of all that is said, the

public is rarely wrong in its judgments. . . . I have learned there is always a public here for the best that we can offer.

In the spirit of Americans who still believed that a useful victory had been won in Europe, Mrs. Fiske compared Major General O'Ryan of the 27th Division with Kean and Booth, and found the soldier mightier than the actor:

How paltry are our paint and powder, our gilt crowns and our tinsel, plumed helmets and our tin swords, our spoken words, compared with the achievement of such a leader and of such men?

The talk ended on that note of humility; but next day the managing director of the Society of Arts and Sciences referred to the gathering in honor of Mrs. Fiske as the most distinguished dramatic dinner ever given. It was a large claim, but probably as many of the great of the theatre had never met in one room, before or afterward.

During the New York run of *Mis' Nelly of N'Orleans*, there were other, less publicized dinners, but dinners that were the beginning of a tradition. Harry Fiske, who had made his way back from bankruptcy, was the host. He had recently taken the parlor floor of an old Greenwich Village house at 66 West 11th Street. With the taste of a connoisseur and the experience of a theatrical producer, he furnished the apartment: colonial furniture, antique pieces and faithful reproductions; costly bric-a-brac that had come as gifts, and from plays in which his wife had appeared; paintings, lithographs and photographs of Minnie by famous artists and photographers, and fine old Japanese prints.

The home in the country which Mrs. Fiske had wanted for so long was still in the future, but the Greenwich Village apartment was a homecoming for the city-bred Harry. There, in surroundings of his choice, he was at his best as host and raconteur and friend of men and women from many walks in life.

Mrs. Fiske was a frequent guest at 66 West 11th Street. On special occasions Harry prepared many-course dinners for her—dinners which he cooked and served with the touch of an epicure. In a sense, the dinners repeated their early days in the house farther uptown, where Minnie had proved hopelessly incompetent in domestic things, and Harry had taken charge. Now they were no longer attempting a full-fledged marriage, which temperaments and circumstance had made unworkable. Limiting themselves to what was possible between them, they were at ease with each other, and their talk at dinner was almost always the happy and brilliant conversation of a genial and admiring host entertaining a great lady of the theatre.

CHAPTER 41

While some of the new generation put their faith in motion pictures, others rediscovered the stage idols of their parents.

One of the latter was Jimmy Kemper, an ambitious young singer of Warrensburg, Missouri. When he was sixteen, his father took him to Kansas City, where they saw Mrs. Fiske in *The High Road*.

After the final curtain, Jimmy found it hard to collect himself or to remember he was in a theatre. Like others under the spell of Mrs. Fiske's art, he had the feeling that confining walls had dissolved between him and infinitely exciting realities. The feeling endured as a steady fire under his own ambitions.

Soon afterward the Kemper family moved to Independence. There, Jimmy became a neighbor of the Trumans, and he joined the circle of friends of Bess Truman, who also had singing ambitions, but he was headed for wider horizons.

Six years after his ambitions had been fired by a middle-aged actress, Jimmy was admitted to the Bush Conservatory in Chicago, where he was looked on as a prodigy.

On Thanksgiving Day, Jimmy found himself in distinguished company. The place was the Elm Street home of K. M. B. Bradley, president and founder of the Conservatory, and the professional artists who were his guests discussed Jimmy Kemper's future. Everyone had a different plan, but the wonderful old pianist, Mme. Julie Rive' King, asked, "What would *you* most like to do, Jimmy?"

Without hesitation he told her, "Mrs. Fiske is playing here in *Mis' Nelly of N'Orleans;* I would like to do for her a sketch I have written."

Mme. King chuckled. "Done! I know Mrs. Fiske and will arrange for an audience for you." She did, and a few afternoons later Jimmy set out for the Powers Theatre. Mme. King, who had played before the crowned heads of Europe, was as excited over the hearing as Jimmy, and she had her protégé, Harold Triggs, learn the background music for Jimmy's sketch.

Mrs. Fiske had written that Mr. Griffith would be at the stage door to conduct Jimmy to her dressing room, but instead there was a doorman, who said, "A singer? Go right in. They're waiting for ya by the work light. Good luck, buddy!"

On the stage, a young man who had just finished his last unsteady notes retreated under the disapproving gaze of a pianist and a man standing by the piano. The two turned on the newcomer. "Come along," the standee told Jimmy, and the pianist asked, "What's your voice?"

Jimmy stuttered, "I'm a baritone, but I came to—"

"A baritone!" the pianist roared. "Those stupid agents know we want a tenor!"

"I brought my accompanist," Jimmy said, "and I—"

The pianist interrupted him coldly. "I have a national reputation—in fact, international. Will I do?" The men's laughter had an ogreish sound.

Jimmy tried again, "But my music was arranged especially to fit the sketch—"

"Forget it." The pianist thrust a sheet of music into his hand. "Here's the song you're to sing, 'Alice, I'm in Wonderland.' It's your solo for backstage atmosphere. If you're a baritone, I'll put the song down a few notes." As he transposed, he muttered, "These damned agents. A baritone!"

Jimmy started to protest again.

"*Sing!*" The pianist roared. He had finished the introduction, and Jimmy sang,

"Alice, I'm in Wonderland. . ."

As he sang, a shaft of light burst across the stage and a woman in dressing gown stood framed in the bright doorway. She advanced in the shaft of light until she was standing near the young singer. As he finished the last note, she threw back her auburn head and cried in a quality of voice Jimmy was never to forget, "That is the voice I looked for all the time we were playing in New York. Young man, please come with us. It is a beautiful voice. Thank you very much." Mrs. Fiske turned suddenly, and in a moment her dressing-room door closed behind her, and the shaft of light was gone.

Jimmy was speechless, the pianist mopped his brow, with a "Thank God!" and the ogres introduced themselves. The man who had stood

313

near the piano was the actor, Ben Lewin, and the pianist was W. Franke Harling, who was later to write the background music of many important Hollywood pictures. The two still had no interest in Jimmy's errand; they expounded on the glamorous tour of *Mis' Nelly*, which had been booked throughout the United States and Canada.

Jimmy would not agree to anything until he had consulted the president of Bush Conservatory.

"Go with Mrs. Fiske, by all means," Mr. Bradley said. "You will have the opportunity to study the greatest personality in the American theatre, her work, her technique and her genius. After the tour we shall be happy to have you back."

A week later Jimmy waited in the railroad station and watched members of the New York company pass on their way to the special cars. Suddenly he saw Mrs. Fiske at the far end of the station, walking back and forth alone. She was dressed in blue and wearing several veils. The youth's first impulse was to go over and ask if there was anything he could do—but he sensed that the actress wanted to be alone. Watching, he observed that the only person who approached her in the station that night was the white-goateed Mr. Griffith, who had been her personal manager ever since she returned to the stage.

But Mrs. Fiske, who kept apart from her company, soon made an exception in the case of Jimmy. Mr. Griffith told the young singer that in all his years with the actress, he had never seen her so interested in a member of her company.

On the train to Minneapolis Jimmy was so excited that he did not sleep a wink, and at rehearsal next day his voice was completely gone. The music for that evening was rearranged, and *Mis' Nelly of N'Orleans* opened in Minneapolis with Jimmy in bed at his hotel. It seemed a bad start for the young singer, but next morning the critics were unanimous in speaking of Jimmy Kemper's beautiful voice, which had lent so much to the atmosphere of the play. Two teachers at Bush Conservatory who had often appeared with the Minneapolis Symphony had asked the critics to be kind. Jimmy was too embarrassed to comment, but Mrs. Fiske was as amused as if she had planned the successful absentee-debut.

The influence of Jimmy's friends did nothing to endear him to the New York cast; at St. Paul, where Jimmy sang for the first time, he overheard slighting remarks about the "debut of the Mystery Baritone." After his solo, he walked to the back of the scenery, alone and miserable. Soon afterward Mrs. Fiske had an exit, and she called Jimmy's name, very softly. When he crossed to her, she whispered, "Your singing is just what the scene has always needed; just the right quality and feeling. It is perfectly beautiful. I am so happy." From the door to her dressing room, she turned and threw him a kiss.

During Holy Week, Mrs. Fiske would not play, and she gave her company a vacation. The New York cast rushed home, and Jimmy returned to Chicago for a happy reunion with the "kids at school." During the week, Jimmy acquired a magnificent wardrobe trunk, and an imported kit bag valued at a hundred dollars. To go with them, Jimmy purchased an expensive velour hat which he fancied had the Barrymore look; and on the advice of friends who warned him that Milwaukee was cold and damp, he bought long underwear.

Jimmy arrived in Milwaukee, tired from the train trip, and he immediately fell asleep in his hotel bed, dressed in the long underwear which was to protect his voice. He was awakened by the clanging of fire engines. Crowds of people seemed to be looking squarely at him. He opened the door, and smoke filled his room. Still half asleep, he put on his velour hat, seized his imported kit bag and, clad in his long underwear, rushed out into the corridor. There he was immediately drenched by water from a fire hose, while firemen shouted, "Get back into your room!"

Fully awakened, Jimmy bravely asked, "Is everything under control?"

"Yeah," one of the firemen shouted, "everything but you!"

It was Jimmy's fate that one of the firemen knew the backstage firemen at the New Davidson Theatre. He told the stagehands, and they told Mrs. Fiske's maid, who told her mistress. Mrs. Fiske laughed heartily, and the next day she called Jimmy into her dressing room. She did not mention his performance at the hotel fire, but asked him to walk with her to the old Jefferson Hotel, where she had rooms. She took his arm and said, "Now talk, Jimmy. Tell me all you can about yourself and don't mind me while I hum the scales just as you do, I am sure, to warm my voice for the evening performance."

Jimmy talked as he had been ordered to, without being sure that Mrs. Fiske heard him through her humming. Without making any direct comments, she began speaking to him of Youth, and how the young often fail to see the proper course. It was her impression that he had too many talents, and she implied that his youth was not likely to be any help in the dilemma. She often wondered why artists and sculptors and writers idealized Youth—Youth that was filled with blunders and lessons to learn, hard and sometimes bitter lessons.

Unlike most women, Mrs. Fiske spoke in general and impersonal

315

terms. The walk was the first of a series of visits during which she gave him useful advice which was mostly lost because of his handicap of youth, as she had foreseen.

In nearly every city she visited, Mrs. Fiske lectured on the protection of fur-bearing animals. After the lecture she would be surrounded by flocks of women who otherwise would have had no hope of meeting the great actress. On these occasions Mrs. Fiske was invariably patient and courteous, but Jimmy sensed that she was bored by groups of women—by most people everywhere, for that matter. For all the unusual attention she paid him, he never flattered himself that he was really close to her; always there was a cool wall of glass between them; and he wondered if anyone had ever known her intimately. Once she told him of her devotion to her cousin, Emily Stevens; there, he felt sure, was a great devotion; perhaps Emily alone could have been really close to Mrs. Fiske, but whether Emily made use of the opportunity, he never knew.

On the western tour, after the closing performance at Salt Lake, the company had just time to rush to the train, which had no diner. By ten the next morning, they were all up and dressed, poised to jump off in search of food at the first stop.

In crossing the desert, the train had fallen behind schedule and it was racing to make up time; it rushed by one town, which the company eyed hungrily in passing, but they were assured that there would be a stop at the next town.

Instead of a town and breakfast, there was a great crash, and the train jarred and shuddered to a stop. Jimmy jumped off into the sagebrush and sand, and through clearing dust he saw what appeared to be a junk yard blocking the track and sprawling away into the desert.

None of the company had been more than bruised in the wreck which had reduced their baggage cars to junk, but the engineer and fireman were pinned under the locomotive. They were still alive and conscious, but beyond hope of rescue by a handful of trainmen and a band of actors. The only one who could do anything for the trapped men was the nurse who traveled with the company. She crawled through the wreckage of painted scenery and theatrical trunks which were lodged against the wheels of the overturned locomotive, and gave both men hypodermics.

With nothing useful she could do, Mrs. Fiske sat alone in the desert by the tracks, watching all that was going on. When Jimmy was passing one of the wrecked cars, he heard a small voice sobbing bitterly.

Through a mess of spilled milk and crushed eggs, he fought his way to the source of the crying—a parrot in a cage. He took the bird to Mrs. Fiske. During the death in the desert she sat alone with the unceasing wind and the empty words of the parrot, whose cage was labeled, "For Hollywood, California."

Hours after the wreck, a rescue train arrived. The son of one of the trapped men was in the crew; but the two under the locomotive were dead. Upon the arrival of the rescue crew Mrs. Fiske went to her stateroom and wrote notes to the wives of the dead men, and began planning how she could get flowers to them.

In the evening the rescue train brought the company back to the little desert town which they had eyed hungrily in the morning; they had now been nearly twenty-four hours without food. The one hotel had a special dinner waiting, and they banished starvation with a huge meal. For the first and only time on the tour, Mrs. Fiske ate with her company, while half the town stood around watching. The shock of cataclysm and death which brought Mrs. Fiske closer to her company seemed to overcome her usual aversion to crowds of strangers, and she proposed that they hire a hall and give an entertainment for the townspeople. During the impromptu show which followed, she sat in the far corner of the room, pleased with everything her company did.

In San Francisco, on their frequent walks, Jimmy usually found Mrs. Fiske in her gayest mood. Once, in Union Square, Jimmy told her how he had come to join her company, and she responded by asking permission to sit on a bench while she laughed. On that afternoon, she said, she had been listening to the agent-sent singers from her dressing room, and waiting to hear the young man of whom Julie Rive' had written so enthusiastically. She had wondered since why he never arrived—and all the time he was in her company, through a comedy of errors.

A few days later at the matinee performance, a famous tenor sat alone in one of the stage boxes, playing to the gallery in dumb show. Jimmy was sharing a Sutter Street apartment with the Harlings, and after the performance Mrs. Fiske asked the three to invite her to dinner that evening. When the invitation was extended, Mrs. Fiske said, "Let's just make it picnic style; it will be fun!" She then explained that she was supposed to dine at the St. Francis with two notables and the famous tenor who had showed off to the matinee audience, but she did not wish to dine with anyone who showed such bad taste.

The Harlings and Kemper had a picnic-style dinner, as Mrs. Fiske had asked, and she did make it fun. She arrived at the apartment in a gay mood, and in honor of the occasion she took off all her veils, observing, "All my relatives say, 'Here comes Minnie with her many veils.' " In one of her few serious moments, she assured Jimmy that he would find acting was not an emotional thing; it was a matter of technique, pure and simple.

She ate heartily and laughed a good deal, observing that wild horses could not have dragged her to dinner at the St. Francis. She took a nap before returning with her hosts to the theatre for the evening performance.

The company's Canadian tour began at Vancouver, British Columbia, in a particularly poor theatre infested with rats and mice. Backstage the animals brought repeated screams from the cast, but Mrs. Fiske only giggled. Once Jimmy heard her cry from her basement dressing room, "Oh, that one was a beauty; he really should go to Hollywood!"

The cast was beginning to tire of the endless tour and its inconveniences, but Mrs. Fiske seemed to gain strength from the road; the signs of fatigue with which she started the tour had disappeared, and she tried to convey to others her love for the country through which they were passing. Just out of Vancouver, when the train was entering the Canadian Rockies, she told him, "Now, Jimmy, I want you to get out on the platform and not even leave it for lunch; send for a sandwich. You will see the most gorgeous scenery in the world. It far surpasses Switzerland."

Jimmy had the country-boy habit of jumping off the train the moment it stopped anywhere. At one beautiful spot where there was engine trouble, Jimmy fell into conversation with another enthusiast from the car ahead, the father of two lively boys, who was greatly excited when he learned that Mrs. Fiske was on the train. Later, when they were on their way again, Jimmy learned that his fellow enthusiast for scenery and Mrs. Fiske was John D. Rockefeller, Jr.

At Calgary, Mrs. Fiske asked Jimmy to arrange a special supper party at the leading hotel, and to be sure that there was a chafing dish with her favorite Welsh rabbit. The supper was in honor of the three Canadian managers who had helped arrange her northern tour. Jimmy and the managers were there before Mrs. Fiske, and when she arrived, Jimmy got the impression of a mischievous imp whom he hardly knew. It appeared that Mrs. Fiske was in the mood to play a new role, but during the evening she played a dozen, including Mis' Nelly and Becky Sharp. She also played an unidentified, impish one that Jimmy took to be a new role, but afterward he guessed that it was Minnie Maddern of the days of *Caprice* and *Featherbrain.*

At first, Jimmy was only a spectator to Mrs. Fiske's act; then he became her stooge. From speaking of the beauty of her beloved Canadian Rockies, she went on, straight-faced, to tell the managers how wonderful the Canadian theatres were, especially backstage. Jimmy looked startled, remembering the rats, and Mrs. Fiske kicked him under the table, squarely on the shin, asking, "Don't you think so too, Mr. Kemper?" While he was still nursing his shin, she answered for him, "Yes, of course you do." During the remainder of the evening, she secured or volunteered Jimmy's agreement to outrageous statements, always with the encouraging kick. The supper ended with his shins black and blue and the bewildered, spellbound managers bowing low and declaring that these had been the most entertaining hours of their lives.

It was very late when the managers had departed, but Mrs. Fiske was still under the excitement of her act; "I don't feel like going to my rooms after this experience," she said. "I must have fresh air." So they walked for a long time through the deserted streets. During their walk Mrs. Fiske asked Jimmy for a true account of an incident which had occurred on their arrival in Calgary. While Jimmy and one of the minor actors were in search of a hotel, Jimmy's companion went out into the middle of the street to ask directions from a traffic policeman. The officer stopped traffic while he supplied the information—and in the midst of it the actor's overstuffed suitcase burst open and spewed out its contents. Calgary citizens screamed with good-natured laughter, but the humiliated actor lost his head and cursed them wildly.

"He missed the opportunity for the best performance in his career," Mrs. Fiske commented. "If he had entered into the spirit of the occasion, he would have won more applause than he would have in a lifetime on the stage!" She sighed for the actor's lost opportunity, and then she laughed as if she were witnessing the scene at the intersection; and she asked naively, "Were there funny-looking things in the bag?"

In Winnipeg the stage door was directly across the alley from the Holy Roller Church, and *Mis' Nelly* had a great deal of competition in the matter of noise. Jimmy was fascinated; he spent every spare moment perched on a scenery crate, looking into the window of the church. Then he began sitting with the congregation and often, during a performance, rushed back to the theatre just before his cue.

Once, during a particularly interesting service, Jimmy was recalled to duty by a frantic stagehand who told him he had missed his cue. Jimmy dashed across the alley and onto the stage for his solo. The performance did not suffer too much, but Jimmy knew he had committed an unpardonable sin.

Usually when a member of the cast marred the performance, Mrs. Fiske spoke her displeasure the moment she made her exit; but this time she went to her dressing room in silence, and Jimmy was left to suffer until after the final curtain, when the maid came with the fateful summons.

Jimmy shivered in his Missouri boots. When he entered the dressing room, he covered his face with his hands, and said, "Mrs. Fiske, I can't look at you."

"Have you learned your lesson, young man?" she asked.

"I feel terrible," he said.

After letting him feel terrible for a minute of silence, she told him, "I knew where you were the moment you failed to pick up your cue— I knew you were Holy Rolling." When he did not deny it, she asked almost in a whisper, "Tell me—it must be very interesting—do you suppose we could slip in and sit in the rear of the church unnoticed?"

Jimmy assured her eagerly that it could be arranged; he already knew the likeable young minister, who would be glad to see that she was seated comfortably without any fuss being made over her. Mrs. Fiske chuckled, "I know you know the leading Holy Rollers by now, and we will go—tonight!" They did.

The western tour of *Mis' Nelly* closed in Duluth in late June. On one of the last evenings, Mrs. Fiske asked Jimmy if he was going to take the southern tour, which Cohan and Harris were then booking in New York. The tour was to begin a month after the company returned to New York, giving them a vacation for the month of July.

The western tour had yanked Jimmy away from Bush Conservatory forever, but it had also awakened plans which stretched into the future. Without too much explanation or even apology, he said he intended to go to New York and remain there. Afterward, he was ashamed of his lack of gratitude, and he was obliged to rationalize it by deciding it was a manifestation of the youth against which Mrs. Fiske had so often railed—youth filled with poor judgment and blunders.

Another woman in Mrs. Fiske's position might have ended their association in a pique, but she said only, "You will love New York and it will be a pleasure to take you there for the first time. By the way, that reminds me, we picked you up in Chicago, and arrangements must

320

be made for you to go to New York." Then she said, simply, "I wish you were going with me on the southern tour. Perhaps you will change your mind."

Jimmy's mind was made up with all the finality of youth. Mrs. Fiske arranged to have him go to New York with the company, as she had promised. On the way east from Chicago on the New York Central, she talked to him at length about New York, telling him all the do's and don'ts gathered from her lifelong experience. She also asked him to call at her office when he was settled, as she wished to give him letters of introduction to some New York managers.

They were nearing New York, and his mind was full of the glamor as he imagined it; he only half-heard Mrs. Fiske's great wisdom, and he took it as a matter of course that she should give him letters of introduction to the leading managers. Mrs. Fiske, who had entered New York countless times in the course of half a century, smiled understandingly through her many veils, and through the wall of glass that separates youth from the wisdom of maturity.

In New York, Jimmy learned from Mrs. Fiske's secretary that the promised letters of introduction to managers were ready. At the theatre where she was rehearsing new members of the cast for the southern tour, he bolted past a surly doorman who refused to let him in. With the doorman screaming in pursuit, he burst onto the stage and disrupted the rehearsal. Mrs. Fiske smiled as she threw up her hands in mock dismay. "Let him come in!" she told the doorman. "This is our Jimmy, our beautiful singer, and I want him to meet the cast." She pushed the rehearsal aside to introduce him, and then said briskly, "Now, I have the letter right here. Use this letter to Colonel Savage first. Be a good boy, and keep in touch with me; but run along now, you're holding up the show."

On the street, Jimmy opened the letter to Colonel Savage:

MINNIE MADDERN FISKE
Office Address
131 West Forty-Sixth Street
New York City

My Dear Col. Savage:
May I introduce to you Mr. Kemper—the bearer of this letter. I have an unusual pleasure in presenting Mr. Kemper, as he is a young man with a really superb gift. Mr. Kemper has a beautiful voice. Among all the singers who, from time to time, have been associated with us in various plays, Mr. Kemper stands almost alone and better than

them all. Personally, I feel sure that Mr. Kemper has a fine future. An association with you will undoubtedly lead to distinguished achievement eventually. Mr. Kemper's voice is simply exquisite. Believe me, my dear Colonel Savage,

Sincerely yours,

Minnie Maddern Fiske

Jimmy Kemper saw Mrs. Fiske at length only twice afterward—once for a chat on the stage of the Henry Miller Theatre in New York, where she was playing *Mary, Mary, Quite Contrary*. At another meeting, Mrs. Fiske, who had long avoided mention of the past, recalled the happy times that she and Jimmy and the Harlings had had on the western tour of *Mis' Nelly of N'Orleans*. She said, "Jimmy, I want you to sing for me, like old times, and I want Frank Harling to play for me." So it was arranged that the three go to the Judson Memorial Church on Washington Square South.

It was a cloudy autumn afternoon when they visited the church. Mrs. Fiske sat alone in the twilight of the auditorium while Jimmy sang and Frank Harling played his accompaniment, like old times. The last song he sang was "There Is Sunlight in Your Eyes," written by Mr. Harling and Ben Lewin, the two who had once appeared as ogres to a very young man from Bush Conservatory. As Jimmy came to the climax of the song, "There is naught in paradise outshines the sunlight in your eyes," the sun burst through the stained-glass windows as if a spotlight man, on cue, had covered him. Mrs. Fiske was greatly moved, and the three were silent for a long time. And then Mrs. Fiske said quietly, "I shall never forget this moment."

The last time Jimmy Kemper sang for Mrs. Fiske was at the old Campbell Funeral Parlor. That time there was no mystical light, unless it was unquenchable dignity and compassion in Mrs. Fiske's face. A young woman had died under tragic circumstances; Mrs. Fiske had stepped in and taken complete charge. At her orders, the funeral parlor was banked with flowers, and the music was to be memorable. She had asked her favorite singers, Mary Garden and Jimmy Kemper, to sing. As it happened, Miss Garden missed a train connection in New England. Only Jimmy sang.

Mrs. Fiske had learned that the favorite song of the dead girl was "Love's Old Sweet Song," and she had Jimmy sing it as a farewell to the one whom love had treated badly.

It was as beautiful and touching a farewell as a loved one ever had. But in life Mrs. Fiske had never known or seen the young woman whom she sponsored so gallantly in death.

CHAPTER 42

Mis' Nelly gave Minnie an interim of security in which she could again look to the future. During the western tour, she read manuscript plays as eagerly as ever, and in mid-tour a slender scenario caught her attention.

The scenario came from Hatcher Hughes, drama professor of Columbia University. In an accompanying letter, Professor Hughes observed that he saw in it a great role for Mrs. Fiske. The comedy began with a prehistoric prologue of a cave woman hesitating between a down-to-earth cave man and a poet. It was followed by a tender and witty modern play in which a young woman and her children chose between a business-engrossed husband and father, and a poet-philosopher whom the mother had once loved. Minnie agreed with Professor Hughes's estimate of the scenario, and she requested that work on the play begin at once.

The completed play was a collaboration bearing the names of Hatcher Hughes and Elmer Rice, who was now firmly established in the ranks of American playwrights.

The Hughes-Rice comedy, *Wake Up, Jonathan*, was written in the summer of 1920, and when Mrs. Fiske returned from her southern tour in *Mis' Nelly*, the production was well under way. It was staged and managed by Harry Fiske and produced by Sam Harris, whom Mr. Fiske characterized as "a lovely fellow and the easiest producer to work with I ever experienced."

Wake Up, Jonathan was a happy production. Its only drawback was the fact that the script called for four children, and child-labor laws in various cities forbade the appearance of any child, however gifted and well-cared-for, on the legitimate stage. The Fiskes solved one-fourth of the problem by engaging Freddie Goodrow for the role of the French orphan. Goodrow created the illusion so well that audiences never doubted that he was French and eight years old. Actually, the

323

appealing child who sat in Mrs. Fiske's lap was twenty-two, and not remarkably small for his age. There was, however, only one Freddie Goodrow, with his gift for making himself appear young and small; other roles were filled by real children, whose mothers were paid to accompany them; and the tour was arranged to avoid cities where child actors were restricted by law.

Wake Up, Jonathan had a successful premiere at Atlantic City two nights before Christmas, 1920. The new year found it a recognized hit in Baltimore. On January 17, it opened at the Henry Miller Theatre in New York.

Nearly half a century before, a little Minnie Maddern had made her New York debut; and in the years since then Mrs. Fiske had had triumphs enough for a dozen lifetimes; and failures enough to leave her forever uncertain. The New York opening found her shaken by apprehensions. But the audience took the play to its heart; the second act ended with an ovation, and the audience declined to settle for Mrs. Fiske's repeated appearance. She responded with a witty and modest curtain speech, closing with an expression of gratitude for the American playwright; and the performance ended in an atmosphere of warmth such as she had supposed was gone forever from the New York stage.

The verdict of the audience was affirmed by the critics, and William Archer, visiting from London, added his praise. Of all the New York critics, Alan Dale of the *American* had the best over-all perspective of Mrs. Fiske's work. A generation before, he had hailed her as "America's great actress," and since then he had analyzed, and praised or damned, every role in which she had appeared. Summing up in his long review, he wrote:

> Not in the halcyon period labeled heyday did Mrs. Fiske give as deliciously and artistically perfect a performance as she did in "Wake Up, Jonathan" last night.
> No, not even in the forgotten days of "Tess" was this actress as subtle, as authoritative, and, above all, as distinct and diction-perfect, as she was in the clever and unusual little play by Hatcher Hughes and Elmer Rice.

It was a providential Indian summer. In its sunshine Mrs. Fiske made hay with *Wake Up, Jonathan* as she had with *Mis' Nelly;* and success gave her the opportunity to live once more in the present.

It was a somewhat tarnished present. The World War had ended in a peace that dispelled illusions about a pretty new world. But the 1920's arrived with another idealistic dream—the Prohibition Amendment—and its attendant realities: an army and navy of bootleggers and rum-runners; homemade gin, and homemade lawbreaking in half the kitchens and bathrooms of the United States. For many, the age was headier than the juniper-flavored alcohol: smugglers and pirates abroad in the land, and the fun of throwing painfully acquired ideals out of the window.

Before the years of accountability, little Minnie Maddern had done her bit toward Prohibition, playing Mary Morgan in *Ten Nights in a Barroom* and drenching her audience in tears as she sang, "Father, Dear Father, Come Home with Me Now." Father was home now, making bathtub gin with the aid of his children; but most of those who had consciously or unconsciously brought about the change contemplated the dream rather than the reality. Minnie was not one of them. A dozen years before, in her dressing room at the Hackett Theatre, she had argued the matter with Evangeline Booth: Minnie in the severe costume of Salvation Nell, and the leader of the Salvation Army, with her bonnet cast aside, sitting at the dressing table, making herself glamorous with forbidden powder and paint.

Miss Booth had pictured the millennium coming in the door as alcohol went out of the window, but the actress's answer was always much the same, "It won't work, Eva. The problem isn't alcohol; it's people. You can't solve people with a law and you'll make drink more attractive by forbidding it."

Miss Booth answered that someday Minnie would see the light.

Minnie never did. Early in January, 1921, she and Harry were among the first to join the Association Against the Prohibition Amendment, whose statement of faith began, "The Volstead law is visionary, unnecessarily drastic, ineffective and blasphemous. It has made lawbreakers of a large portion of our population and is helping create a nation of liars, sneaks and hypocrites. . . ."

A month later, Minnie bought her longed-for home in the country. She had found the place the summer before in the high heart of her beloved Adirondacks; in Big Moose Lake an S-shaped island of about ten acres, and at the narrowest part of the island, Camp Veery, a huge log house with porches to match, board walks, and a boathouse built like a fortress and stocked with flat-bottomed rowboats.

The massive island camp was impractical as a home or investment. But Minnie was an artist. For her the purchase meant the things that could be seen from the great windows—trees and lake and sky; the enchanted forest of hard maple and balsam and pine coming down to sand beaches at the edge of clear mountain water; the cyclical hours of the day and seasons of the year in a setting of nature that requires no upkeep. She had never had anything to do with the management of the houses and apartments in which she had lived, and if there were problems she did not recognize them.

Since the Fiskes' marriage the American climate had changed almost beyond recognition, from the staid 1890's with the exciting whiff of renaissance in the air, to the 1920's with naive disillusionment suddenly replacing naive illusions.

Times had changed, but Minnie was still as incapable as the bride who could not plan a meal or manage a house. Harry, who had always been good at such things, took over at Camp Veery. He arranged for improvements and repairs, bought kitchenware, furnishings and wholesale quantities of food. He hired a cook, housekeeper, handyman and laundress.

At the end of the theatrical season, Minnie and Harry went home to Camp Veery, where they spent the summer of 1922, and many others. They were summers that blended into one another, all much alike, and all with a thrill of delight for Minnie—she never tired of the place.

Her own wants were simple: old clothes, and an occasional meal, paths to walk on in the woods, and a rowboat that took her away from camp to the solitude of quiet water beside quieter shores. Rowing exercised her arms, which had grown too heavy to look their best on the stage, and she fondly believed that exercise would reduce them.

The boat also served as a study and practice stage, where Minnie would work on a humane speech or article, or take up the typescript of a play and practice reading her lines, sometimes sounding off in a voice which filled a quarter of a mile radius of lake and lonely woods.

In camp there was less solitude. Minnie had many friends, and Harry had more; both were generous with invitations, and during the summers at Camp Veery many of her friends and his met for the first time.

With her habitual casualness, Minnie quartered guests in the boathouse, and left them to their own devices. Lunch was one of the few certainties of the establishment. About noon, famished guests would struggle out of the woods near where Mrs. Fiske was drifting in her boat, hail her and persuade her to return to camp so that all might eat.

Evenings in the great log living room were more sociable, with

326

Harry Fiske the perfect host. His own guests were varied of age and sex and interests, while Mrs. Fiske's were chiefly intellectual and earnest-minded women. Harry bridged the gaps with effortless talk, and games to suit every taste, even his wife's. Her childhood had been almost barren of the usual games. Once, she had been exposed briefly to parcheesi. Ever since, she had remembered it wistfully, with a conviction that it was one game at which she could excel. So Harry was almost certain to have a game of parcheesi in progress.

When Minnie won fairly, she glowed with triumphant fulfillment. When she did not win, she was visibly ruffled, and she hurried about the board, counting shamelessly to her own advantage. Thoughtful guests recognized it as the enactment of a childhood fantasy, while others learned by experience not to dispute her counting.

After winning two or three games, Minnie would go up to bed, accompanied by Boca, Harry's soft-eyed fawn-colored bulldog. Soon after the two had gone upstairs, Harry would leave the company long enough to go up and lift the non-jumping bulldog onto his wife's bed. Minnie would pet and talk to Boca until she fell asleep.

Having settled Minnie and Boca for the night, Harry would return to the living room, where he was master of ceremonies and raconteur until the last guest had drifted upstairs to the second-floor sleeping quarters. He then went up to the enormous third-floor attic, where he wrote letters and adapted plays until daylight began breaking over the mountains beyond the lake.

Often he was on his way to bed as his wife, with Boca, was starting out for her morning walk.

Minnie was generally the first to bed at Camp Veery, and the first up in the morning. On one occasion, however, a guest preceded her at both ends of the day. The guest was a lady, pure of speech, with intellectual tastes. When she expressed her intention of retiring early, Minnie against her usual custom offered to find the lady a book to take to bed. There were about two thousand volumes on the camp shelves, and Minnie looked among the new acquisitions, observing, "Mr. Fiske has impeccable taste." She selected a volume, and said, "From the title this must be a most interesting study of child psychology." The guest thanked her, and went her way with the book.

In the morning, when Minnie went to the shelves for a book to take on her morning row, the volume of the evening before was back in its place. Later she commented to Harry on the punctilious return, and he asked the name of the book. When he was told, he exploded into

327

laughter. The title was misleading, he explained, and the book obscene. He had bought it to round out a general selection, and it had never occurred to him that his wife might hit on it as bedtime reading for her proper friend.

After the first shock, Minnie laughed and clapped her hands like a gleeful little girl, as she did when something particularly delighted her. Her own sense of propriety was strong, but she would not have been Mrs. Fiske if she had not recognized a comedy situation when she saw one.

CHAPTER 43

That first summer at Camp Veery was followed by Minnie's tour with *Wake Up, Jonathan,* a tour limited by child-labor laws which blocked the play from the Far West, the South, Chicago and many other large cities. Minnie, who had no child of her own, paid dearly for having stage children.

Off stage, the Fiskes were in tune with the 1920's, where many young couples postponed children or had none at all. In part, the fashion resulted from post-war prosperity, which was only a thin casing over inflation. In another part it was disillusionment over the fact that an American army had gone overseas and failed to return with a new heaven and a new earth. Willy-nilly, the Fiskes were deans of the new fashion, but their experience pointed in the opposite direction.

In recent years, whenever Minnie saw a young woman with a baby, she was moved as by the sight of the Madonna and Child. Once, with happy tears in her eyes, she told the daughter of an old friend, "You have made a wise choice"—as though a baby could only be achieved by a great deal of mental exercise. To her intimate friends she spoke with poignant regret of her early decision not to have children, and to ease her conscience she always ended by arguing passionately that she was not constituted to be a good mother.

Harry had no such conflicts. As he expressed it, he had married, "hoping to lead a child by the hand and answer its questions," but he had bowed to his wife's decision and adjusted his life accordingly.

In the late spring of 1922, with Minnie's tour near its end, Harry had the machinery of Camp Veery ready to start smoothly with his wife's arrival in New York. Harry was equally competent in his apartment on West Eleventh Street, where he was cook and dishwasher as well as lord and master.

One afternoon he came home, bearing groceries as he often did. He rested them on an antique stand while he put away his hat and gloves and walking stick. In that room a hundred portraits of Minnie looked down from among rare Japanese prints, and the chairs held the ghosts of actors who had occupied them on the stage—Mansfield, Barrymore, Power, Arliss, and others of the great.

Harry went to the kitchen with the supplies he had selected at the corner market—tenderloin steak, mushrooms, fresh vegetables and endive; he set them on the immaculate table—and stood aghast as the silence was shattered by the cry of a baby, lusty and piercing. The cry was from his bedroom.

The door which Harry threw open grazed a medley of luggage; he saw the startled faces of his wife and her secretary, Mae Cox. Minnie, with her hat and veils still on, was bending over his bed, diapering a baby.

A generation earlier Harry would have exulted over the scene, but the sight of his more than middle-aged wife engaged in such an occupation struck him as grotesque.

"What in thunder is going on?" he demanded.

Minnie smiled brightly through her veils. "Boysie, don't look so startled. It's only a baby; I've had him for months. He's been touring with me since February; he's already an old trouper!"

Harry asked, "How was I to know that, my dear?"

"Perhaps I forgot to tell you," she conceded.

"And whose infant is this?" he asked.

"Mine, by right of loving and caring for him. He was found in a hotel room in Philadelphia, and I had a friend go to court and secure his custody. He was left in a Gladstone bag, with a strip of adhesive over his mouth so he couldn't cry." She addressed the baby, "Now you can cry all you want to, you darling!"

The darling took her at her word, but Harry made himself heard through the uproar. "And what do you propose to do with this infant?"

"Adopt him, Harry. I shall adopt him as soon as it can be arranged. You have no idea how a baby takes to travel, and sleeping in dressing rooms. But then you weren't born in the theatre!"

He said no more on the subject until Mae Cox was in the kitchen, warming a bottle. "You will do as you please," he said, "but if you keep this infant it will be against my wishes and advice. I will have no part in adopting him; and he is not to bear my name."

Minnie agreed to the stipulation, although she had expected Harry to be overjoyed. She had kept the knowledge of the baby from him

330

only because of her natural secretiveness, and she was so adept that for months she had had a baby with her on tour—and no hint of it had reached the press. The play had been a great aid to the concealment. Three of Minnie's stage children were real children accompanied by their mothers, and they provided protective covering for the extra.

The baby rounded out Minnie's Indian summer. Half a dozen years before, she had gone to Staten Island, homeless and childless, to live with relatives. Now, at the age of fifty-six, she returned from playing a brilliantly successful role, and with her baby she spent the summer of 1922 on the little lake-girt continent which was her home.

She had assured Harry that the baby would not make Camp Veery less idyllic, and she was right. The faithful Mae Cox brought her mother to the island to act as nurse and the two were quartered in the spacious boathouse, and the summer was much like the one before— Minnie's morning walks and rows, the guests' search for her at noon, the evenings in the living room of the lodge, and Harry's all-night hours which ended as his wife was beginning her early day.

The only bugbear was the eternal one—the next play. Minnie had begun tackling the problem the year before, but it was not soon enough.

Near the end of her tour in *Wake Up, Jonathan*, she had still been juggling the possibilities of various revivals: *Mrs. Bumpstead-Leigh*, with May Irwin as Ma; *The Rivals*, in a joint production with Otis Skinner; and *Becky Sharp*, with an accompanying star associate, perhaps Tyrone Power.

Half a lifetime later, Power was remembered best for his performances in Mrs. Fiske's company, and belatedly he realized the magic of the schoolmarm-looking little woman who could call up in an actor greatness which no other director was able to call up afterward. From Rutland, Vermont, Minnie wrote Harry: "Tyrone Power is madly eager to play his old part. . . ."

The actress, too, looked back—in this case because no suitable modern play had come up over the horizon. The nearest approach to it had been *Paddy*, by Lillian Barrett—a play with a brilliant central character, and little else. While she was still in Vermont, Harry wired that Brock Pemberton was interested in producing *Paddy*. Minnie was a little pleased—and a good deal worried. She wrote Harry:

> I am very interested in what you wrote of Mr. Pemberton & Paddy and if you can bring Miss Barrett to realize that it is far wiser to take the time—carefully and deliberately—and determine to make the

331

promising material of "Paddy" into a really full, fine play—(with great chance of success) than to wish it rushed into a production that might court failure—in its present undeveloped—shadowy condition. . . . There is certainly a wonderfully effective part there. . . . At present it is all part and no story—and nothing that grips interest or emotion—or sympathy to hang the part on to. Miss Barrett must get a story. Find a story worthy of the part—& then she should have a big play!

Later the same day, she wrote again:

Darling Boy:
   Will you tell Miss Barrett I honestly think I'm on the trail of a story for "Paddy"? It came into my head to-day and I'll write you about it. Between the three of us—we surely ought to develop a great story—& build a fine play for some not too distant day in the future.

Dearest one
Bunner

Her idea was approved, and Harry collaborated with Miss Barrett while Minnie continued her tour.

By summer Paddy, the brilliant and amoral morphine addict, was placed in a story and surrounded by other characters, but she insisted on shedding them as she shed her responsibilities.

The battle with the too-triumphal character was continued during the summer at Camp Veery, and into the fall. Minnie and Harry had faith in the final version, but not enough to gamble on a New York opening.

Paddy was tried out at Rochester on November 27, with the baby cooing in Mrs. Fiske's dressing room while she did battle on the stage.

The following day the Rochester press gloried in Mrs. Fiske's acting but found the play weak and episodic. *Paddy* moved on to similar judgments in other cities.

As the Fiskes had done with other plays which failed to come to life, they tried to change their luck by changing the name. *Paddy* became *The Last Card*, and finally *The Dice of the Gods*. But it never was a success, although at moments Mrs. Fiske made her spectators believe that they were witnessing a triumph. At Toronto, two days before Christmas, 1922, the *Saturday Night* critic wrote: "However infirm the play may be, it permits of acting in those last minutes that no eye-witness will ever forget."

332

In Chicago Ashton Stevens wrote:

She was so infallible, so unerring, that my absurdly comparing mind began to liken her to that almost unendurably flawless portrait of Hals by Hals that hangs in the Art Institute. I remember I foolishly conjured a picture of Bird Milman hanging on a burnished wire. "But Bird Milman sometimes slips," I told myself wrathfully because Mrs. Fiske didn't.

Between her great moments in the play, Minnie tiptoed about her dressing room, or crooned over the baby, whom she had brought along with full paraphernalia and a nurse. Prohibition had ruled out a champagne-basket crib, but Minnie's mind reconstructed the scene of her infancy, and through her make-up she smiled down on the baby as her pain-wracked mother before her had smiled down on her.

Minnie, too, had suffered; it was still touch and go whether she would die in harness; and the great obstacle to her retiring to her home in the country was her home in the country which required so much money.

For a year Minnie's secretiveness had triumphed over the potentially curious, and her adopted baby remained as unpublicized as the child of some remote farm couple. Once a reporter was curious about the crib in Mrs. Fiske's dressing room, but she put his mind at rest by carrying the baby onto the stage in a scene where the erratic Paddy mothered Italian waifs.

Early in the spring Minnie was invited to help launch the Child Adoption League of New York. The moving spirits of the new organization knew she was generous of her time in good causes, and her public pronouncements made news.

Minnie accepted. She was resting between her tour and her New York opening, close enough to run into town for an afternoon. On the train and in a taxi on the way to the Biltmore, she told herself gleefully, "This is the cream of the jest! They invited me because I am a well-known actress—and I accepted because I have a child; and they don't know it, they don't know it!"

The meeting of the Child Adoption League was presided over by Mrs. Charles Dana Gibson. Other speakers were Henry Morgenthau, Will Rogers, Laurette Taylor, Bishop Thomas Gailor and Honoré Wilson. Governor Alfred E. Smith sent a telegram congratulating the new organization.

When Minnie was called on to speak, she made an impassioned plea

333

for adoptions, urging childless couples and parentless children to pool their heartaches and thereby end them. It was perhaps the only occasion on which she was carried away by her own eloquence. Her audience, too, was carried away. Then, on an inspiration, she threw down her trump card: "All this is from my heart; I have adopted a child; he is now more than a year old!"

The rest of the meeting was a happy uproar from which the actress escaped to her train before reporters arrived in force.

Harry had no such luck. The same afternoon, innocent of his wife's blurting her secret, he set out for a walk with Boca. He closed the door on his apartment and was confronted by reporters from the *World*, and *Times*, and *Tribune*—all of them panting for details about the baby.

It was part of the price of being married to a famous woman. Harry also had to pay on another score. At intervals he had told his wife that it was customary to give a baby a name. She had never quite believed him, and she called the baby playful names, sometimes a new one every few days or hours. The one which had come nearest sticking was "Bolie," a name Minnie had once seen somewhere on a sign. But even she did not think of it as a real name.

The first thing the reporters wanted to know was the baby's name, and Harry could not help them. Holding Boca's leash in one faultlessly-gloved hand and his walking stick in the other, he explained, "The baby has no name."

"No name, after a year?"

"Impossible!"

Mr. Fiske answered with dignity, "I'm sorry. She simply does not call him anything definite. It's Mrs. Fiske's baby and she doesn't have to call him anything if she doesn't want to, does she?" It sounded idiotic, even to him, but farther north, Minnie was interviewed by reporters who were more interested in the actress's plans for the baby than in his name. "Would the baby grow up on the road?"

"Oh, yes, indeed!" she said. "Baby will travel with me always. I couldn't think of leaving him behind in the hands of hired attendants. Besides, a baby's place is with his mother and a mother's place is with her baby. We need each other. We lead lonely lives, we stage folk, loneliest of all when we travel. A baby is wonderful company. A baby fills the house. One never gets lonely with a baby around. . . ."

Minnie's plea for adoptions had been aimed at well-to-do, childless women, but it found other marks—as in the case of her jotting down

334

thoughts on sleepless nights, and pinning them to her nightgown. When her custom became known, women with time for fads had done likewise for a little while. But her most famous emulator was David Belasco, who thereafter kept writing materials beside his bed, and pinned his insomnia-inspired memoranda to his nightshirt.

Mrs. Fiske's foster-motherhood had its impact on the stage, too. That spring there was an epidemic of actresses' breaking into print with declarations that they were about to adopt babies. Marie Dressler rated headlines when she asked the management of the Winter Garden to enlarge her dressing room and put in an extra window in anticipation of a blessed event by proxy; and Laurette Taylor was widely quoted when she observed, in the smart coinage of the twenties, that there was only one thing in the world more noble than adopting a baby, and that was adopting two babies.

Minnie's example influenced stage males as well—and seemingly people with spare babies. While her announcement was still news, a baby boy was left in a suitcase at a hotel in Chillicothe, Ohio. The baby was discovered just before Al Jolson arrived, touring in *Sinbad;* and while actresses basked in the light of publicity for their good intentions, Mr. Jolson arranged for a quick adoption, added a nurse to his retinue, bought a crib and a baby buggy—and moved on to the next town, every inch as much a mother as Mrs. Fiske.

C H A P T E R 44

Mrs. Fiske had accepted *The Dice of the Gods* out of desperation—and the day after, a finished and suitable play fell into her lap: St. John Ervine's comedy *Mary, Mary, Quite Contrary*. It arrived unsolicited from David Belasco, who held the American rights. In an accompanying note, Belasco observed that Minnie Maddern Fiske was the only actress in America who could play Mary Westlake.

Minnie was already committed for the season, but she sighed for a play which she did not have to rewrite. On June 29, she wrote Harry:

Darling Boy

Since writing my letter to you regarding the St. Ervine play—I've been giving the matter still more thought—and going over the possibilities of the part. It seems too bad to let it go—if we can hold it in any way—for a time. The part is delicious, perfect for me—I would be very much at home in it. Not a big—almost classic thing like "Becky" but Oh! so much better than anything else that has lately come to us. It is really a good play, by a real playwright—splendid technique—a finished thing in every respect. . . . Mr. Belasco will find it hard to get anyone to play it. He may be willing to hold it for some time. Do—please let him and Mr. Roeder know my great admiration for the play. Perhaps—even—Mr. Tyler could arrange to get it from Mr. Belasco??? for later? If Mr. Belasco has no one to do it. I really don't know what to suggest—I think the play would tickle New York immensely. It is really clever, brilliant and witty. . . .

Dearest love
Bunner

Man and boy, David Belasco had waited nearly forty years to get Minnie under his management and he could wait a little longer. The play was scheduled for production in the early fall.

The summer of 1923 was much like other summers at Camp Veery, except that the actress studied a different role and the summer was briefer because of the early production. In the matter of costume there was no difference at all because Minnie was free to revel in her disregard of fashion. The clothes she wore were those she had worn the summer before, and the summer before that. And the habit was contagious. Harry had been dressing like a gentleman for most of sixty years, and for half of them he had remonstrated with his wife for her utter indifference to her dress. At Camp Veery Harry had finally discovered the comfort of old clothes; he and Minnie competed with each other in digging out their oldest things. And when one of them unearthed a garment that was sufficiently quaint, it was worn until it fell to pieces.

As Minnie observed, appearing under Belasco's management was like making candy in someone else's kitchen. He provided her with a play that required no heartbreaking rewriting; a perfect theatre; and a brilliant cast, with C. Aubrey Smith for her leading man. From there on, Belasco left the production in the Fiskes' hands. He appeared only twice during rehearsals, once to suggest the addition of a Japanese maid, and once to rearrange some cushions in "a more sexy manner."

Left happily to their own devices, the Fiskes reveled in the superb equipment which Belasco used so unimaginatively; and Harry illuminated the sets from above with a soft natural light which might have come from an obliging sun.

Mary, Mary, Quite Contrary had its premiere at the Belasco Theatre on September 11. Mrs. Fiske was given an ovation by the first-night audience and another the next day by the press:

> Mrs. Fiske is the best we have, and we could need no better. . . . Mrs. Fiske is irresistible . . . one fairly basks in the dazzling glory of an art that seems so fast vanishing from the American theatre. . . . A feat of extraordinary artistry of which only this one woman in the world is capable. . .

Alexander Woollcott summed up:

> It was such a performance as her devotees have in mind when they say there is no comedienne like her anywhere in the world. It was magnificent from the first unmistakable toot of her voice, heard in the offstage babble before her entrance, to the grand moment when oblivious of the sou'wester and rubber boots she happens to have on at that moment, she sweeps out of the room in the most gracious and

337

duchessy manner imaginable. She gave a fillip to Mr. Ervine's comedy which sent us all out into the night a most exhilarated set of mortals. . . .

There was praise for everyone and everything, including Harry Fiske's throwing Belasco's celebrated method of lighting out of the window and introducing his own—although the credit went to the wrong person. Torres wrote:

> A Keats would have found inspiration in that lovely English garden, lighted as no stage garden ever was lighted before. There was magic of a May morning in the soft, warm lighting, the new Belasco system which eliminates footlights, and marks a new era in stage lighting. . . .

Praise was dear to David Belasco, and he soaked up the deserved and the undeserved as it fell upon him like rain. Also, he was profoundly proud of Minnie Maddern. Interviewed by the press, he summed up his favorite actress in five words: "Match her if you can."

Belasco then went on:

> This famous actress, with all the technique of the stage at her finger-tips, should be an object lesson to everyone devoted to the art of acting, and every lover of theatre should glory in her triumph.
>
> There are so few great actors left that we should cherish them with the affection and admiration that they so richly deserve. I want only that Mrs. Fiske shall live in the hearts of the American public as Bernhardt lives in the hearts of the French and Duse is beloved by the Italian. That is her due, for Mrs. Fiske is one of the great artists, not only of this country, but of the world.
>
> With all her greatness Mrs. Fiske has the heart of a child—once again proving that simplicity spells bigness. Neither time nor fame has changed her. She has the same modesty, enthusiasm, lightness, charm and sparkle that distinguished her when she appeared at the Madison Square Theatre, where I was stage manager, years ago. She has, of course, matured and improved her work, but otherwise she is the same. In the past few weeks I've been astounded. I've seen so many men and women of the stage grow not only old, but aged. But Mrs. Fiske is like Peter Pan's sister. At rehearsal it was easier to tire out younger women and she was always the first to come and last to go.
>
> The other day I said to one of my young actresses: "See Mrs. Fiske, listen to her, study her, and then pray to God that when you

have been on the stage as long as she has, your voice, your face and your figure will be as youthful as hers."

For myself, I feel it a great privilege to be associated with Mrs. Fiske, and if anything I am able to do relieves her of any anxieties of stage work I am more than repaid. I have adored her since she was a red-headed girl and I a black-haired boy, and I adore her even more now. I am especially proud to be with her at this time of my life. I would rather have it so than at any other period before the curtain rings down on my last production. Meanwhile I can only add that it gives me the keenest pleasure to brag about Little Minnie Maddern, as she will ever be to me.

The glittering success of *Mary, Mary, Quite Contrary* had the quality of something dreamed up by the wizard of the theatre—and it vanished like a dream. Other productions were scheduled at the Belasco, and when New York had had only its first exciting taste of the play, it was sent on tour.

Minnie had spun lesser successes into two years of touring, yet the Belasco tour of *Mary* went to pieces in a few weeks. By the cold New Year of 1924, with the fireworks of her success still in the sky, the actress found herself among the unemployed.

Once more it was too late for one of the big revivals which the Fiskes had planned for so long; and once more they had to seize on the most promising thing that offered.

It was *Helena's Boys*, dramatized by Ida Erlich from a story by Mary Brecht Pulver, and as usual Minnie had to pitch in and work on rewriting the play.

The result was a pleasant piece which was tried out successfully in Washington. From there it was moved directly to Broadway, opening at the Henry Miller Theatre on April 7.

A few months earlier Minnie had had the New York critics at her feet; now she found them snapping at the heels of her play. Most of them praised her acting, but they branded *Helena's Boys* valueless, and damaged the production.

The attack on the play worried the actress more than such things had ever done before—and by the same token her friends rallied to her defense with remarkable unanimity. Scores of well-known people wrote to the critics, protesting their treatment of *Helena's Boys*; the *New York Times* printed a long, spirited defense of the play by Will Irwin; and the gallant old William Gillette wrote in a shaky hand:

339

SEVENTH SISTER

Dear Mrs. Fiske

I have a letter ready for Broun, and am stopped—or hesitated—by a friend who tells me Broun will print it but follow it with a reiteration of what he said in his review only making it worse. His review was pretty bad. Now I will send it (my letter) along to Broun, if you think the danger of making it worse is not too great. I am afraid of it. Nobody now has the least idea of what he said. It is all over and forgotten.

Kindly wire me Hadlyme Connecticut. If you think not best to rouse Broun, you need not write.

In haste and with sincerest regards to Mr. Fiske and yourself.

William Gillette

The protests of friends could not save a flimsy vehicle—and the final effect on Minnie was tonic. For years she had been appearing in slight and pleasant things. Now she was done with trifles and she vowed that her next play would be a great one, whether modern or ancient.

That was the summer Lotta Crabtree died; Lotta, who had achieved fame and riches in the flimsiest trifles; Lotta, whose dancing feet had woven a spell through the dreams of a baby sleeping in an unprophetic champagne basket.

The death of the hoarding Lotta was almost simultaneous with the death of the fabulous, outgiving Mrs. Jack Gardner. The two events were among the few which Mrs. Fiske recorded in writing—for an article that she never had time to do. She wrote Harry:

For another article the story of that Sunday in Boston when I spent hours with Mrs. Jack Gardner first and immediately after with Lotta. Both great women were passing from us. What a contrast! It was a balmy, lovely day. Unforgettable. In all the years of our friendship I had never known "Mrs. Jack" to look so young and beautiful. Never was she so sweet and enchanting as I found her in that intimate hour, high up in the flower-scented, sunny apartment at the top of the Palace. No empress ever left the world with a grander gesture—I parted from her with a feeling of exaltation. And for an hour I wandered about the Palace alone, as that day there were no visitors but me. I sat in the court, the wondrously beautiful enclosure where the young artist (seeing it for the first time) knelt sobbing

340

upon the flags. I was grateful that I had lived to be actual witness of the bestowal of this matchless gift of a genius-woman upon her fellow countrymen. In sheer romance and beauty has there ever been a gift equal to it? Perhaps not in all history. And that same afternoon I drove out to see Lotta. Lotta sitting in her tiny room, surrounded by her old photographs. Lotta, the incomparable imp of the mining camps and the dance halls, later the cloistered, mysterious little nun of the theatre. I spoke of her early California days. "Romantic," she whispered, "romantic!" Her will was a remarkable document. Judge Chase sent me a copy of it. Lotta was a quarter of a century composing it. The will became an obsession with her. She talked to me about it for days at a time. And the fast and furious melodrama that followed the offering of the will for probate! Ninety-nine impostors attempted to break it. Much of that part of the story is funny, but there is also a good deal that is revolting. Do you remember the day that the little imp stole from me my afternoon reception at Harvard? She must have been seventy then, but she was still a girl in spirit and roguish beauty. The boys had no eyes for any of the girls present— no eyes for me, the guest of honor. Not at all. They formed a dense circle around Lotta. When I was in Boston not long ago Arthur Johnson, trustee of the Museum, said he would like to send me some interesting photographs of Mrs. Gardner. No doubt Miss Donovan will let me have special pictures of Lotta. . .

No doubt Miss Donovan would, but Mrs. Fiske was already embarked on greater projects, and the article was never written.

CHAPTER 45

The production which Mrs. Fiske selected for her first major effort in a dozen years was Sheridan's *The Rivals*, first launched at Covent Garden, London, in 1775.

The last and only noteworthy production of *The Rivals* in the United States had been in 1896, at the beginning of Mrs. Fiske's career—an all-star revival with Mrs. John Drew as Mrs. Malaprop, Joseph Jefferson as Bob Acres, and other roles taken by Nat Goodwin, Julia Marlowe Taber and William H. Crane. In point of talent, the revival had been a great moment of American theatre history; nearly every member of the cast was famous, and knew it. Mrs. Drew had observed that the production, though brimming with artists, was inartistic.

The Fiskes' approach to *The Rivals* was the one they had used in their Manhattan Theatre productions: the best available actor for each role, but no star except the play itself.

During several years of planning the production, Minnie had cast and recast the roles, and the final selections were a work of art. Mrs. Fiske was Mrs. Malaprop; James T. Powers, Bob Acres; Chauncey Olcott, Sir Lucius O'Trigger; Thomas A. Wise, Anthony Absolute; Kenneth Thompson, Captain Jack Absolute; Lola Fisher, Lydia Languish; and Georgette Cohan, Lucy.

The Rivals was under the management of George C. Tyler and Hugh Ford, with the Fiskes directing the production—Harry the general movements on the stage, and Minnie working with the cast on the interpretation of roles.

By ear-to-the-gutter prognostications, the revival was in for a short life and an un-merry one. The sins of concealment and silence of the late nineteenth century had been visited on the children of the early twentieth in the form of sex ignorance; the World War broke down the barriers of silence, and America was being flooded with mildly

342

dirty plays that were no more mature than the curiosity they exploited. That background, it was pointed out, was a guarantee of failure for a play from an age when people took the facts of life for granted.

The prognostications were wrong. Encouraged by veterans whose greatest memories of the theatre centered around Mrs. Fiske, the news spread that *The Rivals* was an experience too epoch to miss. In city after city, people in queues blocks long waited for hours to buy tickets. Before the end of 1924, the production had broken all-time records in Pittsburgh, Baltimore and Philadelphia, and it was still in its infancy.

With unlimited backing and scope, crowned by success, Minnie was free to follow her conviction that the American road was her stage, and New York only one of many cities. As it turned out, in two fabulous years of playing in two hundred cities, the production was never taken to New York.

Although *The Rivals* never went to New York, the critics came to it. Among them, the mountainous Alexander Woollcott, as he called himself, pilgrimaged to Newark to see what New York was missing, and he reported at length in the *Sun* of December 9:

. . . The sight of Mrs. Fiske, Mr. Powers, Tom Wise and Chauncey Olcott dancing a country dance with immense relish is a sight worth several trips to Newark. And Mrs. Fiske herself, what words are there to tell the gusto and the bounce of her performance, the alacrity of her vocabulary? And the snorting apoplexy of her scenes of temper. The huge white wig but lends emphasis to the quizzical tilt of her head and the furbelows of her vast costume seem fairly to billow with enjoyment of every scene. This Mrs. Malaprop is the very pinnacle of Sheridan comedy. She is the dinesaur of all eyes. . .

The Sheridan revival played many record-breaking engagements, but the most famous was at the Hollis Theatre in Boston, which had been timed to coincide with the hundred-and-fiftieth anniversary of the play. On a flower-filled stage, in the costume of Mrs. Malaprop, Minnie began the evening performance by reciting a commemorative poem written for the occasion by the humorist, Oliver Herford. It went in part:

Oh Lud! To think that I have lived to see
The hundred and fiftieth caravanssery
Of the first rendering (as the critics say)
Of Mr. Sheridan's unrivaled play,

"The Rivals"—I remember well the way
The Woollcotts, Brouns and Benchleys of that day,
Kissed us with cudgels, fondled us with knives—
They little guessed that we had charmed lives! . . .

In true Sheridan style, the poem went on to attack the rubbish that was filling the contemporary theatres, and it ended with a toast to art's rebirth, and better days.

For Minnie, art had been reborn; and she had never had better days than the present ones. As a token of her regained greatness, she no longer had to be a star. During the Boston engagement she made the point clear to the *Telegram:*

To the Editor
Dear Sir:—

May I be permitted to correct an impression given in the Telegram's very distinguished review of "The Rivals"?

In the course of the review the company interpreting Mr. Sheridan's play is referred to as "The Mrs. Fiske Company." I shall be grateful if you will allow me to make it clear that the group of players, of which I have the honor of being a member, is associated in the delightful task of reviving the notable old comedy without individual starship or leadership of any sort whatsoever.

> Believe me
> Respectfully
> Minnie Maddern Fiske

With *The Rivals* rolling along under its own power, Minnie resiliently entered on a campaign militating against the cruelty of traps, and advocating that fur farms take their place. Through the seventy-two-week tour there poured a stream of letters and pamphlets, with humane lectures at nearly every stop. Washington was one of the actress's strongholds and there, on March 19, 1925, she was honored for twenty-five years of unceasing devotion to the crusade for "Justice to Animals." The testimonial luncheon was almost a national affair, humanitarians traveling halfway across the continent to honor her.

A few days after Minnie had left, the enemy entered Washington. They arrived in the form of a delegation from the fur industry with a fabulous fur coat which they presented to Mrs. Calvin Coolidge. Photographs of the delegation, with the First Lady in the fur coat, were sent all over the nation.

It was a near mortal blow to the anti-trap campaign, but Minnie

344

rallied her forces to counterattack with letters to the First Lady. Her own diplomatic but compelling letter began:

Dear Mrs. Coolidge:
At the very moment when the American Humane Association is pleading the cause of the fur-bearing animals we have been grieved to see the vast and influential publicity, designed to promote popularity of furs, which has been given through the presentation to you of a regal gift by the American fur manufacturers. . . .
We would not presume to say what you should do. We hardly know what we might ask you to do, but we feel that your great heart, which has had its own tortures and which has repeatedly shown its love for all mankind, will give the best answer.

Mrs. Coolidge's answer came in the form of an announcement that she could not wear the fur coat. And she never did. A few months afterward the Fiskes were guests at the White House. They found the President and his wife charming hosts; and nothing was said about the coat.

In Minneapolis in September, a young beginner, Donald Cook, was engaged as a replacement for the role of Captain Jack Absolute. For a week he had hardly a word from the remote and preoccupied Mrs. Fiske; then it was a perfunctory question about what he was interested in besides acting. He answered "Dogs," with startling results. From a tag-end outsider, he was swept into the fold as the actress's companion, confidant and right-hand man. When he was not on board a train or on the stage, he found himself washing and nursing and feeding and walking a motley procession of rescued dogs. To make their teamwork more efficient, Mrs. Fiske suggested that Mr. Cook take hotel rooms next to her own. And in the late hours, when he was done with dogs for the day, he was kept awake by the tireless clatter of the actress's typewriter as she hammered out humane letters and speeches.

Often Donald Cook was inclined to think that the shortest way to the stage would have been through a school of veterinary medicine, but at rehearsals and in her traveling rescue mission for dogs, Mrs. Fiske made practical suggestions on the science of acting. Before the end of the tour, Donald Cook, the unknown beginner and the dogs' nurse, was regarded as one of the most promising young actors in America.

During the summer *The Rivals* toured the Far West. For the first time since the purchase of Camp Veery, Minnie was unable to vacation there, but she shared in the pleasure of those who could enjoy it. In August she wrote from Seattle:

Darling Boy,
  I am thrilled with all the wonderful news of Camp Veery! . . . I shall be so glad if you will decide to stay at Big Moose through the month of October, which is the most lovely month in the season. I feel deeply about this.
  Tomorrow I am writing you about the visit of a young girl who, if convenient, will arrive on August 28. When you have my letter telling about her visit, you will be more than glad to welcome her.
  I am so hopeful that Robbie and Ada will be able to come to the Camp, and if Robbie cannot, will it not be possible for Ada to come anyway? I tell you who I think would enjoy a visit, if you care to ask her, and that is Miss Norah McLaren, the real estate agent of 63 Washington Square South, but I do not urge it for a moment. She is kind, warm-hearted and genial. Also I know Carolyn would be much benefited by a little visit.
  I cannot tell you how delighted I am about the island, and I again repeat, do make every effort to remain through October. It is wonderful there then. Please do!

All news tomorrow.
Dearest love,
Bunner

A few days later she wrote enthusiastically from Walla Walla:

Darling Boy,
This is the most delicious thing you ever tasted! Do let Lizzie make it for you. Do not forget the large mustard seeds!

She enclosed a recipe for "Minnie Maddern Fiske Rarebit," invented by Mrs. Leotta Swanton. One of the important ingredients was Minnie's own combination of onions soaked in milk; it is suggested that she had collaborated on the recipe, as she had done on so many plays.

Minnie had never found a religion that met her exacting standards, but she had never given up trying. Her search had led in recent years to a study of spiritualism; on December 15, 1925, she wrote Harry from Salina, Kansas:

346

There really seems to be only one intelligent way to go about this Psychical research and that is first of all to read what the really big scientific men who have gone into these matters have to say of them. . . . There is humbug and fraud everywhere. But also there is truth. There is probably more fake and humbug connected with Psychical research and spiritualism than in any other department and it is perfectly obvious why this should be so. Grief, intense curiosity to know of the hereafter and indeed there are so many reasons that it makes it impossible to enumerate them . . .

. . . I know there is a life beyond this life and behind it. I have had three distinct proofs that cannot be disputed or argued aside. It is not a question whether one is interested in a future life or whether one cares to have a future life or wants it, the fact is that it is a fact and once recognized it does to a very great extent alter one's outlook . . .

After more than a year of touring, *The Rivals* was still far from home. Minnie had missed her vacation, and she had not seen Harry in many months; so it was arranged that he spend the Christmas holidays with her in St. Louis.

On December 26, after Harry's arrival, she received a glamorous Christmas present, via long distance. Frank Harling, of *Mis' Nelly of N'Orleans* fame, had made an opera of Mrs. Fiske's *A Light from St. Agnes*, and it had its premiere at the Chicago Civic Opera, with Rosa Raisa singing the role of Agnes.

Minnie's St. Louis engagement kept her from attending the premiere, but she and Harry heard it from their hotel by long distance telephone. Nearly thirty years earlier *A Light from St. Agnes* had been hailed as a classic which did for the one-act play what Bret Harte had done for the American short story. Now, with Harling's music, it was perhaps the first authentic American opera—American in authorship and setting, and in its music, spiced with jazz. Judging by the tumultuous reception, the great Chicago audience recognized it as an event. At the end, the storm of applause which came over the long distance phone was broken only by calls for the composer. When Frank Harling appeared on the stage, he received an ovation of alarming proportions. By the cadence of the applause, the curtain was lowered repeatedly, to be forced up each time by the increasing din . . .

"Miss Raisa has returned to the stage," the telephone voice reported. *"She is kissing Frank Harling . . ."* Presumably the kiss was intended to end the demonstration—but it increased to what sounded like a mob scene.

347

"The women of the audience are storming the stage," the voice interpreted. *"Mr. Harling has just escaped . . . Wait! The stage door must have been blocked. They are pursuing him through the corridor to the lobby! . . . He has escaped—No, the women have caught him! He is surrounded in the lobby. Several of them are trying to kiss him at once. Nothing like this ever happened here! Scores of women are crowding around to kiss Mr. Harling. . . ."*

After the smack-by-smack account over long distance, the tumult from the Chicago Civic Opera died down, and Minnie was informed that Frank Harling had been kissed by at least two hundred hysterical admirers.

More than anything else during her tour, that premiere bridged far-flung islands of Mrs. Fiske's life: from the New Orleans of her birth, to Little Rock where she had made her first stage appearance, to the play she had written as a bride in the 1890's, to the jazz age of the 1920's, in which millions of people had learned to live without ideals and drive without direction.

Later in the holiday season the Fiskes made a flying trip to Chicago for a performance of *A Light from St. Agnes.* The opera was again received enthusiastically, but the most tumultuous cheering Minnie heard in Chicago was in a street near the Loop. It was a spontaneous demonstration for Al Capone, glorified pimp, bootlegger and whole-sale murderer, who had become a hero of an age of spiritual anarchy.

CHAPTER 46

The epic *Rivals* company disbanded in the spring of 1926, an occasion which was recorded in a memorial document. Behind the scenes at the last stand, the stage carpenter took out the tools of writing and set down the following—in calligraphy which slanted alternately to right and left:

Mrs. Fiske.
March 6th 1926
Dear Madame;
We the crew in appreciation of your kindness, courtesy and consideration during our long and happy tour, cannot terminate it without our expression of good will and wishes to you.
May you live as long as you want and never want as long as you live.
H. H. Harris. Carpenter.
Johnson Electrician
A. S. Pearson.—Propertyman.

Along with letters from Lotta, Ellen Terry, George Cable, and others of the great, Minnie put the document away against the writing of her memoirs, which she had agreed to publish serially in the *Saturday Evening Post*.

In mid-June Minnie was free at last to go to Camp Veery. She went by way of Northampton, where she visited with Freddie Goodrow and family—Freddie, who had been such a convincing orphan in *Wake Up, Jonathan* that he was in constant danger of rescue by the Child Labor authorities.

During her stay at Northampton, Minnie was escorted to Smith College, where she donned a black robe and had a hood placed over her head as she received the honorary degree of Master of Arts. The degree was conferred on her as "the foremost living American actress."

349

Thereafter Minnie felt less inferiority in the presence of those who had attended college—but her happiest memories of Northampton centered around the Goodrows.

When her train pulled into the tiny station of Big Moose in the Adirondacks, her mind was still full of the visit. Waiting for her at the familiar station were Harry and an eager group of friends from camp. They greeted her with cries of, "Tell us about Smith! We want to hear all about Smith!"

Minnie thought they were under the impression that she had been visiting the family of the lost playwright, Harry James Smith. "I haven't been in Connecticut," she explained; "I've been at Northampton, and I had a delightful visit with the Goodrows. Freddie—"

"Minnie, the degree!" Harry broke in. "The degree from Smith College!"

"Oh!" She remembered, with comical surprise. "I didn't deserve it, but they gave it to me anyway." She told them briefly about the commencement exercises, but she kept interrupting her account to tell of things that had happened at the Goodrows'.

Summer at Camp Veery was another idyllic one, out of the unlimited supply of summers that would come to the island in the mountain lake. And if there was any catch in it, the only one who gave a visible sign was Boca, the fawn-colored bulldog that belonged to Harry, but loved Minnie more.

That summer Boca began hoarding. Every stick that was thrown to her, or used in a dog-against-human tug of war, she carried to a chosen spot. No stick without the authentic human touch plus her own would do. And however far away on the island a stick was thrown for her, she carried it back to add to her hoard. No visiting dog was allowed near her sacred sticks. And when she had been away from the island, her first rush would be to the heap of sticks; she would look them over, carefully, anxiously. Perhaps she would have known if one of them had been taken away—but no one touched them.

And after every romp and tussle a new stick was added to Boca's tangible record of great days with the people she loved.

Usually it was only when Boca had been away that she was seized with anxiety about the sticks, but sometimes during the day she would rush to the pile and examine it intently. The sticks were always as undisturbed as the woods and the shore and the lake that had no rise or fall of tide. But there was some power which Boca never trusted.

For Minnie, the summer of 1926 was like other enchanted summers at Camp Veery, even to the same old clothes—and the ever-recurrent new role to be studied. The success of *The Rivals* had decided her on other long-planned revivals of the classic comedies; but before the next one could be produced, she had to fill in with a soberer play.

Drifting in her boat or walking in the woods, Minnie studied the role of Mrs. Alving in Ibsen's *Ghosts*—much as she had studied Hedda Gabler while floating down the Rhine, and walking in neat German woods along the river. In those days Emily Stevens had accompanied her, or waited, sometimes impatiently, at a village inn.

The presence of Emily now would have added the final touch of perfection to summer. But Emily never came to Camp Veery. And Minnie no longer saw her in New York except when she went, heavily veiled, into the back of a theatre where Emily was starring and watched her brilliant, estranged cousin with loving pride and regret.

One element of their estrangement was professional. Minnie was too famous for Emily's comfort; and they had been too close for too long. Growing up on the stage with Mrs. Fiske, Emily had learned her cousin's method of acting and acquired some of her mannerisms. And critics found it easy to dwell on her limited resemblance to her cousin: like the time she had asserted her independence of Minnie—in exile on Staten Island—by playing Hedda Gabler. And a critic observed facetiously that Mrs. Fiske's only appearance on Broadway that season was Emily as Hedda.

The professional element was inescapable, but there was another estranging element growing out of Emily's dark moods which had touched her in childhood. They had shut out Minnie long before they had affected her devotion to Harry. After Emily had become a stranger to her cousin, Harry was still her friend, guide and advisor. At any hour of the day or night she might call him from her apartment, near Central Park West. "Boy, I have to talk to you; I need your help." And Harry would drop whatever business he had on hand, or leave whatever friends he was with, and go to her.

It was Minnie's last remaining contact with her cousin, and she did nothing to disturb it. Emily herself finally broke the bond. With the passing of time her summonses became more imperious. Once Harry found it impossible to drop everything, and explained the circumstances to Emily.

Her answer was, "It must be now, or never!"

Later the same evening he hurried to Central Park West and found her door closed and her telephone dead to him. He never saw Emily again, except as a stranger.

In the fall of 1926 when Minnie presented *Ghosts*, Ibsen's study of

351

hereditary syphilis, there was less protest than there had been over the wholesome and bracing *Pillars of Society*. Through the efforts of Mrs. Fiske, more than anyone else, Ibsen had become an accepted fact in America, and through the efforts of many others, sex a much-discussed one. While *Ghosts* toured the eastern states, New York was seeing *Sex, The Virgin Man,* and *The Captive*, with its exploration of lesbianism.

Ibsen was accepted in America, but he had never become popular. For half a century die-hards had resisted his plays as something new—and then they suddenly awoke to the fact that Ibsen belonged to history and was already old-fashioned. There had never been a period of slack water; all of Mrs. Fiske's Ibsen productions had been against the current, one way or the other. And, paradoxically, she had never failed to make money with them.

The paradox had something to do with Mrs. Fiske. In *Ghosts*, one of the elements of success was the almost hypnotic illusion of the "fourth wall," whereby audiences felt that they were seeing and hearing what went on in a room in Mrs. Alving's house, without anyone there for a moment suspecting their existence. Another element of success was the shrewd booking of engagements under the auspices of universities, drama groups and civic bodies.

The tide of time had set against the legitimate theatre no less than it had against Ibsen; motion pictures were engulfing the stage and the road—and Mrs. Fiske, who knew the terrain perhaps better than any other living person, toured dry-shod where others would have foundered.

With *The Rivals* she had committed herself to a series of revivals of great classical comedies; and for the next one she approximated the organization of a national theatre. For a nucleus of such a company, she now persuaded the superb actress, Margaret Anglin, to join forces with her, and she secured Otis Skinner as guest star.

The first production of the Fiske-Anglin Theatre was to be *The Merry Wives of Windsor*, with Mrs. Fiske and Miss Anglin as Mistress Page and Mistress Ford, and Otis Skinner as Falstaff. Like *The Rivals*, the play was strategically chosen: New York had not seen it in a decade, and it had not been on the road in an even longer time. Otis Skinner had appeared the season before as Falstaff in *Henry IV*, and his great success guaranteed his popularity as the fat knight in another play.

At the end of a triumphal New York engagement, Minnie toured through the northeastern states and Canada, more secure about her next season than she had been in years. The only discernible obstacle was Miss Anglin's temperament. On February 21, 1927, Minnie wrote from Chicago:

Darling Boy:
It is too bad that Miss Anglin has desired this long delay in announcing next seasons plans. However, announcements or no announcements, I know you will be firm in following Mr. Erlanger's advice to begin the booking for next season in a week or two . . . The crazy bookings of "The Rivals" cost us a fortune in railroad expenses. We cannot afford this risk in the much larger enterprise of the "Merry Wives."

But apart from all this there must come a time before many weeks when we should make a very earnest request to Miss Anglin that the announcements may be made . . . I am in close personal and friendly touch with Mrs. Sherman, President of the Women's Federation and Mrs. Maud Parks a most powerful woman in the League of Women Voters. Thousands of women are more or less directly under the leadership of these women. I know if I were to write a personal letter to these women, explaining just what our new enterprise is to be both these women would personally read the letter at their respective conventions. . . . To get the full value of our message (or even to get it in at all) it would be necessary to get it to these women not later than the latter part of March. . . . Miss Anglin seems to be by far the best choice for our new enterprise but if she is to be freaky and dissatisfied (as she has been so far) putting stumbling blocks on our way—it might be better to have an understanding with her before long. . . .

In April, Miss Anglin relented, and Harry Fiske released the waiting announcement. The next day he followed it up in greater detail:

From Press Department
FISKE-ANGLIN THEATRE
66 West 11th St. New York City
A plan that has been germinating for some time has reached fruition in the formation of the Fiske-Anglin Theatre, a permanent dramatic organization that is headed by Mrs. Fiske and Margaret Anglin and that will begin operation on an extensive scale next season . . . it will be a migratory institution, not national in name but national in that its offerings will be taken to all sections of the United States. . . .

353

The announcement had been widely distributed when Miss Anglin withdrew from the venture. The Fiske-Anglin Theatre had lived only long enough to embarrass its founder. But Mrs. Fiske had her play for the next season, with Otis Skinner as a co-star. She added Henrietta Crosman to the nucleus of the *Merry Wives* company, and went on with her plans.

The same week in April brought a letter to Mrs. Fiske from President Glenn Frank of the University of Wisconsin, requesting her presence at the seventy-fourth commencement, when she was to be awarded an honorary degree for her services to the American stage. Minnie wired her acceptance.

The actress's visit to the university was a red-letter day for her official hosts, Professor and Mrs. Eugene H. Byrne. In 1900, when Byrne was a sophomore, he had seen Mrs. Fiske as Becky. The result was something he later described as an infatuation never to be lost. In his undergraduate years he went without meals and made long pilgrimages to see Mrs. Fiske whenever she was playing within traveling distance. In 1916, when he was back at the University of Wisconsin, married and a member of the faculty, he usefully delayed an appearance of the actress at Madison. Her company was billed for an engagement which corresponded with the annual visit of the Chicago Opera Company; Professor Byrne wired her to that effect, thereby saving her from a fiasco. The exchange of telegrams led to an exchange of letters, though it was not until Mrs. Fiske's tour in *Ghosts* that the two met.

The only other woman to receive an honorary degree at the seventy-fourth commencement was Maude Adams. Minnie might well have wondered why the actress who had broken herself in the long war with the Theatre Trust and the actress who had thriven as the darling of the Trust, alike, should come to the same platform at the same time to receive identical honors—but if she thought of it at all, she attributed it to the unworldly nature of college presidents and professors. Actually it was the result of a mix-up, and there were red faces at Madison. Professor Byrne writes:

> Glenn Frank was eager to have an actress included, and the name of Miss Maude Adams was proposed. Since she had long since abandoned the stage, it seemed to me questionable thus to belatedly honor her at Wisconsin where she had never in my memory appeared at all. I spoke for Mrs. Fiske, but was outvoted because it was evident that Glenn was for Miss Adams. The President was therefore authorized to send an invitation to Miss A. Weeks passed,

354

and no reply was received. Another vote, and Mrs. Fiske's name went through without opposition. An invitation went forth, but to the consternation of the president, and to the amusement of me and the others, Mrs. Fiske accepted by telegram, and almost at the same time came a delayed letter from Miss Adams, accepting the honor. Glenn and the University had two actresses on hand. Glenn settled it this way: as the escort and host of Mrs. F. it was for me to say to her that she would be given the post of honor by having her degree conferred last. At the same time Miss Adams' escort, Professor James Frances Augustine Pyre, was told to tell Miss A. that she would be given the post of honor, first on the list. We did as we were told, comparing notes before and after . . .

In a letter to Harry, Minnie described her first meeting with Maude Adams:

As we approached we saw the long procession forming. When we reached the spot there was dear little Maude Adams (we were to march one behind the other). She grasped my hand and said in her little halting way, "This is much more terrible than a first night—isn't it?"—I said "No!"

And her great moment:

In a serious tone President Frank called "Minnie Maddern Fiske" and I advanced with trembling knees. And he drew an entirely different picture for me. In effect that we now turned directly away from the world of fancies and whimsies and dreams and fantasy where Miss Adams lived, to the great realities. He said at the last:
"Because you have guarded the sacred flame of quality in a theatre threatened by quantity production, because you have dared to lead the crowd where others were content to follow it, I am happy to confer upon you the honorary degree of Doctor of Letters."
It was so eloquent and so deeply impressive! He's a great speaker and I guess a great man. He may be president some day. They think so, here. I went back to the hotel after it was over and got ready for the dinner given by President and Mrs. Frank—That too—was delightful. A very large gathering. President Frank took Miss Adams in to dinner and Governor Zimmerman took me. Do remind me at Big Moose to tell you how amusing the Governor was and President Frank too. I met Zona Gale and we became very friendly. Miss Adams and I expect to meet here. She lives nearby. I'll tell you more of the charming day at Madison—Save this letter Boy—to refresh my memory for our great book.
The long journey back and forth did me up—I was exhausted when

355

I got to Cinnie's and when I feel a little ill I always get a little upset and foolishly "panicky" about "responsibilities." I am so sorry that I wrote in a way that tho I did not mean it so, I suddenly felt you might think I was sort of sermonizing. But just remember, Boy, that I was really quite broken up by the four long days—on the train and the terrific heat. But there should never be a word from me—darling Boy—even if I was a little ill—while you have been harassed in the city such a long time and I have been in the lovely country. It will be wonderful to get to Big Moose. No peace like that . . . Don't let Bokie go down to her sticks until I come. I want to see if she remembers at once.

Devoted love darling Boy
Bunner

CHAPTER 47

In the fall of 1927, Mrs. Fiske returned at last to Shakespeare. At the age of three she had made her stage debut as the Duke of York. Soon afterward, as the Crowned Child, she had admonished Barry Sullivan to "heed not where perspirers are"; and at eight, as Prince Arthur, she had won honors with the Booths and John McCullough.

After that promising beginning, nearly sixty years had passed without Minnie's playing another Shakespearean role. To some degree it had been a matter of chance. For more than a decade she had planned a production of *Macbeth*, but neither of her choices for the title role —Tyrone Power and Otis Skinner—had been available at the right time.

The fall of 1927 finally found Mrs. Fiske and Otis Skinner rehearsing together in Shakespeare—not as the Macbeths, but as Mistress Page and Falstaff, with Henrietta Crosman as Mistress Ford, in *The Merry Wives of Windsor*. Minnie was the only one of the three who had not appeared in Shakespeare in recent times; but her mind and her art were as flexible as they had been in youth. When her individualistic style of speech did not fit the play, she put it aside like a stage costume and spoke within the limits of Shakespeare's blank verse. In her own modern style of acting she had swayed audiences with a barely-perceptible gesture, but the subtle, watched-for gesture did not go with Mistress Page; when she thought of some piece of deviltry to use on Falstaff, she indicated him with a twinkle while her bare hands slapped her stomach in a way that made the audience roar with laughter; she crawled about under tables on her hands and knees, kicked the rears of prostrate page boys, and thumbed her nose at sundry persons with an Elizabethan gusto.

Harry Fiske's first glimpse of Minnie Maddern had been brought about by his fondness for Shakespeare—a fondness he never lost. *The Merry Wives* was his first Shakespearean production, and he threw

357

himself into it with enthusiasm. He rearranged the text so skillfully that no scholar complained of the liberties; he highlighted the spirit of prank, and staged the play almost too magnificently—with solid stage-sets that were beautiful but heavy; they delayed the shifting of scenes and slowed the play.

It was some time since Shakespeare had been known as a money-maker on the stage; and the Fiskes, who could not afford to lose, were burdened with a cast of forty and a massive production. However, a lively Shakespearean revival with great actors was an event, and Minnie —with her knowledge of the road and her influence with women's clubs and civic groups—was confident of success.

At Minnie's insistence *The Merry Wives* opened out of town. So the official premiere was at Philadelphia on the evening of October 31, 1927; actually the play was launched several hours earlier at the Bellevue-Stratford Hotel.

The opening date was the golden anniversary of Otis Skinner's marriage to the stage. At the luncheon preceding the opening, Mr. Skinner was honored by representatives from every cultural group in Philadelphia—from the Art Alliance to the University of Pennsylvania's English Department. Mr. Skinner's non-stage marriage was honored, too, by the presence of Mrs. Skinner and their gifted daughter, Cornelia; and the play was honored, with Mr. and Mrs. Fiske and Henrietta Crosman at the speakers' table. Horace Howard Furness, editor of the *Variorum Shakespeare*, was master of ceremonies.

During the luncheon it developed that the instigator of that great array of American culture was the late showman, P. T. Barnum. Exactly fifty years before, Mr. Skinner recalled, he had arrived in Philadelphia, equipped only with his ambition and inexperience, and a letter of introduction from Barnum, who was a parishioner of the elder Skinner's New England church. The letter vouched for the young man's moral qualities rather than his acting ability, but it brought him a job at the Philadelphia Museum where, in a Barnum atmosphere of stuffed animals and live actors, Davidge ran a theatre known as the Snake Shop. The patience of the stuffed animals was held up as an example to the young actor when he asked for his eight-dollar-a-week salary—but the job led to an association with the Drews, around the nearby corner—and to fame.

It was the great Barnum, too, who had awakened Harry Fiske's passion for the theatre. Without him, the gathering of culture and the revival of *The Merry Wives* would hardly have happened.

That evening at the Broad Street Theatre, the Philadelphia triumph of *The Merry Wives* was underscored by New York. Twenty members of the Players' Club had come in honor of Otis Skinner's anniversary, and after the final curtain they led an ovation that did not end until there had been speeches by Mr. Skinner, by Mrs. Fiske and by Miss Crosman.

News of the success in Philadelphia sped ahead of the play. In Washington, D. C., on November 21, theatregoers in a queue blocks long stood in the rain all day, waiting to buy tickets.

In her days of proud and uncompromising art, Minnie had observed that if an actor was applauded, he had only himself to blame. In changed times and Shakespearean slapstick, she cultivated every niche where laughter or applause could be induced to grow. On the road she wrote Harry:

> The most valuable part of the Ford scene when he throws the linen about the stage is the throwing of the linen as high as possible toward the ceiling. The comic effect is because very often the large pieces of linen become inflated if they are thrown high enough to the ceiling and the drawers and nightgowns come sailing down filled with wind and it looks awfully funny . . . I added a few more pieces of underwear.

She continued to rely on diplomacy in dealing with her company:

> Sometimes lately the little dance that Miss Crosman, myself and little Robin do at the end of the first Ford scene does not have the same electric effect it always used to have. The reason is that Miss Crosman frequently ends the dance and drops our hands sooner than she used to and so the merry effect of going round and round is not definite. I do not care to speak to Miss Crosman about it and I wish you would speak to her as if you had noticed the change yourself. To get the proper spirit and go into it we should keep on going round and round even if the curtains have closed . . .

The timetable of the *Merry Wives* tour provided for a week's layoff so that most members of the cast could be home for Christmas, or Christmas Eve—depending on how far they lived from Chicago, where the play opened on December 26. Minnie planned to use her fragment of a week resting at the home of friends at Mount Vernon —with a snatch of home Christmas.

Harry had already set his heart on another Shakespeare comedy for the following season. But *The Merry Wives* that had started so

359

profitably was having its first losing week, and Minnie was in a cautious mood. On December 8 she wrote from Buffalo:

> Darling Boy:
> I have received your letter about "Much Ado About Nothing" and the copy of the play. I think it best to put off the reading of the play until the week after next when I am at the Farm . . . It is always so peaceful there with no interruptions and then I can get the best line on it. I shall leave right after the play Saturday night arriving in New York at five Sunday afternoon. Shall I come right to your apartment and have dinner with you? Afterwards I can go out to the Farm. If convenient for you I think it would be very nice to have a little Christmas celebration at your apartment on Friday Dec. 23 for Bolie and Catherine. Of course we will not go in for a large tree as we did last year. We can have a little one and the children will enjoy it just as much.
> I do hope you will be able to have Mr. Enrico do over your apartment sometime during the winter! It is so pretty now with the lovely new furniture, but it does look sort of grimy.
> I am glad we did not dismiss Miss B. I have been watching the second act ensemble carefully and she is a distinct note of value. On the other hand Miss B2 contributes nothing in that ensemble and could be dropped out without any loss whatever. From what I gather Miss B2 is prosperously placed in the world. . . . I don't urge this, I only ask you to take it under consideration as it is right for us to curtail all expenses that can be curtailed without injury to the beauty of the scene. . . .

Minnie had made it part of her humane work to keep presidents, and their wives, and heroes from setting bad examples, In mid-December she wrote Harry concerning the hero of the hour, whose every move was followed by idolatrous millions:

> The Humane Societies throughout the country have had a terrific few days forestalling any attempt on the part of the Mexicans to get Lindbergh to attend a Bull Fight. We are very hopeful that we have succeeded in preventing something that would have dealt the heaviest blow to the Anti-Bullfight Movement ever known. I was obliged to contribute $191.00 toward the fund for telegrams and cables from the money left me by Mr. Ensign. Please do not mention anything about this as it all has to be kept secret for diplomatic reasons.

In the same letter, Minnie concluded plans for Harry to spend New Year's Day with her.

Harry was waiting for her in Chicago, where Minnie had reserved rooms at her favorite old Virginia Hotel. Her room, with a view of the soap factory, was part of the suite she had shared in earlier days with Aunt Mary Maddern and young Emily Stevens. Aunt Mary, sitting at this window, grumbling to herself—snapping into rare spoken words at some teasing from Emily: "Don't talk to me about going to my reward! I'll go to my rest. Rest is all the reward I want."

Emily, standing at this same window, considering the great soap factory in the April rain: "A sight fit to wash away the sins of the world!"

Emily had wearied of trouping while she was still young. As an established star, she would visit only a few of the larger cities, and more recently, she would not leave Broadway at all. Perhaps the memory of the road had caused part of the break with her older cousin, who had mothered and still loved her. But not all of it. From childhood she had loved Harry best; and now even he could not break through her wall of deathly silence.

The old year ended with Saturday. That night, writing memoranda about ways to improve the production and pinning them to her flannel nightgown, Minnie did not even pause for the outburst of auto horns and sirens that escorted 1928 into the icy streets of the city. Her ears were stuffed with cotton.

On Monday, after the evening performance, Minnie was handed a telegram with an impersonal, stunning message from a stranger: Emily Stevens had died a few hours before. Would Mrs. Fiske please send instructions for her funeral?

The stern discipline of the road continued to separate the cousins in death. Minnie stayed with the play, while Harry rushed back to New York.

He was on his way when the morning papers carried the details of Emily's death. The morning of New Year's Day the maid had found Emily unconscious in the freezing living room of her apartment. Miss Stevens, who had been under treatment for a nervous condition, had taken an overdose of sleeping tablets. She had apparently roused herself and attempted to close the wide-open windows looking toward her beloved Central Park, and she had collapsed on the floor in a thin nightgown. She had been taken to a hospital, where she died of pneumonia without regaining consciousness.

Harry reported from New York. He had seen to Emily's funeral and cremation, and was settling her affairs and paying her debts. In

Minnie's name and his own, he did all that parents could have done for a child they had loved. There was rumor about a bogus doctor who had enslaved Emily by making her a drug addict—but nothing could be proved, and the supposed doctor had vanished.

The Merry Wives continued on its tour—west as far as Omaha, south to Louisville, north to Toronto, and east to New York—playing profitable engagements and losing ones. There were minor annoyances:

Our lights are often blatant and glary. They tell me it is because the current is stronger in some places and it can't be helped. I do not know the whys and wherefores, but I do know if you can get for New York and Boston the same deep mellow light we had in Cincinnati it will be of immense help . . .

Later she wrote, half wistfully:

The scenery will need touching up for New York, and the sunflowers are getting very mangy. I wish we could have a couple more sunflowers. Possibly in front of Mrs. Page's house. And I do wish we could have a lilac bush somewhere in the street scene.

Through it all there was Emily, whom Minnie would not give up as lost:

You know that for years I have been interested in Psychical Research. I have been going along sanely and reasonably. I am not one to be deluded. Emily's death affected me so deeply that after the first shock was over my investigations became more intense than ever before. When I tell you of what has developed the past weeks you will be I know deeply interested and perhaps astounded . . . The day will come when all these things that seem supernatural now will seem perfectly natural. . . .
I sought out Booth Tarkington when I was in Indianapolis. I knew that Booth Tarkington had been for years engaged in Psychical Research investigations. Mr. Tarkington came to the hotel and spent several hours with me and never have I experienced such a mental experience. You could not have been long in the presence of Booth Tarkington and not recognize his mind is extraordinarily fine and strong. Mr. Tarkington's sister was a medium. No one knew this outside the family and a few close friends. . . . What he told me of the history of his investigations will certainly astound you. Mr. Tarkington has proved beyond all doubt what many of us are beginning to understand—that there is no death as many people conceive death—and that this life is but a small fraction of the big—universal existence . . . later in Cincinnati in making further investi-

gations I have had some experiences that now at this time seem extraordinary, but which really are not . . .

Harry, the confirmed agnostic, never accepted his wife's proofs; but she at least believed that after Emily's death she had cracked the barrier of silence which she had been unable to penetrate in the last years of Emily's lifetime.

CHAPTER 48

Late in May, 1928, *The Merry Wives of Windsor* company disbanded, and one of the scattering cast wrote in farewell:

Dear Mr. Fiske,

Before I go abroad to France tonight I want to send you my cordial good wishes and my thanks for one of the most delightful and harmonious seasons I have ever known.

To say what I think of Mrs. Fiske would be to run into more superlatives than I should soberly use. She will always remain a joyous theme with me.

To you both I send my adieus and gratitude.

Faithfully yours
Otis Skinner

The "harmonious season" had been a modest triumph for Minnie. *The Merry Wives* was an artistic success that added a few thousand dollars to the Fiskes' late-maturing nest egg. That season, with the legitimate theatre receding before the onrush of motion pictures, other producers had done worse with the works of more currently popular playwrights.

That summer, in the quiet of Camp Veery, Minnie listened to the echoes of the presidential campaign. In true American tradition, both candidates—Herbert Hoover and Alfred E. Smith—had started life in humble circumstances—to meet at last in a spirited contest with only one discernible issue. The lone issue was one the actress considered important, and on September 18 she entered the battle:

Mr. Franklin D. Roosevelt,
Chairman, National Democratic Committee
General Motors Building,
Broadway & 57th Street,
New York City.

Dear Mr. Roosevelt:

This year, for the first time, circumstances will permit me to participate in a presidential election . . . My vote will be cast for Governor Smith.

Governor Smith has brought Prohibition into the limelight . . . He knows what millions of us know, that Prohibition has proved not only a ghastly failure but has become a national curse, bringing upon us appalling intemperance, increase in crime, wholesale official corruption and general contempt of law, besides covering us with obloquy and making us ridiculous in the eyes of the civilized world.

Sincerely yours,
Minnie Maddern Fiske

The Committee was delighted with the forthright declaration, but someone could not resist tampering with it and Minnie protested to Harry:

Today I shall wire you to be firm in not permitting the Democratic headquarters to change one word of my statement. (Of course you are free to cut or add anything you think best—but not anyone else.)—I did not like the cheap, common way they made me speak in their making over my statement—so please make them understand in all kindness & courtesy that I wish the statement to go in as I have written it—exactly—word for word and not a word changed—I know you will copy the statement to make it clean, clear and unmistakable. . . .

Republicans, too, were making hay; Minnie found herself publicized as supporting Mr. Hoover. On October 24 she wrote the director of the Authors', Actors' and Artists' League for Smith:

Mr. Owen Johnson,
Room 247, Hotel Biltmore,
New York City.
Dear Mr. Johnson:

In yesterday's newspaper account of Mr. Hoover's reception by the Republican Theatrical Committee my name was mentioned among those attending, and previously it had been used in announcing the organization's membership. This use of my name was unwarranted. A fortnight ago I was invited to join and in declining I explained that I was an enthusiastic supporter of Governor Smith and had already identified myself with the Authors, Actors and Artists League for Smith.

Sincerely yours
Minnie Maddern Fiske

While Minnie defended herself from foes and friends bent on winning, a few voices cried in the wilderness that there were issues to be faced, issues spawned by eight years of isolation from world affairs, inflation, and an orgy of stock-market gambling. The prophets convinced almost no one but themselves, but there were many takers for the prediction that if Governor Smith were elected president he would bring the Pope to America.

In answer to the new outcry, Minnie expanded her statement:

> The Catholic Church has never for one moment interfered in the present campaign. It is sad to say that portions of the Protestant Church (to which I belong and to which my forefathers belonged for centuries) have interfered with a bigotry that belongs to the Dark Centuries. These self-styled religionists are actually doing what they profess to fear would be done if Governor Smith became our president. . . .

The Authors', Actors' and Artists' League for Smith was one of the largest arrays of talent ever rallied to the support of a candidate. Its 160 sponsors included Ernestine Schumann-Heink, Bud Fisher, Ellery Sedgwick, Anita Loos, Elmer Davis, George Gershwin, H. L. Mencken, Brand Whitlock and Jerome Kern.

The climax of the League's activities was a two-hour rally at the Ambassador Theatre in New York early in November. Minnie was touring in New England; but the radio made absence a relative matter, and she heard the program in her hotel room in Springfield.

So much talent had turned out in support of Governor Smith that the rally had four chairmen: Wilton Lackaye, Marc Connelly, Dan Healey and Heywood Broun. Favored speakers like Irvin Cobb and Augustus Thomas were limited to ten minutes; and one minute or two were allotted to such personages as Eddie Cantor, Alma Gluck and Deems Taylor.

After the speeches, the relay team of chairmen read statements and telegrams from all over the United States. Minnie's statement was the first read and the most wildly applauded. The earnest convert to political duty had spent days on it, trying to make up in one burst for the years when she might have battled for the right to vote or, having the vote, made use of it.

CHAPTER 49

That fall the Fiskes produced *Much Ado About Nothing*. The hit of the entertainment season was Al Jolson's *The Jazz Singer*, historic as the first talking picture and symptomatic in its theme.

A Yale psychologist had just proved that jazz made logical thinking difficult—and a commentator in tune with the times had dismissed the findings with four words: "Who wants to think?"

More exciting activities were available. One of them turned on the discovery that everyone could get rich by buying stocks on margin, and selling them at constantly rising prices.

With their life savings, or borrowed money, millions of Americans were gambling—paying $150 for a share of stock in a motor-car company with one small factory in Indiana, and selling at $155—to see the stock rise to $160. And like teachers egging their pupils on in dangerous games, the President and the Secretary of the Treasury issued periodic statements that the buying of stocks was sound and credit was not overstrained.

There had been one warning sign. Calvin Coolidge had not chosen to run—passing the chairmanship of the mad frolic on to Herbert Hoover. But that decision seemingly came from a chill presentiment in New England bones—not from statistics on savings melting out of banks and factories operating at a loss, producing goods which no one bought.

In that year of the lurid light in the American sky, the Fiskes were among the conservative who had money in the bank and did not gamble in the stock market. Minnie was against all chance-taking, and Harry's only speculation was in the theatre. With *The Rivals* and *The Merry Wives*, a good share of the proceeds had gone to outside backers. In *Much Ado*, Harry saw the opportunity to gather all the profits and make a modest killing.

Minnie questioned whether, in her sixties, she was suited to the role of the youthful Beatrice; and she was opposed to their taking all the risk. The national climate of speculation had stirred no gambling blood in her, but it helped weaken her resistance to the one gamble Harry urged. Two successful revivals had paved the way for a third, and all that remained was for them to harvest the profits. It was a sure thing.

But Harry had never been a businessman.

The one play of Harry's life which had created the perfect illusion was Barnum's *Joseph and His Brethren*, seen through the eyes of a young child. For him *Much Ado* was one more opportunity—perhaps the last—to realize that perfection.

He was even more generous of his time than he had been with the *Merry Wives*, working out the acting version, and reducing the six rambling acts and innumerable scenes to four closely knit acts. *Much Ado* had previously been set and costumed in Tudor or Elizabethan style. With excited and loving research, Harry restored the play to Messina of 1530, with Renaissance Italian architecture and glorious Renaissance costumes; he lavished thousands of dollars on details which not one spectator in a thousand would notice.

Minnie was as prodigal-minded in selecting a cast as Harry was with staging and costuming. She wrote Harry:

> Unless "Much Ado" could be superbly cast I feel we should not produce it. It is not the sort of thing you could scamper through as one can with "The Merry Wives" or "The Rivals." It demands high and noble art, with plenty of time for the careful selection of actors. We should be able to do it perfectly. There is the problem of "Benedict." I have heard that Sothern does play "Benedict" well. I might induce him to do so. What do you think of the idea? . . . For "Hero" we should have one of the most celebrated of the young actresses. What about Helen Hayes or Fay Bainter? Would not Sydney Greenstreet be a good "Dogberry?" "Dogberry," "Pedro," "Leonato" and the "Friar" are magnificent roles. They seem to be as good as either "Beatrice" or "Benedict." The finest sort of actors would have to be engaged to play these parts, one or two of them stars or actors of celebrity if possible. These parts have great scenes which I do not think have ever been properly brought out. So far as I can learn everything has been concentrated on "Beatrice" and "Benedict" and the rest neglected . . . We should be able to reveal the play more truly and beautifully than it has ever been revealed. . . .

Of the actors suggested, they were only able to secure Sydney Greenstreet, and his superb Dogberry justified the selection. Among the others, Ian Maclaren was Benedict to Mrs. Fiske's Beatrice; Charles Dalton, Leonato; Geoffrey Wardwell, Claudio; and Betty Linley, Hero.

It was not quite the cast of Minnie's dream, but it swelled the cost of the production. In the first precarious days on tour, Minnie wrote Harry:

May I draw a check to pay Mrs. Campbell's bill for corsets? This bill should be paid for good reasons which I shall tell you when I see you. Please let me know at once. We must economize in every way and guard every dollar at this time as the bills will press. . . .

With the bills pressing, *Much Ado About Nothing* opened its first important engagement at the Hollis Street Theatre in Boston on November 19. On the opening night Minnie received violets, with a note of good wishes signed, "Your faithful old friend, C. T. Copeland."

Later, Copey gave her his written opinion of the production: the best all-around performance of any play of Shakespeare's that he had seen in many a long year; a brilliant presentation, and to an uncommon degree, pleasing to the eye and ear and mind.

Minnie was counting heavily on support from universities and civic groups; for publicity purposes she prefaced the statement with the comment:

Professor Charles T. Copeland of Harvard, perhaps the most famous and popular professor of English literature in this country, affectionately called by the students and graduates "Copey," saw "Much Ado About Nothing" and wrote as follows. . .

Copeland had written the statement for Mrs. Fiske's use; but he questioned if it would be of any great help. And he shook his head over the introduction. There had been a time, he said, when students were hungry for the classics—but at the moment they were more interested in swallowing live goldfish. And now he lived alone at Sanders Hall. Students still lived there and some of them, he supposed, had intellectual pursuits other than reversing the story of Jonah and the whale. But, mostly, their minds were closed notebooks to him, and his mind was a book they did not bother to open.

Much of it might have been Copey's habitual mournfulness—but no great support for the production came from the universities or anywhere else. On December 11, Minnie wrote from Springfield, Massachusetts:

> Darling Boy
> The play went so superbly to-night even tho' the audience was small that I have great hopes of Philadelphia. . .

The hope seemed justified.

With the new year, *Much Ado* opened at the almost-filled Chestnut Street Theatre; it was praised by the critics, and night after night the audiences were reassuringly large. But the bills still pressed.

Harry had come to Philadelphia to see the turning of the tide—and he stayed to find out why it appeared to be standing still. When he had finished his bookkeeping, he brought Minnie the results. Two columns of figures came within a few dollars of balancing. One represented the irreducible expenses of the production; the other, the receipts from the big theatre with every seat sold.

Harry had gambled all they owned on a production so expensive that it could never repay a dollar of the fortune sunk in it.

On the last nights of *Much Ado* Mrs. Fiske's performances continued almost flawless, but she was conscious of every empty seat in the theatre. There were not many—but every one was a wound through which her last hope bled to death.

When the production closed in mid-January, it had lost the Fiskes approximately a hundred thousand dollars. They had nothing left but mortgaged Camp Veery.

Minnie had no time for a backward look; but for Harry *Much Ado* recaptured the perfect illusion of Barnum's long-ago spectacle. It remained the artistic achievement of his theatre-struck life.

CHAPTER 50

Long ago Edward Sheldon had written a play for Emily, a tender and wistful dramatization of Hans Christian Andersen's *The Little Mermaid*. It ended with the Mermaid—with Emily—one of the Daughters of the Air; not dead and not immortal but developing a soul in the limbo between earth and heaven—the limbo from where Minnie sometimes heard from her through mediums.

Ned Sheldon, too, now lived at the twilight edge of the world. When Minnie called on him in his New York apartment, she found him a beautiful sculptured face, with marble-white hair, above sculptured bedclothes. A face, and a voice that never referred to the blindness and paralysis which had overtaken him.

He talked of world events which he heard over his radio; of current books and plays, and of friends who called on him. More rarely, he spoke of the great production of *Salvation Nell* which had lifted him to fame. But he no longer spoke of writing another play for Mrs. Fiske.

If he had written a last play for her—if he had drawn on Hans Christian Andersen, as he had done for Emily—it would most fittingly have been *The Red Shoes*.

In another century, in the snug little house on Seventy-first Street, Minnie Maddern Fiske had chosen to give up the slippers of domesticity for the red shoes of the stage, thinking she would be able to take them off when she tired. She had tired long ago; but she had never been able to take off the red shoes.

For thirty-five years she had danced over America, in great theatres, and in burlesque houses, and in churches; in far-northern skating rinks under the midnight sun; in tar-paper halls in the southwest desert; in the great Brussels ballroom behind the Denver Theatre with the Rocky Mountain winter howling through the set and snow shifting over the fair women and brave men. She had danced her married life away in

371

far-off places while Harry lived among strangers. She had danced through *The Merry Wives* in Chicago while Emily lay dead in New York.

Many times she had told herself that she could soon take off the red shoes, but something always intervened—the twelve-year war with the Theatrical Trust, bankruptcy, the expensive failure of a production, the expensive purchase of Camp Veery. At the start of *Much Ado*, she had planned her last season on the stage; at its end, she foresaw that the red shoes would never come off while she was alive.

Disaster only quickened Minnie's tempo. While the ruins were being cleared away, she assembled another cast and worked furiously on a revival of *Mrs. Bumpstead-Leigh*.

Harry had finally lost the producing of her plays, and she passed to the management of George Tyler, the man she and Harry had once brought to Broadway—a green beginner from Chillicothe, Ohio. The revival of *Mrs. Bumpstead-Leigh* was swept together in a matter of days, and Mrs. Fiske continued her tour almost without interruption.

Two of Mrs. Fiske's recent productions had never been seen on Broadway: her superb *Rivals*, and her too-superb *Much Ado*. They had never been seen there because she feared the unpredictable New York critics, particularly Heywood Broun, with his power of destruction.

Minnie feared the rough-and-ready showmanship of Mr. Tyler, but she had no say. And on April Fool's Day, 1929, she was pitchforked onto the stage of the Klaw Theatre in New York, with a thrown-to-gether cast in a dated farce.

On that desperate night, Minnie drew on every comedy resource of her sixty years on the stage. She played on her audience like a virtuoso, but she had no illusions about winning over the critics. And after the performance she returned, tired and discouraged, to a hotel room in Brooklyn.

On the rainy and gusty day after, she resolutely opened the New York *Telegram* and read Heywood Broun's review:

> Mrs. Fiske did much last night to lay a ghost which has long per-sisted. At the Klaw Theatre George Tyler revived "Mrs. Bumpstead-Leigh," by Harry James Smith.
> Mrs. Fiske was in no need of a revival. There never has been any good reason why her acting should be haunted. And yet strange wraiths and fallacies cluster around her playing. The curious notion obtains that she is an exotic performer and almost the goddess of the little theatre movement.

In solid fact she is a veteran trouper capable of winning the warm approval of the Elks and Eagles. She can mug and clown with the best of them. Last night she did.

But it would not be fair to let it go at that. Over and above a rabble-rousing performance, which included mild apoplexies for the comic effect, she added certain nice touches which lift competence into something higher.

I wonder why the impression ever got abroad that she was the best girl of the merely intellectual. Probably Ibsen deserves the blame. Because Mrs. Fiske has done him frequently some part of the public opinion has assigned her to a place among the difficult up-lifters.

That is not fair to Mrs. Fiske. It isn't fair to Ibsen. When he has been dead for another hundred years realization will come that he was just as good a showman as David Belasco or Morris Gest. . . .

Occasionally one could hear an interpreter last night explaining to his companion, "She says, 'How are you?' " but the fact that a word or two is lost in transmission does not rob the performance of its values. Perhaps it heightens them.

I would rather hear twenty-five percent of Mrs. Fiske's speeches than get a full hundred percent from any other actress. . . .

That from Heywood Broun, who had more than once made New York seem too hazardous a place for her to appear on the stage!

The other critics did even better; and George Tyler, who had produced well over a hundred and fifty plays, was moved to make a unique statement to the press: "In an experience covering a period of over thirty-five years in theatrical management, the presentation of this play is the first under my direction to bring forth an absolutely united set of overwhelmingly enthusiastic press reviews."

By the grace of genius and a lifetime spent in acquiring skill, Minnie had reconquered New York with a broken sword; *Mrs. Bumpstead-Leigh* served her to the end of the season. By then she had a suitable play.

The new play was *Ladies of the Jury* by Fred Ballard, author of the successes *Believe Me, Xantippe* and *Young America.*

Ladies of the Jury was a slight play. But it had an idea—the role of a New Jersey society matron, serving on a jury for the first time. In the course of three acts, the blundering but common-sense woman talked her eleven associates into changing their verdict from a murder conviction to an acquittal, bringing justice out of the machinery of the law.

Ladies of the Jury was generously staged, and in the brilliant cast Mrs. Fiske found one of her associates from Minnie Maddern days— Wilton Lackaye, who had made a hit as the jealous Portuguese noble- man in *Featherbrain*. A few years later he had created the role of Svengali in *Trilby*, one of the greatest successes in stage history.

The theme of *Featherbrain* had been that women were created to amuse their husbands—the emptier their heads, the greater the mutual happiness. In a long step from that view of the Eighties, Wilton Lackaye and Minnie Maddern met again, in an age where women had begun to serve on juries in murder trials.

In the first act of *Ladies of the Jury*, Lackaye as the Judge and Min- nie as the twelfth juror struck brilliant sparks from each other; the fireworks of the two great virtuosos lingered over the rest of the play— audiences never guessed that age and illness had impaired Lackaye's memory, and the old maestro read each spontaneous-seeming line from a script on his judge's desk.

The play opened in Atlantic City and played at Baltimore and Boston before coming to New York on October 21, 1929. It was still early enough in the season for a Broadway failure to be disastrous, but Tyler was confident, even in the face of seven other openings on the same evening.

The Erlanger Theatre was sold out for the premiere, and that night there was the most impressive parade of motor cars seen in the theatre district that fall. More than impressive, it was historic. Events of the following days were to discourage a repetition for years to come—and when their effects finally wore off, changing conditions made it more practicable to go to theatres by taxi. The parade marked the end of an era.

It began before eight and went on for three-quarters of an hour—a softly-gleaming, slow torrent of cars, with muted motors, gliding up to the entrance of the Erlanger; pausing and gliding on: Hispano- Suizas, Isotta-Fraschinis, Mercedeses, Duesenbergs, Fiats, Rolls-Royces, and an occasional self-conscious Cadillac or Packard. Out of the cars as they came to a stop there hatched the great of New York society and business, their wives and friends and daughters—in evening dress, in furs and jewels and knee-length silk and transparent velvet. The most fortunate of the daughters were escorted by dispossessed princes and mothy counts—the dream of American heiresshood.

It was more than the arrival of a brilliant first-night audience for Mrs. Fiske; it was the last glamorous cavalcade of the 1920's; the paradox of a nation that had withdrawn from the world to self-suffi-

374

ciency—and to top-flight distrust of its own machines and its own men.

It might have been a different parade if the founding fathers had purged children's books of Tory characters, if they had substituted presidents for kings, junior executives for princes, and American stage-coaches for transformed pumpkins.

Many had made the substitution for themselves. Like Minnie, who had rooted her art in native earth and the reality of her own times. But for many others there remained the hiatus, the childhood promise of something more than democratic government could bring—some consummation out of the past of a Europe in whose troubled present they had no wish to share.

The hiatus had never been clearer than it was that night in front of the Erlanger, under the dark October sky of Forty-fourth Street—the parade of exotic cars; exotic furs and fabrics and jewels; the catch of breath and crowd-murmur for a titled head.

Count and prince and old-world vehicle belonged in the parade. Everyone there was a character in a fairy tale that was about to dissolve with the unceremonious ending of an enchantment.

In the theatre the enchantment held. It was packed with the most glittering audience of the year. And in spite of the seven other openings, nearly every important critic was on hand to welcome Mrs. Fiske.

Mortally tired, broke, and pushing sixty-five, she made her first entrance in the courtroom scene as Mrs. Livingston Baldwin Crane, about to become the twelfth juror. She was greeted with such a Niagara of applause that it was minutes before she could be sworn in. Her exchange of fireworks with Wilton Lackaye as Judge Fish kept the theatre charged with electricity and laughter, and at the end of the act she was given an ovation that never slackened until she consented to a curtain speech.

As an actress Minnie dominated the play, kept it vibrating and set its pace with superb authority. As a woman acknowledging the ovation, she was noticeably shy, soft-spoken and humble. She had no illusions about fame, and no sympathy with the "star" acting which had been forced on her—but she was very grateful.

The press next day went on in the spirit of that fabulous first night; reviews that most actresses saw in their young dreams—and only in their dreams after a lifetime on the stage:

> Charles Darnton: Queen of our stage, and when it comes to that, Queen of the whole dramatic world. . . . Mrs. Fiske swung the jury as she might have swung a plume over her priceless head. What a woman and what an actress!

Robert Garland: The Great Lady of the Theatre. She can do no wrong. . . . Something about her I can never put into words. . . Mrs. Fiske, first, last, and always . . . a glittering and glamorous entertainment.

Percy Hammond: Mrs. Fiske's comedy magically employed.

Burns Mantle: The first night's audience kept the walls of the Erlanger trembling. The first actress brings into play that lovely sense of comedy contrast that is hers . . . beautifully and imperturbably herself.

No one has the craft of this great planet among the stars—the richness of her comedy and the matchless pattern of her playing. She is Mrs. Fiske and there can never be another. She is incalculable and altogether peerless.

A day before Minnie had been fighting for survival—fearful that her last hope of a play would be done to death in the canyons of New York. Overnight she was lifted to the pinnacle of fame, where she looked out on a smiling world. That world was hers, her backers assured her. Fame was hers already, and they would raise up a fortune for her. This was the beginning, and the rest would follow in the twinkling of an eye.

To a women long haunted by the fear of poverty in her old age it seemed quite improbable. But she was inclined to believe—because it was no more improbable than the age in which it had been promised.

CHAPTER 51

On her way to Harry's apartment Minnie's path was crossed by a banker.

Walking from the subway, she paused as silk-hatted Tammany dignitaries bore the coffin through the crowd and up the stone steps of the church. For half a block the curb was walled with cars waiting in black immobility, and mounted police sat guard above the citizens who had gathered to see how the mighty had fallen.

Near her, one of New York's finest sat at attention for the passing notable, statue-like and unaware that his mount was eating hothouse roses out of an open car.

"A good use for funeral flowers," Minnie told herself, "but apples would be better for his digestion. I might have bought one from that young man at the subway exit—" The banker had entered the church, where the organ was muttering the "Dead March" from *Saul;* the crowd relaxed—and the policeman came to with a start. Minnie saw the look of hushed consternation as he tightened the reins.

"A good young man," she told herself; he had restrained his horse as gently as if it had been a little child. She went on, thinking kindly of the officer, but disturbed in memory. Perhaps what she had seen was one of the horses of the Apocalypse, eating roses bought on credit for a banker who had shot himself.

In an age as gone as Babylon—a few weeks ago—*Ladies of the Jury* had opened in New York. The most poetic of all the glamorous reviews appeared in the *Wall Street Journal*. It began: "Mrs. Fiske is a white sail in the wind, a slender bark battling fierce waves. . . ."

The review appeared on October 22. By noon the next day it did not require a Freud to interpret the dream of a storm at sea. Wall Street was the white sail in the wind; Wall Street was the slender bark, bat-

377

tling waves of stock that were dumped in ten-thousand- and twenty-thousand-share lots. And at the end of the day the tape was two hours behind in recording the sale of six million shares.

The next day was more alarming, with stocks falling faster than ticker tape dropped on a parade from the Exchange windows. The day after was worse; Montgomery Ward, the people's favorite at 137, was down to 50; and White Sewing Machine, recently selling at 48, was a dollar a share.

And the next month was worse, with the savings of a million citizens wiped out, and stocks still falling. Some banks closed, and some bankers—and more depositors—shot themselves. There were bread lines in the streets; and men with anxious faces—the look of success not quite gone from their clothes—stood on windy corners, offering apples to passers-by.

Once, Minnie remembered, Emily had made a few hundred on a stock-market tip; lost it, and dismissed it philosophically: "They were paper profits and paper losses. After I have a good cry, I'll dry my eyes and start all over."

But this time there seemed no end to losses, and no place to start over.

In Harry's apartment, over the perfect luncheon which he cooked and served, Minnie spoke of the shadow on the land, asking, "When do you think it will end?"

Harry, usually rich in words, answered, "God knows, my dear." He had lost their life savings by failing to compare the cost of a production with its possible revenue. And the masters of American finance were guessing no better. One after another they announced the end of the recession—and the recession deepened and stocks fell faster.

"It would have been so different if we had elected Al Smith," Minnie said.

Harry doubted it. "Mr. Raskob, his campaign manager, told America that everyone could get rich by investing in stocks; and Raskob was one of the powers behind the bull market. The Democrats at least tried to make disaster a bipartisan policy."

Panic and depression had hit the theatre hardest of all. "I saw Mr. Tyler this morning," Minnie said. "He wants me to think about a new play for this winter."

Harry rumbled in protest, "With *Ladies of the Jury* holding up, and other plays closing?"

She reminded him, "It is earning only a few hundred dollars a week.

378

Mr. Tyler thinks a new play would swell the box-office receipts."

"What do you think?"

"My instincts are against it—but you and I know so little about the commercial theatre."

By mid-December they were working on a new production, *The Family Blues* by Hatcher Hughes and Alan Williams. Professor Hughes, with Elmer Rice, had provided Minnie with the delightful *Wake Up, Jonathan*, and more recently Hughes's *Hell Bent for Heaven* had been a Pulitzer prize winner. But the new comedy bore no resemblance to the Rice-Hughes fantasy, and little to Hughes's rugged exploration of a revivalist's sex life. Minnie had accepted it as a half-stunned woman might allow herself to be led through a storm to promised shelter.

The Family Blues was a product of its decade, different from a score of other similar plays only in the matter of chronology. Being the latest, it was a little farther out on the limb of daring.

The comedy shows an evening of the home life of a Park Avenue family in the nineteen-twenties. It begins with the teen-age daughter tiring of her public liaison with a married man and deciding on the novelty of marriage. The son, wearied by examples of promiscuity, brings home a specialty dancer who has offered to be his mistress, and whom he has married instead. At home he is momentarily disconcerted to learn that his bride is one of his father's castoff mistresses.

The father has just been carried in, dazed, after a car crash in company with his stenographer mistress. He calls the name of a former mistress. She is summoned, and arrives with her army major husband. During the ensuing row, the major's wife goes into premature labor. The play ends with the major's wife's baby, by the Park Avenue father, crying upstairs—and the forgiven father beginning his next affair with the night nurse.

As the wife of the busy satyr, Minnie had a more conventional role than many others she had played. But the innocuous part did not reconcile her to a comedy which dared so much for nothing. Its nearest approach to a philosophy was a line spoken by the father. Sobered by near-death and birth and the disillusionment of his son, he observes to his wife:

"Well, thinking isn't going to get us anywhere. . . What would you say to getting out the old yacht and sailing around the world?"

If *The Family Blues* said anything, it was by implication. It implied that endless promiscuity and folly and bootleg liquor left no hangover;

379

and no matter how Americans squandered their money, there would always be plenty more where it came from—and at least one ocean-going yacht in which to escape from the necessity of thinking.

For Minnie there was nightmare in the contrast between the implications of the play and reality: the lengthening bread lines, shivering apple-sellers, and the anxious faces of a people hung over from a national debauch. A month out of its decade, the play was like a drunk swimming in mid-ocean and proclaiming that he knew he wouldn't fall overboard.

The Family Blues opened in Newark on January 27, 1930. It was politely received—but after the performance Minnie collapsed in her dressing room, overcome with shame and humiliation.

Re-named *It's a Grand Life*, the comedy was brought to New York two weeks later. Minnie was prepared to accept any censure the critics might deal out to her. There was no censure; but the critics branded the play as unworthy of the actress—and it closed after a dozen performances.

With the first weakening of the *Grand Life*, George Tyler had consulted the Fiskes, concluding that in such unusual times art might pull a rabbit out of the hat where a commercial effort had produced an egg.

Minnie advised a classical comedy; and while the *Grand Life* was dying, they hastily and extravagantly produced a second revival of *The Rivals*. Almost overnight they assembled a brilliant cast, and the production went ahead with such feverish speed that only a week intervened between the closing of the old play and the opening of the new.

The Rivals opened in New York on March 13, after a tryout at Princeton and a few performances at Springfield, Massachusetts. Minnie was nearing exhaustion from three plays in less than six months; she was fearful of bringing the still-shaky production to New York—but the first night passed with only one serious blunder. From her dressing room she sensed that something had gone wrong on the stage, and when she neared the wings she heard the actors ad libbing. A cue line was repeated—her cue, which she had missed!

As she rushed onto the stage, through the wrong entrance, she heard a titter. The scene was repeated, and the play went on, with the break in the illusion healing over. The final curtain fell in a thunder of applause—but Minnie was still shaken.

It was the first time she had missed a cue since the time she had left Barney Macauley to make his final speech bound and with a gag in his mouth. Anyone could slip once in fifty years, she told herself. But she had slipped.

She did not slip again, and before the end of the week the production was going smoothly.

The four-week New York engagement ended with an ovation and innumerable curtain calls. Before responding, Minnie removed the sharp lines of court plaster converging downward between her eyebrows to suggest age and crabbedness. She removed them hastily and powdered her brows—answering the curtain calls in the costume of Mrs. Malaprop, but with the face of Minnie Maddern Fiske. It was a face the public rarely saw except behind veils or under the make-up of a character: a smiling, grateful face, marked by time, but with the pert profile and haunting eyes of the child who had made her appearance on Broadway sixty years before in *Hunted Down*.

After the final curtain call, Minnie kissed the foreheads of Messrs. Craig and Peters and Powers and Mack, telling each, "You played beautifully tonight!"

In her heart she knew that she, too, had played beautifully. What she did not know was that she had appeared on a New York stage for the last time.

CHAPTER 52

The Rivals had been a successful marriage of business and art. By autumn the honeymoon was over, and Minnie found herself embarked on hateful repertory.

In interviews with Alexander Woollcott she had condemned repertory as outworn, needless, harmful and impossible. Fifteen years had only deepened her conviction. Now she saw the repertory company as a group of workmen who tried to turn out motor cars one day, typewriters the next, and washing machines the day after. They might produce those things, wastefully and after a fashion, but if one of them was ever right it would be at the expense of the others.

But she had to live—and in the early fall of 1930 she threw her fading strength into rehearsing a group of actors. They were not a company and they were not a cast because they did not know what they were going to present.

It was Tyler's ambitious plan for them to rehearse all of Minnie's great successes. In each city, theatregoers would cast ballots for what they wanted to see, and the company would oblige. The leader of the American theatre was to become a player piano, ready to play any tune the public called.

For five weeks they rehearsed madly. Then, with Minnie near exhaustion, they began their nebulous tour through the eastern states, quieter under the pall of depression than she had ever seen them in the dead of winter.

Of all the plays the company had rehearsed, they presented only three: Ladies of the Jury, Mrs. Bumpstead-Leigh and Becky Sharp.

There were few highlights on that autumn tour, but Philadelphia gave Becky a heart-warming reception. On October 24, over thirty years after Mrs. Fiske had made the role famous, the Public Ledger observed:

382

At every point in the play she captured the youthful sparkle of Becky and created the impression of youth.

Which is the measure of Mrs. Fiske's genius . . . she invests the role with all its worldly wisdom, all its brilliant wit, all its misguided courage and all its flashing charm.

And in Pittsburgh a reporter from the *Sun-Telegram* stepped into a mystical dimension of space and time. He had arranged for an interview with Mrs. Fiske at her hotel. When he knocked on the door he heard, or thought he heard, an answering voice. He opened the door— and stepped into a limbo of cold fog and smoke, and pigeons whirred up and flew about him.

At first gasp the reporter thought he had opened a door to an air shaft or roof. When his eyes adjusted to the atmosphere, he made out a room, with the windows wide open, and the slight figure of a woman kneeling by a fireplace, crumbling bread.

Minnie rose, and smiled at the reporter with blue, compassionate eyes. "Those pigeons looked so cold and hungry out on the cornice," she explained as the birds settled down to their meal. "I keep the windows open so they can come in and eat the crumbs I scatter on the hearth. They know me and depend on me."

At Yale, Minnie addressed William Lyon Phelps's class in contemporary drama—and rounded out a paradox.

Shortly before, Gene Tunney, retired heavyweight champion, had addressed the class on Shakespeare. Minnie, in turn, spoke on fighting. Specifically, it was bullfighting. And, like Calvin Coolidge's minister on sin, the actress was against it. She had written a speech for the occasion, but before going to class she received an announcement of a bullfight to be held at Newark, New Jersey. She discarded the written speech and urged the students to join in a protest against the event.

Minnie's address on the drama was never given. Neither was the bullfight. And New Jersey laws were amended to forbid the sport. For Minnie it was the chief victory of her tour.

There weren't many others. One of the few was her revolt against repertory—and that had its price. In December she dropped *Mrs. Bumpstead-Leigh* because her company could not do more than two plays well; and at the beginning of January she parted company with Tyler, who had dreamed of capitalizing on her fame and building up a fortune for her.

The broken tour had brought Minnie as far as Chicago. There she enrolled her company under the management of the Blackstone Company, an enterprise of Tracey Drake, owner of the Blackstone Hotel; Drake was new to theatrical management, but Minnie and Chicago had known each other for half a century.

Ladies of the Jury opened at the Blackstone Theatre on January 12, 1931, and it ran for four almost-prosperous weeks. Minnie was grateful—but the darling of her heart was the next production, *Becky Sharp*.

She was unaware of what the revival of *Becky* revealed; but Ashton Stevens summed up, fatefully and tenderly:

> God did not destine Mrs. Fiske to ever become an ex-actress. She will, I hope, in His good time, die with her make-up on—and possessing then as now the youngest brain in the modern playhouse.
>
> It is a full thirty years since I first saw her "Becky Sharp" and wrote the most intelligent line I've ever written—"Dull people do not like Mrs. Fiske's acting! . . ."
>
> Minnie Maddern Fiske is the most civilizing force the stage has known in my time.

Minnie treasured the review; she was buoyed up by the assurance that she had the youngest brain in the theatre—but she missed the implication of physical failing and the nearness of the time when she would die with her make-up—her red shoes—on.

Becky was given only nine times in Chicago before the company began a tour through the northern Midwest. Wherever they went, *Ladies of the Jury* was well received; Minnie wrote Harry that it caused so much handclapping that she was often embarrassed. Becky embarrassed her in a different way, but she finally attributed its poor reception to the fact that Thackeray was not much read of late.

The company was billed for two performances at Madison, Wisconsin, arriving there at the end of winter. Minnie's first thought was of the Eugene H. Byrnes, who had entertained her when she was receiving her honorary degree. Professor Byrne vividly recalls the resulting visit and Mrs. Fiske's famous encounter with Governor LaFollette. He illuminates the disappointing reception of Mrs. Fiske's last *Becky*.

> It was hard to take in many respects. The lady was old and thin. She wore red wigs of different hue in different acts. Her costumes were extravagant and becoming (but I missed the great green satin gown of 1901 in the ball scene): instead of the white evening dress and white turban of the supper party with Steyne of old, she wore a feathered dress of bright blue which billowed about her as she sank to the floor "done for!" The other women were in indifferent scraps

384

of gowns. It was pitiful, except as one remembers what it had been. (My wife calls my attention to Mrs. Fiske's astonishing ability in that last revival of "Becky" to sink to the floor at the end of the scene with Steyne, crying "I am done for! Done for!" like a young girl, when death was stalking her trail, and she an old woman.)

The house was only partly filled. She noticed it. So did I. Afterward my wife, younger son and I went back. She received us in the make-up and costume of the Pumpernickle scene, sat or half reclined on her cot, saying she did not go out to dinner between performances any more, but was waiting for sandwiches to be brought in to her. She paid much attention to our lad, telling him of her own adopted son, and sharing all her conversation with us with him, and he agape, as well he ought to have been. We remained only a short time, since in the evening she was doing "Ladies of the Jury" and later we were meeting at the Glenn Franks for supper.

Mrs. Fiske struck us as fading physically, wasting away, rather; but the astonishing thing was that her very thinness made her figure in "Ladies" admirable.

At supper there were perhaps a dozen men and women, all of whom had been at the theatre. Afterward we went to the drawing room where a circle for general conversation was formed, Mrs. Fiske and the President sitting on a couch at the top of the group. The general conversation did not go well at first; the lady was tired, and my wife thought we were all cruel to her in expecting anything more from her. Presently Glenn got up, came to my chair, asking me to take his place on the couch beside Mrs. Fiske; he said *sotto voce* he was worn out, but that I could get her to talk, since all wished her to talk!

Sitting beside her, under cover of what was being said near us, I said that the President wished her to talk. She murmured to me in apparent astonishment; "Never can I talk. Not an idea in my head. Absolutely never two in succession." I said help would be given, so somehow she and I threw something into the circle which produced results which were presently to be amazing. The conversation drifted into the subject of the retirement into private life of one devoted to public affairs. To our horror the Governor, with the bluntness of the La Follettes, said across the circle: "Mrs. Fiske, do great artists ever retire?" Mrs. La Follette rattled her beads in embarrassment.

Quickly from Mrs. Fiske: "Governor La Follette, do politicians ever retire?" She had saved the day by creating a general laugh. I interjected something about *"il gran refiuto,"* Dante's phrase for the unheard of resignation of Pope Celestin V. Then Mrs. Fiske, as the laughter left her the floor, said: "Do I understand, Governor, that you are asking why *I* do not retire?" Poor Phil! Again a laugh, and a second triumph for Mrs. Fiske, to which shortly she added a third and even higher one.

It was long past midnight when she rose, and before speaking to anyone else, she held out her two hands toward the poor Governor, saying as he came across to take her hands, "You are a dear young man and I love you." That was the end. None of us ever saw her again. As a performance, considering the whole situation, it was as fine as any I ever saw her give. She swept us all along in admiration for remarkable gifts evoked when needed.

Late in April, the worn actress's tour ended at Lancaster, Pennsylvania—where, in 1895, she had begun her first tour as Mrs. Fiske.

Only her business manager and a few others knew how gallant a tour it had been. On paper, with her salary and percentage of the box office, Minnie had received a handsome sum, while the management lost money. But she had secretly returned most of her earnings so the play could go on.

She finished empty-handed—but her pride had been preserved, and her company had had brief sanctuary from the depression.

CHAPTER 53

On paper the Fiskes still owned Camp Veery, but it was now beyond their finances to set its machinery in motion, and Minnie turned home to a less pretentious place.

A year or two earlier she had bought a house in Hollis, Long Island, and established there her adopted son, Bolie, who was now nine, her secretary, Mae Cox, and Mae's mother and aunt. It was a simple establishment in a commonplace suburb: a small frame house whose only luxuries were an upright piano and shelves of books. The house had two advantages: it was within easy reach of New York, and it was so like countless others that there the tired actress was able to drop into anonymity.

From Lancaster Minnie returned to Hollis, racked by internal pain which had exhausted and frightened her on her tour. A celebrated physician was called in and began treating her, but he avoided naming her ailment. Harry, in whom the doctor confided, also avoided mention of the diagnosis, but fear was stamped on his large handsome face. And while Minnie rested and read plays and made plans, she clipped hopeful newspaper stories on the conquest of cancer.

One of the new plays she read was a comedy by Carlos Drake, son of her Chicago producer. In the play the role of Kate Gordon had been written to her measure. After one reading, she wired her acceptance of it for fall production.

In that same April, Sid Grauman offered Minnie a spring engagement in Los Angeles in *Mrs. Bumpstead-Leigh*. The producer apologized for not being able to offer her more than a flat $600 a week for a six-weeks engagement—but the depression was a grim fact, and he had been obliged to scale down his prices.

Harry was outraged. Six hundred dollars a week for the First Lady of the theatre, who had several times refused three hundred thousand for a season! He would not permit it.

Minnie had just returned from touring. Better than Harry, she knew the condition of the theatre.

She wrote her will and last requests, and crossed the continent once more for six weeks of spirited horseplay in the old farce. On the way, she stopped over in Chicago to discuss her next production with young Carlos Drake.

The engagement at the Mayan Theatre in Los Angeles was a happy event. At its end, Sid Grauman made the statement that Mrs. Fiske in *Mrs. Bumpstead-Leigh* had been the most enjoyable experience in his career. And Minnie had enough strength left to address an open letter to the children of California, urging them to oppose the cruelties of rodeos.

It was all she had left. She had been underweight when she started to California, and she returned to Hollis, emaciated and almost unable to take any food.

Her earlier fine plans had included summer at Camp Veery, where she could rest while working with Carlos Drake on his play—but an angel with a flaming estimate of costs kept her and Harry away from their Adirondack home. In the meantime, her playwright had moved to Westport, Connecticut, and she arranged to work with him there.

Three weeks after her return from California Minnie left, alone, for Westport.

Carlos Drake was destined to be Mrs. Fiske's last playwright and to take part in a larger drama than the one he had written for her. In an article published in *Town & Country* he gives clear glimpses of her from her arrival at Westport to her last performance on the stage.

When I met her I was shocked at the change in her appearance since I had seen her last in Chicago. She was emaciated, and seemed very weak. Getting out of the train, she handed me an envelope on which she had written the names and addresses of her husband and myself. "Just in case something happened," she informed me with a chuckle. "You see—I had it pinned here, to my cloak! . . ."

Mrs. Fiske made it clear that she didn't want any visitors, didn't want anyone to know she was there. She was delighted with the musty old house, a house which had stood almost two hundred years. . . . In the drawing room, arranged like a studio, she enjoyed sitting on the floor with her back against the sofa, with notes scattered about on either side of her, while I sat on a low chair nearby and tried to remember all that she said.

The first evening she had some appetite, and demanded a cocktail before dinner. "We'll celebrate," she said, "even if I pay for it with some perfectly monstrous nightmares. I think this is fun. Here I am—old enough to be your great-grandmother—visiting you God knows where in the country. It's quiet, and far-away, and odd, and I like it. Only I don't feel a bit like your great-grandmother."

"Why should you?" I replied. "I don't feel a bit like your great-grandchild."

"My dear, this question of age is a ghost story. It is with any actress. But you see, I'm a thousand years old. And I'm tired. And I can't eat much. I like your line in the play about my being ageless. One gets to that point. I once knew a woman who thought she was the reincarnation of Thais, a woman over a hundred. She has become ageless—as I have."

"And of whom are you the reincarnation?" I could not help asking.

She smiled. "Of a great many people. I'll tell you about them sometime. Aren't you convinced you've lived before? I am. I'll go on living, too, long after this uncomfortable body of mine can't digest even the food I'm taking tonight. . . ."

I used to write in the mornings while Mrs. Fiske slept. She would take what I had written after luncheon, and through the afternoon, sitting out-of-doors in a lawn-chair, would read it, and make notes. . . .

Every evening about ten o'clock we would walk down a little hill from the house to the mailbox, a distance of about four hundred yards each way—the only exercise she would take. She would walk slowly, holding my arm. I was greatly concerned about her condition. She seemed to be living entirely on nervous energy, and was not eating enough to maintain her strength. . . When she tried forcing herself to eat she suffered stomach pains and nausea. . . ."

At work, there were flashes of her vital self:

Mrs. Fiske laughed, caught hold of my arm, and pulled herself up from the floor. "I'll show you this scene. Watch! This is the drawing room. I'm off-stage. I come in, unnoticed. I come in all the way. No escape. There's your couple—the wretches! I see them. I stop. Like this. I draw myself up. I say 'Goddamn!' "

Her voice rang out like a pistol shot. Then we both laughed heartily.

"Of course, I'd prefer you didn't write it that way," she added. . . . "But that's what I mean by making it natural. . . . Whatever you do, don't be old-fashioned and sentimental in your writing! . . ."

She was amused one day to receive a note from her adopted son, aged nine, who was attending a boys' camp. "My hut," he wrote, "is nice. There are nice boys in the hut." That was all; no affectionate heading, and no signature.

"That's my idea of a thoroughly business-like letter!" she laughed. "He ought to be successful in a bank."

Mr. Fiske came out from New York, and spent a weekend. He, like myself, was anxious about her health. I got him aside.

"Have you ever known her to be this way?"

"Never," he said.

"What is it? What's the matter?"

"The doctors," he informed me, "call it 'delayed fatigue.' She's still tired from her California tour. When she gets back to the city she can rest—not see anybody at all. Rehearsals won't begin for another three weeks. I'm sure she'll be better then."

Rehearsals began at the end of September, in the bare Engineers' Hall on Fortieth Street. Minnie commuted from Hollis, staying only a few hours and taking liquid nourishment. She appeared stronger after her rest, but in a few days her strength began to ebb. When she could no longer make the trip to Hollis, she took a room at the Murray Hill Hotel.

For years Minnie had stayed away from the Murray Hill, confiding that its corridors were haunted by the fair-haired Emily, who had often stopped there with her as a child. Now she was closer to the lost girl than she had been during their years of estrangement, and she was grateful for the familiar old hotel. It was only a few blocks from Engineers' Hall, where Harry had set up a steamer chair for her in a room next to the rehearsal hall.

She was now able to rest continuously except for the brief time she was practicing her part—but her strength continued to ebb. Less than two weeks before the scheduled opening in Rochester, Minnie's doctor gave the order that she must stop—and director and playwright were left with a production and a booked tour—minus the all-important star.

In the emergency, and because of her great friendship for Mrs. Fiske, Henrietta Crosman agreed by long distance to take the role of Kate Gordon temporarily, although it meant dropping her own plans.

Minnie's strength was still failing, but she insisted on being present when Miss Crosman arrived. The two embraced; she introduced her successor to the company, and said good-bye to each one. She then returned to Hollis—leaving Henrietta Crosman with the task of learning a long and exacting role in a little over a week.

It was the first time in Minnie's life that she had failed a play, and it weighed heavily on her. Lizzie Maddern, her own mother, had danced in ballet when she had to fight for every breath, and she had continued to dance when she was dying. In Minnie's own company, Maurice Barrymore had fought the death of his mind; he had given magnificent portrayals of Rawdon Crawley while he struggled in a twisting jungle, fighting to distinguish between fancy and reality. It seemed a weakness on her part to fail a production because of mere illness.

Her conscience was eased a little when *Against the Wind* opened at Rochester on schedule. It was a magnificent act of devotion on Miss Crosman's part—but there were limits to what even love and loyalty could do in a week with a role written for someone else. The reviews were indifferent.

From Rochester *Against the Wind* moved on to Cleveland. Again the reviews were disappointing, although they found less fault with Miss Crosman's heroic effort than with the play—without Mrs. Fiske there to dazzle them with something beyond the lines.

In the Long Island suburb, in her little house, Minnie lay in bed with the disappointing reviews scattered about. She asked herself, "What am I doing here, when a play needs me on the road?"

When she could find no good answer, she ordered Mae Cox to pack, and summoned her doctor, telling him, "Patch me up somehow."

She arrived in Cleveland on Wednesday, October 21—and was put to bed in a hotel, with Miss Cox and a trained nurse watching over her. She was too weak to see anyone, but she rested more happily, close to her play; and she was cheered by minor dividends from her career. One of them was the October *Good Housekeeping*, which had just appeared. In that issue she was featured as one of the twelve greatest living American women. Her fellow great included Jane Addams, Ernestine Schumann-Heink, Helen Keller, Willa Cather and Carrie Chapman Catt.

As another, odd dividend, Minnie had a telephone call from a very new actor who had been inspired by her stage career. The actor was Alexander Woollcott, making his first stage appearance in *Brief Moment*, which was trying out in a nearby theatre. Woollcott greeted her with, "You've been responsible for this!" She chuckled over the conversation when she reported it to Carlos Drake. "They *will* act!" she said.

There had been press rumors that Mrs. Fiske declined to appear in *Against the Wind* because she didn't have sufficient faith in the play. Pitifully weak, she left her bed to rehearse with the cast on Thursday.

"We'll show those fellows!" she cried to her young playwright. "We'll whip it into shape. Don't worry! I'm much better. I ate something today."

She rehearsed again on Friday, and the next afternoon she faced her first audience in the role of Kate Gordon.

Minnie's confidence inspired the other players. She missed some of her own lines, but she was quick, versatile, charming; the matinee was a success. At the end, when she had taken many curtain calls and Drake was assisting her to her dressing room, she said brightly, "There! I told you! But, by heavens, young man, we've got a lot of work to do yet on that manuscript!"

In the evening Minnie repeated her valiant performance; and the company moved on to its big test in Chicago. Everyone was cheered by the finale of the Cleveland engagement, but Minnie paid for it. On Sunday in Chicago she could not eat or sleep. On Monday at rehearsal she stumbled through her lines like a somnambulist, and Harry was unable to conceal his anxiety.

Few plays have opened in fairer or fouler weather. Minnie had been the darling of Chicago for most of a lifetime; a glorification of her as one of the twelve greatest American women was on the newsstands; the scene of her play was fashionable Lake Forest, and the advance publicity had been thorough. Against all that was the fact that Minnie was dying.

On the opening night of October 26, her dressing room was almost hidden under an avalanche of flowers and messages. Among the telegrams from people Minnie had never even met was one saying—I'LL BE THERE TO GIVE THE LITTLE GIRL A BIG HAND. TEXAS GUINAN. And out front, the Blackstone was packed with Fiske fans, Chicago society, reporters and critics.

The curtain rose on the Sutherlands' living room, empty at the moment, with the sounds of a tennis match coming through windows open to the terrace, and a light breeze stirring the curtains. Characters drifted on and off, but the audience hardly noticed them, waiting for Mrs. Fiske.

She came; and she looked so small, so frail! The audience burst into applause. It continued. She stood with one hand on the back of a chair, supporting herself weakly, and smiled—a tired smile. I could see that she was making a tremendous effort, and I could sense the amazed, questioning feeling on the part of the audience. "Is it really she?"

Many people in our audience that opening night must have felt like shouting to Mrs. Fiske to stop. It was agonizing to watch her—that great artist in such a condition! Her lines were dragged out. A film seemed to have settled over memory, and when she came to places in her part where the lines were a trifle unfamiliar she would pause, grope for words, then, falling back on her theatrical instinct, say whatever occurred to her. But with all her weakness there was a tragic determination in her manner which had a stirring effect. Several times during the second scene of the first act she tottered, and appeared about to fall, and at such moments the audience held its breath, and sighed with relief when she regained her equilibrium and fresh impetus. . . . She got through it somehow. I was backstage then, and as the curtain fell I ran to where she was standing, holding on to a prop, with her eyes closed, and her lips tightly drawn.

"Keep the curtain down!" ordered Mr. Fiske. She was mumbling aloud lines of the final act.

We carried her to her dressing room where the nurse gave her a stimulant. It revived her. "It's going so badly!" she burst out in a passion.

"On the contrary, it's splendid!" I lied.

She gave me a flashing look, then shook her head wearily.

Mr. Fiske was gravely concerned. I spoke of stopping the performance.

"Stop? What are you saying?" she exclaimed, overhearing us. "Who's talking of stopping? I've never done such a thing in my life! Don't be ridiculous!"

I went into the dressing room of the leading man. "I've never known anyone like her!" he cried. "She's inhuman! Her will is incredible!"

During the second act she was firmer in her lines. While off-stage, waiting for her entrance, she sat in an armchair, propped up with pillows, the nurse on one side of her, Mae Cox on the other. Mr. Fiske held the script, and watched for her cues. When the time came he touched her arm, and said gently, "Now, Minnie—" The other members of the cast, going on and off, paused to give her a word of encouragement.

She carried on. She supported the play. The other characters seemed to revolve about her, like puppets on wires attached to her frail body. The atmosphere was tense.

"She can do anything she puts her mind to," muttered Mr. Fiske grimly.

The first scene in the last act. An emotional part. She carried it off splendidly. When the curtain fell the audience refused to stop clapping. Mrs. Fiske took a call. I stood in the wings, and saw her beckoning to me. They were calling, "Author!" and I had to go out and say something. I went out and faced them. "My friends—" I mumbled a few words. Mrs. Fiske came to my side, took my hand. She would do this—after all she had been through. . . .

After the final curtain Minnie was carried to her dressing room in a state of collapse. Her thoughts were still on the play, and through her press agent she implored the critics not to judge the play by that night; it hadn't had a fair chance.

Ashton Stevens and several other critics were too touched to write anything at the time. Those who did write took circumstances into account. In the next day's Chicago *Tribune* Charles Collins observed:

> So far as Mrs. Fiske's performance is concerned it was verbally uncertain and physically feeble last night because of her recent illness. She seemed as frail as Duse on her farewell tour, and her grip on her material was insecure. Final appraisal of the characterization should be reserved until later in the engagement.

Tuesday night Minnie seemed near death on the stage, but she kept on her feet to the final curtain. On Wednesday she gave a matinee as well as an evening performance. On November 1, Ashton Stevens wrote:

> Mrs. Fiske has done another beautiful and Fiskian thing for the calling which she honors and which despite its occasional lack of pride honors her. . . . As she gets better the play gets better. And never in my life have I been more eager for the success of a debatable manuscript. For if all goes well with "Against the Wind," it means that the indubitable First Actress and most gallant lady of the theatre is herself again.

A crisis had passed; Minnie seemed to gain strength with each performance. After a particularly successful matinee, her face was alight with a mischievous whimsical expression as she greeted Harry and Drake in her dressing room. Holding out both her hands, she told them gaily, "You wouldn't believe me, would you, you two? Well, most people have to be shown before they'll believe anything!"

It was not renewed strength Minnie had discovered—only the way of giving her ultimate reserves. When they were gone, she drove herself by force of will alone, to the end of her sixteenth Chicago performance. In hypnotized awe, her last audiences watched two plays by the same name acted on the same stage. The slight comedy with many characters, and the more somber play with only one, a small, determined, dying woman beating up against the wind of eternity.

394

C H A P T E R 54

When Minnie was taken home to Hollis, her physician was out of town.

In the emergency, Harry called in the able Dr. Walter Bensel, who shook his head over the patient. It was simple enough, he said, but she had done such an utter job of exhausting herself and wrecking her digestion. And in the process, she had damaged her overstrained heart. If that could be kept going, there was a chance of repairing the other wreckage.

Dr. Bensel said nothing about cancer, and he was surprised when Minnie asked about it. It was a case of intestinal poisoning that would have been no great problem if it had been treated earlier.

There was a touch in irony in Minnie's celebrated physician's having treated her for the wrong disease. But she only felt grateful for the news—and for Mae Cox, her faithful secretary, who now took charge.

Minnie rested with new peace of mind. Resting was all she was able to do. Her exhaustion devoured rest and sleep, and was never satisfied. In Chicago she had agreed to a month of recuperation before resuming *Against the Wind*. The month passed unnoticed. It was lengthening into two when she began actively thinking about the work that must go on if she went on living.

Camp Veery had been spacious enough to hold the Fiskes' separate lives and circles of friends, the outgrowth of years of enforced separation. But the Greenwich Village apartment was Harry's personal place; the house in Hollis was Minnie's; and they had no thought of living under the same small roof. Harry came out from New York every week or so and spent an evening with her. Together they talked of a spring tour and discussed plans for the future.

Early in February Minnie's heart began to falter. But when Harry visited her near the middle of the month, he found her in good spirits—though she seemed unusually frail and weak—and he was assured that she was out of danger.

Throughout her life Minnie had the power of giving people vivid dreams. One of her admirers from the days of *Caprice* records that on the night of February 14, 1932, he dreamed of being in a theatre with an altar on the stage, or in a church with the trappings of a theatre. Mrs. Fiske was there, sometimes busying herself at the altar and sometimes mingling with the audience or congregation—a performance where the sacred and the profane had become indistinguishable, and priestess or player and communicant met face to face.

The dreamer had never heard Minnie's dictum, "Theatres, too, can be holy places." But the dreamer divined her belief. The next day, with the dream still pervading his consciousness, he read of her death.

Harry, at his apartment, was notified by telephone. Gallant, as always, his first thought was for two girl art students he was guiding through the Depression; he broke the news to them so they would not meet it, unprepared, in the evening paper. He then opened the envelope which Minnie had given him before her California trip. Her final instructions were partly typed and partly written, on three different kinds of paper, but they were simple and direct:

An inexpensive coffin. There were to be no flowers. Her body was to be taken to Harry's apartment. No one was to look on her face. Harry was to be kind to reporters, who had been kind to her. He was to be kind to all of them—and send them all away. Only Harry and Merle Maddern and Mae Cox were to attend the brief service and cremation.

Of those who attended the last rites for Mrs. Fiske: Merle Maddern, on the New York stage and radio, carries on the Maddern tradition to this day. Mae Cox, and her mother, kept faith with Mrs. Fiske by raising the adopted Bolie. He received a good education—and eventually his draft notice. He married; and through the foresight of his guardians he was able to lead the life of his own choosing, free from the notoriety and reportorial prying that could so easily have come to a boy adopted by one of the great. Harry Fiske outlived Minnie by ten years, dying after a long illness in 1942. During that long twilight, Harry made various attempts to find a place for himself in the theatre and on the radio—but the great years, and the golden touch, had become memories.

In the press rooms of a nation, editors and critics were left to decide on Minnie Maddern Fiske's place in history. Most of them agreed that with Terry and Bernhardt and Duse gone before her, Mrs. Fiske had been the last of the great final flowering of the legitimate stage and there would never be another like her.

There were also the dissenters.

George Jean Nathan questioned whether she had been an actress at all, let alone a great one.

Stark Young conceded that she had been one of the half dozen whom he would rather see than all the others. But he weighed her as an intellectual, and found her wanting in some of the requirements set forth in an essay by Marcel Proust.

Minnie had believed with shining faith in the indestructibility of the spirit; that she would truly begin living when she had laid aside the body, of which she had never been greatly enamored. If she were right, as she had often been, she was in a position to take amused interest in the press debate.

Without doubt she bore up under Nathan's question of her art; she might have reminded him, as she once did Alexander Woollcott, "I never said I could act."

She must have taken unholy glee in failing the requirements of an obscure essay by Proust. Better than Stark Young, she knew that the solemn ranks of the intellectuals were not for a kindred spirit of St. Francis of Assisi, who preached to the birds and called the animals "our little brothers"—with an insight six hundred years deeper than science.

Proust—"no doubt a dear young man"—would never have approved a woman who repeated to herself with childlike faith:

> He prayeth best, who loveth best
> All things both great and small;
> For the dear God who loveth us,
> He made and loveth all.

Many things barred Minnie from the solemn ranks: qualities of heart and imagination, an inner climate of humor, and a feeling of oneness with bird and tree and evening star.

All that did not prevent her from having one of the good minds of her time, or from being for thirty-five years the leader of her profession. And for a dozen, its solitary conscience. Her war with the Theatre Trust had been fought for a high stake of civilization, the coming of age of the American theatre.

Technically, Minnie won that impossible fight. But it was an empty victory. While she and Frohman fought through the years, the living theatre ebbed from stage to screen.

The change in itself gave Minnie no regrets. She had never been dismayed by new things; only by the trivial uses made of them. While

397

other actors and critics jeered at moving pictures, she prophesied that they would develop a higher art than the stage had ever known.

What she did not foresee was that the methods and spirit of the Trust would at least temporarily conquer the new medium; that its producers would by-pass civilization and turn the theatre back to an adolescent level of entertainment.

In immediate results, Minnie lost the great battle of her life. When she died from its after-effects, the American theatre, now of the screen, was a self-styled industry, complacent under the guidance of Will Hays, the dead hand of Warren Harding.

It was a turn of history which should have troubled the departing actress less than her fellow citizens who were left to calculate the hazards of prolonged adolescence in a world where dangers came of age so quickly.

Minnie Maddern Fiske had done her part. The red shoes were off at last. And the bringing to age of the American theatre was left to other playwrights and other players, and to the public in whom Minnie had unshaken faith.

APPENDIX

Plays and casts of characters with
which Minnie Maddern Fiske
was associated

Produced plays written by
Minnie Maddern Fiske

Fontenelle—A Romantic Drama in Four Acts by Harrison Grey Fiske and Minnie Maddern Fiske played by Mr. James O'Neill

The Countess Roudine—A Drama in Four Acts by Minnie Maddern Fiske and Paul Kester played by Modjeska

The Rose—Pathetic Play in One Act by Minnie Maddern Fiske played by Rosina Vokes, later used by Felix Morris

Moses—A Comedy Farce from the German in Two Acts—Adapted by Minnie Maddern Fiske played by Felix Morris

The Eyes of the Heart—Drama in One Act by Minnie Maddern Fiske played by George Arliss and others

Not Guilty—Drama in One Act by Minnie Maddern Fiske played by Mrs. Fiske and others

A Light from St. Agnes—Tragedy in One Act by Minnie Maddern Fiske played by Mrs. Fiske and others

John Doe—by Minnie Maddern Fiske

Plays written by
Minnie Maddern Fiske
but not produced

Selma
Florian
Verrick
The Girls of Cloverton
Common Clay (scenario)
Kathryn (scenario)

Some parts played by
Minnie Maddern as a child

Duke of York in *Richard III*
Willie Leigh in *Hunted Down* (6 years)
Prince Arthur in *King John* (9 years)
The Crowned Child in *Macbeth*
Damon's Son in *Damon and Pythias*
Little Fritz in *Fritz, Our German Cousin*

Paul in *The Octoroon*
Franko in *Guy Mannering*
Sybil in *A Wolf in Sheep's Clothing*
Mary Morgan in *Ten Nights in a Barroom*
The Child in *Across the Continent*
The Boy in *Bosom Friends*
Alfred in *Divorce* (5 or 6 years)
Lucy Fairweather in *The Streets of New York* (9 years)
The Gamin and Peachblossom in *Under the Gaslight*
Marjorie in *The Rough Diamond*
The Girl in *The Little Rebel*
Adrienne in *Monsieur Alphonse*
Georgie in *Frou-Frou*
Hendrick and Meenie in *Rip Van Winkle*
Eva in *Uncle Tom's Cabin* (12 years)
Dollie in *Chicago Before the Fire*
Hilda in *Karl and Hilda* (5 or 6 years)
Ralph Rackstraw in *Pinafore*
Clip in *A Messenger from Jarvis Section*
The Sun God in *The Ice Witch*
François in *Richelieu*
Louise in *The Two Orphans*
The Widow Melnotte in *The Lady of Lyons* (9 years)
Ralph Rackstraw in Hooley's Juvenile *Pinafore*

Other plays in which
Minnie Maddern appeared
as a star

The Puritan Maid by Ver Planck and Devereux
The Professional Beauty by Ver Planck and Devereux
The Storm Child
The Child Wife
Lady Jemima
Mila, Queen of the Natchez
Frou Frou—Adaptation by Augustin Daly
Featherbrain—Adaptation of *Tete de Linotte* by Steele MacKaye

399

Theatre Programs
New York, Tuesday, February 7, 1871
Lina Edwin's Theatre
720 Broadway
Lina Edwin   Proprietor & Lessee
Immense Success
of
Laura Keene
in
Dion Boucicault's Best Play
"HUNTED DOWN"
or, *The Two Lives of Mary Leigh*
Cast of Characters
Mary Leigh, *the artist's wife*
Miss Laura Keene
John Leigh, *Royal Academician*
Mr. Frank Mordaunt
Sir Arthur Glangurrig
Mr. Hart Conway
Count De Willidoff, *a broken-down gambler*..........Mr. George Becks
John Smith, *a London footman*
Mr. M. Rainford
Jeemes Jenkins, *a London butler*
Mr. F. Dovey
Clara, *a model*...Miss Emma Maddern
Mrs. Bolton Jones..Miss Amelia Harris
Fanny, *nursemaid to Mary's children*
Miss Emma Warren
Maud Leigh....Miss Charlotte Groves
Willie Leigh, *aged 6 years*
Little Minnie Maddern

Grand Opera House
R. L. Marsh   Lessee and Manager
Milwaukee, Wisconsin
March 5th, 6th and 7th, 1882
The Charming Young Actress, Miss
MINNIE MADDERN
First Presentation here of
Chas. Callahan's romantic comedy drama,
"FOGG'S FERRY!"
Supported by a strong and specially selected Dramatic Co. Under the Direction of *Jno. H. Havlin*
Cast of Characters
Chip............Miss Minnie Maddern
Zebulon Fogg, *a Ferryman*
Harold Forsburg
Gerald White........W. A. Whitecar
Bruce Rawdon..........Chas. Mason
400

William Still, *a Still One*
Wm. Cullington
Judge Norwood.........F. Armstrong
Bolter.................J. F. Hennegan
Blanche Norwood
Miss Helen Sedgwick
Mrs. Fogg...........Miss Kate Beebe
Martha Blodgett....Miss Lillie George
Author's Note: This production opened Monday Evening, May 15th, 1882, at the Park Theatre, New York.

The Academy of Music—Chicago
Dan'l Shelby, Sole Proprietor and Manager

Gentlemen will Confer a Favor on the Management if they will kindly Applaud with the *Hands* and not the *Feet*
Grand Opening!
Monday, August 27th, 1883
Engagement of the Young American Artiste
MINNIE MADDERN
supported by
Mr. George Morton
and her own Selected Company, under the management of
Legrand White
in a Romantic Comedy, *written expressly for Miss Maddern*, entitled
"JUANITA"
by Charles Callahan
Juanita..........Miss Minnie Maddern
Jasper Deering....Mr. George Morton
Don Miguel Valdez.Mr. A. W. Purcell
Philip Deering......Mr. Robert Scott
Dr. Barbour..........Mr. O. W. Eagle
Diego..............Mr. C. R. Burrows
Victor Young....Mr. H. Percy Brooke
Cadger.......Mr. Henry V. Donnelly
Officer...............Mr. J. T. Booth
Billy Newt......Miss Lillian Wallack
Geraldine Floyd...Miss May Wheeler
Barbara Fenn......Miss Ada Morton
Mrs. Heloise Fenn..Miss Adele Clarke
Mannela..........Miss Alice Stickney
This Theatre is Lighted Throughout with the Edison Incandescent Light

---

Grand Opera House
St. Louis
One Week, Commencing Sunday, Nov. 16, 1884

The Charming Young Emotional
Artiste,
MINNIE MADDERN
Under the Management of
Mr. Charles Frohman
In Her Recent New York Triumph
"CAPRICE"
A Comedy-Drama, in Four Acts by
Howard P. Taylor
Aided by an auxiliary of picked players
Mercy, *a Rustic Maiden*
    Miss Minnie Maddern
Jack Henderson.....Mr. Henry Miller
Philander Potts....Mr. J. W. Summers
Jethro Baxter......Mr. J. T. Herndon
Wally Henderson....Mr. H. P. Brooke
Jerome Henderson..Mr. Errol Dunbar
Harry Woodthorpe
    Mr. Harold Russell
Erastus Whiting
    Mr. Norman Campbell
Tobias Wheeler.......Mr. Cyril Scott
Timothy..........Mr. Robert Sinclair
Williams, *a Servant*..Mr. F. W. Strong
Emma Watson.........Mary Maddern
Millie Wetmore ⎱ Miss Lillian Wallack
Jake Baxter....⎰
Edith Henderson..Miss Jenny Williams
Campers, New Year's Callers, Etc.
Author's Note: In "Caprice" Minnie
Maddern sang "In the Gloaming."

The Lyceum Theatre—New York
Steele MacKaye General Manager
September 15, 1885
MISS MINNIE MADDERN
In an entirely new version of Sardou's
"Andrea" written especially for her by
Mr. MacKaye
"IN SPITE OF ALL"
Cast of Characters
Alice Clandenning
    Miss Minnie Maddern
Stella, *Prima Donna of the Comic*
Opera..........Mme. Selina Dolaro
Bessie, *Mrs. Clandenning's maid*
    Miss Lillian Wallack
Louise, *Stella's maid*
    Miss Marie Hartley
Carrol Clandenning
    Mr. Eben Plympton
Herr Antonius Kraft, *Impresario*
    Mr. Richard Mansfield

Mr. Hartmann, *Jeweler*
    Mr. John A. Lane
Jack Knickerbocker, *the Brother*
    Mr. Joseph Frankau
Call Boy, *of the Theatre*
    William Payson
Under the Immediate Direction of
Mr. Steele MacKaye

Tremont Theatre
Boston
Week of November 20, 1893
Engagement of
MINNIE MADDERN FISKE
Under the Management of
Mr. A. M. Palmer, in
"HESTER CREWE
A Play in Four Acts, by
Harrison Grey Fiske
Cast of Characters
Sir Kenneth Gordon, Bart.
    Mr. Charles J. Bell
Rev. Matthew Parmlee
    Mr. Courtenay Thorpe
Major Tom Crawford
    Mr. Arthur Lawrence
Kit Crewe........Mr. George Trader
Professor Planchetti—Mr. Lionel Bland
Caleb Hethcote.....Mr. James Garrett
John Mumford....Mr. Carl St. Aubyn
Peter Stork......Mr. Harry Randolph
Jerry Billings...Mr. Arthur Lawrence
Sam..............Mr. Clifford Leigh
Hackett...........Mr. Edwin Miller
Lady Violet Ormsby
    Miss Anna O'Keefe
Jerusha Lane......Miss Adele Clarke
Madame Planchetti
    Miss Mary Maddern
Mrs. Willoughby Vane
    Miss Eleanor Lane
Hester Crewe.............Mrs. Fiske
The play produced under the personal
direction of *Mrs. Fiske*
The Incidental Music composed by
Mr. Charles Puerner
Orchestra under the direction of
Mr. E. N. Catlin

Empire Theatre
Broadway and 40th Street, New York
Charles Frohman   Manager
Special Matinee, Thursday, February
15, 1894, in aid of the

Maternity and Training School
Departments of the
Hannemann Hospital
MINNIE MADDERN FISKE
in
"A DOLL'S HOUSE"
Drama in Three Acts, by Henrik Ibsen
Cast of Characters
Helmer........Mr. Courtenay Thorpe
Krogstad...Mr. William H. Thompson
Dr. Rank......Mr. Vincent Sternroyd
Porter...............Mr. Frank Bailey
Mrs. Linden...Sydney Cowell Holmes
Ellen...........Miss Bijou Fernandez
Anna................Miss Alice Leigh
Ivar ....Johnny McKeever
Bob................Little Mabel Bell
Emmy...........Edith Wachterhauser
Nora......................Mrs. Fiske

Grand Opera House
San Antonio, Texas
Saturday, Jan. 18, 1896
"THIS PICTURE AND THAT!"
A Comedy in One Act by
Brander Matthews
Cast of Characters
Mrs. Willoughby..Miss Ida Waterman
Major John Strong, U.S.A.
Mr. James Neill
Dr. Daulton, formerly Surgeon,
U.S.A...........Mr. Frank R. Mills
A Porter of the Hotel
Mr. Harry De Vere
"THE WHITE PINK"
A Comedy in One Act from the French
of Alphonse Daudet, by
Harrison Grey Fiske
Cast of Characters
Vidal, *member of the national*
assembly.........Mr. Albert Gran
Virginie, *his daughter, aged 21*
Miss Helen Macbeth
Cadet Vincent....Mr. Frank R. Mills
The Marquis, *aged 16*......Mrs. Fiske
"A LIGHT FROM ST. AGNES"
A Tragic Sketch in One Act by
Minnie Maddern Fiske
Cast of Characters
Michael Kerouac.....Mr. James Neill
Father Bertrand.....Mr. Albert Gran
'Toinette...................Mrs. Fiske
Note: The records of a small community in Louisiana tell of the life and
402

works of a certain Agnes ———. Her
name and remarkable works are remembered with love and reverence.

Duquesne Theatre
Pittsburgh, Pa.
Saturday, March 14, 1896
"CESARINE"
A Drama in Three Acts
("La Femme de Claude") by
Alexander Dumas, fils—
English Version by *Alice Kauser*
Cast of Characters
Claude Ruper........Mr. James Neill
Cantagnac, *a Prussian Spy*
Mr. Frank R. Mills
Antonie, *Claude's Pupil*
Mr. Albert Gran
Rebecca..........Miss Ida Waterman
Edmee...........Miss Mary Maddern
Cesarine...................Mrs. Fiske
Followed by
"NOT GUILTY"
A Dramatic Sketch in One Act by
Minnie Maddern Fiske
Cast of Characters
Mr. Knowlton, *a lawyer*....Mr. Mills
Mother Francesca, *Superior of the*
Convent............Miss Waterman
Margaret, *Adelaide's daughter*
Miss Macbeth
Debbe, *an old servant*....Miss Maddern
Adelaide..................Mrs. Fiske

Garden Theatre
New York
Beginning March 16, 1896
MINNIE MADDERN FISKE
in
"MARIE DELOCHE"
—THE QUEEN OF LIARS—
by
Alphonse Daudet and *Leon Hennique*
adapted from the French by
Harrison Grey Fiske
directed by
Henry Greenwall and Company
Cast of Characters
Marcel Nattier...........James Neill
Pierre de Sonnancourt, *a priest*
Frank R. Mills
Paul de Brives............Albert Gran
Jacques Olivier.......Lyster Sandford
Gaston...............Harry De Vere

Countess Nattier...Miss Ida Waterman
Lucile de Brives..Miss Helen Macbeth
Mere Andre......Miss Mary Maddern
Marie Deloche..............Mrs. Fiske

Garden Theatre
New York
Beginning Thursday, March 19, 1896
"A DOLL'S HOUSE"
Play in Three Acts by Henrik Ibsen
Directed by
Henry Greenwall & Company
Cast

Torwald Helmer.........James Neill
Krogstad.................Albert Gran
Dr. Rank...............Frank R. Mills
Porter................Harry De Vere
Mrs. Linden...........Ida Waterman
Ellen.................Helen Macbeth
Anna.................Mary Maddern
Nora......................Mrs. Fiske
followed by
"A LIGHT FROM ST. AGNES"
Tragic sketch in One Act by
Minnie Maddern Fiske
Cast

Michael Kerouac.........James Neill
Father Bertrand.........Albert Gran
'Toinette...................Mrs. Fiske

McVicker's Theatre—Chicago
Second Week—Beginning Monday,
April 6, Ending April 11, '96
MINNIE MADDERN FISKE
Under the direction of
Henry Greenwall & Company
"CESARINE"
A Drama in Three Acts
("La Femme de Claude")
by Alexander Dumas, fils
English Version by *Alice Kauser*
Cast of Characters

Claude Ruper........Mr. James Neill
Cantagnac..........Mr. Frank R. Mills
Antonie..............Mr. Albert Gran
Daniel...........Mr. Lyster Sandford
Rebecca...........Miss Ida Waterman
Edmee...........Miss Mary Maddern
Cesarine....................Mrs. Fiske
Preceded by
"THIS PICTURE AND THAT"
A Comedy in One Act by
Brander Matthews

Author's Note: "Cesarine" opened in
New York at the Garden Theatre,
March 24, 1896.

McVicker's Theatre
Chicago
Beginning Monday, April 13, 1896
MINNIE MADDERN FISKE
Under the direction of
Henry Greenwall & Company
"DIVORÇONS"
A Comedy in Three Acts by
Victorien Sardou
Cast of Characters

Des Prunelles—*age 40*..Mr. James Neill
Adhemar.............Mr. Frank Mills
Clavignac...........Mr. Albert Gran
Bastien, *a servant*..Mr. Lyster Sandford
Joseph, *a waiter*......Mr. Albert Gran
Commissary.........Mr. B. C. Barrett
Madame de Brionne
Miss Ida Waterman
Mlle. De Lusignan
Miss Mary Maddern
Josepha.........Miss Helen Macbeth
Cyprienne.................Mrs. Fiske
Policemen, Waiters, etc.
Supper served in the last Act
furnished by Auditorium Annex

Grand Opera House
H. Greenwall   Lessee and Manager
New Orleans, La.
One Week Commencing
Sunday, Dec. 13, 1896
MINNIE MADDERN FISKE
Under the direction of
Mr. A. M. Palmer presenting
"THE RIGHT TO HAPPINESS"
A Three-act Comedy of Sentiment,
from the German by
Marguerite Merington
Cast of Characters

Doctor Lee....Mr. James M. Colville
Raymond Winfield....Mr. Barton Hill
Douglas Colbert..Mr. Alfred Hickman
Edgar.............Mr. Charles Stevens
Simon.............Mr. Byron Ongley
Lily.................Miss Belle Stokes
Helen *(Winfield's daughter)*
Miss Rebecca Warren
Mrs. Bessell......Miss Mary Maddern
Madeline *(Winfield's daughter, a*
cripple).................Mrs. Fiske

Fifth Avenue Theatre
Broadway and Twenty-Eighth Street
New York City
Henry C. Miner,
Sole Proprietor and Manager
Beginning Tuesday Evening,
March 2, 1897
MRS. FISKE
and
A Specially Selected Company
presenting
"TESS OF THE D'URBERVILLES"
A Play in Four Acts
Dramatized by *Lorimer Stoddard,*
from the novel by *Thomas Hardy*
Cast of Characters
Angel Clare..........Edward M. Bell
Alec Stoke D'Urberville
Charles Coghlan
John Durbeyfield *(otherwise Sir John)*
W. J. LeMoyne
Abraham Durbeyfield..Namon Fowler
Farmer Crick......W. L. Branscombe
Jonathan ⎱ ⎰...Wilfrid North
Tim ⎰*dairymen*⎱. Alfred Hickman
James ⎱ ⎰W. E. Butterfield
Bailiff..............W. L. Branscombe
Joan Durbeyfield......Mary E. Barker
Tess......................Mrs. Fiske
'Liza Lu................Edith Wright
Marian ⎱ ⎰......Annie Irish
Izz ⎰*dairymaids*⎱..Bijou Fernandez
Retty ⎱ ⎰...Nellie Lingard
Constables, etc.
The Entire Production under the
direction of Mrs. Fiske
The Scenery painted by Joseph Physioc
and Seymour D. Parker
The Incidental Music composed by
Charles Puerner
Costumes by Windsor

Grand Opera House
Chicago, Ill.
Thursday Evening, Nov. 17, 1898
Engagement of
MRS. FISKE
and Her Company
Presenting on Thursday Night
(only time)
"LITTLE ITALY"
A Tragedy in One Act by
Horace B. Fry

404

Cast of Characters
Fabio Ronaldi...Frederic de Belleville
Michele..............Wilfrid North
Gioja.....................May Follis
Giulia.....................Mrs. Fiske
The people of the Italian Quarter
By members of the Hart Conway
School of Acting
Followed by
"DIVORÇONS"
A Comedy in Three Acts by
Victorien Sardou
Cast of Characters
Henri des Prunelles
Frederic de Belleville
Adhemar Gratignan........John Craig
M. Clavignac..........Wilfrid North
Jamarot, *commissary of police*
John Jack
Guiseppe, *head waiter at Dagneau's*
Frank McCormack
Bastien..................James Morley
Madame de Brionne....Sydney Cowell
Mlle. de Lusignan..........Olive Hoff
Josepha.............Gertrude Norman
Cyprienne.................Mrs. Fiske
The scenery by Frank E. Gates and
Edwin A. Morange
The incidental music arranged by
Charles Puerner
Costumes by Windsor

Fifth Avenue Theatre
Broadway and Twenty-Eighth Street
New York City
Edwin Knowles Sole Manager
Commencing Monday Evening,
February 27, 1899
Carriage Parties Received at
28th St. Entrance
MRS. FISKE
"MAGDA"
A Play in Four Acts by
Hermann Sudermann
Cast of Characters
Lieutenant-Colonel Schwartze,
retired........Frederic de Belleville
Pastor Heffterdingt, *of St. Mary's*
John Craig
Dr. von Keller, *Privy Councillor*
Tyrone Power
Lieutenant Max von Wendlowski
Frank McCormack

Von Klebs, Major-General, *retired*
                    Wilfrid North
Professor Beckmann..Frank Opperman
*Schwartze's children by his first
marriage*
Magda...................Mrs. Fiske
Marie...........Gertrude Norman
Augusta, née von Wendlowski,
    Schwartze's second wife
                    Mary E. Barker
Franziska von Wendlowski, *her
    sister*................Sydney Cowell
Mrs. von Klebs......Gertrude Bennett
Mrs. Ellrich...............Olive Hoff
Mrs. Schumann....Dolores Marbourg
Theresa.................Edith Wright
    The Scenery by Frank E. Gates and
        Edward A. Morange
        Costumes by Windsor
The Fifth Avenue Theatre Orchestra
    under the direction of
        Maurice Z. Hanan

Fifth Avenue Theatre
Broadway and Twenty-Eighth Street
            New York City
Edwin Knowles   Sole Manager
    Commencing Monday Evening,
        March 20, 1899
            MRS. FISKE
        "FROU-FROU"
    A Play in Five Acts
by *Henri Meilhac and Ludovic Halevy*
        Cast of Characters
Henri De Sartorys
            Frederic de Belleville
Paul De Valreas...........John Craig
Brigard...............Tyrone Power
Baron De Cambri......Wilfrid North
Pitou.............Frank McCormack
Pierre..................George Bonn
Georges...................Ipha Dahl
Gilberte...................Mrs. Fiske
Louise....................Olive Hoff
Baroness De Cambri..Gertrude Bennett
Pauline...............Sydney Cowell
Zanetto.............Gertrude Norman
Governess...........Ethelwyn Hoyt
Rosine..............Leonora Stonehill
    The Scenery by Frank E. Gates and
        Edward A. Morange
        Costumes by Windsor

The Fifth Avenue Theatre Orchestra
    under the direction of
        Maurice Z. Hanan

Fifth Avenue Theatre
Broadway and Twenty-Eighth Street
Edwin Knowles   Sole Manager
    Week commencing Monday Evening,
        April 11, 1898
            MRS. FISKE
        First Time in America
    "A BIT OF OLD CHELSEA"
        A Play in One Act, by
        Mrs. Oscar Beringer
        Cast of Characters
Jack Hillier, *a sculptor*
            Forrest Robinson
Artists
    Phil McDonnell......Wilfrid North
    Jim Dixon..........George Trader
    Paul Raymond...Frank McCormack
Alexandra Victoria Belchamber, *a
    flower girl*...............Mrs. Fiske
            Followed by
    "LOVE FINDS THE WAY"
*A Comedy of Sentiment, in Three Acts
        (from the German)
    by Marguerite Merington*
        Cast of Characters
Doctor Lee......Frederic de Belleville
Douglas Colbert.....Forrest Robinson
Raymond Winfield....Verner Clarges
Edgar Townsend......George Trader
Simon.................Wilfrid North
William...........Frank McCormack
Leslie................Lotta Linthicum
Mrs. Bessell...........Sydney Cowell
Winfield's daughters
    Madeline................Mrs. Fiske
    Helen.............Alberta Gallatin
Jane................Dorothy Chester
    The Scenery by Frank E. Gates and
        Edwin A. Morange
        The Incidental Music by
            Charles Puerner
        Costumes by Windsor

Fifth Avenue Theatre
Broadway and Twenty-Eighth Street
            New York City
Edwin Knowles   Sole Manager
    Commencing Monday Evening,
        March 13, 1899

405

MRS. FISKE
"A BIT OF OLD CHELSEA"
A Play in One Act by
Mrs. Oscar Beringer
Cast of Characters
Jack Hillier, *a sculptor*....John Craig
Artists
Phil McDonnell......Wilfrid North
Jim Dixon............Tyrone Power
Paul Raymond...Frank McCormack
Alexandra Victoria Belchamber, *a*
flower girl................Mrs. Fiske
Followed by
"LOVE FINDS THE WAY"
A Comedy of Sentiment, in Three Acts
(from the German)
by Marguerite Merington
Cast of Characters
Doctor Lee......Frederic de Belleville
Douglas Colbert...........John Craig
Raymond Winfield....Tyrone Power
Edgar Townsend...Frank McCormack
Simon..................Wilfrid North
William.................George Bonn
Leslie.....................Olive Hoff
Mrs. Bessell..........Sydney Cowell
Winfield's daughters
Madeline.................Mrs. Fiske
Helen............Gertrude Bennett
Jane................Gertrude Norman
The Scenery by Frank E. Gates and
Edward A. Morange
The Incidental Music by
Charles Puerner
Costumes by Windsor

Fifth Avenue Theatre
Broadway and Twenty-Eighth Street
Edwin Knowles   Sole Manager
Beginning Tuesday Evening,
September 12th, 1899
Carriage Parties Received at
28th St. Entrance
MRS. FISKE
Presenting for the first time in this city
"BECKY SHARP"
A Play in Four Acts by
Langdon Mitchell
Founded on Thackeray's *Vanity Fair*
Cast of Characters
The Marquis of Steyne
Tyrone Power

Sir Pitt Crawley, Bart.
Robert V. Ferguson
His Sons
Pitt Crawley........Charles Plunkett
Rawdon Crawley
Maurice Barrymore
William Dobbin.......Wilfrid North
George Osborne......Stanley Rignold
Joseph Sedley, *of Bogleywollah,*
India..............William F. Owen
Major Loder............E. L. Walton
Lord Bareacres.....W. L. Branscombe
Lord Tarquin..........Frank Reicher
Lord Southdown...Frank McCormack
The Duke of Brunswick—B. B. Belcher
Prince Peterwaradin......Paul Weigel
Tommy Raikes.........Walter Pleugh
General Tufto.............Neil Grey
Ranelagh.................Henry Stokes
Blenkinsop............George P. Bonn
German Students
Fritz.................Frank Reicher
Max...................Paul Weigel
Bowles.............W. L. Branscombe
Raggles.............Arthur Maitland
Landlord of the "Elephant," *at*
Pumpernickel...........Otto Meyer
Becky Sharp................Mrs. Fiske
Amelia Sedley.......Zenaide Williams
Miss Crawley..........Ida Waterman
The Marchioness of Steyne
Jean Chamblin
Lady Bareacres......Francesca Lincoln
Lady Blanche Thistlewood, *her*
daughter................Olive Hoff
Lady Jane Crawley..Leonora Stonehill
The Duchess of Richmond
Josephine Roberts
The Duchess of Buccleugh
Agnes Bruce
Briggs, *Miss Crawley's companion*
Mary Maddern
Fifine.................Ethelwyn Hoyt
Guests, etc.: Gertrude Norman, Dirce
St. Cyr, Mary MacNamara, Gloria
Alonzo, Helen Henry, Alma Whitsell,
Sidney Mather, Arthur W. Row, William
W. Brown, R. B. Keggerais,
Frederick Kingstone, H. F. Anderson,
Albert Reed, R. F. McCoy, Cortland
Hopkins.
The play produced under the direction
of *Mrs. Fiske* and *Fred Williams*
Scenery by Henry E. Hoyt

406

Costumes designed by Percy Anderson, of London and made by M. Herrmann and W. Dazian
Wigs by Charles Meyer and Charles L. Lietz. Shoes by John Azzimonti.
Properties by William Edgerly and Joseph Turner
The Fifth Avenue Theatre Orchestra under the direction of Maurice Z. Hanan

Manhattan Theatre
Broadway and Thirty-third Street
New York City
Harrison Grey Fiske—Manager
Beginning Tuesday Evening, Sept. 24, 1901
"MIRANDA OF THE BALCONY"
by *Anne Crawford Flexner*
founded on the Novel by
A. E. W. Mason
Cast of Characters
Luke Charnock......Robert T. Haines
Ralph Warriner..........J. E. Dodson
Major Ambrose Wilbraham
Etienne Girardot
Sir George Crowninshield
Edward Lester
M. Fournier..............Max Figman
Viscount Steignton...Jefferson Winter
Captain Grant-Duff..Bertram Godfrey
Mr. Jermyn........Frank McCormack
Jaynes................Phillips Smalley
Carlos..................Bessie Harris
Hassan Akbar...Frederick C. Bertrand
Hamet...............Jefferson Winter
Rustum..............Charles O. Shaw
Cassim................Edward Davis
Selam.................Burton Adams
Lady Donnisthorpe
Kate Pattison Selten
Miranda Warriner..........Mrs. Fiske
Jane Holt.................Annie Irish
Lady Ethel Mickleham..Emily Stevens
Thompson...........Victoria Addison
Guests at Lady Donnisthorpe's:
Louise Delmar, Dorothy Stanton, Mary Maddern, Ella Miller, Josephine Wyndham, Jessica Penn, Katherine Kaye, Marion Wolsey Cate, James Henderson, Claus Bogel, H. Hartwell Sleight, J. Cleaney Mathews, W. C. Raue, Edward Stockton, and Frank Alliston.
Play in 4 Acts—5 Scenes

Scenery painted by
Messrs. Gates and Morange
The Manhattan Theatre Orchestra under the direction of Charles E. Puerner
The Spanish Song in Act III and incidental music composed by Charles E. Puerner
Gowns by White, Howard and Company, Worth and Mme. Virion
Moorish and Arabian costumes by Maurice Herrmann
The play produced under the direction of
Mrs. Fiske and *Max Figman*

Manhattan Theatre
Broadway and Thirty-third Street
New York City
Harrison Grey Fiske—Manager
beginning November 25, 1901
"THE UNWELCOME
MRS. HATCH"
*Play in Four Acts—Four Scenes
by Mrs. Burton Harrison*
Cast of Characters
Richard Lorimer, *a successful financier*..............J. E. Dodson
Paul Trevor, *a wanderer and idealist*
Robert T. Haines
Jack Adrian, *affianced to Gladys*
Jefferson Winter
Mr. Cleeve, *Mr. Lorimer's attorney*
Max Figman
Freddy Brenton, *affianced to Dolly Gay*...............Phillips Smalley
Jones, *a private detective*
Frank McCormack
Elihu G. Carmichael
Frederick Bertrand
Butler...............Charles O. Shaw
Footman.................W. C. Raue
Delivery Boy..........George Odell
Mrs. Richard Lorimer
Eleanor Moretti
Gladys Lorimer........Emily Stevens
Marian Lorimer (*"Mrs. Hatch"*)
Mrs. Fiske
Lina Thurston...........Annie Irish
Dolly Gay...............Rose Stuart
Bridesmaids to Gladys
Ethel Gilmour.....Victoria Addison
Muriel Chauncey......Helen Ashley
Beatrix Callendar....Katharine Kaye

Agnes, *a gem of the old country*
Annie Ward Tiffany
Coralie.................Louise Delmar
Chambermaid...........Edith Talbot
Maria, *the lame child*....Lillian Claire
Members of the "Little Wings" club,
Park Loungers, etc.,
by Misses Miller, Maddern, Penn, Eldridge, and Messrs. Bogel, Sleight, Mathews, Henderson, Anderson and Denton
Children from the East Side
Play produced under the direction of
Mrs. Fiske and *Max Figman*
The scenery painted by
Messrs. Gates and Morange
The gowns by White, Howard and Company and Madame Virion
The Manhattan Theatre Orchestra under the direction of Charles Puerner

Manhattan Theatre
Broadway and Thirty-third Street
New York City
Harrison Grey Fiske—Manager
January 20, 1902
"A BIT OF OLD CHELSEA"
A Play in One Act by
Mrs. Oscar Beringer
Jack Hillier, *a sculptor*
Robert T. Haines
Artists
Phil McDonnell..Frank McCormack
Jim Dixon..........Phillips Smalley
Paul Raymond.......James Young
Alexandra Victoria Belchamber, *a*
flower girl...............Mrs. Fiske

Manhattan Theatre
Broadway and Thirty-third Street
New York City
Harrison Grey Fiske—Manager
May 6, 1902
"TESS OF THE D'URBERVILLES"
A Play in Four Acts by
Lorimer Stoddard
from Thomas Hardy's novel
Cast of Characters
Angel Clare...............John Craig
Alec Stoke D'Urberville
Frederic de Belleville
John Durbeyfield, *otherwise Sir John*
John Jack
Abraham Durbeyfield...Emily Stevens

408

Farmer Crick.............Claus Bogel
Dairymen
Jonathan Kail....Frank McCormack
Amby Seedling..Charles J. Burbidge
Bill Lewell............Phillips Smalley
Bailiff............Charles J. Burbidge
Joan Durbeyfield......Mary E. Barker
Tess...................Mrs. Fiske
'Liza Lu................Lillian Claire
Dairymaids
Marian.............Eleanor Moretti
Izz...................Helen Ashley
Retty...............Nellie Lingard
Constables, Etc.
The Scenery painted by Joseph Physioc and Seymour D. Parker
The incidental music composed by
Charles Puerner
The Manhattan Theatre Orchestra under the direction of Charles Puerner

Manhattan Theatre
Broadway and Thirty-third Street
New York City
Harrison Grey Fiske—Manager
May 21-1902   Wednesday Afternoon
"A DOLL'S HOUSE"
A Play in Three Acts by
Henrik Ibsen
Cast of Characters
Torwald Helmer.........Max Figman
Krogstad................James Young
Dr. Rank.................Claus Bogel
Porter.............Charles J. Burbidge
Mrs. Linden..........Eleanor Moretti
Ellen...................Helen Ashley
Anna.................Mary Maddern
Ivar...................Queenie Phillips
Bob....................Harry Wright
Emmy.............Blanche Alexander
Nora.......................Mrs. Fiske
The Manhattan Theatre Orchestra under the direction of Charles Puerner

Manhattan Theatre
Broadway and Thirty-third Street
New York City
Harrison Grey Fiske—Manager
Double Bill
May 26, 1902
"LITTLE ITALY"
A Tragedy, in One Act, by
Horace B. Fry

Cast of Characters
Fabio Ronaldi....Frederic de Belleville
Michele...................Claus Bogel
Gioja................Helen Stevenson
Giulia......................Mrs. Fiske
People of the Italian Quarter, Etc.
Followed by
"DIVORÇONS"
A Comedy in Three Acts by
Victorien Sardou
Henri des Prunelles
                    Frederic de Belleville
Adhemar Gratignan......Max Figman
M. Clavignac............James Young
Jamarot, *Commissary of Police*
                    Claus Bogel
Giuseppe, *head waiter at Dagneau's*
                    Frank McCormack
Bastien.................James Morley
Madame de Brionne.......Florida Pier
Mlle. de Lusignan..Marion Ten Eyck
Josepha..............Victoria Addison
Cyprienne..................Mrs. Fiske
Sergeants-de-ville, Waiters, etc.
The Scenery painted by
Gates and Morange
The Costumes by White, Howard and
Company, and Madame Virion
The Manhattan Theatre Orchestra
under the direction of Charles Puerner

Manhattan Theatre
Broadway and Thirty-third Street
New York City
Harrison Grey Fiske, Manager
November 19, 1902
"MARY OF MAGDALA"
by Paul Heyse
A Drama in Five Acts
Persons Represented
Caiaphas.................M. J. Jordan
Aulus Flavius........Henry Woodruff
Haran...................Scott Craven
Jotham...................Max Figman
Joab.....................James Young
Gamaliel...........Frank McCormack
Judas, *of Kerioth*.......Tyrone Power
Simon....................W. B. Mack
Quintus................Sydney Smyth
Marco............Herbert McKenzie
A Torch Bearer........Henry Haskins
Mary, of Magdala.........Mrs. Fiske
Rachel..................Rose Eytinge
Miriam..................Ida Hamilton

Romans, Soldiers, Hebrews, Priests,
Men and Women of Jerusalem, Egyp-
tian Dancing Girls, etc. by Misses
Spencer, Maynard, E. Harris, Lee,
Clowes, Morris, Nordstrom, Wain-
right, C. Harris, Maddern, Stevens,
Noel, Berrell, Piggott, Doyle, Hall, B.
Doyle, Chamberlin—Messrs. Jewett,
Ornton, Slevin, McClure, Thompson,
Raymond, Le Rendu, Koe, Hammond,
Carson, Briscoe, and others.
The play produced under the
Direction of Mrs. Fiske
Incidental Music composed and
selected by Charles Puerner
Manhattan Theatre Orchestra under
direction of Charles Puerner
Scenes for Acts I, II, V painted by
Gates and Morange—Scene for
Act III by Homer F. Emens
The Scenery constructed by
George Ormston
Costumes by Percy Anderson of
London—made by Maurice Herrmann
Wigs by Charles L. Leitz
Furniture, Properties and Effects by
James Caldwell

Manhattan Theatre
Broadway and Thirty-third Street
New York City
Harrison Grey Fiske, Manager
October 5-10, 1903
A Drama in Four Acts, entitled
"HEDDA GABLER"
by Henrik Ibsen
Cast of Characters
Jörgen Tesman......William B. Mack
Assessor Brack........Henry J. Carvill
Eilert Lövberg......Hobart Bosworth
Hedda Tesman............Mrs. Fiske
Mrs. Elvsted..........Carlotta Nillson
Miss Juliana Tesman...Mary Maddern
Berta....................Belle Bohn

Manhattan Theatre
Broadway and Thirty-third Street
New York City
Harrison Grey Fiske, Manager
September 14, 1904
MRS. FISKE
and the
Manhattan Company
Presenting a Comedy in Four Acts

409

(Five Scenes)
Founded on Thackeray's *Vanity Fair*
entitled

"BECKY SHARP"
by Langdon Mitchell
Cast of Characters
The Marquis of Steyne. .George Arliss
Sir Pitt Crawley, Bart.
Robert V. Ferguson
His Sons
Pitt Crawley.......William B. Mack
Rawdon Crawley.......John Mason
William Dobbin...Henry J. Hadfield
George Osborne......Stanley Rignold
Joseph Sedley, *of Bogleywollah,*
India............Frank J. McIntyre
Major Loder.........Roydon Erlynne
Lord Bareacres.....W. L. Branscombe
Lord Tarquin......Harry S. Hadfield
Lord Southdown. .Robert V. Ferguson
The Duke of Brunswick
Charles Terry
Prince Peterwaradin. .Ludwig Lederer
Tommy Raikes.......Edwin Brewster
General Tufto.............Neil Grey
Ranelagh...............James Morley
Blenkinsop...............James Edlam
German Students
Fritz..............Ludwig Lederer
Max.............Harry S. Hadfield
Bowles.............W. L. Branscombe
Raggles...................E. Seber
Landlord of the "Elephant" *at*
Pumpernickel...........Otto Meyer
Becky Sharp...............Mrs. Fiske
Amelia Sedley.......Laura McGilvray
Miss Crawley..........Kate Fletcher
The Marchioness of Steyne
Anne Gregory
Lady Bareacres......Cecilia Radclyffe
Lady Blanche Thistlewood, *her*
daughter.............Emily Stevens
Lady Jane Crawley.....Lucy Spencer
The Duchess of Richmond. .Mary Page
The Duchess of Buccleugh
Gertrude Graham
Briggs, *Miss Crawley's companion*
Mary Maddern
Fifine...............Frances Welstead
Guests, etc.—Ethel Howard, Marie
Frederick, Kate Oglebay, Daintry
Yates, Robert J. Wurster, Walter G.
Hendrix, William A. Sheehy, Lydian
Durrett, William Hamilton, George C.
410

Smiley, James Duncan and J. H. Carter.
Scenery by Gates and Morange
Costumes designed by Percy Anderson,
of London and made by M. Herrmann,
W. Dazian and Madame Freisinger
Wigs by Charles Meyer and
Charles L. Lietz
Properties by William Edgerly,
Joseph Turner and James Caldwell
The Manhattan Theatre Orchestra
under the direction of
Frederick W. Ecke

Manhattan Theatre
Broadway and Thirty-third Street
New York City
Harrison Grey Fiske—Manager
Beginning Thursday Evening,
November 17, 1904
MRS. FISKE
and the
Manhattan Company
In a Drama in Four Acts, entitled
"HEDDA GABLER"
by Henrik Ibsen
Cast of Characters
Jörgen Tesman......William B. Mack
Assessor Brack.........George Arliss
Eilert Lövberg............John Mason
Hedda Tesman.............Mrs. Fiske
Mrs. Elvsted........Laura McGilvray
Miss Juliana Tesman...Mary Maddern
Berta..................Emily Stevens
Scenery by Gates and Morange
Mrs. Fiske's Gowns made by
Madame Freisinger

Manhattan Theatre
Broadway and Thirty-third Street
New York City
Harrison Grey Fiske—Manager
December 12, 1904
MRS. FISKE
and the
Manhattan Company
presenting a New Play, in Five Acts,
entitled
"LEAH KLESCHNA"
by C. M. S. McLellan
Cast of Characters
Paul Sylvaine.............John Mason
Kleschna, *known as Monsieur*
Garnier.........Charles Cartwright
Schram..............William B. Mack

General Berton......Edward Donnelly
Raoul Berton...........George Arliss
Valentin Favre.......Etienne Girardot
Herr Linden......Robert V. Ferguson
Anton Pfaff...........Charles Terry
Johann.............H. Chapman Ford
Reichmann..........Monroe Salisbury
Baptiste.................James Morley
Leah Kleschna.............Mrs. Fiske
Madame Berton......Cecilia Radclyffe
Claire Berton...........Emily Stevens
Sophie Chaponniere..Frances Welstead
Frieda....................Marie Fedor
Charlotte..............Mary Maddern
Scenery by Gates and Morange
Properties by James Caldwell
Mrs. Fiske's costumes by
Madame Freisinger
The Manhattan Theatre Orchestra
Under the direction of
Frederick W. Ecke

Manhattan Theatre
Broadway and Thirty-third Street
New York City
Harrison Grey Fiske—Manager
Wednesday Afternoon, March 29, 1905
THE MANHATTAN COMPANY
appearing in Three One-Act Plays
by MRS. FISKE
"THE ROSE"
Count Choteau de Rohan
George Arliss
Frederick, his physician
Edward Donnelly
Baptiste, his valet....Etienne Girardot
Marie, Countess de Rohan
Gertrude Graham
'Tilda, her maid........Lucy Spencer
"A LIGHT FROM ST. AGNES"
Michel Kerouac...........John Mason
Father Bertrand......William B. Mack
'Toinette.............Fernanda Eliscu
"THE EYES OF THE HEART"
Monsieur d'Ancelot.....George Arliss
Paul, his son........Edward Donnelly
Monsieur Grasset..Robert V. Ferguson
Remy, his son.......Monroe Salisbury
Didier, an old servant.William B. Mack
Mignon, M. d'Ancelot's orphan
grand-daughter.......Emily Stevens
Annette..............Mary Maddern
An Errand Boy.........Charles Terry

Manhattan Theatre
Broadway and Thirty-Third Street
New York City
Harrison Grey Fiske—Manager
Three Matinees
Tuesday, Wednesday, Thursday,
April 24, 25, 26, 1906
MRS. FISKE
and the Manhattan Company
"THE EYES OF THE HEART"
by Mrs. Fiske
"DOLCE"
A One-Act Comedy
by John Luther Long
Dolce, Contessa di Cassali,
formerly the singing girl of Little
Italy.....................Mrs. Fiske
Shandon, an American artist
John Mason
Servant.................Charles Terry
"A LIGHT FROM ST. AGNES"
by Mrs. Fiske
The Manhattan Theatre Orchestra
Under the Direction of
Frederick W. Ecke

Lyric Theatre—New York
Sam S. and Lee Shubert
Lessees and Managers
Week Beginning Monday Evening,
November 19, 1906
Under the Direction of
Harrison Grey Fiske
MRS. FISKE
and
The Manhattan Company
Presenting a Play in Four Acts, Entitled
"THE NEW YORK IDEA"
by Langdon Mitchell
Cast of Characters
Philip Phillimore......Charles Harbury
Mrs. Phillimore, his mother.Ida Vernon
The Reverend Mathew Phillimore,
his brother..........Dudley Clinton
Grace Phillimore, his sister
Emily Stevens
Miss Heneage, his aunt
Blanche Weaver
William Sudley, his cousin
William B. Mack
Mrs. Vida Phillimore, his divorced
wife...................Marian Lea
Brooks, her footman..George Harcourt
Benson, her maid..........Belle Bohn

411

Sir Wilfrid Cates-Darby.George Arliss
John Karslake............John Mason
Mrs. Cynthia Karslake, *his divorced
wife*....................Mrs. Fiske
Nogam, *his valet*......Dudley Digges
Tim Fiddler......Robert V. Ferguson
Thomas, *the Phillimores' family
servant*...............Richard Clark
The Production staged by
Mr. and Mrs. Fiske
The Scenery painted by
Gates and Morange, & built by the
George W. Ormston Company
The properties by Edward Siedle
Mrs. Fiske's costumes by Howard and
Company, Dustan and Arnold,
Constable & Company

Shubert Theatre
New Orleans
Beginning October 28, 1907
Harrison Grey Fiske presents
MRS. FISKE
and The Manhattan Company
in
"TESS OF THE D'URBERVILLES"
*A Drama in Four Acts by
Lorimer Stoddard based on the
novel by Thomas Hardy*
Cast of Characters
Angel Clare...........Guy Bates Post
Alec Stoke-D'Urberville.George Arliss
John Durbeyfield.....Charles Harbury
Abraham Durbeyfield...Emily Stevens
Farmer Crick......Robert V. Ferguson
Jonathan Kail......Frank McCormack
Amby Seedling.........Charles Terry
Bill Lewell.......Bernard Cavanaugh
Bailiff................William Jackson
Joan Durbeyfield......Mary E. Barker
Tess......................Mrs. Fiske
'Liza Lu.................Lillian Claire
Marian.........Florence Montgomery
Izz...................Merle Maddern
Retty.................Laure Donalde
(Southern Tour)

Shubert Theatre
New Orleans
Beginning November 4, 1907
Harrison Grey Fiske presents
MRS. FISKE
and The Manhattan Company
in "LEAH KLESCHNA"

A Play in Five Acts by
C. M. S. McLellan
Cast of Characters
Paul Sylvaine..........Guy Bates Post
Kleschna, *known as Monsieur
Garnier*...........Charles Harbury
Schram............Bernard Cavanaugh
General Berton.....Frank McCormack
Raoul Berton............George Arliss
Valentin Favre....Robert V. Ferguson
Herr Linden..........William Jackson
Anton Pfaff.............Charles Terry
Johann...................John Elliott
Reichman..............Henry Powers
Baptiste.................Paul Judson
Leah Kleschna..............Mrs. Fiske
Mme. Berton....Florence Montgomery
Claire Berton..........Emily Stevens
Sophie Chaponniere....Laure Donalde
Frieda................Merle Maddern
Charlotte..............Mary E. Barker
(Southern Tour)

Lyric Theatre—New York
Sam S. and Lee Shubert
Lessees and Managers
Week Beginning Monday Evening,
December 30, 1907
MRS. FISKE
and
The Manhattan Company
presenting
under *Harrison Grey Fiske's* direction
A Play in Four Acts entitled
"ROSMERSHOLM"
by *Henrik Ibsen*
Translated by *Charles Archer*
Cast of Characters
John Rosmer, *of Rosmersholm, for-
merly clergyman of the parish*
Bruce McRae
Rebecca West, *in charge of Rosmer's
household*................Mrs. Fiske
Rector Kroll, *Rosmer's brother-in-
law*...................Fuller Mellish
Ulric Brendel..........George Arliss
Peter Mortensgard, *editor of the
"Beacon"*...........Albert Bruning
Madame Helseth, *housekeeper at
Rosmersholm*.Florence Montgomery
The play produced under the direction
of *Mr. and Mrs. Fiske*

Hackett Theatre
42nd Street between Broadway &
8th Ave.—New York
Beginning Tuesday Evening,
November 17, 1908
Harrison Grey Fiske presents
MRS. FISKE
and The Manhattan Company
in
"SALVATION NELL"
A Play, in Three Acts, by
Edward Sheldon
Characters

Jim Platt..............Holbrook Blinn
Major Williams.......David Glassford
Sid J. McGovern........W. T. Clarke
"Squirt" Kelly ....Eugene Reed
Kid Cummin ......Robert Evans
Al McGovern.............John Dillon
Chris Johnson.........Thomas Carroll
Callahan.................E. F. Nagle
Jerry Gallagher....Judge R. Downing
Joe Madden............R. C. Beecroft
Denny Giffen..............Mark Ross
Tommy Blake............Frank Foley
Blumenthal........Herbert Heywood
O'Rourke..⎤ ⎡.Frank Hilton
O'Brien....⎬ *Policemen* ⎨.H. Heywood
Butler.....⎦ ⎩..E. W. Short
Dr. Benedict..........Edwin Brewster
Jimmy Sanders..........Antrim Short
Baxter...................Robert Evans
Bradley..................Eugene Reed
Paddy............Clarence Rockefeller
Bob....................Frank De Gez
Pete....................Jesse Keppler
Packey.............Clarence Williams
Nell Sanders...............Mrs. Fiske
Lieutenant O'Sullivan *("Hallelujah*
Maggie")............Mary Madison
Myrtle Odell............Hope Latham
Susie Callahan..........Grace Shanley
Old Mary.............Mary Maddern
Mrs. Flanagan.....Lelia Romer Tyler
Mabel Keeney..........Elsie Romayne
Sal....................Merle Maddern
Rosie Hubbell............May Barton
Frau Schmidt...........Petra Folkman
Mame Marsh...........Elsie Romayne
Mrs. Spratt..........Mabel Stoughton
Mrs. Baxter.............Gilda Varesi
Mrs. Mellen............Mona D. Ryan
Jennie..............Constance Abbott
Mamie.................Corinne Ford

Salvationists, Musicians, Street
Vendors, etc.
The play produced under
Mr. and Mrs. Fiske's personal direction
Act I painted by D. Frank Dodge,
Acts II and III by Ernest Gros
Scenery constructed by the
George W. Ormston Company
Properties by the Siedle Studio
Costumes by Freisinger
Music Program under the Direction of
Mr. Henry Burck

Lyceum Theatre—New York
Daniel Frohman, Proprietor & Manager
Week Beginning Monday Evening,
March 28, 1910
Harrison Grey Fiske presents
MRS. FISKE
and The Manhattan Company
in
"PILLARS OF SOCIETY"
A Play in Four Acts
by *Henrik Ibsen*
Cast of Characters

Karsten Bernick.......Holbrook Blinn
Mrs. Bernick, *his wife*...Virginia Kline
Olaf, *his son*...........Gregory Kelly
Martha Bernick, *his sister*...Alice John
Johan Tonnesen, *Mrs. Bernick's*
younger brother....Edward Mackay
Lona Hessel, *her stepsister*..Mrs. Fiske
Hilmar Tonnesen, *Mrs. Bernick's*
cousin..............Cyril Chadwick
Dr. Rorlund, *a schoolmaster*
Henry Stephenson
Merchants
Rummel..............Fuller Mellish
Vigeland..........Wilfred Buckland
Sandstad............T. N. Heffron
Krap, *Bernick's chief clerk*
R. W. Tucker
Dina Dorf, *a young girl living in*
Bernick's house......Merle Maddern
Aune, *foreman of Bernick's shipyard*
Sheldon Lewis
Jacob, *a servant*......R. Owen Meech
Mrs. Rummel.............Mabel Reed
Mrs. Holt..............Florine Arnold
Mrs. Lynge..........Veda McEvers
Hilda Rummel......Helena Van Brugh
Netta Holt.............Helen Fulton
Townspeople, Sailors, Steamship
Passengers, Etcetera

413

The play produced under the
personal direction of
Mr. and Mrs. Fiske
The scenery painted by Ernest Gros—
built by the George W. Ormston
Construction Company

Lyceum Theatre—New York
Daniel Frohman, Proprietor and
Manager
Week Beginning Monday Evening,
April 11, 1910
Harrison Grey Fiske presents
MRS. FISKE
and The Manhattan Company

The Performance Will Begin with
"THE GREEN COCKATOO"
Grotesquerie, in One Act by
Arthur Schnitzler
Followed by
"HANNELE"
A Dream Poem, in Two Parts by
Gerhart Hauptmann
(Translated by *Mary J. Safford:*
Metrical passages by *Percy MacKaye*)
Cast of Characters
Hannele....................Mrs. Fiske
Gottwald, *a schoolmaster*
Holbrook Blinn
Sister Martha, *a deaconess*..Alice John
Paupers
Tulpe, *an old beggar woman*
Florine Arnold
Hedwig, *a dissolute woman*
Mabel Reed
Pleschke, *a beggar*....Sheldon Lewis
Hanke, *a young ne'er-do-well*
R. W. Tucker
Seidel, *a wood cutter*
Edward Mackay
Berger, *a magistrate*......Paul Scardon
Schmidt, *a beadle*......T. N. Heffron
Dr. Wachler........Henry Stephenson
In her delirium Hannele imagines
she sees:
Mattern, *the mason, her father*
Fuller Mellish
A Woman's Figure, *her dead mother*
Virginia Kline
A Tall Dark Angel..Wilfred Buckland
First Angel...........Merle Maddern
Second Angel.........Veda McEvers
Third Angel........Helena Van Brugh
414

Sister Martha...............Miss John
The Village Tailor....R. Owen Meech
Gottwald..................Mr. Blinn
Pleschke..................Mr. Lewis
Hanke....................Mr. Tucker
Seidel....................Mr. Mackay
A Stranger..................Mr. Blinn
Four White-Robed Youths—
Misses Mercer, Marstrand,
Droste and West
Mourners—by Misses Arnold, Mary
Maddern, Fulton, Reed; Messrs. Meech,
Arundel, Harrison and others
Many Large and Small Angels of Light
and Gottwald's Pupils
The play produced under the
personal direction of
Harrison Grey Fiske
Music for *Hannele* composed by
Max Marschalk
Symphonic Orchestra—under direction
of Alexander Z. Birnbaum
Scenery painted by Ernest Gros and
built by George W. Ormston
Construction Company
The costumes by Freisinger
The properties by the Seidle Studios

Lyceum Theatre—New York
Daniel Frohman, Proprietor and
Manager
West 45th Street Near Broadway,
New York
Week Beginning Monday Evening,
March 20, 1911
Harrison Grey Fiske presents
MRS. FISKE
and The Manhattan Company
in
"BECKY SHARP"
A Play in Four Acts by
Langdon Mitchell
Founded on Thackeray's *Vanity Fair*
Cast of Characters
The Marquis of Steyne
Henry E. Dixey
Sir Pitt Crawley, Bart.
Robert V. Ferguson
His Sons
Pitt Crawley...........Paul Scardon
Rawdon Crawley.Henry Stephenson
William Dobbin........Lewis Howard
George Osborne......Reginald Mason

Joseph Sedley, *of Bogleywollah, India*
Harold Russell
Major Loder.............Ivan Simpson
Lord Bareacres........R. Owen Meech
Lord Tarquin.........Harry L. Fraser
Lord Southdown.......R. V. Ferguson
Tommy Raikes.........Gregory Kelly
General Tuffo........George McLeod
Ranelagh................Herbert Holt
Blenkinsop.........Henry Mathewson
German Students
Fritz................Ralph Harlow
Max...............Thomas Clifton
Bowles............Frederick Marshall
Raggles.............Harold Mathews
Landlord of the "Elephant"
at *Pumpernickel*.......Carl Hartberg
Becky Sharp...............Mrs. Fiske
Amelia Sedley......Helena Van Brugh
Miss Crawley.........Florine Arnold
Briggs, *Miss Crawley's companion*
Mary Maddern
Lady Bareacres.........Veda McEvers
Lady Blanche Thistlewood,
her daughter......Constance Jackson
Lady Jane Crawley.......Sophie Blair
Fifine.............Marianne Marstrand
The Play Produced under
the Direction of
Mr. and Mrs. Fiske
Scenery by Gates and Morange
Costumes designed by Percy Anderson,
of London and made by W. Dazian
and Madame Freisinger
*Author's Note: This Revival of "Becky
Sharp" began May 26, 1910, in St. Louis
at the Olympic Theatre.*

Lyceum Theatre
Daniel Frohman, Proprietor & Manager
West 45th Street Near Broadway,
New York
Week Beginning Monday Evening,
April 3, 1911
Harrison Grey Fiske presents
MRS. FISKE
and The Manhattan Company
in
"MRS. BUMPSTEAD-LEIGH"
*A Comedy in Three Acts by
Harry James Smith*
Cast of Characters
Justin Rawson.......Charles Harbury
Miss Rawson, *his sister*....Kate Lester

Goeffrey Rawson, *his younger son*
Malcolm Duncan
Anthony Rawson, *his elder son*
Douglas J. Wood
Stephen Leavitt..........Paul Scardon
Mrs. Stephen Leavitt....Veda McEvers
Peter Swallow........Henry E. Dixey
Kitson...................Cyril Young
Mrs. De Salle..........Florine Arnold
Mrs. Bumpstead-Leigh......Mrs. Fiske
Violet De Salle...Kathlene MacDonell
Nina..............Helena Van Brugh
The play produced under
the direction of
Mr. and Mrs. Fiske
Scenery by D. Frank Dodge
*Author's Note: Peter Swallow was
played by Holbrook Blinn—Chicago—
week of Oct. 31, 1910. Peter Swallow
was played by Henry E. Dixey—New
York—Apr. 3, 1911, for 6 weeks. Peter
Swallow was played by Tim Murphy
for remainder of engagement. Peter
Swallow was played by Malcolm Dun-
can on summer tour, 1911.*

The Empire Theatre
Thursday, Friday and Saturday,
Oct. 19, 20, 21, 1911
Syracuse, N. Y.
Harrison Grey Fiske presents
MRS. FISKE
and The Manhattan Company
in
"THE NEW MARRIAGE"
*A Comedy in Four Acts, by
Langdon Mitchell*
Cast of Characters
Wilmer Bromley.......Joseph Kilgour
Agnes Bromley.............Mrs. Fiske
Mrs. Ellicot..........Elizabeth Fagan
Blanche Ellicot..........Anne Bradley
Mrs. Cantrip...........Hattie Russell
Horace Byethorne........Shelley Hull
Leona Byethorne......Gladys Hanson
John Goodloe.......Edward Donnelly
Jane Goodloe......Edwalyn O'Connell
Luke Horaby........Douglas Paterson
Jennie Gunn.......Helena Van Brugh
Kokosura...............T. Tamamoto
Antoine.................J. T. Chaille
Emilia..................Gilda Varesi
The Play Produced by
Mr. and Mrs. Fiske

415

The Scenery Painted by
Ernest Gros

Broadway Theatre
Brooklyn, New York
Beginning November 27, 1911
Harrison Grey Fiske presents
MRS. FISKE
and The Manhattan Company
in
"MRS. BUMPSTEAD-LEIGH"
A Comedy in Three Acts by
Harry James Smith
Cast of Characters

Justin Rawson......Henry Stephenson
Miss Rawson, his sister..Hattie Russell
Geoffrey Rawson, his younger son
Shelley Hull
Anthony Rawson, his elder son
Douglas Paterson
Stephen Leav...c......R. Owen Meech
Mrs. Stephen Leavitt......Gilda Varesi
Peter Swallow.........Joseph Kilgour
Kitson...................Cyril Young
Mr. De Salle...........Florine Arnold
Mrs. Bumpstead-Leigh......Mrs. Fiske
Violet De Salle.......Francesca Rotoli
Nina...............Helena Van Brugh
The Play Produced under
the direction of
Mr. and Mrs. Fiske
Scenery by D. Frank Dodge

Princess Theatre
Toronto, Canada
January 17, 1912
Wednesday Night Only
First Time on Any Stage
"JULIA FRANCE"
A Play in Three Acts by
Gertrude Atherton
Cast of Characters

Julia France...............Mrs. Fiske
Mrs. Edis...............Gilda Varesi
Fanny Edis......Kathlene MacDonell
Mrs. MacManus.......Florine Arnold
Mr. Pirie..........Henry Stephenson
Mrs. Winstone..........Hattie Russell
Daniel Tay..............Shelley Hull
Mrs. Morison.......Helena Van Brugh
Mr. Morison.........Douglas Paterson
Denny...............R. Owen Meech
The play produced by Mrs. Fiske

416

Empire Theatre
Broadway and 40th Street, New York
Charles Frohman, Manager
Week Beginning February 26, 1912
Harrison Grey Fiske presents
MRS. FISKE
and The Manhattan Company
in
"LADY PATRICIA"
A Comedy in Three Acts
by Rudolf Besier
(by arrangement with
Charles Frohman)
Cast of Characters

Dean Lesley........Henry Stephenson
Michael Cosway..........Leslie Faber
Bill O'Farrell.............Shelley Hull
Baldwin................Ernest Stallard
Ellis...................Lewis Howard
John.....................Cyril Young
Robert.........Frederick Roland
Lady Patricia Cosway......Mrs. Fiske
Mrs. O'Farrell.........Emily Fitzroy
Clare Lesley.............Maud Gilbert
The Play Produced by Mrs. Fiske

His Majesty's Theatre
Montreal—Canada
Week Beginning Monday,
October 14, 1912
Harrison Grey Fiske presents
MRS. FISKE
and The Manhattan Company
in
"THE HIGH ROAD"
A Pilgrimage, in Five Parts
by Edward Sheldon

Winfield Barnes.......Frederick Perry
Alan Wilson..........William Lewers
John Stephen Maddock..Arthur Byron
Silas Page...............Charles Fisher
Harvey Lawrence, the Governor's
Secretary............Lewis Howard
Martin Denison, the Governor's
Stenographer.........Barrett Clark
Scott, the Governor's door-keeper
Harry J. Holliday
Cornelius Murray, Chairman of the
National Committee.Aldrich Bowker
Leslie Farley, Vice-chairman of the
National Committee...Joseph Selman
James R. Kenyon, Treasurer of the
National Committee....M. B. Snyder
Robert Lyons, Chairman of the

Finance Committee..Philip Gresham
Leet, *Mr. Barnes' butler*.H. J. Holliday
An Expressman.......Charles Burleigh
Mary Page................Mrs. Fiske
Esther, *Miss Page's maid*.Nina Melville
   The play produced under
     the direction of
   Mr. and Mrs. Fiske
   The scene in Part I painted by
     Homer F. Emens
   The scenes in Parts II, III, IV
   painted by Gates and Morange
   Properties by the Seidle Studios
   Jean Drouin, Musical Director
Author's note: Opened in New York
at Hudson Theatre, November 19, 1912.
Author's Note: During the early sum-
mer of 1913 Mrs. Fiske was filmed as
Tess in "Tess of the D'Urbervilles" by
Famous Players Film Co. (Adolph
Zukor, President) Daniel Frohman—
Intermediary. The picture—superior
for its day—has been destroyed.

Nixon's Apollo Theatre
Atlantic City, N. J.
Beginning Monday, February 16, 1914
Harrison Grey Fiske presents
MRS. FISKE
and The Manhattan Company
in
"MRS. BUMPSTEAD-LEIGH"
A Comedy in Three Acts
by *Harry James Smith*
Cast of Characters
Justin Rawson.......Aldrich Bowker
Miss Rawson..........Grace Griswold
Geoffrey Rawson.......Fleming Ward
Anthony Rawson.....Kenneth Hunter
Stephen Leavitt.......Francis Dossert
Mrs. Stephen Leavitt....Nina Melville
Peter Swallow.......Malcolm Duncan
Kitson..................Alfred Helton
Mrs. De Salle...........Kate Mayhew
Mrs. Bumpstead-Leigh......Mrs. Fiske
Violet De Salle............Fay Bainter
Nina...................Marion Pullar
   The Play Produced under
     the Direction of
   Mr. and Mrs. Fiske
   Scenery by D. Frank Dodge

Broad Street Theatre
Philadelphia

Samuel F. Nixon   Managing Director
Two Weeks, Beginning Monday,
   Oct. 12, 1914
Harrison Grey Fiske presents
MRS. FISKE
in
A Comedy in Three Acts, entitled
"LADY BETTY MARTINGALE"
or
The Adventures of a Lively Hussy
by *John Luther Long* and
Frank Stayton
   The Persons of the Play
Canon Slowpeek.......Sidney Herbert
Lady Betty Martingale, *a widow, his*
   daughter.................Mrs. Fiske
Lady Fewits, *her gossip*
               Marie Chambers
Sir Ricochet Rascible....Arthur Elliott
Lord John Derring, *alias "Jock"*
   Rumple..................Eric Blind
Mr. Terram-Tyke, *a solicitor*
               Thomas Louden
Suggs, *a gaoler*......Percy D. Standing
Mrs. Suggs..............Alice Belmore
Hyx................Henry Warwick
Slib, *a scullion*........Alfred Hemming
Marrons, *maid to Lady Betty*
               Anne Faystone
Proxit, *maid to Lady Fewits*
               Nina Melville
Time: 1760   *Place:* England
   The Play Produced by *Mr. Fiske*
   The Incidental Music Composed by
     William Furst
The Scenes Painted by Homer Emens
The Costumes Designed by Percy
   Anderson and Executed by
     B. J. Simmons & Co.
   The Wigs by W. Clarkson
The Properties from the Seidle Studios
Author's Note: During the latter part
of 1915 Mrs. Fiske was filmed as Becky
Sharp in a motion picture titled "Vanity
Fair" wherein the play "Becky Sharp"
by Langdon Mitchell was not used.
"Vanity Fair" was made by Thomas
A. Edison, Inc. A poor picture for its
day it is preserved in the Film Library
of the Modern Art Museum, New
York.

Tremont Theatre
Boston

467

Jno. B. Schoeffel, Proprietor and
Manager
Week of October 23, 1916
Madison Corey & Joseph Riter
present
MRS. FISKE
(by arrangement with
Harrison Grey Fiske)
In "The Comedy with the Message of
Gaiety and Kindness"
"ERSTWHILE SUSAN"
(Founded on Helen R. Martin's Novel,
"Barnabetta")
by *Marian de Forest*
Cast of Characters
Barnaby Dreary, *the tinsmith*
Walter Wilson
Jacob Dreary, *the stage driver,*
Barnaby's son . . . . . Robert Stowe Gill
Emanuel Dreary, *the tinsmith's*
helper, Barnaby's son . . . . Rikel Kent
Abel Butcher, *the hotel-keeper's*
son . . . . John Daly Murphy
David Jordan, *the lawyer from*
Reading . . . . Henry Mortimer
Robert Marsh, *the Governor of*
Pennsylvania . . . . Hugh Chilvers
Absalom Puntz, *the attorney and*
undertaker . . . . Sol Aiken
Juliet Miller—Erstwhile Susan, *the*
elocutionist from Iowa . . . . Mrs. Fiske
Barnabetta Dreary, *the household*
drudge . . . . Madeline Delmar
Ramah Schwenkfelders, *the fiancee*
of Jacob . . . . Wylda Millison
Mrs. Winthrop, *the sister of Jordan*
Anita Clarendon
Alice Winthrop, *the cousin of Jordan*
Frances Stirling Clarke
Helen Meredith, *the other cousin of*
Jordan . . . . Ethel Craven
The Mennonites
Joseph Yoder . . . . Samuel Aidenfelder
Abraham Wackernagel
Henry B. Folger
Em. Wackernagel
Virginia Chauvenet
Jennie Getz . . . . Anna Reader
Sheba Yoder . . . . . . Eleanor McMurtie
Staged Under the Personal Direction of
Harrison Grey Fiske

Criterion Theatre
New York

418

Broadway at 44th Street
Mr. Hackett   Lessee & Manager
November 19, 1917
Klaw & Erlanger and George C. Tyler
present
MRS. FISKE
in
"MADAME SAND"
A Comedy in Three Acts
by *Philip Moeller*
Under the direction of *Arthur Hopkins*
The Players
in the order of their appearance
Rosalie . . . . Jean Robb
Madame De Musset . . . . . . Muriel Hope
Paul De Musset . . . . Walter Schellin
Casimir Dudevant . . . . Ben Lewin
Buloz . . . . Walter Kingsford
Heinrich Heine . . Ferdinand Gottschalk
Alfred De Musset . . . . Jose Ruben
Madame Julie Aurore Lucille
Amandine Dudevant George
Sand . . . . Mrs. Fiske
Doctor Giuseppi Pagello
John Davidson
Lucretia Violente . . . . Olin Field
Mlle. De Fleury . . . . Marjorie Hollis
Mlle. Rolande . . . . Inogen Fairchild
Mlle. De Latour . . . . Caroline Kohl
Franz Liszt . . . . Owen Meech
Frederic Chopin . . . . Alfred Cross
Lackey . . . . Charles Peyton
Guests at the Reception of the
Baron de Rothschild
Settings and costumes designed by
Rollo Peters
Gowns by Madame Freisinger
Author's Note: "Madame Sand" moved
to Knickerbocker Theatre and opened
Dec. 31, 1917—2 changes in cast:
Rosalie—Alexa Fior, & Paul De Musset
—France Bendtsen.

George M. Cohan Theatre
Broadway & 43rd Street, New York
Beginning Monday Evening,
April 15, 1918
Harrison Grey Fiske
(By arrangement with Klaw &
Erlanger and George C. Tyler)
presents
MRS. FISKE
in
"SERVICE"

A Play in Two Acts
by *Henri Lavedan*, of the
Academie Francaise
(English Version by
William C. Taylor)
Cast of Characters
Colonel Eulin...............Lee Baker
Lieutenant Eulin......Georges Flateau
General Girard..........Roger Lytton
The Minister of War.......Rikel Kent
Madame Eulin..............Mrs. Fiske
Pauline....................Alexa Fior
Produced and Staged by *Mr. Fiske*
Presented by arrangement with
Madison Corey
The scenes from the studios of
Gates and Morange

The American Red Cross
(*by Arrangement with Klaw and
Erlanger, Cohan and Harris and
George C. Tyler*)
presents
"OUT THERE"
A Dramatic Composition in Three Acts
by *J. Hartley Manners*
Produced Under the Personal Direction
of the Author
PART ONE
INSPIRATION
*A room in a lodging house during the
autumn of 1915*
" 'aunted" Annie..Miss Laurette Taylor
"Princess" Lizzie.....Miss Helen Ware
"Old Velvet".......Miss Beryl Mercer
'erb...............Mr. H. B. Warner
Monte...........Mr. James T. Powers
Dr. Hanwell........Mr. George Arliss

PART TWO
DEVOTION
The "Orange Walk"
The Surgeon.......Mr. George Arliss
The Irishman....Mr. Chauncey Olcott
The Cockney.......Mr. O. P. Heggie
The Canadian...Mr. James K. Hackett
The Scotchman
          Mr. George MacFarlane
The American..Mr. George M. Cohan
Gabrielle............Miss Julia Arthur
The Help.......Miss Laurette Taylor

PART THREE
REVELATION
Division 1—Mrs. Hudd's Rooms
Mrs. Hudd........Miss Beryl Mercer
Miss Elizabeth Hudd.Miss Helen Ware
Herbert Hudd......Mr. H. B. Warner
Mr. Montague Marsh
          Mr. James T. Powers

Division 2—A Public Place
The Nurse.......Miss Laurette Taylor
Mrs. Minnie Maddern Fiske
will deliver a Red Cross Appeal written
expressly for these gala performances
and following this
Mme. Eleanora de Cisneros
will sing
*Author's Note: Toured the U.S.A. dur-
ing May of 1918 to raise funds for the
Red Cross.*

Henry Miller's Theatre
New York
Henry Miller, Manager
February 4, 1919
Messrs. Cohan & Harris
present
MRS. FISKE
*In a Comedy of Moonshine, Madness
and Make-Believe*
"MIS' NELLY OF N' ORLEANS"
by *Laurence Eyre*
Under the Direction of
Harrison Grey Fiske
Cast of Characters
Angelique............Gertrude Chase
Zephyrine................Eva Benton
Delphine Falaise.....Madeline Delmar
Félix Durand.......Georges Renavent
Unc' Boze...............Joseph Dunn
Père André Clément.....Frederic Burt
Nelly Daventry............Mrs. Fiske
Georges Durand....Hamilton Revelle
Mélanie Cardanne.........Zola Talma
Masquers, Singers, etc.: The Cohar
Quartette, Messrs. Hindermeyer, Fergu-
son, Mathieu, Gallagher and Misses
Chase, Keane, Kissler and Chester.
Acknowledgment to Mr. George W.
Cable for his services as an authority
on the Creole.
The scenery designed and painted by
Homer Emens

419

The gowns by Helen Sheppard
The costumes by Freisinger

Henry Miller's Theatre
New York
Beginning January 17, 1921
Sam H. Harris
presents
MRS. FISKE
in a Comedy
"WAKE UP, JONATHAN"
In a Prologue and Three Acts
by Hatcher Hughes and Elmer E. Rice
Under the direction of
Harrison Grey Fiske
Cast of Characters

Jonathan Blake.........Charles Dalton
Marion Blake...............Mrs. Fiske
Helen Blake...............Helen Holt
Junior Blake..............Frank Hearn
Peggy Blake..............Lois Bartlett
Chippy Blake.............Nadia Gary
Bernard Randall......Donald Cameron
Stephen Brent..........Fleming Ward
Adam West..............Howard Lang
Jean Picard..........Freddie Goodrow
Jennie................Edith Fitzgerald
Scenes by Gates and Morange
Marionettes designed by Michael Carr
made by the Wits and Fingers Studio
operated by Remo Buffano with the
assistance of Ester Stocktop, Lugarda
Harling and Will Chambers
The music composed and arranged
by W. Franke Harling

Cort Theatre
Chicago
Beginning Monday Evening,
January 29, 1923
Mr. H. H. Frazee
Presents
MRS. FISKE
In a Play in Three Acts
"THE DICE OF THE GODS"
by Lillian Barrett
Direction of Harrison Grey Fiske
Cast

John Henderson.....Donald Cameron
Buchanan Laurence..Edward Donnelly
Roger Canby............Sidney Mason
Dr. Henry Arnold....Joseph Macaulay
Parsons...............Wallis Roberts
Charles...............Francis Sadtler

420

Giuseppi Alfano......France Bendtsen
Mr. Sullivan.........William T. Clark
Michele.............Rodolfo Badaloni
Pasquale...............Virginia Smith
Giovanni...........William Lambert
Salvatore..............Frederick Scott
Patricia Baird—"Paddy"....Mrs.. Fiske
Charlotte Baird........Ernita Lascelles
Dolly Laurence........Helen Jackson
Suzanne...............Clelia Benjamin
Elise....................Evelyn Orton
Mary McCafferty.....Maggie Weston
Francesca.............Eunice Osborne
Marie................Caterina Barone
Beatrice............Henrietta Jordan
Lucia..................Nera Badaloni
Mrs. Fiske's Costume in Act I from
Milgrim's, New York, in Acts I and
II from the Flambeau Shop
Scenes Designed and Painted by
Gates and Morange
Author's Note: The New York open-
ing of "The Dice of the Gods" was at
the National Theatre April 5, 1923.

Belasco Theatre
West 44th Street, near Broadway,
New York
under the sole management of
David Belasco
Beginning Tuesday Evening,
September 11, 1923
David Belasco
by arrangement with
Harrison Grey Fiske
presents
MRS. FISKE
in
"MARY, MARY,
QUITE CONTRARY"
A Light Comedy by St. John Ervine
Characters in the Order of Their
Appearance

Mrs. Considine......Winifred Fraser
Sheila, her niece......Nora Swinburne
Geoffrey, her son......Francis Lister
Sir Henry Considine, K.C.M.G.,
formerly Governor of Andabar,
her brother-in-law..C. Aubrey Smith
Rev. Canon Peter Considine, M.A.,
Vicar of Hinton St. Henry, her
husband..............Orlando Daly
Mary Westlake—Mrs. James
Westlake.................Mrs. Fiske

Tori, *Mrs. Westlake's Maid*
Naoe Kondo
Mr. Hobbs, *her manager*....A. P. Kaye
Jenny, *a parlor maid*..Audrey Cameron
Ellen, *the house maid*..Gladys Burgess
Miss Mimms..........Florence Edney
Mr. Beeby..............Lennox Pawle
Scenery by Ernest Gros
Designs by W. Harris, of London
Scenes built by Charles Carson
Gowns and hats by Philip Roman

Henry Miller's Theatre
New York
Beginning April 7, 1924
MRS. FISKE
in
"HELENA'S BOYS"
A Comedy in Three Acts by
Ida Lublenski Erlich
Dramatized from a story by
Mary Brecht Pulver
The play directed by
Harrison Grey Fiske
Produced and Managed by
Charles L. Wagner
Cast of Characters
Helena Tilden.............Mrs. Fiske
Harold Beansy.........Gay Pendleton
Henry................Reggie Sheffield
Moresby Girald.........Ralph Shirley
James Truesdell....William Courtleigh
Tot Raymond...........Irene Purcell
Ann Kimball..........Elaine Temple
Tibby McNair..........Louie Emery
Mr. Parr..............Carlton Rivers
Lucy................Eunice Osborne
Richard.............John A. Willard

Hollis Street Theatre
Boston
Beginning January 12, 1925
"THE RIVALS"
A Comedy in Three Acts
(and Ten Scenes)
by *Richard Brinsley Sheridan*
Staged by *Harrison Grey Fiske*
Management—*George C. Tyler* and
Hugh Ford
Cast of Characters
Sir Anthony Absolute
Thomas A. Wise
Captain Jack Absolute
Kenneth Thomson

Faulkland...................Fred Eric
Bob Acres...........James T. Powers
Sir Lucius O'Trigger.Chauncey Olcott
Fag...................Percival Vivian
David................George Tawde
Thomas..............Walter Woodall
Mrs. Malaprop..............Mrs. Fiske
Lydia Languish............Lola Fisher
Julia Melville.............May Collins
Lucy................Georgette Cohan
Costumes by Eaves Costume Company
Wigs by Berner
Settings designed by David S. Gaither
Constructed by Liberty
Construction Company
and painted by P. Dodd Ackerman
Scenic Studios
Author's Note: This engagement was a
150th anniversary of the first perform-
ance of Sheridan's "The Rivals" which
took place at Covent Garden, London,
January 17, 1775.

Mansfield Theatre
47th Street, West of Broadway
New York
Week Beginning Monday Evening,
January 10, 1927
MRS. FISKE
in
"GHOSTS"
A Drama in Three Acts
by Henrik Ibsen
Cast of Characters
Mrs. Helen Alving, *widow of Captain*
Alving, Chamberlain to the King
Mrs. Fiske
Oswald Alving, *her son, a painter*
Theodore St. John
Pastor Manders......Walter Ringham
Regina Engstrand, *Mrs. Alving's maid*
Jarvis Kerr
Jacob Engstrand, *her father; a*
carpenter........William C. Masson
The Play Staged by
Harrison Grey Fiske
Production Designed by David Gaither
Built by Butler & Heywood
Painted by Kennell and Entwistle

Knickerbocker Theatre
Broadway and 38th Street, New York
Week Beginning Monday Evening,
March 19, 1928

MRS. FISKE and OTIS SKINNER
with
HENRIETTA CROSMAN
in
"THE MERRY WIVES OF
WINDSOR"
A Farcical Comedy in Five Acts
by *William Shakespeare*
Produced and Directed by
Harrison Grey Fiske
Persons Represented
Sir John Falstaff.........Otis Skinner
Master Fenton, *a gentleman*
Geoffrey Wardwell
Robert Shallow, *a Justice of*
Gloucestershire........Owen Meech
Abraham Slender, *his nephew*
France Bendtsen
Two Gentlemen dwelling at Windsor
Francis Ford.....Lawrence H. Cecil
George Page.......Henry Mowbray
Sir Hugh Evans, *a Welsh parson and*
schoolmaster.........Hannam Clark
Doctor Caius, *a French physician*
Rodolpho Badaloni
Host of the Garter Inn
William C. Masson
Followers of Falstaff
Bardolph.............Tracy Barrow
Pistol....................Will Geer
Nym................Horace Cooper
Cricket.................Mary Walsh
Bede..................Ella Houghton
Robin, *Falstaff's page*...Virginia Smith
Peter Simple, *servant to Slender*
Burford Hampden
John Rugby, *servant to Doctor Caius*
George Le Soir
Mistress Ford.....Henrietta Crosman
Mistress Page..............Mrs. Fiske
Anne Page, *her daughter*
Elaine Temple
Mistress Quickly, *servant to Doctor*
Caius..............Eleanor Gordon
Servants to Ford
Robert.................Boyd Zook
John..................Rene Roberti
Windsor Townspeople—Marion Pullar,
Ester Gustafson, Marie Blackwell, Kay
Barnes, Nera Badaloni, Mary Walsh,
Ella Houghton, Rene Roberti, Boyd
Zook, Douglas Barrington and Julian
Garfield

Play edited and arranged by
Harrison Grey Fiske
The scenes designed and painted by
Gates and Morange
The costumes designed by
Henry Dreyfuss
The dances directed by
Esther Gustafson
The furniture and properties
designed by France Bendtsen
The women's costumes made by
Madame E. S. Freisinger
The men's by the
Eaves Costume Company
The wigs by Berner
The shoes by Barney's

Broad St. Theatre
Philadelphia
Beginning Tuesday, Christmas Night,
December 25, 1928
THE MRS. FISKE COMPANY
in
"MUCH ADO ABOUT NOTHING"
A Comedy in Four Acts
by William Shakespeare
Produced and directed by
Harrison Grey Fiske
Persons Represented
Don Pedro, *prince of Aragon*
Pedro De Cordoba
Don John, *his bastard brother*
Charles Warburton
Claudio, *a young lord of Florence*
Geoffrey Wardwell
Benedick, *a lord of Padua*
Ian Maclaren
Leonato, *Governor of Messina*
Charles Dalton
Antonio, *his brother*.....Owen Meech
Followers of Don John
Boraccio............Frank Webster
Conrade..............Harry Green
A Page..................Elsie Keene
Friar Francis.........Horace Pollock
Dogberry, *a constable*
Sydney Greenstreet
Verges, *a headborough*
Dallas Welford
Watchmen
George Seacole.......Tracy Barrow
Hugh Oatcake.........Evan March
A Sexton..............George Le Soir

Balthasar, *a singer attendant on Don Pedro*..............Frank Webster
Hero, *daughter to Leonato*
Betty Linley
Beatrice, *niece to Leonato*
Mrs. Fiske
Gentlewomen attending on Hero
Margaret...........Virginia Phillips
Ursula.................Mary Walsh
Singers, Musicians, Watchmen, Attendants, etc.: Victor Ferrani, Stanley Rignold, Harold Setliff, Emmet Shields, Kay Barnes, Ingrid Dillon, James, Charles and Vincent Lepari.
The play edited and arranged by
Harrison Grey Fiske
The scenes designed and painted by
Gates and Morange
The costumes designed by
William Weaver and made by Eaves
The dances by Ruth Ingalls
Music directed by Bernard Molé

Klaw Theatre
251 West 45th Street, New York City
Charles Bottine   Manager
Week Beginning Monday Evening,
April 1, 1929
MRS. FISKE
In the Farcical-Comedy
"MRS BUMPSTEAD-LEIGH"
by *Harry James Smith*
Directed by *George C. Tyler*
The Cast
Justin Rawson...........Fuller Mellish
Miss Rawson........Jennie A. Eustace
Geoffrey Rawson.....Edmund George
Anthony Rawson.......John Anthony
Stephen Leavitt.......William Lorenz
Mrs. Leavitt...........Valerie Valaire
Peter Swallow..........Sidney Toler
Kitson................Dallas Welford
Mrs. De Salle..........Stella Mayhew
Mrs. Bumpstead-Leigh......Mrs. Fiske
Violet De Salle.......Eleanor Griffith
Nina.................Doris Freeman
Scenery designed and painted by
Gates and Morange
Costumes and Millinery by
Lucille, New York, designed by
Evelyn McHorter
Furniture by Wm. Bradley Studios

Erlanger's Theatre
44th Street, West of Broadway,
New York
Week Beginning Monday Evening,
October 21, 1929
MRS. FISKE
In a New Comedy
"LADIES OF THE JURY"
by *Fred Ballard*
Staged by *Harrison Grey Fiske*
Direction *A. L. Erlanger* and
George C. Tyler
Characters
THE JURY:
Mrs. Livingston Baldwin Crane
Mrs. Fiske
Lily Pratt.............Claire Grenville
Cynthia Tate.........Eunice Osborne
Mayme Mixter........Hallie Manning
Mrs. Dace................Elsie Keene
Mrs. Maguire............Marie Hunt
Jay J. Pressley..........George Farren
Spencer B. Dazey.....Sardis Lawrence
Alonzo Beal...........J. H. Stoddart
Tony Theodophulus....Vincent James
Steve Bromm.........Walter Kinsella
Andrew MacKaig......George Tawde
THE OTHERS:
Judge Fish..........Wilton Lackaye
Halsey Van Stye...H. Dudley Hawley
Rutherford Dale...C. W. Van Voorhis
Dr. Quincy Adams James, Jr.
William Lorenz
Art Dobbs, *court officer*...Al Roberts
Mrs. Gordon—Yvette Yvet—
Germaine Giroux
Evelyn Snow.............June Mullin
Susanne.................Vanda Curci
Clerk of the court.....Edward Powell
Court reporter.......Virginia Murray
Scenery designed and painted by
Gates and Morange
Mrs. Fiske's dresses designed by
Evelyn McHorter and executed by
Lucille, New York
Author's Note: The Erlanger Theatre was later known as St. James Theatre.

The Cort Theatre
48th Street, East of Broadway,
New York
Week Beginning Monday Evening,
February 10, 1930

423

MRS. FISKE
In a New Comedy in Three Acts
"IT'S A GRAND LIFE"
by *Hatcher Hughes* and *Alan Williams*
Staged by *Harrison Grey Fiske*
Direction *A. L. Erlanger* and
George C. Tyler
Characters

Austin Tyler..............Cyril Scott
Helen Tyler................Mrs. Fiske
Jean Tyler............Leona Beutelle
Timmy Tyler....Andrew Lawlor, Jr.
"Doc" Burdette...Raymond Van Sickle
Nikolas Van Tyle......Gene Gowing
Major Richard Dale....Robert Barrat
Mercedes Dale......Germaine Giroux
Validia Sierra........Virginia Venable
Dr. Moran............William Lorenz
Reporter on the *New York Times*
C. W. Van Voorhis
Reporter on a Tabloid
Walter Kinsella
Joseph................Edward Powell
A Trained Nurse.........Elsie Keene
Dresses designed by Evelyn McHorter
and executed by Lucille, N. Y.
Scene painted by Gates and Morange
Properties by William Bradley Studios
Draperies by S. Weiss and Son

Erlanger's Theatre
44th Street, West of Broadway,
New York
Beginning Thursday Evening,
March 13, 1930
"THE RIVALS"
A Farcical-Comedy in Three Acts
by *Richard Brinsley Sheridan*
Staged by *Harrison Grey Fiske*
Direction *A. L. Erlanger* and
George C. Tyler
Cast of Characters

Sir Anthony Absolute......John Craig
Captain Jack Absolute....Rollo Peters
Faulkland..........Pedro De Cordoba
Bob Acres...........James T. Powers
Sir Lucius O'Trigger....Andrew Mack
Fag..................Percival Vivian
David................George Tawde
Thomas.................Dann Malloy
Mrs. Malaprop............Mrs. Fiske
Lydia Languish.......Margery Maude
Julia Melville............Betty Linley
Lucy................Georgette Cohan

474

Settings by Gates and Morange
Construction by Frank Dwyer Inc.
Costumes by Eaves Costume Co.
Designed by William Weaver
Properties and furniture by
William Bradley Studios
*Author's Note: This is the last engage-
ment Mrs. Fiske played in New York.
Erlanger's Theatre was later known as
the St. James Theatre.*

The Playhouse
Wilmington, Delaware
MRS. FISKE
(Her First Repertoire Season)
In the Farcical Comedy
"MRS. BUMPSTEAD-LEIGH"
by *Harry James Smith*
Staged by *Harrison Grey Fiske*
Direction
*A. L. Erlanger Amusements Enterprises
Inc.* and *George C. Tyler*
October 3, 1930
Characters

Justin Rawson.......William Ingersoll
Miss Rawson, *his sister*
Ethel Strickland
Anthony Rawson, *his elder son*
Robert Leslie
Goeffrey Rawson, *his younger son*
Sherling Oliver
Stephen Leavitt........Sydney Booth
Mrs. Stephen Leavitt
Jeannette Dowling
Peter Swallow........Edmund Elton
Kitson................Thomas Shearer
Mrs. De Salle........Eleanor Gordon
Mrs. Bumpstead-Leigh......Mrs. Fiske
Violet De Salle...........Mona Smith
Nina.................Marga la Rubia
Scenery Designed and Painted by
Gates and Morange
Constructed by Frank Dwyer, Inc.
Costumes by Lucille, New York
Designed by Evelyn McHorter
Furniture by William Bradley Studios

Broad Street Theatre
Philadelphia
Beginning Thursday, October 23, 1930
MRS. FISKE
Her First Repertoire Season in
"BECKY SHARP"
*A Comedy in Four Acts by
Langdon Mitchell*

(Founded on Thackeray's
Vanity Fair)
Staged by *Harrison Grey Fiske*
Direction *A. L. Erlanger Amusement
Enterprises, Inc.* and *George C. Tyler*
Characters
The Marquis of Steyne
William Ingersoll
Sir Pitt Crawley, Bart.
Edmund Elton
His Sons
Pitt Crawley........Kemble Knight
Rawdon Crawley.....Sydney Booth
William Dobbin............Will Geer
George Osborne......Sherling Oliver
Joseph Sedley, *of Bogleywollah,
India*.................Edward Butler
Mr. Loder..............Robert Leslie
Lord Bareacres.......Thomas Shearer
German students
Fritz.................Vincent James
Max................George Siebold
Bowles...............Thomas Shearer
Raggles................Vincent James
Becky Sharp................Mrs. Fiske
Amelia Sedley........Marga la Rubia
Miss Crawley.........Eleanor Gordon
Lady Bareacres.......Ethel Strickland
Lady Blanche Thistlewood, *her
daughter*...............Mona Smith
Lady Jane Crawley......Alice Cowan
Briggs, *Miss Crawley's companion*
Jeannette Dowling
Fifine..................Mary Emerson
Guests, Aides, Servants, etc.
Scenery designed by David S. Gaither
Constructed by Frank Dwyer, Inc.
Mrs. Fiske's costumes designed by
William Weaver—others by Eaves
Costume Co. and Brooks Costume Co.

Blackstone Theatre
Chicago
Beginning Monday, Jan. 12th, 1931
MRS. FISKE
In a New Comedy
"LADIES OF THE JURY"
by *Fred Ballard*
Staged by *Harrison Grey Fiske*
Cast of Play
THE JURY
Mrs. Livingston Baldwin Crane
Mrs. Fiske
Lily Pratt...........Ethel Strickland

Cynthia Tate.......Jeannette Dowling
Mayme Mixter...........Elsie Keene
Mrs. Dace..............Alice Cowan
Mrs. Macguire........Eleanor Gordon
Jay J. Pressley......William Ingersoll
Spencer B. Dazey.......Luke Conness
Alonzo Beal...........Kemble Knight
Tony Theodophulus....Vincent James
Steve Bromm.........E. N. Johnstone
Andrew McKaig.....Thomas Shearer
THE OTHERS
Judge Fish...............James Seeley
Halsey Van Stye.......Edward Cullen
Rutherford Dale.......Sherling Oliver
Dr. Quincy Adams James, Jr.
Will Geer
Art Dobbs............Edward Butler
Mrs. Gordon—Yvette Yvet—
Marga la Rubia
Evelyn Snow...............Eve Kohl
Susanne...............Mary Emerson
Clerk of Court.......George Seibold
Scenery designed and painted by
Gates and Morange
Constructed by Frank Dwyer
Dresses of Mrs. Fiske designed by
Evelyn McHorter,
executed by Lucille, N. Y.

Mayan Theatre
Pasadena, California
Beginning Monday Evening,
May 25, 1931,
Sid Grauman
by arrangement with
Harrison Grey Fiske
presents
MRS. FISKE
and Her Company
in
"MRS. BUMPSTEAD-LEIGH"
by *Harry James Smith*
Cast
Justin Rawson........Frank Dawson
Miss Rawson..............Mary Hill
Geoffrey Rawson.......Melville Ruick
Anthony Rawson......John Davidson
Stephen Leavitt.......Bram Nossen
Mrs. Leavitt........Helen H. Holmes
Peter Swallow......Charles Dow Clark
Kitson.................George Kirby
Mrs. De Salle...........Eva Condon
Mrs. Bumpstead-Leigh......Mrs. Fiske

425

Violet De Salle.........Lurene Tuttle
Nina..............Donella Donaldson

Blackstone Theatre—Chicago
Edwin Wappler   Manager
Beginning October 26, 1931
MRS. FISKE
in
"AGAINST THE WIND"
A Play in Three Acts by
Carlos Drake
Staged by *Harrison Grey Fiske*
Direction—*The Blackstone Company*

Cast of Characters

Frederick Sutherland...Charles Dalton
Martha Sutherland.........Alice John
Frederick Sutherland, Jr..Hugh Rennie
John Sutherland......Reed Brown, Jr.
Kate Gordon ("Tawny")...Mrs. Fiske
Isabelle Caraway........Terry Carroll
Irene Deering.....Olive Reeves Smith
Phoebe Carter...........Elsie Keene
Ghita................Virginia Venable
Wesley Ross........George A. Lessey
Paul Paige................Isham Keith
Ellis.......................Carl Reed
Anna...................Olivia Anders

426

INDEX

429

430

432

433